Ninja Hacking

Ninja Hacking
Unconventional Penetration Testing Tactics and Techniques

Thomas Wilhelm

Jason Andress

Bryan Garner
Ninjutsu Consultant

Joshua Abraham
Technical Editor

AMSTERDAM • BOSTON • HEIDELBERG • LONDON
NEW YORK • OXFORD • PARIS • SAN DIEGO
SAN FRANCISCO • SINGAPORE • SYDNEY • TOKYO

Syngress is an imprint of Elsevier

Acquiring Editor: Rachel Roumeliotis
Development Editor: Matthew Cater
Project Manager: Laura Smith
Designer: Alisa Andreola

Syngress is an imprint of Elsevier
30 Corporate Drive, Suite 400, Burlington, MA 01803, USA

Library of Congress Cataloging-in-Publication Data
Application submitted

British Library Cataloguing-in-Publication Data
A catalogue record for this book is available from the British Library.

ISBN: 978-1-59749-588-2

Printed and bound by CPI Group (UK) Ltd, Croydon, CR0 4YY
Transferred to digital print 2012

Typeset by: diacriTech, India

Working together to grow
libraries in developing countries

www.elsevier.com | www.bookaid.org | www.sabre.org

ELSEVIER   BOOK AID International   Sabre Foundation

For information on all Syngress publications visit our website at *www.syngress.com*

Contents

About the Authors

Thomas Wilhelm has been involved in Information Security since 1990, where he served in the U.S. Army for 8 years as a Signals Intelligence Analyst/Russian Linguist/Cryptanalyst. A speaker at security conferences across the United States, including DefCon, HOPE, and CSI, he has been employed by Fortune 100 companies to conduct risk assessments, participate and lead in external and internal penetration testing efforts, and manage Information Systems Security projects.

Thomas is also an Information Technology Doctoral student who holds Masters degrees in both Computer Science and Management. Additionally, he dedicates some of his time as an Associate Professor at Colorado Technical University and has contributed to multiple publications, including both magazines and books. Thomas currently performs security training courses for both civilian and government personnel through Heorot.net, and maintains the following security certifications: ISSMP, CISSP, SCSECA, and SCNA.

Jason Andress (ISSAP, CISSP, GISP, GSEC, CEH, Security+) is a seasoned security professional with a depth of experience in both the academic and business worlds. He is presently employed by a major software company, providing global information security oversight, and performing penetration testing, risk assessment, and compliance functions to ensure that the company's assets are protected.

Jason has taught undergraduate and graduate security courses since 2005 and holds a Doctorate in Computer Science. His research is in the area of data protection, and he has contributed to several publications, writing on topics including data security, network security, and digital forensics.

About the Ninjutsu Consultant

Bryan R. Garner (CHT, fifth-degree black belt in Bujinkan Budo Taijutsu/Ninjutsu, Security Specialist) holds a Shidoshi level teaching license in the Bujinkan Martial Arts system and has trained in Ninjutsu for more than 10 years. He has been involved in martial arts since he was 5 years old, receiving two Shodan ranks previously in other martial art styles. Sensei Garner has trained in Japan, as well as attended many seminars throughout the United States to further his training. He currently runs his own Ninjutsu Martial arts school in Colorado Springs and works as a full-time Security Specialist for a large corporation.

About the Technical Editor

Joshua Abraham (aka Jabra) joined Rapid7 in 2006 as a Security Consultant. Josh has extensive IT Security and Auditing experience and has worked as an enterprise risk assessment analyst for Hasbro Corporation. Josh specializes in penetration testing, web application security assessments, wireless security assessments, and custom code development. He has spoken at Black Hat, DefCon, ShmooCon, Infosec World, CSI, OWASP Conferences, LinuxWorld, and the SANS Pentest Summit. In his spare time, he contributes code to open source security projects such as the BackTrack LiveCD, BeEF, Nikto, Fierce, and PBNJ.

Introduction

BOOK OVERVIEW AND KEY LEARNING POINTS

This work is not what most people would expect to read when they pick up a "hacking" book. Rather than showing the reader how to perform traditional penetration test attacks against networks and systems, we will be taking an unusual journey, intended to expand the mind of the reader and force them to see system and network security from a completely different perspective.

Ninja Hacking provides the reader with a unique perspective of how to conduct unorthodox attacks against computing networks using disguise, espionage, stealth, and concealment. Many books on hacking discuss traditional methods used to gather information from corporate networks and systems. However, there are many infiltration techniques that are unconventional, which can yield greater access into a target network. By blending ancient practices of the Japanese ninja with current hacking methodologies, additional attack vectors can be realized.

Ninja Hacking explores historical Ninjutsu techniques and relates them to real-world penetration tests and hacking efforts in a manner that expands the mindset, tools, and methods of information of security experts who are intent on covertly assaulting a target network.

BOOK AUDIENCE

This book will provide a valuable resource to penetration testers and security professionals, as well as to network and systems administrators. The information provided on unconventional attacks can be used to develop better and more specific defenses against such attacks, as well as to provide new angles for penetration testing.

Those in management positions will find this information useful as well, from the standpoint of developing better overall defensive strategies for their organizations. The concepts discussed in this book can be used to drive security projects and policies, in order to mitigate some of the larger issues discussed.

HOW THIS BOOK IS ORGANIZED

This book is composed of 17 chapters, in six major sections:

- Ninjas and hacking – Chapters 1 and 2
- Tactics – Chapters 3 and 4
- Disguise and impersonation – Chapters 5, 6, and 7
- Stealth and entering methods – Chapters 8, 9, 10, and 11
- Espionage – Chapters 12, 13, 14, 15, and 16
- Escaping and concealment – Chapter 17

Because of the content and organization of the topics in this book, it is not necessary to read it from front to back or even in any particular order at all. In the areas where we refer to information located in other chapters in the book, we have endeavored to point out where the information can be found. The following descriptions will provide you with an overview of the content of each chapter.

Chapter 1: The Historical Ninja

In this chapter, we take a look at parallels between the historical ninja and modern hackers. By understanding the pressures of war and society at the time, we can better understand how ninja culture and their skills were shaped. We also contrast the ninja against the samurai, and compare the ethics between both groups. By the end of the chapter, we will be able to identify similarities and differences between modern-day white hats who perform more traditional attacks and those people working in special units who conduct unorthodox attacks.

Chapter 2: The Modern Ninja

Once we understand the historical ninja, we can extrapolate the skills necessary to perform modern-day unorthodox attacks using the ninja philosophy as a framework. We examine the differences between white hat versus black hat hackers, and identify functional gaps between these two groups – gaps that can be filled with ninja hackers, whom we refer to as Zukin. Once we identify these gaps, we examine ethical questions about the role of Zukin and merge ancient teaching about war and conflict with today's virtual world.

Chapter 3: Strategies and Tactics

Sun Tzu's "The Art of War" provides us with a wealth of knowledge that can be applied to a ninja hacking project, which can be augmented with both historical ninja strategies and tactics, and modern-day studies of war and conflict. The strategies discussed in this chapter include some important topics, such as laying plans, waging war, maneuvering, and the use of spies. We also examine briefly how female ninjas were used in ancient Japan.

Chapter 4: Exploitation of Current Events

In this chapter, we will examine psychological operations to a greater extent and build on what the ninja were experts at – playing on people's fears. When combined, the strategies used by the ninja in feudal Japan, espoused by Sun Tzu, and methods of psychological warfare published by the U.S. military, can provide an effective base of knowledge, in which to conduct devastating attacks against target systems, all without being detected.

Chapter 5: Disguise

In this chapter, we examine the ways that the ninja, modern attackers, and penetration testers have used people's predisposition to trust authority to their advantage. By following their examples, and most importantly creating our own ways of disguising ourselves, we can acquire a heightened level of trust by using uniforms and badges to gain elevated access, posing as vendors, or presenting ourselves as someone that the target might normally do business with.

Chapter 6: Impersonation

In this chapter, we cover the use of impersonation in penetration testing. This may appear to be a simple thing – assume a disguise and play a role; however, if we need to avoid detection at all costs, impersonation becomes a much more complicated endeavor. If we decide to conduct an attack using pretexting, we need to make sure that our disguise is perfect, and that our knowledge, language, understanding of geography, and understanding of human psychology is exceptional for the task at hand.

Chapter 7: Infiltration

In this chapter, we cover various infiltration tactics. We discuss topics such as bypassing locks without leaving direct physical evidence and working around some of the more common biometric systems such as fingerprints or voice recognition systems. We also delve into the use of trusted networks in order to ease the penetration or attack of logical systems.

Chapter 8: Use of Timing to Enter an Area

In this chapter, we cover the use of timing in attacks. When entering a location, whether from a physical or logical standpoint, timing is a key component to the attack. Timing can allow us to pass completely unnoticed, walking into a building with a crowd, or sending a cache of covertly collected data out over the network. Timing attacks such as tailgating can allow us to enter a facility or network behind a legitimate user, avoiding the notice of security systems and physical access controls.

Chapter 9: Discovering Weak Points in Area Defenses

In this chapter, we look at a variety of methods to discover weak points in area defenses. We discuss traffic patterns, both from a physical and a logical standpoint, and tools that we might use to find such patterns where they exist, and how we can go about disrupting traffic patterns in order to cover our other activities and stop or delay other events from happening. We also look at guns, gates, and guards, from both logical and physical angles. Finally, we cover information diving.

Chapter 10: Psychological Weaknesses

In this chapter, we discuss the use of psychological weaknesses to manipulate our targets. We discuss social engineering as a science, and we refer to the framework used by the ninja; the five elements: earth, air, fire, water, and void; the five weaknesses: laziness, anger, fear, sympathy, and vanity; and the five needs: security, sex, wealth, pride, and pleasure.[1]

Chapter 11: Distraction

In this chapter, we discussed the use of big events to distract the targets of our attack. Using such distractions can ensure that we are able to carry out our main attack unmolested while everyone is concerned with the deliberately noticeable attack that we have set to draw their attention. Multipronged attacks such as these can allow us to approach a target from multiple angles, as well as use timing to make our attacks more effective by including distractors, or cause a distraction with the attacks themselves.

Chapter 12: Concealment Devices

Because the primary job of the ancient ninja was espionage, in this chapter, we will look at how we can develop our own espionage tools, focusing specifically on mobile devices. There are some limitations that we need to be aware of, and countermeasures that could thwart our endeavors to gain access to data. We will also see how we can smuggle data out of facilities without detection using concealment methods that hide data in broad daylight.

Chapter 13: Covert Listening Devices

In this chapter, we cover a variety of covert listening devices that are available for our use. Although a broad range of eavesdropping tools is available, we concentrate on the more passive methods of eavesdropping. We also cover the use of software methods such as keystroke loggers and spyware. Last but not the least, we look at less common methods of listening on communications such as van

Eck phreaking, listening to keyboard emissions, and watching fluctuations in LED indicators on devices.

Chapter 14: Intelligence

In this chapter, we discuss the various techniques involved in intelligence gathering and interrogation. Such tactics may vary in scope and severity, depending largely on the party doing the intelligence gathering or interrogation and the setting, in both the political and geographical sense. Some portions of this chapter discuss activities that are out of scope for standard penetration testing, but we cover them in the context of both historical use by the ninja, and modern use in the real world by various parties.

Chapter 15: Surveillance

In this chapter, we discuss surveillance and we talk about some of the places from where we can gather data on companies and individuals. We talk about the tools that we can use for location tracking and various methods that might be used to detect surveillance. Additionally, we discuss the use of antisurveillance devices and methods.

Chapter 16: Sabotage

This chapter discusses the use of sabotage. Although sabotage is not frequently used in penetration testing, it was used historically by the ninja, and it is regularly put to use in various conflicts and by criminal organizations. We cover logical sabotage, which, when used with care, can actually be very useful in a penetration-testing scenario. We also discuss the use of physical sabotage, including targeting communications, hardware, and access controls.

Chapter 17: Hiding and Silent Movement

When a compromise is accomplished, it is the time when stealth is most needed. In this chapter, we will look at ways to hide our attack location and activities. We examine the ways that system and network administrators search for intruders and find countermeasures that will ensure our activities are undetected.

Conclusion

Researching and writing this book has been a great adventure for the authors, and we hope that you enjoy the end result. Although we obviously do not cover every variation and possibility for unconventional attacks, we hope that we can expand the arsenal of the reader and enable you to become better at not only executing these sorts of attack, but defending against them as well. In your efforts, always remember *ishi no ue ni san nen*.[2]

Endnotes

1. Hayes S. The ninja and their secret fighting art. Tuttle Publishing; 1990. 978-0804816564.
2. Хмельницкая Областная Федерация Киокушинкай Каратэ. ФИЛОСОФИЯ КЬОКУСИНКАЙ КАРАТЕ Kyokushin Tetsugaku. www.tsunami.km.ua/philosophy/philosophy.html; 2010 [accessed 18.06.2010].

The Historical Ninja

1

In the news, we are constantly hearing about malicious hackers who were able to achieve incredible success against large corporations, stealing millions of dollars worth of data. Yet, we wonder why these large corporations succumb to the malicious attacks in the first place, considering the resources available. Government systems, with threats coming from across the globe, are successfully compromised; yet, the governments cannot put together an effective shield to prevent the attacks in the first place. These events should make us wonder how the extremely proficient malicious hackers could ever succeed – the answer is twofold:

1. They do not have to play by anyone's rules.
2. They think differently.

By not having to play by anyone's rules, they can try different types of attack vectors, without having to worry about scope statements and get-out-of-jail-free letters – they are free to try anything they want. The advantages of thinking differently mean that they can try unconventional attacks against targets; there are no limitations to their creativity and freedom to try new things, even if the attacks result in shutting down systems or destroying data. The truly talented malicious hackers are unique and quite a challenge to stop.

Because malicious hackers are real, it is critical for security engineers tasked with defending systems to understand how the "enemy" thinks … and that is part of what this book is about. We will be taking a look at how to think unconventionally, learn how to conduct attacks against our own systems, and understand what can be done by malicious hackers against both corporate and government systems.

SHINOBI-IRI (Stealth and Entering Methods)

Many of the techniques discussed in this book will be outside the realm of traditional penetration-testing environments; however, understand that all these techniques can and have been used in today's cyber world. To learn how to think unconventionally, we will delve back into history and examine some extraordinary hackers from ancient Japan – the ninja.

Ninja Hacking. DOI: 10.1016/B978-1-59749-588-2.00001-9

We will attempt to emulate the mind and follow the teachings of the ancient ninja, so that we can create and execute unorthodox attacks against computer networks, systems, and facilities. We will also attempt to understand how to better be prepared for such attacks, should they target our organization. While this seems like an odd task to attempt, we will find that there are numerous parallels between the philosophy of the ninja and the philosophy of some of the more successful hackers – both malicious and friendly.

To understand the ninja, we have to understand the samurai and the feudal system of ancient Japan, for the ninja were defined by their times and foes. Both the ninja and samurai stand out in history primarily because their culture was not significantly influenced by western society until the 1800s. As a result, their culture and philosophy was developed independent of foreign moralities and viewpoints (Chinese influence is the primary exception). Because of the lack of influence by western society, it is difficult for most Westerners to understand the mindset of the times when the ninja were influential in Japan. While this book is by no means meant to be an historical tome on the ninja, we will be looking at the history of both the samurai, feudal Japan, and how the ninja profession was shaped.

The samurai were the militaristic upper-class of ancient Japan and had far reaching authority to shape both history and the countryside of the nation. The samurai were considered the elite and would (theoretically) dole out justice within their community or across the countryside during their travels. Samurai could be hired on as mercenaries as needed or retained as part of a standing army by a warlord. Without a doubt, the samurai defined how war was conducted in ancient Japan and were considered a standard of chivalry. However, chivalry has its shortfalls – specifically the need to follow ethical standards. The ninja eschewed such shortcomings, which is why they became such an important force in Japanese politics and war.

Born out of necessity because of constraints in their ethical code, called Bushido, the samurai were unable to do some of the more nefarious types of attacks or clandestine political operations. The ninja were able to fill that vacancy; however, it should be understood that the job of a ninja was not something anyone ever aspired to become – ninja existed because there was no other choice, either because of the pressures of war, the Japanese culture, or their inability to compete with samurai directly. The life of the ninja was not considered glorious or honorable – in fact, the ninja were often despised by Japanese culture; yet, they were sometimes tolerated because of their usefulness by the ruling class. This tolerance was sometimes cast aside – there were more than one occasion when ninja strongholds were attacked solely on the desire to eradicate the threat the ninja posed to those in power.

The line between samurai and ninja weren't always well-defined, either. In some cases, samurai would also perform the duties of a ninja, as dictated by the needs of the ruling warlord. Because of the disgraceful nature of the ninja, all ninja would disguise their true nature with that of a different profession, whether it was as a farmer, an entertainer, a priest, a fisherman, a merchant – or even a samurai. There have been many famous samurai who were thought to have also performed duties as a ninja; the need for clandestine operations in times of conflict was simply unavoidable.

Because of the militaristic training, the samurai were quite capable of performing this dual role.

In this chapter, we will look at the history of the ninja. But because of the inter-relationships between the samurai and the ninja, we must also understand the samurai as well. Once we understand the histories of both cultures, we can then begin to understand how we might integrate the philosophy of the ninja into the modern world of information security.

THE HISTORICAL SAMURAI

Hollywood has portrayed the samurai in various lights – sometimes good and sometimes evil. As with everything in history, the samurai cannot be easily defined in such simplistic descriptions. There were certainly samurai who abused their power, just as there were samurai who upheld the "greater good." To understand the historical influence of the samurai, we have to examine the philosophy and writings of the time.

The dominant philosophy of the samurai was that of Bushido (Bu-shi-do), which literally translated means Military-Knight-Ways.[1] In general, the samurai attempted to uphold the traditions of Bushido, even though there was no written version of this code of honor. However, there were some writings over the centuries that did have some influence on the samurai – both in terms of military conduct and philosophy.

Bushido

The samurai, and Bushido, were discussed in detail by Dr. Inazo Nitobé in his work titled *Bushido, the Soul of Japan*, originally written in 1900, intended for western audiences. Dr. Nitobé described Bushido as an ethical system that influenced all of Japan.[1] For the samurai, Bushido was the "noblesse oblige of the warrior class"[1] and provided the samurai with a moral compass in which to conduct their affairs.

WARNING

Bushido should not be confused with the western philosophy of chivalry, however. Because Japanese cultures developed in such a significantly different manner than western cultures, there are very distinct differences between the two; the use of *seppuku*, or the act of intentionally disemboweling oneself, is not seen in the histories and stories of knights from Europe. These differences between cultures must be understood so that parallels are not unintentionally drawn between these two militaristic classes.

Although Bushido was never formalized in written form, there were many scholars and warriors from Japan who wrote about their opinion and insight as to what it meant to be samurai. These writings, along with oral traditions, were used to teach newer generations of samurai what was required of them in service of their warlord. These teachings were restricted only to those things considered critical for a warrior, however. According to Nitobé, there were three areas that the samurai focused all their effort on: wisdom, benevolence, and courage.[1] The samurai were "essentially a man of action. Science was without the pale of his activity. He took advantage of it in so far as it concerned his profession of arms. Religion and theology were relegated to the priests; he concerned himself with them in so far as they helped to nourish courage [...] literature was pursued mainly as a pastime, and philosophy as a practical aid in the formation of character, if not for the exposition of some military or political problem."[1]

The Book of Five Rings

Similar to Sun Tzu's *The Art of War*, the *Book of Five Rings* is a treatise on military strategy. The *Book of Five Rings*, written by Miyamoto in the 1600s, broke the samurai strategy down into five elements or rings: Ground (strategy), Water (the warrior's spirit), Fire (fighting), see Figure 1.1, Wind (military traditions), and Void (balance of all things).[2] As a way of thinking in order to properly follow "the Way" of Bushido, Musashi outlined the following nine tenets[2]:

1. Do not think dishonestly.
2. The Way is in training.
3. Become acquainted with every art.
4. Know the Ways of all professions.
5. Distinguish between gain and loss in worldly matters.
6. Develop intuitive judgment [sic] and understanding for everything.
7. Perceive those things which cannot be seen.
8. Pay attention even to trifles.
9. Do nothing which is of no use.

These tenets, when applied to the different "rings," provided a path in which samurai could follow and stay within the moral guidelines of Bushido. While Musashi's treatise on strategy is worth reading in its entirety (even for those who are just interested in ninja hacking), we will focus on some specific excerpts.

The Ground Book

The *Ground Book* discusses strategy with regard to victory on the battlefield. Musashi summarized the job of the samurai as "the Way of the warrior is to master the virtue of his weapons."[2] He then discusses the advantages and disadvantages of each weapon used during his period of Japanese military campaigns. This is in contrast with that of the ninja, in that the ninja had to learn how to use everyday items as weapons, since possession of military-type weapons would make them stand out if they were in the disguise of any profession, other than samurai.

The Water Book

The *Water Book* focuses on the samurai's spirit; although the book focuses primarily on the fighting spirit, the writings were applied to every aspect of a samurai's

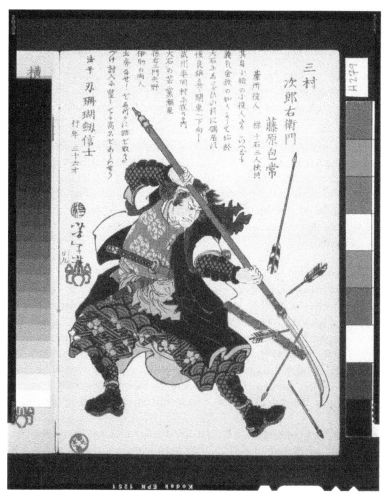

FIGURE 1.1 Illustration of Samurai Blocking an Arrow Attack.[3]

Miscellaneous Items in High Demand, Prints & Photographs Division, Library of Congress, LC-USZC4-8655
(color film copy transparency)

life – not just in combat. The idea behind water is that it is fluid, not rigid. When using the sword, although the attacks by samurai may seem stiff and regimented, the true mindset is that of calm and an absence of tenseness.[2]

What distinguishes the samurai from the ninja regarding spirit is the emphasis on "the cut," which is discussed at length and can be summed up in the words "Although attitude has these five divisions, the one purpose of all of them is to cut the enemy. There are none but these five attitudes."[2] While ninja may use diversion and attempt to avoid combat, depending on the situation, the spirit of the samurai is to win in combat.

The *Fire Book*

In the *Fire Book*, the author focuses on fighting, but expands into the fighting spirit of the samurai. The real crux of this book is in the following passage:

> *The training for killing enemies is by way of many contests, fighting for survival, discovering the meaning of life and death, learning the Way of the sword, judging the strength of attacks and understanding the Way of the "edge and ridge" of the sword.*[2]

As we can see, the emphasis is again on winning in combat, which is how battles were won on the battlefield. However, the *Fire Book* does not contain any information about feints or the use of deceit to trick the enemy, yet still let them seem the victors in battle. This absence of falsities in battle in the *Book of Five Rings* is because of the emphasis meeting in battle, instead of avoiding it. When we take a look at the ninja, we will see that the samurai and ninja have completely different viewpoints on the goals of battle.

The *Wind Book*

Understanding different schools of martial arts is an important part of the samurai's ability to be effective in combat, according to the *Wind Book*. However, the different schools referred to in the *Wind Book* focus on the same things found under the *Water Book*, which include the use of the long sword, the short sword, gaze, use of feet, and speed. The focus again is meeting an opponent in a battle to the death. This is in contrast with the ninja in that one of the goals of the ninja was to complete their mission, which was often that of a clandestine nature – face-to-face confrontations to the death were usually the rare exception, and would usually result in the compromise of the mission.

The samurai had a strong bond with their sword, which has been called the "soul of the samurai."[1] According to Nitobé, the sword was the physical representation of his own loyalty and honor and wore them even in the most trivial of activities outside of his home.[1] As we will see later, this is in contrast to how the ninja perceived their sword – as a tool.

The *Book of the Void*

The concept of void is an integral part of Japanese culture and is basically the belief in nothingness, whether it is emptiness or the unknown. The idea of void is included in both samurai and ninja teachings and is an essential part of their understanding of the world. According to Musashi, the *Book of the Void* requires samurai to understand other martial arts, but to never stray from "the Way."[2] By doing so, the samurai understands multiple disciplines without deviating from Bushido.

Hagakure (In the Shadow of Leaves)

Another treatise in Bushido was written by Yamamoto Tsunetomo in the 1700s and varies dramatically from the teachings of Musashi in certain areas. Tsunetomo summarizes the role of the samurai early on in the writings: "For a warrior there is nothing other than thinking of his master. If one creates this resolution within himself, he will always be mindful of the master's person and will not depart from him even for a moment."[4] The book, *Hagakure*, includes numerous stories of samurai, interspersed with explanations of what is Bushido. The examples in the *Hagakure* are a bit heavy-handed, compared to the descriptions of Bushido by Nitobé, and it describes many scenes in which the samurai committed (or should have committed) *seppuku* (Figure 1.2), in order to regain their honor over some grievance or mistake on the part of the samurai. According to Masaaki Hatsumi, the current grand master of Ninjutsu, or the art of the ninja, the examples in the *Hagakure* illustrate that the samurai "did not reach the highest level in martial arts, and their experiences and writings are mere illusion."[5]

One area that the *Hagakure* matches with that of the *Book of Five Rings* is that a samurai should have the mindset of attacking one's foe. In the *Hagakure*, the author states that "it is a principle of the art of war that one should simply lay down his life and strike. If one's opponent also does the same it is an even match.

FIGURE 1.2 Samurai and General Akashi Gidayu About to Perform Seppuku Circa 1582.[6]

Fine Prints: Japanese, pre-1915, Prints & Photographs Division, Library of Congress, LC-DIG-jpd-01517
(digital file from original print)

Defeating one's opponent is then a matter of faith and destiny."[4] In the case of the author's own views regarding how to best be samurai, he provided the following guidelines[4]:

- Never to be outdone in the Way of the samurai
- To be of good use to the master
- To be filial to his parents
- To manifest great compassion and to act for the sake of man.

Surprisingly, these guidelines are similar to those of the ninja – what is different is how they are executed during their duties.

Samurai Weapons

The samurai were well versed in multiple weapons of their time, including even the gun.[2] However, the primary weapon most associated with samurai is the katana, referred to by Musashi as the long sword, which could "be used effectively in all situations."[2] Additionally, the companion (short) sword (also referred to as a *wakizashi*) was used in confined spaces, the bow at the commencement of battle, the spear used on the battlefield, the halberd as a defensive weapon, and the gun for inside fortifications.[2]

The samurai did not have to worry about being seen in public with weapons – in fact, the samurai were given their first sword at the age of five. Afterwards, the samurai were always close to their sword and carried it with them whenever they left their home[1]; the sword was an integral part of the samurai's life (Figure 1.3).

We will see a stark contrast with the ninja, which did not venerate their weapons, but saw them as simply tools to accomplish their mission. We will also see that because of necessity, the ninja used common farmer tools as weapons, in order to avoid suspicion. However, for the samurai, the sword embodied much more than just a weapon to be used on the battlefield; it was venerated and kept as a family heirloom.

THE HISTORICAL NINJA

It is difficult to assemble the history of ninja, since public opinion of ninja was so negative. Historians of the time preferred to record events from the perspective of the warlords or the samurai – discussions of the use of ninja in these campaigns were often ignored or relegated to footnotes. However, the ninja have a long history and have been involved in battlefield campaigns, political assassinations, clandestine operations, and information-gathering activities, just to name a few. In order to be successful in their profession, they had to use a different set of ethics than the samurai, which was the basis for their being despised by Japanese society.

FIGURE 1.3 Samurai Wielding the Katana, Wearing the Wakizashi.[7]

Miscellaneous Items in High Demand, Prints & Photographs Division, Library of Congress, LC-USZC4-8658
(color film copy transparency)

Ninja also used a variety of weapons, designed to provide stealth, fortification infiltration, confusion in cases of armed conflict, and crossing obstacles of various nature. As mentioned earlier, all the weapons were considered to be tools only and not venerated or ritualized. Ninja chose to use whatever weapon would achieve success in their mission, which can be summed up as "to observe, to spy, to predict, and to stop danger."[8]

Although the historical ninja is somewhat shrouded in myth, we will attempt to discern reality from fiction, starting with different stories of famous (or infamous) ninja.

Origins of the Ninja

Although the identity and skills of ninja were perfected in Japan, there is a belief that a lot of the foundations of Ninpō were imported from China, through immigration of warriors, scholars, and priests; over the centuries, this imported wisdom was refined and codified into what is now understood as Ninpō.

The areas of Japan with the greatest ninja history were Iga and Koga, which consisted of over 70 families dedicated to perfecting the ninja arts.[9] Each of these families developed their ninja skills to meet their particular requirements and geographical locations; however, the skills were eventually collectively known as *Ninjutsu*. During political crisis and war, the provincial warlords throughout Japan would hire ninja operatives to perform covert activities. One of the more famous ninja families was led by Hanzo Hattori, who was employed by the Shogun Ieyasu Tokugawa as the director of the Shogun's secret police; Tokugawa referred to Hattori as "a bushi (samurai) from the remote province of Iga,"[9] which illustrates the blending of samurai and ninja.

The current style of Ninjutsu – the Togakure ryu – was established eight centuries ago and originated from the Iga province[9]; the Togakure ryu focused on 18 areas of training[9]:

1. Seishin teki kyoyo (spiritual refinement)
2. Tai jutsu (unarmed combat)
3. Ninja ken (ninja sword)
4. Bo-jutsu (stick and staff fighting)
5. Shuriken-jutsu (throwing blades)
6. Yari-jutsu (spear fighting)
7. Naginata-jutsu (halberd fighting)
8. Kusari-gama (chain and sickle weapon)
9. Kayaku-jutsu (fire and explosives)
10. Henso-justu (disguise and impersonation)
11. Shinobi-iri (stealth and entering methods)
12. Ba-jutsu (horsemanship)
13. Sui-ren (water training)
14. Bo-ryaku (strategy)
15. Cho ho (espionage)
16. Inton-jutsu (escape and concealment)
17. Ten-mon (meteorology)
18. Chi-mon (geography)

Many of these skills were used by other professions, especially the samurai; however, ninja perfected and modified each area as needed, to meet their particular needs.

The depth of knowledge in each area of training within each ninja clan varied, depending on the location of the ninja family and the requirements of the missions. Because Japan had so many different terrains, families would only be able to train

> **NOTE**
>
> Although we will try and integrate many areas of training of the historical ninja into modern applications of hacking techniques, understand that hacking is a relatively new profession and does not have the centuries traditional ninja skills have had in order to perfect their art. While this book examines ways to integrate the mindset of the ninja into today's technological world, we are only laying a foundation for future generations of ninja hackers to build upon.

in the geographical surrounds they lived in – it would not be practical for a ninja growing up in the mountainous regions of Japan to be able to train effectively in Sui-ren. This geographical limitation also restricted their ability to practice different disguises they would assume; again, someone who grew up in mountainous regions would have a harder time successfully disguising themselves as a saltwater fisherman.

Lineage

The traditions of Ninpō have been primarily passed down orally through the generations; ninja were trained by heads of family and Chūnin only in various discrete forms. There were never any "ninja schools" or dojos. Ninjutsu was a strictly hidden family practice only; however, some ninja wrote their knowledge in the form of scrolls. The Togakure ryu has a distinct lineage of grand masters[9]:

1. Daisuke Togakure
2. Shima Kosanta Minamoto no Kanesada
3. Goro Togakure
4. Kosanta Togakure
5. Kisanta Koga
6. Tomoharu Kaneko
7. Ryuho Togakure
8. Gakuun Togakure
9. Koseki Kido
10. Tenryu Iga
11. Rihei Ueno
12. Senri Ueno
13. Manjiro Ueno
14. Saburo Iizuka
15. Goro Sawada
16. Ippei Ozaru
17. Hachiro Kimata
18. Heizaemon Kataoka
19. Ugenta Mori
20. Gobei Toda
21. Seiun Kobe

22. Kobei Momochi
23. Tenzen Tobari
24. Seiryu Nobutsuna Toda
25. Fudo Nobuchika Toda
26. Kangoro Nobuyasu Toda
27. Eisaburo Nobumasa Toda
28. Shinbei Masachika Toda
29. Shingoro Masayoshi Toda
30. Daigoro Chikahide Toda
31. Daisaburo Chikashige Toda
32. Shinryuken Masamitsu Toda
33. Toshitsugu Takamatsu
34. Masaaki Hatsumi

A cursory examination of the names in this list provides insight into how the passing of ninja traditions was primarily through family. The greatest impetus for this is that families kept their knowledge secret, for fear that they would be discovered and their entire family would be eliminated; since self-preservation was a key component to the survival of the individual ninja, a hierarchy of leadership was developed. The hierarchy within a ninja operation consisted of three levels: jōnin, chūnin, and genin. These different positions within the organization may have followed family lines, but communication between each position was extremely regulated, for fear of discovery.

Ninja Hierarchy

The jōnin (meaning "High-man") position was considered the head of the organization and would obtain requests from different provincial leaders or daimyo. The jōnin had the duties of understanding the current political situations in the different provinces, accepting and declining jobs, ensuring the security and loyalty of the various chūnin (the middlemen) under his command, and setting high-level assignments to be completed.[10] In order to preserve his own identity, however, the jōnin remained anonymous to those under him; orders would be sent by couriers that would be ignorant of their duties and the identities of both the jōnin and the chūnin.[10]

The chūnin ("middle"), commander in the ninja hierarchy, was responsible for selecting genin (the field agents) for specific operations sent down by the jōnin. It was possible that the jōnin would send out counter-productive orders to multiple chūnin for a couple reasons – the first being a diversion and the second to test the loyalty of the chūnin. The chūnin translated the strategies from above into tactics for the field agents, yet would not participate in any field operations themselves.[10]

The genin ("lower") was the individual who actually conducted the espionage; they were the field agents of which myths are made. Following the orders from the chūnin, the genin would conduct their missions to the best of their abilities, oftentimes without knowing the entirety of the tactics behind the mission. Information flowing between the genin and the chūnin was often also anonymous, in order to protect the identity of the chūnin, should the field agent be captured.

Stories of Ninja

To get an idea of what role ninja performed, there are a few different stories that we can examine. Although there are undoubtedly some inaccuracies, there are some stories that are more recent that can be verified through artifacts. In Chapter 2, "The Modern Ninja," we examine some of the history and modern interpretation of Nin-jutsu and Ninpō; however, since the information about them come from within the lineage of that martial art and philosophy, we will restrict our examination of the ancient ninja to that of historical accounts.

Yakushimaru Kurando

As we discussed, espionage was the primary role of ninja; however, in some cases, they were called upon to perform more active roles. In 1336, Emperor Go-Daigo was held captive by Ashikaga Takauji.[5] A ninja by the name of Yakushimaru Kurando was tasked with the job of rescuing the emperor and did so by infiltrating the compound in which the emperor was being held by impersonating as a lady in waiting.[5] According to legend, Kurando was able extract the emperor from his captors by carrying the emperor on his back while fending off the enemy[5] until another provincial lord was able to arrive on the scene.

Yasusuke Sawamura

In 1853, the most publicized ninja activity in Japan was the invasion of Commodore Matthew Perry's "black ships" by Yasusuke Sawamura. Commodore Perry had arrived in Japan to conduct trade and establish political ties with Japan; however, the Japanese were unsure as to the real intentions of Commodore Perry and sent Sawamura to gather intelligence on the foreigners.[10] The ninja was successful in accessing the Commodore's ships and stole documents as both proof of their success and to bring back information that might be useful; the documents stolen are preserved to this day, which were "extolling the delights of French women in bed and British women in the kitchen,"[10] information that lacked in strategic value and serves as evidence of the lack of linguistic experience of the invaders.

Sandayu Momochi

In 1579, samurai and general Nobunaga Oda was traveling through the Iga province and was thrown from his horse. Nobunaga came to believe that his fall was an ill omen and ordered his son – Katsuyori – to attack the ninja in the province. Sandayu Momochi, in a feat that demonstrated his ability to perform on the battlefield, defeated Katsuyori's forces in what became known as the battle of Tensho Iga no Ran.[10]

The loss infuriated Nobunaga who then personally led an invasion in 1581, which decimated most of the residents; the remaining survivors sought refuge deeper in the mountain regions of Iga.[10] Although eventually defeated, the battle of Tensho Iga no Ran illustrated the versatility of ninja both off and on the battlefield.

Goemon Ishikawa

Sometimes, the stories of a ninja are embellished, as is the case of Goemon Ishikawa (Figure 1.4). Similar to the tales of Robin Hood, Ishikawa's history as a ninja has been transformed over time, to be made more unbelievable, yet entertaining. Similar to Robin Hood, Ishikawa supposedly stole from the rich and gave to the poor; however,

FIGURE 1.4 The Character Goemon Ishikawa.[11]

Fine Prints: Japanese, pre-1915, Prints & Photographs Division, Library of Congress, LC-DIG-jpd-00654

(digital file of 620a, left panel, from original print)

as the story goes, Ishikawa and his family were put to death because of his assassination attempt on daimyo Toyotomi Hideyoshi in the 16th century.

Ninja Code of Ethics

Gathering accurate information on the history of Ninjutsu is difficult; understanding the ethics and motivations of ancient ninja is almost impossible to gather. We will look at a couple of areas to see what types of ethics were followed by ninja: first, we will look at some writings from an earlier grand master on the subject; then, we will examine different examples to see how they correspond.

Writings of Takamatsu

Toshitsugu Takamatsu, the 33rd grand master of the Togakure ryu, wrote to his pupil and eventual 34th grand master, on the historical purpose of the Ninjutsu. In his writings, Takamatsu identified four priorities[9]:

1. Stealthy reconnaissance is the ninja's chief contribution to victory. […]
2. Universal justice and a peaceful balance in society are the ninja's motivations. […]
3. The ninja relies on the power of universal laws to fulfill his intentions. […]
4. The ninja works to accomplish his goals by having others unknowingly act out his wishes for him.

Historical Examples

In the tale of Yasusuke Sawamura, who acquired documents from Commodore Perry's ships, we see that stealthy reconnaissance was indeed a function of the ninja's profession.

Yakushimaru Kurando's efforts to rescue the emperor can loosely be seen as the working of universal justice and a peaceful balance; however, it is tenuous, at best, since there were certainly political issues that played a part in the conflict between those who supported the emperor and those who had captured him. To understand better the ideals of justice and balance, we need to examine how the influence of ninja dissipated over the years. According to Hayes, "it was peace, not defeat in battle, that caused the final demise of the ninja clans."[10] Peace came about because of the unification efforts in the 16th century which reduced the need for the special skills of ninja; rather than attempt to fight unification by supporting continued conflict, history shows that the ninja were integrated into the political reality of the times. Ninja families, like many others in the country during the centuries of civil war, would have undoubtedly desired a more stable country that would ensure the safety of their future generations and improve their own economic situation.

When Takamatsu wrote that the ninja rely on universal laws, he was discussing the need to do whatever it takes to succeed in their mission. Yakushimaru Kurando's daring rescue of the emperor provides a good example of a ninja doing more than would be expected under the circumstances. As already discussed, Kurando was able to thwart numerous attackers while simultaneously protecting the emperor from harm or recapture.

Ninja Weapons

The tools of the ninja were adapted from common, everyday items, in order to prevent arousal of suspicion. This is not to say that ninja were incapable of handling martial weapons in time of war; in case of armed conflict between warring nations, many able-bodied men were mustered into an army and were trained in such weapons as the halberd (used to knock over opponents, whether they were on foot or on horseback) and the spear (not intended to be thrown, but used during attacks).[9]

TIP

One of the hackers' greatest skills is to be able to look at an object differently than others and to identify uses that do not conform to their intended design. Although we will be discussing traditional tools and weapons of ninja, it is important to understand that these tools were shaped out of everyday objects, such as nail-removers, harvesting tools, and clothing accessories. A practical exercise would be to examine items within one's own workspace and see how it could be modified or used in a covert manner.

The traditional weapons of war were not used during typical espionage assignments, unless that assignment required the ninja to adorn themselves in samurai gear. To avoid suspicion, ninja would modify everyday items to provide concealment for secret communiqués or act as weapons. Because the tools were objects used every day during the course of the ninja's daily activities (whether as a farmer, fisherman, and so on), they had to be practical and functional – the level of reverence given to the samurai swords of the time was simply not applied to common utilitarian items found in a workshop or within the sphere of one's profession.

Tools of the Trade

As ninja assumed identities of the working class, they learned to adopt tools of their trade into weapons or means of improving their espionage capabilities. Farmers had access to harvesting tools; fishermen had access to nets and spears; and everyone had access to walking staffs. Knowing how to use weapons was only half of the ninja's skill set – the ability to transform nonweapons into weapons was the other half. Just like hackers of today, ninja were able to see things differently and modify things to make them useful in nontraditional ways.

Shinobigatana (Ninja Sword)

The ninja sword was shorter than those used by the samurai – the shorter length allowed ninja to travel undetected easier and fight more efficiently within enclosed spaces, such as hallways or thresholds. The sword was by no means ornamental like the samurai counterpart; intended to be utilitarian, the sword was often crafted simply and roughly in a home workshop.[9] The shinobigatana was used to help climb walls or open containers – whatever was needed at the time.

Kyoketsu Shoge (Blade and Chain Weapon)

A hooked blade with an attached 18-foot cord that is tied to a metal ring at the opposite end seems like a specialty weapon; however, these items were used in the farmer's field to control livestock and harvest vegetation. In the hands of ninja, it was used to slash, stab, or ensnare the enemy; it could also employed as a climbing device or used to haul equipment over walls.[9]

Kusarifundo (Weighted Chain)

The weighted chain of a ninja was used by farmers to secure animals or items; however, when used against a person, especially when surprised, the kusarifundo could be a deadly weapon. Easy to conceal, the chain could be withdrawn unexpectedly; when possessed by someone from the laboring class, it would not arouse suspicion by soldiers or guards. The kusarifundo was used by ninja to strike or entangle the enemy or their weapon – 18 to 30 inches in length, the chain was composed of non-reflective steel.[9]

Toami Jutsu (Use of Fish Nets)

Beyond the traditional use of catching fish, the net was used by ninja as traps that could slow or capture pursuers, including multiple attackers; nets could be set as traps in wooded areas and within corridors as needed. In the right surroundings, especially near water, nets were commonly found and would not be seen as a weapon by guards or soldiers.

Shuriken (Throwing Blades)

By far, the most recognizable weapon of ninja was the "throwing star." However, what is being sold as ninja shuriken in specialty and knife shops is not what was used in ancient Japan by ninja, which is much lighter and thinner than contemporary "toys." There are two types of shuriken. Hira shuriken were flat plates of metal that had anywhere from three to eight points – the points were not exaggerated, but formed natural angles. Originally, they were used to pull out nails; the hira shuriken had a hole in the center and were thin, which allowed ninja to carry and conceal numerous shuriken. The hira shuriken were used not as weapons, but as means of distracting or discouraging pursuit – aimed for the face or used as caltrops – the shuriken would cause the pursuer to pause and doubt their resolve, which might be enough of a distraction for the ninja to escape.[9] The bo shuriken resembled a knife and was also used as a means of distraction. Usually, not long enough to inflict mortal wounds, the bo shuriken would still be able to cause fear in an attacker, which again may be enough of a distraction to slow or halt the pursuit.

Clothing Accessories

Beyond tools and trade instruments, ninja could conceal items on their person that were hidden either by their dress or part of it. Kunoichi, or female ninja, would conceal in their clothing and hair items such as daggers, drugs, explosives, and wire (which could be used offensively, defensively, or as sabotage).[9] However, more mundane items could be used as well.

Staffs and Canes

Staffs and canes themselves performed the function as a defensive or offensive weapon. The disguise of an elderly person with a cane was certainly not out of the ordinary in ancient Japan (or today, for that matter). Bo-jutsu, or stick and staff fighting, was practiced throughout all the classes, including both peasants and samurai. The ninja could use any length staff, but they specialized in shinobi-zue (ninja canes) that were designed to appear as walking sticks, but provided concealment for weapons, including blades, chains, and darts.[9] Canes were also modified to conceal messages and used as breathing tubes under water and blowguns. The exact purpose of the cane for ninja was more than to provide stability for the owner as they walked the streets and outdoors – it was to provide a weapons platform that allowed them to succeed in hostile activities.

Tessen (Iron War Fan)

Tessen was designed strictly for war, or as a symbol of authority, and was often constructed from a single sheet of iron.[9] Other methods of construction included the use of iron ribs, which would allow the fan to fold; this alternative construction could be designed in such a way that the existence of the ribs were concealed, making the *tessen* look more like a common clothing accoutrement. The *tessen* would be able to deflect the blow of a sword, as well as an offensive weapon, whether it targeted the lower ribs, kidney, or neck of the attacker.[9]

SAMURAI VERSUS NINJA

Now that we have discussed the samurai and ninja individually, we can see differences between the two classes. In this section, we will compare the two directly, with a bit of a different perspective – that of modern-day penetration testing and cyber warfare. We will make note along the way some variances between the classes and how the differences pertain to network and system security; however, the examples in this section are just the start of understanding how Ninpō can be applied to modern situations.

Ethical Differences

Although we discussed ethics of the ninja, we did not go into much detail – we primarily just looked at examples of historical ninja to see how they behaved and extrapolated from that what the ethics might be. The reason we did not get into that much detail is that the ethics of the ancient ninja is quite complex. The samurai had centuries of development for Bushido, but nothing like that existed for ninja. Although the more educated ninja were aware of the writings of the times regarding strategy and warfare, ninja had to inject a different mentality in order to do things that were considered dishonorable in their society. This different mentality could be the result of the origins of the ninja, which came from dissidents, hermits, and outcasts – these people were already outside of society's influence. Over the years, these outcasts would take advantage of their history and social status in order to perform espionage and sabotage effectively; eventually, skills were honed and what is now known as Ninjutsu was defined.[8]

The ethics of the ancient ninja was voiced by grand master Toshitsugu Takamatsu, in which he said that "family, community, homeland, and 'appropriateness' determine when a ninja should act, not power, money, political obligation, or thrill of violence and adventure."[9] When compared with the ethics already discussed, there seems to be a parallel between that of the ninja and that of the samurai. However, there are significant differences in light of the family histories of each class.

The clearest way of differentiating the samurai and ninja is in relation to their interaction with society – samurai were ingrained into society; ninja accepted that they were outside of society. If we think about how this parallels today's society of white hats and black hats, we can see similarities, as long as we generalize. White hats have developed their own code of ethics through various organizations; black hats work outside any established code. White hats seek industry recognition through certification; black hats most often avoid drawing attention to themselves and rarely have certifications.

The comparisons of white hat/black hat with samurai/ninja can persuade us to see that information security is about confrontation. Those intent on protecting systems and networks are modern-day samurai, while those capable of maliciously infiltrating systems and networks are modern-day ninja – the level of skill of each class determines how well they succeed.

Battlefield Use

Samurai were very capable battlefield soldiers of their age, who would dedicate themselves to perfecting their art. Ninja were also just as dedicated to their art, but rarely were ninja placed into open armed conflict; each class had their strengths and uses and were applied appropriately.

Samurai had legitimate power and authority within Japanese society and were seen as protectorates. Because of this responsibility, there were expectations that the samurai would act honorably and conduct themselves on the battlefield with intense dedication, even if that dedication resulted in the loss of their lives. Ninja had no such expectations of honor placed on them by society and would exercise their skills in any way that ensured their safety; death of a ninja meant that the act of espionage failed, since a dead ninja could not relay acquired secrets. An emphasis on avoiding conflict and staying alive was strong within ninja teachings, which is contrary to that of the samurai.

In today's cyber warfare, direct conflict is expected by security professionals, and metrics are developed to gauge the successes of failure of these professionals and the devices that protect corporate or government data. White hats attempt to follow the latest security trends, expand their knowledge of both reactive and proactive techniques, and try to demonstrate their expertise each year in anticipation of annual reviews.

Very capable black hats, on the other hand, focus strictly on success of the mission – obtaining data without authorization or damaging systems. They are not concerned with how well they know the latest security trends, because they set the trends by discovering new ways to exploit target systems. They are concerned with how well they can avoid detection and how well they can evade those who have discovered their activities.

What we have not seen to any great extent in modern cyber warfare is the use of black hats by government or corporations against rivals. Some evidence exists that China is doing just that,[12] which may be a prelude to the use of black hats by all countries that have a stake in global cyber warfare. If such a use of black hats by governments becomes a reality, then the parallels between the ancient ninja and modern-day black hats would be even greater.

Weapons

Samurai typically came from affluent families that could afford to pay for the weapons, armor, and horses used by the samurai in times of both war and peace. The weapons and armament used were often crafted by skilled artisans and would be revered as a family treasure for generations.[9]

The weapons of the ninja were fashioned from everyday items and were not handled with reverence or spirituality – they were simply tools of the trade.[9]

In the contemporary world, acquiring significant talent is usually reserved for large corporations and government agencies, who can afford to equip their security professionals with advanced tools (often with high-cost licenses). White hats will have greater financial backing to attend training, improve network defenses, than black hats. Malicious black hats cannot typically afford the high-dollar software and must rely on open-source applications to conduct their activities.

NOTE

There is also another component (besides cost) to the black hat's impetus toward the use of open-source tools not usually found in commercial software . . . anonymity. Even if we assumed that commercial software is faster and more reliable, the risk of being associated with a specific attack because of purchase and registration information is too much of a risk for most black hats.

Black hats simply do not have the financial backing that white hats have; to be successful, the black hat often has to make do with whatever they can acquire, just the same as the ninja who crafted their blade from a random piece of steel found on a farm.

Despite the similarities between black hats and ninja, these are not interchangeable terms. In ancient Japan, there were ninja and common criminals – to lump these two types of people into a single group reflect a lack of understanding the larger picture; lumping black hats and ninja hackers into a single group has the same issue of shortsightedness. The difference between criminals and ninja can be broken down into ethics, motivation, and techniques. The common criminal (which is the category that the typical black hat falls into) is typically motivated by greed or self-interest; their actions are geared toward improving their own situation – not that of society or their country. The ancient ninja had very strong ethics and – as we will see throughout the rest of the book – conducted themselves in a manner that benefited their family, their community, and their homeland.[9] A parallel in today's world of these types of qualities can be found in people working in special forces, government intelligence agencies, and law enforcement who may perform duties that would be perceived as illegal or malicious by foreign countries. It is to these people this book is written for as well as those security professionals who want to improve their situational awareness and skill sets when conducting professional penetration tests against corporate assets. It should be noted (and will be noted often throughout this book) that there will be plenty of examples of activities that are *way outside* the scope of a traditional penetration test. By no means are we suggesting that all (or any) of the techniques discussed in this book be used in a typical information assurance project – however, we want everyone to be aware of the techniques that have and will be used in today's cyber warfare arena.

Summary

By now, we can begin to see that this book is dramatically different than most "hacker" books; we will be examining ancient methods of espionage and applying them to today's cyber security environment. By looking at the ninja from feudal Japan and understanding their function in their society, we can see how there is a need and use for a similar mindset in contemporary life. Governments and global companies are beginning to productively employ nefarious hackers to spy on their rivals, and the methods being used are frighteningly similar to those used by ancient ninja.

To understand the historical role of ninja, we have to understand the rise and employment of samurai; we must look at the ethics of the samurai and their dedication to Bushido to truly comprehend why ninja were a necessary component of the political environment of feudal Japan. Without this strict code of the warrior, ninja would not have found a niche to fill during the civil wars – a niche that was considered unethical, yet necessary.

However, it is important to understand that the niche could not have been filled with any type of person – it was filled by a group of people dedicated to improving their skills that matched or exceeded those of the samurai or the traditional warrior. The remainder of this book will be focusing on identifying advanced skills that meet or exceed traditional penetration-testing skills; although some of these skills will be impractical to employ in a pentest project, understanding the limitations of traditional pentesting and the capabilities of unorthodox hacking methods will improve the information security defensive measures of an organization.

By expanding our skill in unorthodox attacks – regardless of whether or not they are used in a penetration test – we can exceed the abilities of traditional penetration test engineers by understanding advanced intricacies of espionage and deception.

Endnotes

1. Nitobé I. The Project Gutenberg EBook of Bushido, the Soul of Japan, by Inazo Nitobé. The Project Gutenberg. [Online]. www.gutenberg.org/files/12096/12096-h/12096-h.htm; 1904 [accessed 1.07.10].
2. Musashi M. A book of five rings. [mobi]. MobileReference; 2009. B001VLXNUQ.
3. Miscellaneous Items in High Demand, Prints & Photographs Division, Library of Congress, LC-USZC4-8655 (color film copy transparency). www.loc.gov/pictures/item/2005678559; [accessed 1.07.10].
4. Tsunetomo Y. Hagakure: The book of the Samurai. Tokyo, Japan: Spastic Cat Press; 2009. B0035LCAPY.
5. Hatsumi M. Advanced stick fighting. New York: Kodansha International; 2005. 4-7700-2996-9.
6. Fine Prints: Japanese, pre-1915, Prints & Photographs Division, Library of Congress, LC-DIG-jpd-01517 (digital file from original print). www.loc.gov/pictures/item/2008660383; [accessed 1.07.10].
7. Miscellaneous Items in High Demand, Prints & Photographs Division, Library of Congress, LC-USZC4-8658 (color film copy transparency). www.loc.gov/pictures/item/2005678562; [accessed 1.07.10].
8. Zoughari K. The ninja: ancient shadow warriors of Japan. Rutland (VT): Tuttle Publishing; 2010. 0804839271.
9. Hatsumi M. Ninjutsu: history and tradition. Burbank (CA): Unique Publications, Inc.; 1981. 0865680272.
10. Hayes SK. The ninja and their secret fighting art. Rutland (VT): Charles E. Tuttle Company; 1981. 0804816565.
11. Fine Prints: Japanese, pre-1915, Prints & Photographs Division, Library of Congress, LC-DIG-jpd-00654 (digital file of 620a, left panel, from original print). www.loc.gov/pictures/item/2009615613; [accessed 1.07.10].
12. Bryan K. Capability of the People's Republic of China to Conduct Cyber Warfare and Computer Network Exploitation. U.S.-China Economic and Security Review Commission. [Online] www.uscc.gov/researchpapers/2009/NorthropGrumman_PRC_Cyber_Paper_FINAL_Approved%20Report_16Oct2009.pdf; 2009.

The Modern Ninja

It is sad to say, but the modern vision of a ninja conjured up in most people's minds is what has been paraded across the big screen by Hollywood in their oft-failed attempts to portray their interpretation of historic Japanese culture and war. If the modern vision of a ninja is not an image of a person garbed in all-black pajamas swinging from tree to tree or walking on the air, it is that of some self-proclaimed ninja caught on camera by news agencies doing foolish things, such as trying to bring a sword to a gun fight, or impaling himself on a metal fence. Either way, the reality of what the historical ninja actually was has been almost obliterated.

There are some who have continued to carry the traditions of the historical ninja into today's world, especially in the study of Ninjutsu. However, the question of the role of a ninja in today's world is a difficult one to answer; most answers, by those that have actually studied and practiced Ninjutsu, tend to espouse Ninjutsu as a highly effective method of self-reflection and internal growth. It is hard to justify the need for advanced self-defense and espionage tactics when one lives in the well-manicured world of suburbia and works in the forests of cubicles, faxes, and copiers. Although some may have visions of brutally destroying uncooperative fax machines, the combat techniques of Ninjutsu serve better within the confines of a dojo.

However, if we examine Ninjutsu tactics within the virtual world, we may find some interesting applications. Although we cannot rely on muscle memory to physically protect us against a physical attack, we can use the teachings and techniques of Ninpō to better understand the chaotic and anarchistic world of the Internet, and how to best conduct attacks and defensive maneuvers to obtain victory against our adversaries – or at least elude defeat. In the information system security world, those that would best benefit by examining the tactics of the ninja include anyone who conducts professional penetration testing, or administrators intent on protecting corporate and government networks and systems. Traditional methods, used by penetration test engineers and administrators within the cat-and-mouse game of identifying flaws within the network or system before anyone else, have been effective in most instances; however, current defensive and penetration-test methodologies have inherent flaws in that they still abide by restrictive codes of ethics to keep a penetration test project from getting out of control. The flaws come in the form of preventative constraints in the types of attacks that can be used, identification of off-limit

Ninja Hacking. DOI: 10.1016/B978-1-59749-588-2.00002-0

systems or networks, time limitations within the project, and business-related "political" minefields that must be avoided. Worse yet, the mindset of the defender and attacker can be the greatest weakness in the whole penetration test process; if the players in this event cannot mentally escape the societal and ethical restrictions that inherently come with being part of the corporate culture, effective tactics will be left unused and vulnerabilities will be left undiscovered. To truly understand the threats against a target system, the attacker must be capable of easily discarding societal pressures and norms and examine attack vectors that are unconventional and radical; otherwise, penetration tests become rote, repetitive, and ineffective.

One challenge facing those that are willing to shed the orthodox methods of conducting a penetration test is dealing with the question of ethics; many professional penetration testers are constrained by rules of ethics, whether from a certification body or within formalized business policies. There seems to be a general misconception that unorthodox methods of attack, including those used by the historical ninja, are somehow unethical. To understand why "unorthodox" does not equate to "unethical," a better understanding is required on the true nature of ethics, and how it is defined.

When the topic of ethics comes up in conversation within the context of penetration testing, the dichotomy between white hat and black hat hackers is often bantered about without properly defining the differences. In typical discussions, the label of "unethical" is often tied to the activities of black hats, whereas white hats are assumed to be the ones who act ethically. Unfortunately, ethics is perceived differently by different cultures and groups within the hacking community, and really does not belong in the discussion surrounding the differences between white hats and black hats.

Applying ninja tactics to modern-day penetration testing may seem anachronistic; however, there are many lessons that can be used to improve the technique of professional penetration testers – the most significant lesson being how to think like a ninja. By shifting one's perceptions about how to conduct attacks against network systems, the penetration test engineer can provide better value to the customer by identifying and exploiting vulnerabilities that may have been undiscovered otherwise.

MODERN-DAY NINJUTSU

In Chapter 1, "The Historical Ninja," we examined the historical ninja, and the environment they lived in, which shaped the way they performed espionage work. Times change, and if we are to employ ninja tactics into penetration testing, we need to see how Ninjutsu has evolved over the last few centuries.

When we discuss the modern-day ninja, we have very limited examples to look toward; because of the nature of war and peace, numerous traditional Ninjutsu techniques have suffered and been lost over the ages. The most notable example of modern-day Ninjutsu that was able to persevere despite the threat of time is the Bujinkan Organization, founded by thirty-fourth Grandmaster of the Togakure School, Dr. Masaaki Hatsumi. Within the Bujinkan Organization exist nine different martial arts lineages;

however, only three of these schools of thoughts within the Bujinkan Organization's current teachings can be considered unique to Ninjutsu, and Ninpō:

- Togakure-ryū
- Kumogakure-ryū
- Gyokushin-ryū

The other six lineages taught within the Bujinkan, intended to provide survival techniques for the ninja who become embroiled in combat, involve martial arts that are also used extensively by other traditions, including those displayed by samurai in ancient Japan (Garner B. personal communication, December 14, 2000).

Within each of these three unique Ninpō lineages, there are numerous tactics and skills that were shared in common – the differences between the lineages are largely centered on what tactics were emphasized, based on regional influences. These shared tactics and skills make up the following Shinobi Happō Hiken[1]:

1. Taijutsu, Hichō-justsu, Nawa-nage (body skills and rope throwing)
2. Karate Koppō-Taijutsu, Jūtaijutsu (unarmed fighting)[A]
3. Bō-jutsu, Jō-jutsu, Hanbō-jutsu (staff and stick arts)
4. Sō-jutsu, Naginata-jutsu (spear and halberd arts)
5. Senban-nage, Ken-nage-jutsu, Shuriken (throwing of blades)
6. Ka-jutsu, Sui-jutsu (use of fire and water)
7. Chikujō Gunryaku Hyōhō (military fortification, strategy and tactics)
8. Onshin-jutsu (concealment).

These eight branches have evolved and been rebranded over the hundreds of years of their formal existence, but they provide the student of Bujinkan Ninjutsu a structured method of training and a solid understanding of what the ninja skill set consisted of in times past. Additional martial techniques that aided ninja in their missions were added as needed, including the use of a short sword, truncheon, and metal fan.[1]

WARNING

It should be pretty obvious, but the application of any martial arts in a real-world situation, outside of a training environment, is dangerous. Although the areas of Shinobi Happō Hiken were listed here, it does not mean they should be incorporated into professional penetration tests. The objective of this chapter is to understand that ninja had a very specific type of skillset, intended to keep them alive and successful in their era ... and how we need to come up with our own skillset that follows the philosophy of Ninpō.

Although these eight methods make up the core of Ninjutsu, there is an additional component that has been brought forward in time that make Ninjutsu unique in the

---

[A]Taijutsu is another term for unarmed fighting and is used extensively to describe Koppō-Taijutsu and Jūtaijutsu within Ninjutsu.

martial arts; specifically, a mindset that permits the ninja to be successful in their unique role in unconventional warfare. In an effort to define the mindset of a ninja, Hatsumi stated[1]:

> *The spirit of the ninja is [...] based on the principle of bearing insults and swallowing the desire for revenge. In other words, the fundamental rule of the ninja when faced with an enemy's attack is to evade it naturally and disappear, using Ninpō Taijutsu (concealment skills sometimes referred as "Tongyō no Jutsu"). Only when no other option is left open would a ninja make use of natural principles and methods to fell his opponent.*

The traditions of the Bujinkan have been studied and used in training throughout the world, including military academies; however, popularity in the art has fluctuated over the years and been strained because of undesirable individuals with preconceived notions who misunderstood what Ninjutsu teachings truly encompassed. Those with misconceptions were typically interested in tactics popularized in the movies, including use of poisons, deadly traps, and brutal techniques designed to severely hamper pursuing enemies (Garner B. personal communication, December 14, 2000). Although, historically, the ninja used such techniques, the essence of ninja training was not one of aggression, but of evasion, as stated by Hatsumi, which unwaveringly precludes the use of deadly force unless absolutely necessary.

Although Hatsumi succinctly described what the spirit of a ninja entails, it is important to again stress the mission of a ninja was not to meet in face-to-face battle with the enemy; rather, the mission of a ninja was to subvert the enemy's efforts through strategic employment of espionage, unconventional warfare, and guerilla warfare without detection. Absence of detection is such a critical component of a ninja's activity that Ninjutsu has also been described as "if you can see it, it's not Ninjutsu" (Garner B. personal communication, December 14, 2000).

As mentioned in Chapter 1, "The Historical Ninja," the motivations of ninja were not one of greed or self-interest. Toshitsugu Takamatsu, the thirty-third Grandmaster of Togakure-ryū wrote that "family, community, homeland, and 'appropriateness' determine when a ninja should act, not power, money, political obligation, or thrill of violence and adventure."[2] The belief structure that benefiting family, community, and homeland come first in any decision to act is the essence of the Ninpō ethical framework; it is this ethical framework we will reference extensively to throughout this book.

WHITE HATS VERSUS BLACK HATS

In this book, we will identify similarities between professional penetration testers and practitioners of Ninjutsu. However, we also need to understand the function of those that attack networks and systems within the realm of computer security, and distinguish between what has become a popular method of identifying "good guys" and "bad guys" – white hat hackers and black hat hackers, respectively. The concept of two types of "hats" originate from old Westerns movies, where the good guy wears a white cowboy hat and combats those with nefarious intent, who can be identified by their black cowboy hats. It would be fantastic if it was just as easy to identify the "criminal" element in computer crimes by what type of hat they wear, but reality is much more difficult to paint in colors of black and white.

Many definitions of a black hat hacker try to intertwine the concept of ethics and morality with the activities of these "bad" hackers. The problem with including ethics in any definition is that ethics is a matter of perspective; hypothetically speaking, a hacker located in China who attacks government systems within the United States may be seen as one of the good guys to the Chinese government in certain circumstances, whereas that same hacker would be seen as one of the bad guys to those living in the United States. The inability to distinguish the good guy from the bad guy when incorporating ethical perspectives necessitates the need to define white and black hats differently.

To complicate matters, there have been others who have suggested gray hat hackers also exist, which can be identified as hackers who fall somewhere in between the actions of white and black hats. Gray hat hackers theoretically have the benefit of additional flexibility in conducting attacks when compared with white hats, yet somehow avoid the negative social (and legal) stigma of being a black hat hacker, because they don't break the spirit of the law. The disadvantage of adding the concept of a gray hat into the mix means that it makes defining boundaries even that much more difficult when trying to distinguish differences between appropriate and inappropriate behavior.

Black Hat Hackers

In an effort to remove confusion and perspective from the definition of white hat and black hat hackers, we can simply center our definitions around the concept of "permissions." If we define a white hat hacker as someone who has permission by the system owner (typically a high-level manager) to attack a computer system, and a black hat hacker as someone that does not have the necessary permissions, we reach a much clearer understanding of what the differences are between the two groups. The important part in labeling white hats and black hats is removing the concept of morality and ethics from the definition. But what does this mean in practice, then, if we are going to remove ethics from the definition, and how can we justify the use of black hats?

In the reality of cyber warfare or industrial espionage, using our definition of a black hat, those individuals attacking a foreign or competitor's system would certainly be categorized as black hat hackers because they would be attacking without the approval of the system owners; however, the attackers would be motivated to conduct their attack within the belief that it benefits either family, community, homeland, or a combination of each; by framing their activities within this ethical framework, their attack would be seen as legitimate and appropriate by both the attacker and those who would benefit from the attack (such as a government entity).

It seems difficult to justify the notion that black hats are potentially beneficial; however, we have already examined how ninja played a part in the development of Japan to undermine armies. To understand the need for unconventional warfare in modern times, we can also look at the need and existence of special military forces, which are designed to conduct clandestine and unconventional warfare and train insurgents in espionage and military tactics.[3] An argument can be made that there is a need for clandestine operations in cyber space, just as there is a need to conduct special ground operations in foreign countries by special force teams. This forces us to accept the notion that black hats can do good, at least from a particular perspective.

White Hat Hackers

Now that we have a better understanding of what a black hat is, and the beneficial use of unconventional tactics by clandestine teams, let's see if we can understand the role of a white hat better. When we mention professional penetration testing, or ethical hacking, we conjure up images of professional engineers conducting an attack within a predefined scope of operation. In some cases, the scope can be extremely restricted, certain hacking tools may be excluded, and certain systems designated as "off limits." Although this may allow the system owners to better understand the risk of a specific threat, penetration testing within a defined scope that limits the actions of the penetration test engineer does not provide the system owner a true understanding of the risks that confront an organization. To identify all threats, and thus the true risks to a network or system, the penetration test engineers must be given unrestricted "movement" to conduct their attacks. The disadvantage to a comprehensive risk assessment and penetration test is often time and money, which forces a lot of organizations to tighten down the scope of the penetration test. Depending on the level of support, the black hat hackers may have significant funding, significant time, significant resources, or a combination of all three, in order to conduct their attack; white hat hackers working for the benefit of corporations rarely have this luxury. To make the most of the funds and time available, penetration testing by white hat hackers is therefore restricted within scope requirements. To ensure repeatability and cost-effectiveness, methodologies are used by the penetration test engineers. The specific methodology used may be obtained through open sources, such as the Information Systems Security Assessment Framework (ISSAF), Open Source Security Testing Methodology Manual (OSSTMM), the Open Web Application Security Project (OWASP), or government documents; or the methodology may be developed in-house by the penetration testers themselves by blending different methodologies and frameworks and regulatory requirements.

Regardless of which method is used, the techniques and tools tend to be similar between the methodologies. The use of methodologies does provide some significant advantages, and can be used to find the threats to a system or network using well-known attack vectors.

To complicate matters, those who conduct professional penetration tests under the guise of a white hat hacker are often indoctrinated in information security "best practices" when conducting assessments. This indoctrination exhibits itself in the penetration test by favoring repetitiveness over ingenuity; however, professionals who have substantial experience in penetration testing will be able to modify and adopt their attacks in a way that deviates from published methodologies. New attack methods within the realm of white hats are relegated to research and development departments within universities and companies. When compared with black hat hackers, white hat penetration test engineers only improve their methodologies when someone else in the community has released a new approach, or they dedicate time to improve their own approach. It is unfortunate that many new attack vectors are developed by those considered as black hats by the information system security community – malicious hackers. To be truly effective in a professional penetration test, white hat hackers must expand their mindset to be closer to that of a black hat hacker.

Ninja Hackers – or *Zukin*

How should we identify those individuals who attack a system with the permission of the system owner using unconventional means that are outside the boundaries of accepted methodologies? The term white hat hacker cannot work because they do not default to the use of unconventional attack methods. The term gray hat hacker cannot be used either, because the very definition of a gray hat hacker includes the use of illegal, or nonconsensual, attack methods against a target system or network. And because the attack is being done with permission, the black hat hacker moniker has to be excluded. To properly define such an individual, we need to come up with a new term; in this book, we will use the phrase "ninja hackers" and "Zukin" to identify these professionals, and investigate methods to become a ninja hacker ourselves.

SHINOBI-IRI (Stealth and Entering Methods)

A "Zukin" is the name for the old traditional black mask that ninja wore during certain missions. It allowed them to conceal their identity and reduce their chance of being discovered. We will be using the term "Zukin" throughout this book to denote ninja hackers – and to distinguish ourselves from the traditional black, gray, and white hat hackers.

The use of unconventional methods during a professional penetration test has both disadvantages and advantages. To understand both, we need to identify exactly what we are talking about when we refer to unconventional penetration test tactics. This book breaks out numerous unconventional attack methods into different chapters and discusses disguise, infiltration, impersonation, stealthy entrance, surveillance, espionage, escape, concealment, and even sabotage – areas that are often outside traditional penetration test methods. In those rare occasions where a methodology includes an unconventional attack within a penetration test, the penetration test engineer is often still restricted on how far he or she can go and what type of "damage" he or she can do against the target system, which can be something innocuous as placing a text file on the system, or something worse such as deleting database records. Again, restrictions placed on a penetration test engineer during an assessment prevent a full understanding of the true potential of a vulnerability and effectiveness of an attack vector, resulting in misleading results.

Restrictions on unconventional attack methods exist because of the fear of negatively impacting the target system, especially if the target system is mission-critical to a business unit. The system owners may be apprehensive about system crashes and other disastrous events if they allow attacks that are outside the industry's "best practice" to be performed against their assets. The types of attacks that are often conjured up by the imagination when thinking of unconventional attacks include denial-of-service attacks, and buffer overflows that crash a system; however, the traditional penetration testing attempts to produce results without doing any harm to systems and prefer to identify and demonstrate risks to administrators and management. If we are to integrate Ninpō and penetration testing into a coherent tactic, we have to acknowledge that attacks that crash a system or deny access to a system are inherently contrary to ninja hacking, because it draws attention to ourselves and our attack, which needs to be avoided at all costs, according to the traditions of Ninjutsu. One of the duties within the Togokure-ryu, as written by Toshitsugu Takamatsu, requires that the ninja[2]:

> *Move undetected into the enemy's area of influence and gather pertinent information about the enemy's strength and weaknesses. Escaping in a manner that prevents his presence from ever being known, the ninja then returns to his allies with the knowledge that will permit an attack at the most opportune time and place, leaving the enemy bewildered by the fact that the attack "just happened" to befall them at their weakest point.*

Therefore, the methods of a ninja hacker, using unconventional attacks, could be used against any type of system – even critical systems – because the Zukin techniques should never affect the day-to-day operations of the target under attack, yet still identify vulnerabilities that could devastate the owners of the system if the vulnerabilities were exploited by nefarious attackers.

A negative side-effect of ninja hacking is that only a few potentially exploitable vulnerabilities are identified during the attack. The ability to avoid detection is threatened when multiple attacks are attempted against the target system. A Zukin needs to identify the best approach to infiltration and compromise before the attack, and carry out that attack to its (hopefully) successful conclusion. Only if unsuccessful in the initial attack would a ninja hacker attempt a second ingress (unless the second ingress was part of the attack plan, but we will get into that discussion in Chapter 3, "Strategies and Tactics"). The advantage to this method of attack is that resources are conserved and focused; the disadvantage is that only one attack vector is identified, tested, and exploited. However, this disadvantage does not invalidate a penetration test.

> **TIP**
>
> Within an effective incident-response program, an organization should be ready to deal with unplanned and unconventional events, which is exactly how a ninja hacker conducts his or her attacks.

Although only a single attack vector is identified and used, there is great benefit in conducting a penetration test that uses highly skilled engineers, capable of great creativity and understanding on how to use unconventional methods, to gain entry into a target system or network. In addition, any success can be seen as an indication that an organization's incidence response, vulnerability identification, patch management, security policy, and security training programs need additional improvements. For an organization that is truly interested in improving its security posture, any successful attack – especially those provided by highly skilled engineers versed in the use of unconventional tactics – provides a wealth of valuable information that can be used to the advantage of the organization and its stakeholders.

Additional benefits and disadvantages in using ninja hackers will be discussed throughout this book, but when used correctly, the benefits can significantly outweigh the disadvantages, especially because ninja hacking is the closest an organization can come to understanding the threats and capabilities of black hat hackers. However, not every organization can immediately benefit from a professional penetration test conducted by Zukin. If an organization does not have an effective security policy, incident response team, vulnerability identification program, risk-assessment group, or an understanding of the existing threat vectors, it would be wasting its time and resources by requesting a penetration test using unconventional methods; a better alternative would be to begin with audits, risk assessments, and eventually penetration tests using traditional methodologies. Once all other efforts have been exhausted to identify vulnerabilities within an organization, only then should the management pursue more aggressive and comprehensive penetration tests, such as those used by ninja hackers. Penetration tests using traditional methodologies will identify vulnerabilities that should be expected and are well known throughout the information system security community – penetration tests using unconventional methodologies will identify those exploitable vulnerabilities nobody expects, and which pose the largest threat to an organization, primarily because they go undetected for days, months, years, or indefinitely.

ETHICS OF A MODERN-DAY NINJA

The ethics of a modern-day ninja aren't significantly different from those from history. Toshitsugu Takamatsu's words, where "family, community, homeland, and 'appropriateness' determine when a ninja should act, not power, money, political obligation, or thrill of violence and adventure,"[2] can still define how a ninja should act in today's world. Any attempt to add additional rules to Takamatsu's definition would hinder the ninja from successfully completing the mission. For Zukin, Takamatsu's definition provides a solid foundation in which to conduct attacks.

Some organizations within the information security community have tried to define ethics for community members; in some cases, the ethics had to be revised because they hampered organizational security. Take, for example, the The (ISC)² © Code of Ethics in the beginning of this millennium. An "Objective for Guidance" published in 2000 "discouraged certain common but egregious behavior" including "consorting with hackers."[4] The absurdity of this guideline as a method of defining ethics can be seen in the numbers of government agency employees attending hacker conventions, especially DefCon and H.O.P.E. To understand the techniques, tactics, and mindset of black hat hackers, white hat hackers need to have some level of interaction with them, instead of trying to recreate black hat attacks through research and development labs. The shortsightedness in The (ISC)² © Code of Ethics guideline against consorting with hackers was eventually recognized, and has since been modified to "discourage such behavior as associating or appearing to associate with criminals or criminal behavior."[5] It wouldn't take too much effort to imagine a scenario where white hat hackers need to violate the modified guideline in order to understand, replicate, and protect against a new form of attack by black hat hackers. Advocates of the guideline would most likely point out that (1) it is only a guideline, and does not *require* adherence, and (2) violation of the guideline would be a rare occurrence for most professionals. However, the very existence of the guideline demonstrates the societal pressures placed on white hat hackers, which constrains their actions and modifies their perspective to favor repetitiveness and use of "best practices" over ingenuity and unconventional tactics.

Historical ninja ethics were developed to increase survival in historical, brutal Japan during both times of war and peace. To understand the relevance in today's hacker world, let's dissect "family, community, homeland, and appropriateness" individually.

Modern Ninja Ethics – Family

The identification of family as the first ethical determinant in defining the actions of a ninja is based on the inherent societal bonds that exist in Japanese culture. Today, the level of affinity toward family doesn't exist as strongly as in times past, even in Japan. However, if we expand on the definition of "family" to include coworkers and close friends, we can create a level of loyalty that loosely mirrors the ethics of the historical ninja. To apply the loyalty to family on a more modern level, we can take a look at a professional penetration test team; the capabilities and effectiveness of any penetration test team is directly related to the support received both internally (other penetration test engineers) and externally (organizational support). Without support from team members and upper management, any penetration test effort will be significantly undermined.

Application of ninja family ethics is unlike today's corporate environment and would require serious dedication by all team members toward a common goal.

Support for Zukin should not end at 5 p.m., when most people leave for work; just as knowledge surrounding the art of Ninjutsu was passed down and around within the family, knowledge within the Zukin family should also be shared with the same fierce intensity of the historical ninja, whose life depended on the sharing of knowledge within his family. This not only expands the knowledge base within the penetration test team, it also promotes an environment of learning and loyalty, which can be seen in modern Bujinkan dojos.

Another advantage of applying ninja family ethics to modern penetration testing is that the effectiveness of the penetration test team increases; team members are able to understand each other's strengths and limitations better without fear of rejection or consequences. In addition, any identified weaknesses can be compensated for by other "family" members. Communication is also improved because all members understand that teamwork is essential to the completion of the penetration test project; in addition, the members of the team succeed, or fail, as a team.

The best example of how ninja family ethics works in modern times would again be special forces units assigned to the military. Special forces units are designed to work as a cohesive unit, capable of surviving without immediate external support. Each member has a duty to perform, yet continuous and cross-training is an on-going activity, even during a mission. Team members are highly reliant on each other, yet are capable of independent action as required. Communication is essential, and long-term support – both internal and external – is critical toward the success of the mission.

Modern Ninja Ethics – Community

The organizational structure of the Japanese community was illustrated in the leadership organizational structure within the ninja clans. The hierarchy within a ninja guild consisted of three levels, with jōnin ("upper") being the head of the organization, genin ("lower") being the field agent actually conducting the espionage, and chūnin ("middle") being the assistant and middle-man between the jōnin and genin. These levels extended along all caste lines and within the ninja's extended community. A nobleman may have the position of jōnin, whereas a farmer might have fulfilled the role of genin. The job of a ninja was often secondary to their role within the community; however, the role of a ninja was a critical component of the progress made by the community in the larger theater of national politics.

Ninja communities were often small in comparison with other provinces within Japan. The profession of a ninja was not selected out of desire, but desperation, or determined by birth. In order to be able to stand up against the military might of the other hostile provinces, the ninja had to learn unconventional warfare and become "criminals" in order to survive. To protect their citizens, an intricate method of anonymity was established around the community caste system.

As mentioned in Chapter 1, "The Historical Ninja," the communication channels were created in such a way as to hide the identity of those in the different levels, in case an agent was compromised. Similar examples exist in the modern world,

> **NOTE**
>
> Although we discuss anonymity a lot within a discussion about community, it is important to understand that because of the seriousness of the risks involved by ninja, the community as a whole had to support the idea of anonymity for the greater good of the community.

especially among criminal organizations. The best example of the use of multitiered players of covert operations would be in credit card fraud.

One example of credit card fraud involves a company (such as a credit card processing center) that is attacked in order to obtain legitimate credit card information; the first layer of attack is done by the "harvester." After the harvester obtains the credit card data, they sell it to middlemen who buy the data and resell it to others willing to create replica cards. Very rarely do any of the actors ever meet face-to-face; rather, they attempt to maintain their anonymity in case someone in the chain is arrested and investigated.

Criminal organizations are not the only community that uses anonymity to protect its members – police have been using the "Crime Stopper" program to increase arrests and convictions of felonious criminals. The program is designed to protect the identity of anyone willing to provide information about a crime from initial contact with police, until the trial's conclusion. Identity was kept from others, including other witnesses, the accused, and those within the judicial system.

Another example for the need to create anonymous communication channels would be when national agencies conduct surveillance against foreign governments, in order to protect the agents, whether they are citizens of the foreign country or not. Unfortunately, the model may not be used, as demonstrated in the case of Robert Hanssen who sold the identity of informants and double-agents to Russian intelligence officials. However, history teaches us that the model works very effectively. For additional proof, we can simply look at resistance movements during World War II, and the Underground Railroad within the United States before the Civil War.

Applied to professional penetration testing, anonymity of the penetration test engineers can be extremely beneficial, especially when conducting physical penetration tests. If the stakeholders – especially security officers and network administrators – are capable of recognizing those individuals who will attempt to infiltrate a facility without proper identification and clearance, then the penetration test will not succeed in identifying exploitable vulnerabilities. Even during penetration tests where everything is done over the network, location of the attack systems used during the penetration test should be unknown by those defending the target systems. Otherwise, the system and network administrators may simply block network access to the attack systems, which again would prevent a full understanding of the exploitable vulnerabilities within a network. By encouraging loyalty to the community on the part of the penetration test engineers, and insulating them from others, the effectiveness of a penetration test is improved.

Modern Ninja Ethics – Homeland

Most professional penetration testers do not have to be confronted with aligning their activities within the best interest of their nation; however, some of the best examples of cyber warfare demonstrate how nationalism can play into the activities of hackers. Some groups are heavily aligned with national assets, such as those being created within the U.S. Air Force Cyber Warfare command. Other groups are either loosely associated with governments or are simply supporting their government's views through cyber attacks, such as hackers in Russia and China who have conducted attacks against foreign entities; granted, Russia and China are the most recent examples of large-scale support for hacking activities – however, they are not the only ones who have done so, and certainly won't be the last.

Care is obviously needed when dealing with penetration testing at this level; however, when combined with family and community ethics, nationalism can be a strong motivator for success in a penetration test effort, for either black hats or white hats. Outside of government support, nationalism can play a part in improving corporate assets, as well as stimulate research.

Corporate espionage does not simply occur within the borders of one's own country, especially in today's Internet world. By understanding the attack vectors against any company, which often include corporate spying originating in foreign countries, penetration test engineers can be part of the nationalistic efforts to improve the technological advantages of their own nation, which benefits its citizens.

Modern Ninja Ethics – Appropriateness

The order in which loyalties were listed by Toshitsugu Takamatsu was doubtfully arranged randomly, which means that appropriateness is the last consideration made before conducting an attack against a target. However, it seems that the loyalties are meant to be taken as comprehensive; in other words, all conditions of ethics must be met before conducting an attack. In a case where an attack would benefit the Zukin's family, community, and nation, they would not be able to morally commit themselves to the attack if the attack was inappropriate. According to Takamatsu, "universal justice and a peaceful balance in society are the ninja's motivation. The ninja does not use his advanced skills and powers for mere self-protection or greed-inspired profit."[2]

The wisdom of Takamatsu regarding appropriateness surrounding the motivations of the ninja can easily be applied to modern ninja, as well as those working in the information technology field. Although it may be financially beneficial to conduct attacks against a system for nefarious reasons – even under the guise of doing it for family, community, and homeland – it may not be the appropriate thing to do.

When combined, "family, community, homeland, and appropriateness" provide the penetration test engineer a better set of ethical guidelines than those espoused by groups within the information system security community. Unfortunately, codification of ethics down too far, such as that found in the guideline discouraging "consorting with hackers,"[4] has negatively impacted the capabilities of numerous professionals in charge of corporate and national security. A ninja hacker must be aware of the societal influences that exist and constantly extolled, and avoid accepting them simply because it is considered "best practice" by others.

Summary

At first glance, the application of ninja techniques, training, and ethics to penetration testing will seem inappropriate to many within information system security. However, traditional methods of conducting penetration testing has some significant, and potentially insurmountable obstacles in determining the effectiveness of a network's security posture, and efficacy of security training and policies designed to reduce risks of compromises.

Current penetration test methodologies are not designed to teach unconventional methods of attack, which often are the most successful in infiltrating a network and avoiding detection; this makes unorthodox attacks the most dangerous to an organization, especially when conducted by those with malicious intent. To truly understand the risks faced by an organization requires a unique type of penetration test, where the penetration test engineer must be capable of examining attack vectors that are unconventional and radical, which requires the organization to perform threat modeling against all systems, including those that were created "in-house." Once these threat models are understood, there must be unique ethical standards placed on the engineer; "best practices" and societal constraints imposed on the engineer (without truly examining the impact of those constraints on the engineer's ability to successfully detect risks) could significantly hamper the engineers effectiveness, leaving corporations and countries exposed to real and exploitable vulnerabilities.

By looking back into history and identifying commonalities between professional penetration testing and the ninja's mission of subverting the enemy's efforts through strategic employment of espionage, unconventional warfare, and guerilla warfare without detection, we have the potential to improve our ability to detect flaws within our client's overall security posture, thus making our family, community, and homeland safer.

Endnotes

1. Hatsumi M. The way of the ninja: secret techniques [Jones B, Trans.]. Tokyo: Kodansha International; 2004.
2. Hatsumi M. Ninjutsu: history and tradition. Burbank: Unique Publications; 1981. 0865680272.
3. Special Forces. Ft. Bragg. [Online]. http://web.archive.org/web/20080822224340/www.bragg.army.mil/specialforces; 2008 [accessed 01.07.10].
4. The (ISC)² © Code of Ethics. Archive.org. [Online] http://web.archive.org/web/20001217152500/isc2.org/code.html; 2000 [accessed 01.07.10].
5. The (ISC)² © Code of Ethics. *(ISC)²* ©. [Online] www.isc2.org/ethics/default.aspx; 2009 [accessed 01.07.10].

Strategies and Tactics

In Chapter 2, "The Modern Ninja," we examined different aspects of historical ninja and applied them to modern equivalents, which gave us a mindset that we can use to conduct unorthodox attacks against target systems. However, a mindset is only part of the equation – in this chapter, we will examine strategies and tactics that would be compliant with our new mindset. Fortunately, we do not need to create these strategies and tactics on our own; we can look back through history and see what has worked for both the ninja and warriors in the past and apply the techniques to professional penetration testing.

Before we delve into the discussion of strategies and tactics, we need to differentiate the differences between these two terms. A strategy is an overall plan, intended to reach a high-level goal; while a tactic is the actual attack designed to support the strategy. As an example of the difference between strategy and tactics we could use the following: ninja hacking will almost always include a need to be undetected, which we can include in our overall strategy. A tactic that we could use to support our strategy of stealth could be the use encrypted channels.

Now that we understand the difference between strategy and tactics, our understanding of historical texts on the topic of warfare will be easier to dissect and use for our own needs. One of the more well-known recordings of military strategy is the collection of Chinese writings titled *The Art of War*, which we will examine extensively throughout this chapter and book. There is historical evidence that ninja, samurai, and warlords knew about *The Art of War*; but even if that was not the case, the writings provide a solid understanding of how to conduct both orthodox and unorthodox attacks against a target with the goal of complete victory. Within *The Art of War* are numerous topics, or aspects, necessary for conducting a successful military campaign. Although most of these topics could be applied to ninja hacking, the four topics we will focus on include Laying Plans, Waging War, Maneuvering, and The Use of Spies – these four topics of *The Art of War* have some interesting applications to espionage and unconventional warfare, which can greatly benefit a professional penetration test engineer in discovering exploitable vulnerabilities.

Laying Plans involve understanding the campaign strategy and developing plans that support the strategy. A lot of emphasis is placed on understanding the enemy to include their defenses, mindset, capabilities, public/political support, and military options. Within *The Art of War*, the topic of Waging War examines battlefield strategies that help ensure victory or identify situations that foretell defeat. Although some advice may seem more like tactics, we will see that the writings on Waging War are intended to provide the military general with a solid understanding of the ways and means of conducting war, rather than provide specifics that may or may not work depending on the situation.

In *The Art of War*, Maneuvering examines conditions on the field of battle and how terrain and environmental circumstances can be best leveraged for a successful military campaign. Although the writings were designed to instruct commanders on physical fields of battle, there are many excerpts that can be used in a virtual military campaign as well. The topic "The Use of Spies" not only focuses primarily on saving a commander's resources for future campaigns but also examines the different roles a spy can play in order to obtain information about the enemy.

In this chapter, we will look at excerpts from *The Art of War* on Laying Plans, Waging War, Maneuvering, and The Use of Spies, which will allow us to develop a loose strategy in support of ninja hacking. Once we understand the strategic wisdom from *The Art of War* and how it can be applied to ninja hacking, we will be able to develop tactics that support our strategy, which in turn will make us more successful as professional penetration test engineers, intent on using unorthodox techniques to discover and exploit vulnerabilities within target systems and networks.

One additional topic we will examine in this chapter is the historical use of women within Ninjutsu. Although we will not be discussing specifics and differences between women and men in a professional penetration test, we will discuss women ninja (kunoichi) from the perspective of how they took advantage of the enemy's preconceived viewpoints. By the end of this chapter, we will be able to apply solid strategies against our targets by understanding the teachings within *The Art of War* and how to exploit opponent's presumed beliefs regarding their system and network defenses.

Before we begin our look at strategies and tactics according to Sun Tzu, we should keep in mind the wisdom of Toshitsugu Takamatsu, the thirty-third grand master of Togakure-ryū when he stated that[1]

> *Stealthy reconnaissance is the ninja's chief contribution to victory. The ninja should move undetected into the enemy's area of influence and gather pertinent information about the enemy's strengths and weaknesses. Escaping in a manner that prevents his presence from ever being known, the ninja then returns to his allies with the knowledge that will permit an attack at the most opportune time and place, leaving the enemy bewildered by the fact that the attack "just happened" to befall them at their weakest point.*

THE ART OF WAR – BREAKING THE RULES

Initially written in the sixth century B.C., *The Art of War* is a compilation of military wisdom that has been analyzed and annotated by scholars throughout history and translated into multiple languages[2]; the writings are considered a seminal work on military strategy and tactics and are used at both military academies and military history programs alike to teach students how wars are won. Although there is a question as to who the actual author of *The Art of War* was, it has generally been acknowledged to be Sun Tzu, a successful Chinese military general. Sun Tzu's effectiveness as a general is illustrated in the introduction to *The Art of War*, as translated by Lionel Giles in 1910, where he presented the following bit of biography on Sun Tzu[2]:

> *Sun Tzu Wu was a native of the Ch`i State. His Art of War brought him to the notice of Ho Lu, King of Wu. Ho Lu said to him: "I have carefully perused your 13 chapters. May I submit your theory of managing soldiers to a slight test?" Sun Tzu replied: "You may." Ho Lu asked: "May the test be applied to women?" The answer was again in the affirmative, so arrangements were made to bring 180 ladies out of the Palace. Sun Tzu divided them into two companies, and placed one of the King's favorite concubines at the head of each. He then bade them all take spears in their hands, and addressed them thus: "I presume you know the difference between front and back, right hand and left hand?" The girls replied: Yes. Sun Tzu went on: 'When I say "Eyes front," you must look straight ahead. When I say "Left turn," you must face towards your left hand. When I say "Right turn," you must face towards your right hand. When I say "About turn," you must face right round towards your back.' Again the girls assented. The words of command having been thus explained, he set up the halberds and battle-axes in order to begin the drill. Then, to the sound of drums, he gave the order "Right turn." But the girls only burst out laughing. Sun Tzu said: "If words of command are not clear and distinct, if orders are not thoroughly understood, then the general is to blame." So he started drilling them again, and this time gave the order "Left turn," whereupon the girls once more burst into fits of laughter. Sun Tzu: "If words of command are not clear and distinct, if orders are not thoroughly understood, the general is to blame. But if his orders ARE clear, and the soldiers nevertheless disobey, then it is the fault of their officers." So saying, he ordered the leaders of the two companies to be beheaded. Now the king of Wu was watching the scene from the top of a raised pavilion; and when he saw that his favorite concubines were about to be executed, he was greatly alarmed and hurriedly sent down the following message: "We are now quite satisfied as to our general's ability to handle troops. If We are bereft of these two concubines, our meat and drink will lose their savor. It is our wish that they shall not be beheaded." Sun Tzu replied: "Having once received His Majesty's commission to be the general of his forces, there are certain commands of His Majesty which, acting in that capacity, I am unable to accept." Accordingly, he had the two leaders beheaded, and straightway installed the pair next in order as leaders in their place. When this had been done, the drum was sounded for the drill once more; and the girls went through all the evolutions, turning to the right or to the left, marching ahead or wheeling back, kneeling or standing, with perfect accuracy and precision, not venturing to utter a sound. Then Sun Tzu sent a messenger to the King saying: "Your soldiers, Sire, are now properly drilled and disciplined, and ready for your majesty's inspection.*

They can be put to any use that their sovereign may desire; bid them go through fire and water, and they will not disobey." But the King replied: "Let our general cease drilling and return to camp. As for us, We have no wish to come down and inspect the troops." Thereupon Sun Tzu said: "The King is only fond of words, and cannot translate them into deeds." After that, Ho Lu saw that Sun Tzu was one who knew how to handle an army, and finally appointed him general. In the west, he defeated the Ch`u State and forced his way into Ying, the capital; to the north he put fear into the States of Ch`i and Chin, and spread his fame abroad amongst the feudal princes. And Sun Tzu shared in the might of the King.

Although the actions of Sun Tzu beheading women can certainly be considered extreme, the story can be seen as a method of illustrating the single-focused mindset required of a successful military leader, and the ruthlessness needed to win wars. Naturally, times have changed our opinion of what effective punishment should be during times of war, but the same mindset remains a requirement in today's world.

The question remains, however, whether or not Sun Tzu's teachings on how to conduct a military campaign has any relevance in a professional penetration test. To see if we can take the military wisdom of Sun Tzu and apply it to today's information security environment, we will examine different passages from *The Art of War* and discuss them in detail. What we will find is that the wisdom from 2500 years ago can be applied even to the virtual world.

LAYING PLANS

While we will look at those passages from Sun Tzu's *The Art of War* that have a greater impact on understanding unorthodox attack methods, we will also examine those passages that defines a military campaign and how they relate to penetration testing. This exercise in merging ancient teachings with security professional methodologies requires a significant philosophical analysis of Sun Tzu's words within the context of today's security environment, which is exactly what we will be doing throughout this chapter.

As mentioned previously, Laying Plans involves understanding the campaign strategy and developing plans that support the strategy and is the first chapter in Sun Tzu's work. The placement of this chapter within the body of *The Art of War* indicates that this is a fundamental framework that must be comprehended and adhered to, in order to be successful in war. We have an advantage in that Sun Tzu's work has been analyzed and annotated over the centuries, in an effort to more clearly define the exact meaning behind each verse. This will help us better understand what Sun Tzu was attempting to convey and provide insight into how we can apply the message to our own objectives as ninja hackers. So let us begin our journey of discovery and look at some excerpts from the first chapter of *The Art of War*. Again, this exercise will consist of a significant philosophical analysis of Sun Tzu's words within the context of today's security environment.

Five Constant Factors

If we want to conduct a traditional penetration test, the "five constant factors" would not apply; however, if winning at all cost is the motivator behind the attack against a target system or network, then it is essential to understand Sun Tzu's philosophy. These five factors are intended to provide a moral framework and justification for when and why one would go to war.

3. The art of war, then, is governed by five constant factors, to be taken into account in one's deliberations, when seeking to determine the conditions obtaining in the field.

4. These are: (1) The Moral Law; (2) Heaven; (3) Earth; (4) The Commander; (5) Method and discipline.

5, 6. The MORAL LAW causes the people to be in complete accord with their ruler, so that they will follow him regardless of their lives, undismayed by any danger.

7. HEAVEN signifies night and day, cold and heat, times and seasons.

8. EARTH comprises distances, great and small; danger and security; open ground and narrow passes; the chances of life and death.

9. The COMMANDER stands for the virtues of wisdom, sincerely, benevolence, courage and strictness.

10. By METHOD AND DISCIPLINE are to be understood the marshaling of the army in its proper subdivisions, the graduations of rank among the officers, the maintenance of roads by which supplies may reach the army, and the control of military expenditure.

11. These five heads should be familiar to every general: he who knows them will be victorious; he who knows them not will fail.[2]

Although these passages are not specific to Ninpō, they are critical components to waging war, even in information system security and especially in cyber warfare. We discussed Ninpō ethics in Chapter 2, "The Modern Ninja," which relates directly with the concept of Moral Law, as espoused by Sun Tzu. Heaven and Earth, in terms of a professional penetration test, encompass all activity within the actual penetration test, to include information gathering, attack tactics, enumeration, and exploitation of vulnerabilities. The Commander represents multiple members on a penetration test team, to include functional manager, project manager, penetration test team lead, and the team's champion, which is often a high-level manager. Method and Discipline are the tools, resources, and processes used by management to successfully complete a penetration test project within well-defined time, cost, and scope.

Heaven and Earth

Mastering Heaven in ninja hacking could be easily translated into understanding the patterns of a system or network, including those that work on the targets. By mastering Heaven, a ninja hacker will understand how to best take advantage of a target company's system activity and when workers are conducting business; often, an attacker will decide to conduct attacks during specific times of the day, depending on whether they want to blend in with normal business traffic or avoid detection and operate when all workers have left for the day.

NOTE

The application of ancient Chinese philosophies to penetration testing does not have to be ingrained in the psyche of the penetration test engineers; however, understanding these philosophies will help understand how the ninja perceived the world and the circumstances that influenced their special brand of warfare.

Earth, in a virtual world, could be seen to reference the connectivity "landscape" of the Internet and the target network. By mastering Earth, a ninja hacker will understand how to best take advantage of the network "landscape," whether it is attacking through multiple hops, conducting bandwidth-consuming attacks, avoiding detection by firewalls and intrusion detection systems (IDS), and identifying and exploiting vulnerabilities.

Earth could also represent the physical world in which penetration tests are conducted. A penetration test engineer could focus on physical attacks and attempt to walk through the door of a corporate facility by using techniques such as social engineering, tailgating, entering through unsupervised doors including loading docks, or hanging out in the smoking area and entering with other employees.

Together, Heaven and Earth encompass all the activity performed by security engineers during the course of the penetration test. Understanding both aspects of a penetration test is critical; otherwise, the engineers will be caught (by attacking during the wrong time) or miss opportunities (by attacking with the wrong tactics). Used together, the ninja hacker can meet the overall strategy of avoiding detection and confrontation.

The Commander

The other two "heads" deal with management, which are also essential components of a successful penetration test. As mentioned previously, the Commander refers to numerous individuals within an organization, to include a functional manager, project manager, penetration test team lead, and the team's champion. Figure 3.1 is a typical organizational structure within a professional penetration test and illustrates decision-making within the team.

In a corporate environment, the team champion, as seen in Figure 3.2, is often an upper-level manager who will support the efforts of the penetration test team across the larger corporate organization. The higher up the managerial chain the team champion is, the better the penetration test team and its projects will be supported and defended. In terms of governmental efforts, the team champion could be a high-level commander who has authorized the activities of a professional penetration test team

Team champion
(C-level)
PenTest
manager
Project
manager
PenTest
engineer
PenTest
engineer
PenTest
engineer

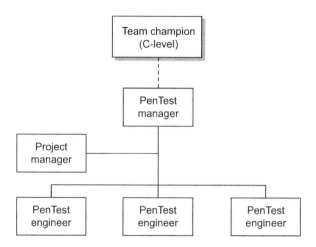

FIGURE 3.1 Typical Organizational Structure of a Penetration Test Team.

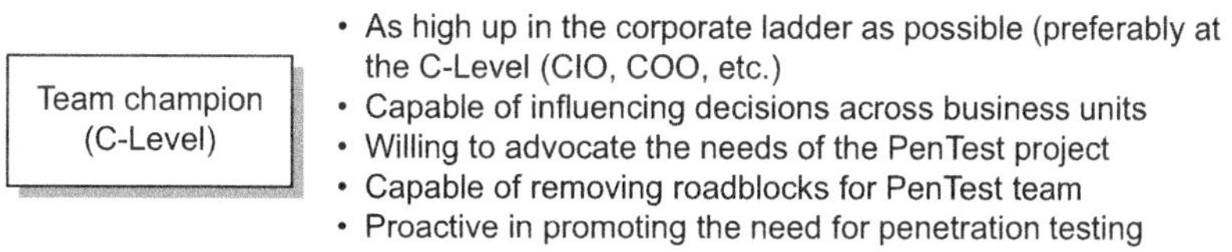

Team champion
(C-Level)
• As high up in the corporate ladder as possible (preferably at the C-Level (CIO, COO, etc.)
• Capable of influencing decisions across business units
• Willing to advocate the needs of the PenTest project
• Capable of removing roadblocks for PenTest team
• Proactive in promoting the need for penetration testing

FIGURE 3.2 Team/Project Champion.

or supports cyber defensive measures and research. In malicious attacks not supported by national organizations, the team champion could be anyone who provides financial, resource, or training support for the malicious endeavor.

To overcome obstacles, the team champion is often called upon to settle differences, encourage discourse, and increase the chances of success for the penetration test project. The ability to influence participation and cooperation across functional units is an important skill, which can improve the success of a penetration test. Without a team champion, the penetration test project will often fail.

The inclusion of a talented project manager can greatly improve the chances of success for penetration test projects. In large organizations with a permanent penetration test team, the project manager is often someone intimately familiar with penetration testing, as seen in Figure 3.3.

One mistake often made by management interested in starting a professional penetration test team is to select an engineer within the organization to be the project manager. The profession of project manager is dramatically different than that of an engineer; throwing an engineer into the job of project manager – especially without proper project management training – is a great way of ensuring that a penetration test project will fail.

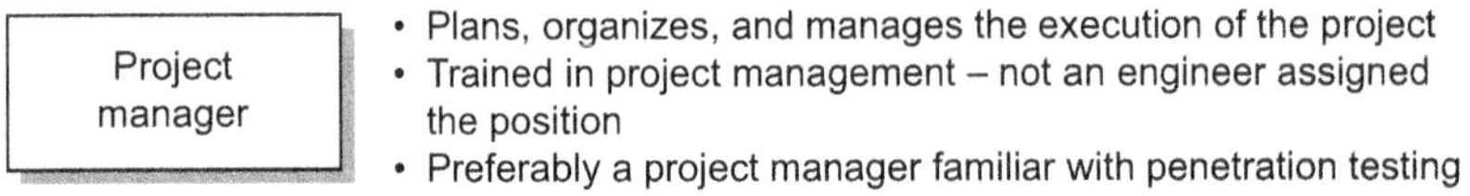

FIGURE 3.3 Project Manager.

Method and Discipline

Method and Discipline are the tools, resources, and processes used by management to successfully complete a penetration test project within well-defined time, cost, and scope. The project manager will have a significant amount of input and work within these two factors. Method and Discipline would focus primarily on project management processes across all stages of a penetration test project, including the following:

*   Conceptual stage
*   Planning and design stage
*   Executing stage
*   Closing stage

Modern project management methodologies can provide a significant number of processes that are useful within a penetration test; however, there are additional needs surrounding system and network attacks that require an expanded understanding of project management. Numerous published processes (such as those available to an accredited professional management professional (PMP) through the project management institute) must be adjusted to meet these additional needs. A thorough discussion of the unique project management requirements needed within a penetration test is outside the scope of this book and has already been addressed in the book titled *Professional Penetration Testing: Creating and Operating a Formal Hacking Lab* (ISBN: 978-1-59749-425-0, Syngress).

Warfare Is Based on Deception

In Chapters 5 and 6, we will examine different ways to deceive victims. One of the reasons we use deception is because it is much quicker to obtain information through social engineering than it is to try and compromise a computer network and its internal systems. However, Sun Tzu provides many more reasons why we should employ deception in our attacks.

18. All warfare is based on deception.

19. Hence, when able to attack, we must seem unable; when using our forces, we must seem inactive; when we are near, we must make the enemy believe we are far away; when far away, we must make him believe we are near.

20. Hold out baits to entice the enemy. Feign disorder, and crush him.

[...]

24. Attack him where he is unprepared, appear where you are not expected.

25. These military devices, leading to victory, must not be divulged beforehand.[2]

Sun Tzu recognizes in the previous verses that deception is a critical component in war. To apply these words to a penetration test, we must be able to catch the system administrators and network security engineers unprepared and unawares.

Deception, regarding "unable" and "inactive," implies to the ninja hacker that any attack against a target system or network must be seen as incapable of success. A targeted probe using numerous versions of malformed packets against a target system might alert a network security engineer and make them react to the probe; while a default scan launched from a proxy server located in a country well known for simplistic and automated attacks may be ignored by the same security engineer. Although we may know how to quickly and effectively attack a system, it is prudent to not reveal our capabilities early in our attack so that our target administrators underestimate our skills.

Inactive could be interpreted a couple different ways. The first way would be undetectable, such as the use of secure tunnel over well-known ports. The second way would be that the activity is so slow that network security devices in a target network would not detect them because a certain threshold was not reached.

Deception surrounding location is something already familiar with most penetration test engineers, who have to deal with network security engineers "cheating" during an announced penetration test. It is not uncommon for network and system engineers to intentionally block access to penetration test engineers through the use of firewalls, in order to provide an inaccurate picture of a system and its security posture. Penetration test engineers often create proxies or attack servers in unexpected locations, in order to appear as legitimate systems and not as hacking platforms.

"Hold out baits" would certainly fall within the context of social engineering, which we will discuss extensively throughout this book. Social engineering typically plays on people's desire to

- be helpful
- be greedy
- be afraid
- avoid confrontation
- avoid embarrassment

Greed seems the most obvious when talking about baiting someone, but we will examine numerous ways to bait people into complying with our own desires during a penetration test.

Attacking from unexpected directions is the best way to avoid detection. When it comes to penetration testing, network and system security personnel are often caught expecting attacks to originate from outside the company. Internal systems, vendor networks, and employee systems are often relegated to secondary efforts when securing a network from malicious attacks; which makes them our primary target. It is often easier to enter a network because an employee opens up an e-mail with a malicious attachment that gives us administrator access on the system by establishing a reverse shell, than it is to conduct head-on attacks against firewalls from an attack platform located on the Internet. In a physical attack, it may be easier to enter through a loading dock entrance, than through the front door where a security guard is stationed. We need to focus our energy looking for unexpected locations of ingress; as part of a security life cycle, most of the expected avenues of attack will have already been thought of and hardened. Our job as ninja hackers is to identify the ways into a network that nobody thought of before … where they are unprepared for our attack.

WAGING WAR

Waging War, within the writings of Sun Tzu, examines battlefield strategies that help ensure victory or identify situations that foretell defeat. A lot of discussion focuses on actual costs and political treats to protracted campaigns, which can certainly have a bearing on penetration testing in general. However, there are a couple passages that can provide the ninja hacker an advantage when conducting unorthodox attacks. Despite the fact we have talked about slowing down attacks to avoid detection, there is a fine line where we proceed too slowly and jeopardize our own success.

It also behooves us to focus on our goal – successful penetration of a target system or network. Often, we become distracted with how clever we can be or exploring the entire system; what we need to do is make sure that the objective of our mission is always solid in our thoughts and prevent ourselves from deviating from the project scope.

No Cleverness in Long Delays

Penetration tests employ very skilled engineers to conduct the attacks, and the engineers typically draw a large salary. Because of this, management tries to maximize profit by speeding up penetration test. Although this could be detrimental in a ninja hacking environment where the primary goal is success – not speed – there are times when penetration test projects should be pushed along. Sun Tzu recognized that warriors can grow weary in prolonged or delayed campaigns.

> 2. When you engage in actual fighting, if victory is long in coming, then men's weapons will grow dull and their ardor will be damped. If you lay siege to a town, you will exhaust your strength.

> [...]

5. Thus, though we have heard of stupid haste in war, cleverness has never been seen associated with long delays.[2]

Professional penetration testing is expensive. Prolonged attacks against a target system or network may not be the most efficient use of time, resources, and money; nor does it reflect well on the hacker's skills if a project extends past a reasonable amount of time. Sometimes projects are longer than expected because the penetration test engineer cannot stay within the project scope. With ninja hacking, there's only a need to find one way in, not all exploitable attack vectors.

A prolonged penetration test project also negatively affects the enthusiasm and energies of the penetration test team. It is natural for a person's interest to taper off over time, and security engineers are no exception. One task that constantly plagues a project manager is ensuring that the quality of work performed by team members is consistently high across the entire project. Because of the unique nature of a penetration test, where discoveries and exploits occur toward the end of the engagement and not at the beginning, any loss of enthusiasm by the penetration test team members endangers the success of the project. Energies need to increase the longer the penetration test engagement – not lessen. Therefore, projects need to be developed in such a way that victory is quick, not prolonged.

Rousing Anger

In information security, there is an advantage to remaining objective and unattached during a penetration test; in war, this sort of indifference can do more harm than good. In order to endure prolonged campaigns, there has to be a reason to fight; anger and rewards are great motivators.

16. Now in order to kill the enemy, our men must be roused to anger; that there may be advantage from defeating the enemy, they must have their rewards.

17. Therefore in chariot fighting, when ten or more chariots have been taken, those should be rewarded who took the first.[2]

Although there is a pervasive belief that a paycheck should be sufficient reward, this is not often the case for those within the information technology field, especially those working as penetration test engineers. These professionals are often guided by different motivations and include[3] the following:

- Developing knowledge
- Creating intricate and beautiful systems
- Proving potential
- Making money
- Helping others
- Enhancing career growth

If the penetration test engineer is not rewarded properly, depending on what motivates them, the project may not be as successful as hoped. Sun Tzu recognized back in sixth century B.C. that a lack of rewards beyond a paycheck would enervate the soldiers, while rewarding soldiers for exceptional service would assists the war effort. The trick is to reward the soldiers in a way that matches their particular motivation.

An astute project manager who has worked with the team for an extended length of time will be able to identify what motivates the project members and reward them accordingly. The penetration test engineer will be consistently focused on the project scope throughout the entire length of a project as long they can perceive the possibility of rewards beyond their paycheck. As for ninja hacking, although we identified in Chapter 2, "The Modern Ninja," that family, community, homeland, and appropriateness as ethical constraints (and possible motivators) for conducting an attack in the first place, there often still needs to be a reward system in place to keep the engineers motivated throughout the entire project life cycle.

Victory – Not Lengthy Campaigns

War, for war's sake, is doomed to fail. There must be a conclusion to any campaign, including penetration test projects. Without a foreseeable finality, warriors get tired and begin to look for other outlets to distract them. It is important for project managers to provide an end-date to all campaigns.

> *19. In war, then, let your great object be victory, not lengthy campaigns.*[2]

Although we already discussed the need to keeping a project within time, cost, and scope previously in this chapter, we need to understand the criticality of doing so. Sun Tzu's dictum should be foremost in the minds of all team members, not just the project manager. In the corporate world, ninja hacking can benefit the organization greatly, as long as the scope is understood and followed. There is no benefit in conducting an attack that does not take advantage of the unique nature and skill set of the team members, who have learned how to expand their skills beyond traditional and orthodox methodologies.

MANEUVERING

Maneuvering examines conditions on the field of battle and how terrain and environmental circumstances can be best leveraged for a successful military campaign. A lot of what Sun Tzu wrote deals with taking advantage of terrain; however, there are some passages that fit well into our concept of ninja hacking and focus primarily on when and how to strike. Within the virtual world of the Internet, the timing and tenacity of our attacks will be critical components in our attack.

Using traditional methods of penetration testing, attacks are often dictated as to when and how they can occur – customers may dictate that there can be no attacks during business hours, no use of tools that *might possibly* damage systems, communicate with network security before an attack begins, only target-specific systems can be probed, etc. If both the attacker and defender know how and when the attack will be conducted, the true nature of a systems or networks security posture is inaccurate. To truly understand how secure a system is, the attack team must be permitted to devise strategies and tactics that make sense to them. For ninja hackers, they must also perform their attack in a manner that avoids detection.

Practice Dissimulation

The ability to provide the enemy believable, yet false, information during an attack can be the difference between victory and defeat. In penetration testing, we use social engineering to deceive our victims – this is not just a good idea, it is fundamental to combat.

> *15. In war, practice dissimulation, and you will succeed.*[2]

One of the hardest things for people to do in the security industry is to lie; but lie we must. Whether it is through social engineering, malformed packets, use of false identity, or mislabeling malicious data to appear legitimate, we must lie to be effective as ninja hackers. This is no easy task because IT and security often encourage open and accurate communication. At Colorado Technical University, there is a course that teaches penetration testing. A requirement for this course is that the students have to go out in their community and social engineer someone; they must obtain some sort of information to which they should not have access. Examples of successful social engineering efforts on the part of the students include obtaining social security numbers, PIN numbers, authorization codes at checkout stands, mothers' maiden names, dates of birth, and more. However, most students are not successful in social engineering; others are not successful until many weeks after the class begins, primarily because they do not know how to truly lie. In the beginning, they have gotten too nervous in their attempts to wrangle unauthorized information out of others; in time, they finally get the courage up and successfully social engineer others and get a passing grade for their efforts.

Lying takes practice. The ninja from ancient Japan had to be quite effective at lying, considering their life depended on others believing the lie. In ninja hacking, failing to convince others does not have the same level of consequences; even with a "get out of jail free" note from the client, the worst case scenario is a night in jail while events are being sorted out and phone calls are made. It is important to have – in advance – direct cell phone numbers along with any alternative phone numbers on hand before we begin any social or physical attacks; this will save us quite a headache in the long run.

Strike Fast – Strike Wisely

Although brute-force attacks have their place in both modern penetration testing and feudal Japan, it is rarely the attack of choice for the ninja; strategic and pinpoint attacks are much more the appropriate tool for the ninja. Sun Tzu recognized the advantage of precise attacks as well.

18. In raiding and plundering be like fire, in immovability like a mountain.

19. Let your plans be dark and impenetrable as night, and when you move, fall like a thunderbolt.

[...]

21. Ponder and deliberate before you make a move.

22. He will conquer who has learnt the artifice of deviation. Such is the art of maneuvering.[2]

Repeatable, low-level processes (not to be confused with high-level frameworks and methodologies) within professional penetration testing are rare; within ninja hacking, they are even rarer. Once a ninja hacker uses a tactic against a target, reuse of the tactic in a later penetration test increases the risk of being caught since others are now aware of that method. Ninja hackers must be meticulous in formulating their attack so that they will not be detected, and the best way is to constantly create new tactics.

TIP

Some of Sun Tzu's wisdom may seem contradictory; on one hand, he suggests patience and other times he promotes blitzkrieg-type attacks. Experience in penetration testing is probably the best way know what the speed of one's attack should be. However, like all great military commanders, studying the campaigns of others is essential "homework." As ninja hackers, we need to examine as many different attacks as possible and learn from their victories and defeats. A great place to start is the FBI's Cyber Investigations Web site: fbi.gov/cyberinvest/cyberhome.htm.

For example, let us assume a ninja hacker attacked a system, which had an FTP service running. In this case, there was a way to compromise the FTP service using a buffer overflow attack. Once the system administrators find out about the successful attack, they will be *much more* aware of the risk of buffer overflows to their system and will undoubtedly start paying more attention to patching the host applications. If the ninja hacker were to attack a different remote-access application on the system, the chances of success would undoubtedly drop and the chances of being caught would increase. Once the initial compromise was successful, a ninja hacker must focus on a completely new attack vector; to do otherwise is to simply perform a professional penetration test using traditional methodologies.

Studying Moods

The ability to understand the moods of your opponents allows insight into how to best attack them. Sun Tzu also wrote that *"if you know the enemy and know yourself, you need not fear the result of a hundred battles."*[2]

29. A clever general, therefore, avoids an army when its spirit is keen, but attacks it when it is sluggish and inclined to return. This is the art of studying moods.

30. Disciplined and calm, to await the appearance of disorder and hubbub amongst the enemy:—this is the art of retaining self-possession.[2]

Taking advantage of your opponent's weaknesses is paramount to a successful campaign; but to know their weaknesses requires a deep understanding of what both motivates them and exhausts them. Even more important is we need to identify our own weaknesses, including how we perform attacks and develop preconceived ideas. If we can understand our own patterns and biases, we can modify them to be less predictable and more effective in our careers.

We should also learn to be methodical and deliberate in our attacks, even if they appear to be chaotic and unfocused. In Chapter 10, "Psychological Weaknesses," we will discuss in detail the concept of "the five weaknesses," which are laziness, anger, fear, sympathy, and vanity. These are balanced by "the five needs," – security, sex, wealth, pride, and pleasure. By understanding the "fives," we can identify our weaknesses and the weaknesses of others.

THE USE OF SPIES

As ninja hackers, we need to be comfortable with the concept that we are spies. Our activity often generates a lot of animosity directed at us. The use of "spies" is critical to identify weaknesses that are both known and unknown to the system or network administrators. As ninja hackers, it is our job to pry secrets out of the target, the target's administrators, and support systems that have elevated levels of trust.

However, most of the time, system and network administrators do not want us to find out these secrets; disclosure of vulnerabilities tends to make the administrators appear incapable (which is rarely the case). Identifying misconfigurations, weak procedures, and improper resource management are the "skeletons in the closet" that must be dragged out into the open in order to improve security postures. Although it is not the job of the ninja hacker to sooth the bruised egos of administrators whose systems and networks were compromised, it is still necessary to promote a positive atmosphere so that security postures improve.

Five Classes of Spies

Sun Tzu identified five different types of spies used during a military campaign. In ancient Japan, the ninja were experts in spying for military commanders; Sun Tzu recognized five distinct roles for spies, all used by the ninja in different circumstances.

6. Knowledge of the enemy's dispositions can only be obtained from other men.

7. Hence the use of spies, of whom there are five classes: (1) Local spies; (2) inward spies; (3) converted spies; (4) doomed spies; (5) surviving spies.

8. When these five kinds of spy are all at work, none can discover the secret system. This is called "divine manipulation of the threads." It is the sovereign's most precious faculty.

9. Having LOCAL SPIES means employing the services of the inhabitants of a district.

10. Having INWARD SPIES, making use of officials of the enemy.

11. Having CONVERTED SPIES, getting hold of the enemy's spies and using them for our own purposes.

12. Having DOOMED SPIES, doing certain things openly for purposes of deception, and allowing our spies to know of them and report them to the enemy.

13. SURVIVING SPIES, finally, are those who bring back news from the enemy's camp.[2]

The question is how each one relates to an organized attack against a target system of network. From a technical perspective, none of these types of spies have to actually be persons – in the virtual world of networking – all of these spies could be bots and applications running to provide us a comprehensive understanding of our target. Let's look at some potential tools and concepts that would fit each description.

Local Spies

"Inhabitants of the district"[2] could include vendors, contractors, delivery companies, and utility companies – anyone or thing that supports the day-to-day business of the target organization. In ninja hacking, exploitation of the trust relationship between these groups and the target organization would improve our ability to conduct reconnaissance of the facility and network infrastructure.

Local spies would come under close scrutiny – more than employees and inward spies. When conducting physical attacks, discrepancies in appearance, mannerisms, or vernacular will alert corporate security quickly. The use of disguises by the ancient ninja is an interesting topic, which we will examine much closer in Chapter 5, "Disguise," and Chapter 6, "Impersonation."

When conducting virtual attacks, discrepancies in originating IP addresses, protocols, and timing become the triggers for security alerts. We will need to use methods of disguising our communications through use of fraudulent certificates, anonymous relays, packet manipulation software, and exploitation of trusted networks.

Although local spies are under greater scrutiny, they are typically deployed before other spies. It is much more difficult to obtain inward or converted spies, forcing us to start locally. There are some advantages in using local spies in that they are easily disposed of. If we social engineer someone over the phone using a fake identity, once we hang up the phone we can simply discard that identity. Inward and converted spies are not so disposable – it takes a significant amount of work to get someone (or something) on the inside. In some cases, an inward spy is impossible to deploy until a local spy has been successful. An example would be the success of an local spy (masquerading as an IT technician) is essential before an inward spy (keylogger/camera/wireless access point) can be engaged.

Inward Spies

It would be an incredible fortune if we could get one of our own ninja hackers employed within the target organization. In cases of national and corporate espionage, this may be a realistic possibility. Chances are, however, that our only option is persuade current employees to assist in our effort to infiltrate their organization, networks, and resources. The employees who become inward spies do not necessarily have to know what job they are fulfilling in our campaign; they just have to be participants.

From the perspective of a physical attack, an inward spy could be anyone who provides us useful information, to include help desk, human resources, janitorial, and support personnel. Pretexting, baiting, and impersonation are highly successful methods of obtaining information from inward spies and will be discussed later in this book. In a virtual attack, inward spies can be any device or application that provides access to sensitive data that should normally only be obtainable from within the organization. Key loggers, cameras, wireless access points, voice recorders, malware that opens up reverse shells, and network sniffers all fall within the definition of inward spies.

Converted Spies

From a professional penetration testing situation, it is hard to identify a converted spy – there is not much of a chance that someone is spying on the penetration test team or their systems. Network and system administrators may block the access of systems known to be owned by penetration testers, but that is purely defensive in nature, not offensive which requires the use of spies. In corporate and national espionage, the use of converted spies would be much greater. The difficulty is identifying the enemy's spies and using them to our own advantage. We do not necessarily need to get them to support our cause, but rather feed misinformation back to the enemy.

One way to think about converted spies with regard to penetration testing is to look at compromised systems as "converted." The ability to use a target system as a pivot point to conduct additional attacks, or at the very least understand the internal network, is extremely advantageous to penetration testers. The difficulty lies in obtaining a system; however, obtaining this system is paramount, according to Sun Tzu, who said:

> 25. *The end and aim of spying in all its five varieties is knowledge of the enemy; and this knowledge can only be derived, in the first instance, from the converted spy. Hence it is essential that the converted spy be treated with the utmost liberality.*[2]

Therefore, we need to focus on obtaining access to a target system as soon as we can, in order to be successful in our penetration test. Easier said than done, certainly, but something to keep foremost in our minds while we work through the rest of this book.

Doomed Spies

Within the concept of ninja hacking, doomed spies would be alerts, applications, or network devices that distract our target from our real attack vector. We must use doomed spies in such a way that our target does not know we were the ones who triggered the alerts; it must seem as if any alerts were caused naturally (power outages), simply random, or from another source – someone they would typically expect. Any method of distraction would work as long as it prevents our true attack and identity from being discovered. In Chapter 11, "Distraction," we will discuss distraction extensively, and in Chapter 16, "Sabotage," we will also be looking at ways to manipulate data and install rootkits.

TIP

As a project manager, the idea of spending time and resources on a part of the project that is intentionally doomed to fail seems counterproductive. In traditional penetration testing projects, this is probably true; however, the use of unorthodox attacks requires subterfuge and the inevitable – and intentional – failures.

In some cases, multiple teams of ninja were used to conduct an attack against a target. The jōnin would send two or more teams with an expectation that one team would fail and provide a distraction for the other team. Each team was unaware of the other, and the information provided to the teams would be different, in case of capture. The team that was expected to fail might have been provided misinformation as well, making them the doomed spies (B. Garner, personal communication, December 14, 2000).

Surviving Spies

A successful campaign relies on surviving spies. The data retrieved during a spying attempt can provide sufficient information to conduct a successful attack against a target. In the case of the virtual world, most of the data we obtain would be reliable and accurate. Only when we encounter network security devices like Honeypots can we question our data. Automated attacks against Honeypots often fall for the deception; however, human interaction with a Honeypot often betrays its intent and can be avoided in the future.

Rewards for Spying

Everyone who participates in a professional penetration test should be properly compensated for their efforts – same with warriors in a military campaign. However, Sun Tzu espoused that spies should receive extra compensation.

14. Hence it is that which none in the whole army are more intimate relations to be maintained than with spies. None should be more liberally rewarded. In no other business should greater secrecy be preserved.[2]

The last quote was included primarily to promote the career of those who can understand and conduct unorthodox attacks within the framework of corporate and national security. Penetration test teams are often seen as an operational cost to an organization, when in truth the findings of security professionals involved in identifying and verifying network and system exploits provide an actual financial benefit; executive officers are beginning to use their security program as a way to differentiate their company from competitors. Eventually, those organizations that take security seriously will make gains in the competitive market over those who fail to understand the importance of security. In other words ... engineers: do not sell yourself short; managers: pay your staff what they are truly worth.

PRECONCEIVED NOTIONS

Everyone has preconceived notions about how things work in the world, and as Zukin, we need to be able to take advantage of our victims' world views. A classic example of the ancient ninja's manipulation of preconceived notions was the use of women ninja or kunoichi. Women in ancient Japan were often relegated to minor roles in society and were not considered as capable; however, the ninja saw a significant way of exploiting preconceived notions about women and used those notions to their own advantage.[1] One of the more famous examples of women ninja was Mochizuki Chiyome, who created a school for orphaned girls and trained them to be ninja spies. These girls were also trained to work as *miko*, or shrine attendants, within temples throughout Japan. The placement of ninja in positions of trust throughout Japan increased the awareness of political events and gave Mochizuki Chiyome and her clan additional influence and power. Her spies were able to not only gather information about regional conflicts, but seed rumors and misinformation, collect information about fortress layouts, and manipulate commanders.[4]

Although there is a wealth of history surrounding kunoichi, the purpose of this section is to recognize the possibility of exploiting preconceived notions on the part of administrators within the target organization. Administrators have a well-defined viewpoint of what a penetration test consists. Whether or not their understanding is accurate is immaterial; what they perceive as part of a penetration test is preconceived. We can take advantage of that preconception and use it to make our attacks more successful by using similar psychological warfare tactics used by kunoichi.

Psychological Warfare

According to the Department of Defense, psychological warfare (PSYWAR) is "the planned use of propaganda and other psychological actions having the primary purpose of influencing the opinions, emotions, attitudes, and behavior of hostile groups in such a way as to support the achievement of national objectives,"[5] and is a subset of study within psychological operations (PSYOP). Psychological operations can be broken down into two categories – strategic and tactical. Strategic PSYOP is defined by the availability of time to develop vulnerabilities, and tactical PSYOP targets existing vulnerabilities.[5] Each category has different objectives within the framework of conducting PSYWAR, especially in professional penetration testing. The objectives for both strategic and tactical PSYOP include[5] the following:

Objectives (Strategic)

a. To support and explain a nation's policies, aims, and objectives;

b. To relate those policies and aims to the aspirations of the target audience, where practical;

c. To arouse public opinion or political pressures for or against a military operation;

d. To influence the design of enemy strategy and tactics;

e. To support economic and other non-violent forms of sanctions against an enemy;

f. To stimulate dissension between enemy military and political elites;

g. To undermine confidence in enemy leadership and war aims;

h. To lower the morale and efficiency of enemy soldiers and civilians, seeking a reflection of lower morale and efficiency in the combat zone;

i. To encourage disaffection in the enemy nation on the part of religious, ethnic, social, political, economic, and other elements having grievances against the government or against each other;

j. To interfere with control systems or with communications;

k. To elicit the moral or active support of neutral nations or perhaps to insure continued neutrality;

l. To make friendly leaders stronger and enemy leaders weaker;

m. To give hope and moral support to resistance elements in the enemy area;

n. To support a counterelite;

o. To gain support in newly liberated-areas;

p. To augment or complement tactical propaganda operations.

Objectives (Tactical)

a. To lower the enemy's morale and combat efficiency;

b. To increase the psychological impact of combat weapons;

c. To confuse the enemy;

d. To facilitate the occupation of enemy areas by delivering ultimatums and giving rally or surrender directions;

e. To support strategic PSYOP by furnishing more detailed and timely knowledge of local vulnerabilities which may be used in strategic plans and operations;

f. To give information and directions to friendly elements operating in the enemy combat zone;

g. To give specific and direct support to tactical commanders on short notice;

h. To build a favorable image of our soldiers and leaders.

In truth, each objective could have some physical or virtual representation within information warfare, especially on the national level. In smaller situations, such as a professional penetration test, a few stand out as more useful than others.

Influence the Design of Enemy Strategy and Tactics
Unless administrators are unaware of an upcoming penetration test, system and network professionals become hyperattentive to activities within their field of responsibility and are on the lookout for any anomalies that would indicate an ongoing attack. Unfortunately, this type of attention is not representative of day-to-day operations and skews the findings of the penetration test. However, we can use the increased surveillance to our benefit by influencing the administrators to make mistakes.

From a strategic perspective, when a penetration test is being negotiated, we can incorporate requests and information into the statement of work that have no relevancy to the actual penetration test. We can include factually false data in the project scope and communications that cause administrators to look in the wrong direction and perform activities that are impotent in detecting our activities, which provides additional confusion and misdirection that we can take advantage of as Zukin. As an example of indirect influence within a physical penetration test, we could request initial information on buildings or campuses that we are not truly interested in examining; requests for the names and phone numbers of facility personnel, hours of operation, and a list of activities within the facility in our initial information exchange with the target organization may filter down to security personnel. Subconsciously, the security personnel would focus more on the facilities that we are not interested in and away from the buildings that we actually want to enter.

Indirect influence within a network and system attack could materialize in a similar manner. By asking numerous questions about firewalls and Internet-facing systems, we could subconsciously influence security engineers to focus their attention on log data within the network's DMZ; if our original intent was to attack the system from a vendor or internal network location, this distraction would give us a serious advantage in conducting our attacks without notice.

Interfere with Control Systems or with Communications

One way to avoid detection is to remove those systems and network devices that provide alerts to security engineers. There have been numerous exploits published that target firewalls, intrusion detection systems, reporting protocols, and back-end applications/databases that communicate with network defense systems. One potential tactic would be to remove the "eyes" of the security engineers and take down those devices that provide the engineers a way to monitor the target networks and systems.

In a physical penetration test, disruption of power is by far the most useful method of removing control systems and communication. In case power disruption is not an option, there are other vectors that can be examined, including private branch exchange (PBX) communication servers, network closets, closed-circuit television camera (CCTV), digital video recorder boxes, or even the CCTV cameras themselves. Attacks do not have to happen simultaneously, either; to deflect suspicion, it would be more prudent to eliminate these systems over time and without a pattern so that security personnel will assume that the outages are "bad luck" or the result of poor quality. Naturally, if this is part of a professional penetration test, the rules of engagement need to include permission to conduct these types of attacks.

Lower the Enemy's Morale and Combat Efficiency

Administrators are already overloaded with the number of systems and network devices they must maintain. Adding a penetration test project into their daily routines adds additional stress. If we want to lower their morale and ability to defend against our attacks, we need to add additional stress into their lives. Remember, the objective of ninja hacking is to use unorthodox methods to successfully penetrate a target network. With that in mind, attack vectors that lower morale include negatively influencing administrator's personal and work lives.

Disruption of a person's daily routines adds additional stress. If we know who the system administrator is of the target system, we may find it prudent to disrupt their routines (assuming they do not know about the penetration test or us). Although the following examples are not nice, they certainly would be effective: phone them at 2 A.M. in the morning, send them e-mails allegedly from the company's human resources department with a problem regarding their health insurance, or leave a note on their car window, complaining about how they parked (especially if they parked perfectly). The primary goal here is to add stress, lower their morale, and decrease their ability to detect your activity.

Confuse the Enemy

There are numerous ways to confuse an enemy, especially during a professional penetration test: attack systems that are unrelated to the penetration test project; send malformed packets that actually do not do anything malicious; launch an attack, and stop randomly; send numerous blank e-mails to administrators; have balloons delivered to administrators' cubicles. All these actions tend to perplex IT personnel who expect logical events to occur during a penetration test. By performing inexplicable and never-before-seen actions during the project, we can confuse our opponents and distract them so they do not detect our actual attack. As Sun Tzu said, "*do not repeat the tactics which have gained you one victory, but let your methods be regulated by the infinite variety of circumstances.*"[2]

Manipulating the Enemy's Perception

Kunoichi were very effective in altering opponent's perception about the capabilities and threat of the ninja operative, by exploiting the biases of the enemy toward women. In combat, the manipulation of perception "takes to form of displays, feints, or demonstrations (which reduce enemy maneuver of fire-induced force attrition), or a combination of displays, feints, and demonstrations. All contribute to delaying premature achievement of friendly cumulating points," where culminating points is defined as "when the strength of the attacker no longer decisively exceeds that of the defender."[6] To put it in other words, as ninja hackers, we need to become experts in modifying the perceptions of administrators – using deception – in a way that improves our chances of success.

The military offensive strategic goals are[6] as follows:

- Influence enemy perception of friendly operational intent (objectives), and by extension, strategic ends.
- Induce incorrect enemy conclusions and decisions about friendly forces being allocated to fight the battle.
- Induce incorrect enemy conclusions about force dispositions.
- Induce incorrect enemy conclusions about the nature and extent of air and naval support to the ground maneuver.

The last goal does not have any real bearing on the virtual world; what it intended to convey is the use of additional combat assets that assist the main battle force, which works well in military and cyber-warfare campaigns. However, if we try to apply the intent of the last goal to professional penetration testing, we could rephrase it to: "induce incorrect enemy conclusions about the nature and extent of the types of penetration test efforts." In other words, we should keep the administrators unaware of any planned physical attacks, social engineering efforts, or targeted attack vector.

Operational Intent

The goal of "Influenc[ing] enemy perception of friendly operational intent (objectives), and by extension, strategic ends,"[6] with regard to professional penetration testing is obtainable if we keep the project scope and system target range broad. Based on personal experience, system administrators and managers prefer to keep the scope and IP range as small as possible since the adverse condition is perceived to be more difficult to remediate once vulnerability findings are enumerated. Penetration testers prefer a large list of target systems for a couple reasons: they can charge more for the project since they have to examine more systems (which does not really relate to the topic at hand); additional systems increases the chance of identifying an exploitable vulnerability or attack vector.

One of the "soft spots" of a network or system is back-end support devices and applications. Often, administrators overlook the support systems as potential targets; in some cases, the support systems are entirely owned and administered by other teams or business units, making a concerted effort to mitigate vulnerabilities and maintain proper patching procedures difficult. When it comes to penetration testing projects, these back-end systems may or may not be included; however, for any ninja hacking project, they should almost always be made available, in order to truly understand the target systems' security posture.

Allocation of Friendly Forces

A method of how to induce incorrect enemy conclusions and decisions about friendly forces being allocated to fight the battle would be to mislead the system and network administrators as to who will be working on the project and for how long. We can accomplish this goal by expanding the window of attack to multiple weeks or months; this will allow us to pick and choose the moment we actually begin the attack. Using deceptive practices, we can launch small attacks targeting systems that have no value to our project, which would draw attention away from our true attack vector as well as masquerade our intended manpower used when we launch our real attack.

We can also induce incorrect decisions by submitting questions about irrelevant network or system attributes. If we intend to ignore the network devices in our attack, we may ask an extraordinary number of questions about routers, switches, firewalls, network protocols, and topology. The administrators may be misled into believing that our primary goal is hack the network, and that the project engineers would be experts in that type of attack. They would not only be unconsciously drawn toward placing extra efforts on monitoring network equipment but also be prone to ignore system attacks, at least initially.

Force Dispositions

Administrators will have a preconceived notion of how a penetration test should be conducted using orthodox methods. To "induce incorrect enemy conclusions about force dispositions,"[6] we need to alter the methods. As ninja hackers, this should be easy since our goal is to use unorthodox methods to exploit our targets. However, there is a dilemma – whenever we use a tactic, even once, it no longer can be considered unorthodox if its use is detected and understood by the opposition. In fact, all of the tactics discussed in this book should be considered "detected and understood" by anyone responsible for defending a system from a malicious or planned attack. It will be up to the reader to devise their own attacks, using the example tactics as a guide. Otherwise, administrators will be able to predict the disposition of the ninja hacker, once they too have read this book.

One of the best ways to create new attack techniques is to have brainstorming sessions within the project team; new ideas or successful attack techniques from the past can be reexamined to see if they can be applied to the current project, and what modifications can be made to make it unique and less likely to be expected by the target systems' administrators.

Summary

Sun Tzu's *The Art of War* provides us a wealth of knowledge that can be applied to a ninja hacking project, which can be augmented with both historical ninja strategies and tactics and modern-day studies of war and conflict. The strategies discussed in this chapter included some important topics, such as Laying Plans, Waging War, Maneuvering, and the Use of Spies. We also examined briefly how women ninja were used in ancient Japan; more importantly, we expanded on why they were used and how preconceptions about penetration testing could be exploited to our advantage.

Laying Plans involves understanding the campaign strategy and developing plans that support the strategy. Although Sun Tzu emphasizes attacking numerous aspects of a nation state, including political and public support, the battlefield strategies provided by Sun Tzu can be applied to the virtual world during our efforts to compromise target systems and networks. The strategies within Laying Plans will be used to describe how to develop competent tactics and provide a solid understanding of the ways and means of conducting "war" – virtual or physical.

In the writings on Waging War, Sun Tzu provides us with some insight on how to conduct war, rather than provide specifics which may or may not work depending on the situation. The art of how to conduct attacks against systems that we extrapolate from Sun Tzu's writings can be augmented with traditional ninja strategies, including stealth and reconnaissance. We just need to be wary of delaying or dragging out our attacks; rather, once an attack vector is decided on, we need to act with conviction.

Maneuvering, with regard to penetration testing, emphasizes what we should and should not allow within our ninja hacking project. System owners and administrators prefer to have restrictive projects, in order to control the impact on their business unit. Ninja hackers must fight against this tendency since limiting the scope and range of an attack cannot provide a true view of a system's security posture. Although ninja hacking is not the first step in understanding the vulnerabilities within a system or network, it is by far the most effective since ninja hacking focuses on attacks that go undetected for long periods of time – assuming they are detected at all.

The use of spies examines the different roles a spy can play in order to obtain information about the enemy. In this chapter, we expanded on Sun Tzu's descriptions on the five types of spies and how they could be used in both physical and network-based penetration. Sun Tzu suggests that all five types of spies must be used in order to be successful; the availability of the different types within a ninja hacking project really depends on the resources and time of the team, and if there is national support behind the project.

In Chapter 4, "Exploitation of Current Events," we will examine some tactics that support the strategies discussed in this chapter; however, in Chapter 4, "Exploitation of Current Events," we will examine psychological operations to a greater extent and build on what the kunoichi were experts at – playing on people's fears. When combined, the strategies used by the ninja in feudal Japan, espoused by Sun Tzu, and methods of psychological warfare, published by the United States military, can provide an effective base of knowledge, in which to conduct devastating attacks against target systems – all without being detected.

Endnotes

1. Hatsumi M. Ninjutsu: history and tradition. In: Furuya D, editor. Burbank (CA): Unique Publications Ltd; 1981.
2. Sunzi. The art of war. (Lionel G, Trans.). Obtained online at www.gutenberg.org/etext/132; 2007 [Original work published 1910].
3. Glen P. Leading geeks. San Francisco (CA): Jossey-Bass; 2003.
4. Hayes SK. Ninja volume iv: legacy of the night warrior. Burbank (CA): Ohara Publications Inc; 1984.
5. Tims FM. New indicators of psychological operations effects. American Technical Assistance Corporation; Obtained online at www.dtic.mil/cgi-bin/GetTRDoc?AD=ADA0 15004&Location=U2&doc=GetTRDoc.pdf; 1975 [accessed 01.07.10].
6. Department of Army. Battlefield deception: chapter 2 – battlefield deception at the operational level of war. Obtained online at www.fas.org/irp/doddir/army/fm90-2/ 90-2ch2.htm; 1988 [accessed 01.07.10].

Acknowledgment

We fully acknowledge use of Chapter 8, "Management of a PenTest," from Thomas Wilhelm's Professional Penetration Testing: Creating and Operating a Formal Hacking Lab, ISBN 978-1-59749-425-0, Syngress.

Exploitation of Current Events

4

People tend to get enthralled with current events, especially those related to disasters, threatening situations, or the latest escapades of their favorite Hollywood stars. As Zukin, we can take advantage of human nature in a way similar to black hats that use spam and malicious Web sites to lure unsuspecting Internet users into installing malware; however, it is much more difficult to conduct pin-pointed attacks against a specific set of employees using the same tactics used by malicious hackers that can spam millions of users in the hope of catching a handful of victims. As Zukin, we need to conduct multipronged focused attacks in a way that appears to be legitimate and do not prompt suspicion.

Because targeting people can increase our chances of being detected, we need to be very careful in deciding to use current events to exploit systems – in order to reduce the amount of contact with others, the attack method most suited to ninja hacking in obtaining our goals of exploiting current events without raising suspicion is to conduct spear-phishing attacks that masquerade as someone within the organization or a trusted service. Masquerading as a person within the target company increases the chance of a victim trusting us, whether in the form of e-mail, phone call, or other social engineering attacks. However, we will also discuss another method of masquerading as a trusted entity by appearing as a legitimate service or Web site on the Internet. For broader attacks, perceptively aligning ourselves with other, more respectable Web sites, will allow us to obtain an aura of reliability.

Another type of attack we will examine is how to exploit windows of opportunity when a computer is known to be vulnerable. With the right "persuasion," especially by exploiting people's fears, we can get malware installed on the target organization's systems without having to create brand new exploits. Done right, the victim will feel better and more secure while providing us with access to their systems, which is exactly what we want as Zukin.

PLAYING ON PEOPLE'S FEARS AND CURIOSITY

In difficult economic times, mergers, reductions in force, promotions, and other "water cooler" type of topics are hot on everyone's mind. The fear of having one's job terminated is a great distracter during the course of business, and the hint of

Ninja Hacking. DOI: 10.1016/B978-1-59749-588-2.00004-4

news will entice employees to do things they aren't supposed to do, such as clicking on links and opening e-mail attachments against their better judgment. Even when there isn't a threat of unemployment, there are other enticements that can be used to exploit people's human nature toward curiosity. By playing on people's interest in the unknown, we can also manipulate their actions and again make them act against their better judgment and training.

We will also be examining techniques used by malicious hackers to coax Internet users to visit dangerous sites while still maintaining the mantle of trustworthiness. By using sites that already have substantial trust among Internet users, we can obtain a perception of trust by tacitly aligning ourselves with those trustworthy Web services.

E-mail Attacks

Companies have expressed the dangers of suspicious e-mails and "spear-phishing" attacks to their employees for years. Unfortunately, employees continue to compromise corporate networks by doing what they shouldn't – opening attachments and clicking on links. Although there is some definite value to conducting an attack by sending e-mail to company employees with dangerous links or attachments, to do so with ninja skills requires a different approach. To be successful as a ninja hacker, we will combine the traditional spear-phishing e-mail attacks with our ability to go unnoticed during the attempt.

An example of an attack that targets a specific set of users is the "Times Reader" attack that feigned to come from the *New York Times*. The attack targeted a finite set of companies, including just six domains; a public sector company, a law firm, an online gambling company, and three chemical companies.[1] Although the reasoning behind the pin-point attack is unknown, the attack seems to have been thwarted before it could reach the intended victims.

Although the Times Reader attack lacked some focus in its target in the fact that it targeted multiple, unrelated organizations, it does provide some direction in how to conduct our own attacks. Some of the more important elements are as follows:

- Employment of a well-known software application name
- Limiting the amount of victims to reduce suspicion
- Appearing to come from a legitimate source

Even though the attack was thwarted because of a third-party monitoring organization, not all attacks are prevented so easily. To increase our ability to evade detection, we would want to target a subset of potential victims, and send out e-mails that purport to originate from inside the organization, or from a trusted source. An example of an attack using just this type of technique was disclosed January 2010, by a victim law firm that claimed Chinese companies were able to break into the law firm and obtain sensitive information about one of their clients. A representative from the law firm indicated that e-mail attacks targeted individuals within the law firm, and appeared to have been sent from within the organization itself.[2] The intent of the attack was to get victims to click on malicious links, which apparently failed; how the illicitly gained information was actually obtained was not explained, but the representative indicated that it was not through the e-mail attack because the context of the e-mails appeared oddly worded.

Now that we identified how focused attacks are conducted, let us look at a successful attack that has had a global impact. In December 2009, Google, Adobe, and other large companies were the target of attack supposedly by Chinese groups. The phishing attacks used zero-day exploits, attached to e-mail messages that "didn't cast a wide spam net to get their victims like a typical botnet or spam campaign... [but rather] started out with 'good intelligence' that helped them gather the appropriate names and email addresses they used in the email attacks."[3] Hunting for intellectual property and the names of Chinese dissidents, the attack used numerous different platforms and attack vectors against the target companies, including PDF files and Microsoft Excel spreadsheets loaded with different Trojan malware. The attacks themselves would target employees using familiar contacts.[3]

NOTE

Most of the commercial and open-source penetration testing exploit platforms have prefabricated documents that can be built into PDF or Microsoft Word documents containing selectable exploits. Although they do work, the content is extremely generic and can raise suspicion among recipients. If we want to conduct a ninja hacking attack, these options are too coarse. Remember, "if you can see it, it's not Ninjutsu" (Garner B. personal communication, December 14, 2010).

The combination of a zero-day exploit, multiple attack vectors, focused attacks against employees, and depth-of-knowledge regarding employee contacts is a laudable effort and something to emulate when conducting our own ninja hacking attacks.

Bad News

Although we may not have our own zero-day exploit, we can still exploit target systems by combining the best techniques in spear-phishing with lessons learned from the historic ninja. Instead of global political battles, we can focus on the politics within an organization as a means of enticing our victims to install our malware. Even in good economic times, there is always fear lurking within an organization. Although not an exhaustive list by any means, the following topics are touchy subjects that can make most employees nervous and concerned: insurance, job security, and organizational mergers.

WARNING

These tactics will work in the right circumstances, but to reduce the chances of getting caught, extra precautions may need to be made: location of download servers containing malware should have legitimate-sounding names, and be placed strategically to avoid suspicion (overseas locations may not be the best option); contact numbers (if used) might want to be directed to throw-away cell phones with no history (and not the home office of the penetration test team); and target employee information should be well vetted before sending out a single e-mail.

Change or Loss of Insurance

The cost of insurance continues to climb, and yet is an important consideration for most family bread-winners. The loss of insurance, or a potential increase in the cost, could negatively impact a family and is therefore a potentially effective attack vector when e-mailing a target victim with attached malware.

Here is a list of legitimate events that can grab the attention of our target, which can be used along with an attachment containing a malicious payload:

- Change in legal marital status
- Change in number of dependents
- Change in employment status
- Change in work schedule
- Change in a child's dependent status
- Change in place of residence or worksite
- Change in your health coverage or spouse's coverage
- Change in an individual's eligibility for Medicare or Medicaid
- A court order

If the e-mail is written in a way that indicates a change to their insurance has been made, then the target is more likely to click on the attachment than if the e-mail is purporting to simply provide information. Regardless of which approach we use, we should restrict the number of e-mails sent out to as few as possible, in order to remain undetected and appear more legitimate.

NOTE

Human psychology is an interesting thing; if we state in our e-mail that the target is required to open an attachment to obtain further information, they may become cautious and not click on the attachment. However, if we state that the attachment is simply "additional information," they may not click on it due to indifference. From a ninja hacking perspective, it may make more sense to accept the less risky option, and use verbiage within our e-mail that doesn't insist the victim act on the new information, and simply let curiosity work in our favor, or to disguise our actions with more plausible explanations, such as "for security purposes, we have encrypted the attachment…"

One additional note is that any attachment sent to the target victim must appear legitimate. We must have text within the attachment that actually relates to the message subject and e-mail content, such as a resume (with malware) sent to a human resources department. If we know which insurance agency is used by the target company, we may be able to find suitable documents on the Internet. Otherwise, federal or state documents might be just as suitable for our attacks. As an example, the U.S. General Accounting Office has a searchable index of insurance information that impacts government employees, small business owners, veterans, and so on. A list of usable PDF documents can be found by visiting www.gao.gov/docsearch/locate?& keyword=health+insurance

Loss of Job

When economic times become difficult, companies often need to lay off employees. When the rumors of layoffs begin to circulate, it may be perfect timing to launch an e-mail attack regarding unemployment benefits or job opportunities. Similar to e-mails regarding health insurance, e-mails must appear legitimate and contain subject lines and content that appears to be pertinent and authentic.

If we decide to play on the fears of our target, we can provide them with information about unemployment benefits and requirements, job training options, educational benefits for the unemployed, and any state or federal documents that explain their rights regarding unemployment. If we instead focus on manipulating the target's hopes, we can send e-mails containing potential job opportunities or information about upcoming job fairs in their field of expertise. Naturally, we would include attachments with malware imbedded that would exploit their system to our advantage. But by playing on the target's fears or hopes, we increase our chances of them opening the attachments; and by including authentic and potentially valuable information, we reduce the suspicions of our targets.

Mergers

Similar to the threat of job loss, organizational mergers, buy-outs, and divestitures are dangerous to people's careers; employees may get reassigned at best, or terminated at worst. Therefore, any tidbit of information regarding potential acquisitions or mergers becomes keenly interesting.

SHINOBI-IRI (Stealth and Entering Methods)

How many targets should we include in an e-mail attack campaign? If we were simply interested in penetrating systems without regard to being caught, the answer would be "as many as we can." However, since our goal is to remain undetected throughout the attack, and since e-mail attacks are often used at the beginning of a campaign, as Zukin, the answer may be as few as "one."

Large attacks are best saved for traditional penetration tests – surgical strikes are more appropriate for long-term projects with high-value targets where success is critical. By limiting the number of victims to less than a handful, we increase our stealth; if additional targets need to be added later, so be it.

To reduce suspicion, information should be generic; if the content of the e-mail is extracted from news sources, accuracy and relevance are increased. If the information contained in the e-mail is considered of significant value to the victim, they may actually pass on the information to others in the organization. Although this may seem beneficial, the more people that view the e-mail, the greater chance of our attack being discovered.

Search Engines

Although we have lauded the strategy of maintaining a low profile in order to avoid detection, we need to examine additional attack vectors used by malicious hackers in exploiting systems during larger-scale attacks. The historical ninja, although exceptionally skilled at evasion and deception, were quite capable of participating in major combats between large armies. Since victory was paramount, the ninja would use whatever attack method was the most appropriate for the situation. If it makes sense to expand our breadth of attack, we should do so.

As mentioned earlier, it is possible to have victims visit dangerous sites while still maintaining the mantle of trustworthiness. A way to do so is to increase visibility on search engines through high-index placement or use of advertisement. Using search engines to attract victims is not new; Google has been eliminating malicious Web sites for years.[4] The advantage we have over other attack attempts is we want to add focus to our attacks, not just try to exploit the greatest number of computer systems possible. Naturally, our success rate will be less than optimal, but if we can get a single foothold in the target corporation's network, then we can claim success.

Advertising Links

Getting target users to install malware on their corporate systems is no easy task –it requires that we provide them with something the target believes is useful or required. If we want to remove suspicion from the victim's mind, we need to also do so in a manner that appears we are legitimate sources for software or document downloads.

Advertisement on search engines is an obvious place to begin. Sites such as Google have effective advertisement campaigns that allow the advertiser to focus on a select audience. Options that allow us to focus our attack include demographics, location, and languages. Although granularities of these options are fairly limited, we can concentrate our attacks within select states or provinces.

After we focus our attack using the demographics, location, and languages options available to us, we can word the advertisement to meet our particular needs and potential target audience. Unfortunately, even if we're lucky enough to get our intended victim to visit our site, we still have to entice them to download malware. Using some of the message subjects discussed earlier, we may be able to convince the victims to view our documents preloaded with malware. Obviously, the possibility for success using this option is low; however, again all we may need is one victim. Cost is also a consideration – if we attempt to use advertisement to attract a small sector of targets, we may have to advertise for a long period of time before we snag our victim so that we can move onto the next part of our attack.

TIP

To reduce our chance of being caught, we can design our Web site to only serve malware to select a range of domains. Programming languages used to provide Web site content can be written to present different pages and documents to different IP addresses (such as PHP's $_SERVER['REMOTE_ADDR'] function). Using our programming skills, we could provide pages without malware to everyone other than our intended victims, thus avoiding detection and removal from advertisement campaigns. It should be noted that the use of proxies, such as tor, would make this type of attack unsuccessful, unless the company we are targeting is the one pushing the use of the proxy.

Advertisements on search engines may not be the best solution. If we can focus our advertisement dollars to Web sites that attract our target victims, placement of ads may produce much better results. Web sites are less discriminating when it comes to hosting advertisement, which we can use to our advantage. Successful examples of this type of attack have been found on popular Web sites, such as DrudgeReport. com, Lyrics.com, Horoscope.com, and Slacker.com, where PDF documents, containing malicious code, were uploaded to victim systems after advertisement links were clicked.[5] Again, these types of attacks are broad, but we may be able to focus our attacks better if we can better identify which Web sites our target victims use.

Fan Sites

Creating Web sites that focus on the target corporation can help us attract victims to our Web site. There are numerous Web sites dedicated to news and events surrounding corporations – some of them are negative (hatewalmart.com), some of them are humorous (peopleofwalmart.com), and some of them are positive (walmartstores. com). We can increase our chance of attracting employees from a target company if we create a Web site that focuses specifically on their employer.

Content becomes an issue when we create a fan site; we may be able to simply import news from other Web sites through the use of feed aggregators, but that may not be enough to attract our intended victims. However, the use of advertisement and fan sites together may provide us with the right volume of fruitful visits, leading to a successful compromise of the target corporate systems.

EXPLOITING PATCH WINDOWS AND PROCESSES

Exploiting a corporate environment's patching process is a much more complicated endeavor than soliciting victims to visit a Web site where malware is served. However, the ability to compromise patch servers has an enormous negative impact on the security of a corporation. If it's possible to connect and exploit a patch server during a professional penetration test, there are much more serious issues surrounding the corporate security that desperately need to be addressed.

What we will examine is how to take advantage of the human element within the patching process, and see how we can exploit people's behavior and fears to afford us an opportunity to exploit their systems. We will also look at some advanced techniques to exploit vulnerabilities identified in announced patches.

Patch Windows

Finding zero-day exploits is a difficult and time-consuming process. Wouldn't it be nice if someone told us what exactly was vulnerable in an application or operating system? Turns out, every time a patch is announced and released, we are given all the information about the vulnerability and where it can be found within the vulnerable software.

In order to identify exactly what changed, we need to have two things:

- The prepatched application
- The postpatched application

Using tools such as IDA Pro, and the binNavi plug-in for IDA Pro (available at zynamics.com), we can identify changes that are made at the assembly-language level. Once we know what has changed, we can create exploits that target the vulnerability that is being patched. The process of reverse engineering patches is becoming more and more established; it has even been suggested that the process could be automated, as discussed in the paper by Brumley, Poosankam, Song, and Zheng. In their paper, the authors proposed that exploits could be generated rapidly and accurately before systems are widely patched. In their experiments, they were able to generate a viable exploit in 30 s[6] – considering that it takes 24 h for 80 percent of all computer systems to even check for the availability of a patch, rapidly generating an exploit would be extremely beneficial for the ninja hacker.

Although the techniques and skills needed to conduct this type of attack is extensive and could consume all the pages of this book, what we will be focusing on in this chapter is how to exploit the delay between the release of the patch, and when the patch is actually installed in vulnerable systems.

In small companies, the patching process relies on the operating system's built-in automatic updating service. Since most systems using this method are patched relatively quickly, the window of opportunity to exploit vulnerable systems is small. In large organizations, the window of opportunity is more complex, since patches may negatively impact performance and availability, especially critical systems. National Institute of Standards and Technology (NIST) Special Publication 800-40 suggests that patches go through a process where an organization must[7]:

- Determine the significance of the threat or vulnerability
- Determine the existence, extent, and spread of related worms, viruses, or exploits
- Determine the risks involved with applying the patch or nonpatch remediation
- Create an organization-specific remediation database
- Test remediations
- Deploy vulnerability remediations
- Distribute vulnerability and remediation information to administrators
- Verify remediation

The time allowed to perform all these steps will vary, but once in a while a patch is deemed so critical that it must be installed almost immediately. Based on the list of tasks that must be performed just to install a patch, it is safe to assume that most patches take weeks or months before they are installed. We can take advantage of this time lag by generating our own exploit, which we disguise as the real vulnerability patch. The trick then becomes to get the users to install them on their system.

In a large organization, we also have to contend with the reality that corporate patch processes usually occur without user interaction. Employee systems usually have processes that automatically fetch and install patches once they have been vetted by the organization. To be successful, we must circumvent the patch process and convince the employees to install our malicious patch before the real patch hits their system and eliminates our ability to exploit the employee's system. Another option is to create an executable that we say is a patch, but is really malicious code instead.

Installing Malicious Software Locally

E-mails, containing malware, requesting corporate employees to install patches have been successful for many years. Once the employee clicks on the e-mail attachment posing as a patch, their system is compromised with the included malware. Often, the malware has nothing to do with the actual security vulnerability, and is simply a ruse to get the victim to install the malware.

As Zukin, we could do the same thing, but then we have to run the gambit of e-mail scanners that might detect our malware. Even if we have a zero-day exploit, the system may be configured to deny execution of exploit code in our attachment. The advantage to including malware within the e-mail is that our identity will be secure, since our attack cannot be traced back without extensive malware analysis. The disadvantage is that our target victim's e-mail server may filter out attachments, meaning we would need to find another way to get the victim to install our malware – for example, through a remote download.

Installing Malicious Software Remotely

Similar to installing malicious software locally, when we perform remote attacks we are hoping the system user will install malware. In this case, we will provide the victim with a link to a remote server to download our malware. Using a remote server, we can push our malware over secure channels to avoid detection from network-based intrusion detection systems and avoid antivirus detection applications within the e-mail server. The disadvantage to this approach is that our malware server is easily traceable. However, if we can limit our use of the malware server to as few attacks as possible, then we can avoid having the server blocked or placed on a blacklist. Although not the best solution with regard to maintaining stealth, remote malware servers can be relocated to new IP addresses relatively easy, along with domain names.

Patch Processes

As mentioned earlier, there are many steps that are part of the patch process for government or large organizations. The process outlined earlier is difficult to interrupt or modify – since the process is internal to the organization, the possibility of outside influence is remote.

There are a couple options still available to us outside the formal process, and those are timing and exploitation of third-party support.

Patch Tuesday

There are well-known patch days, in which millions of systems around the world are downloading and installing patches. The number of patches is published in advance and the fixes are detailed to some level of detail. For system administrators and security engineers actively engaged in patch management, it is difficult to provide false patch data.

However, with the general populous, monthly patch days are events that slow systems and complicate lives; in short, it's an annoyance that is endured, not examined. It is exactly at this time that we can take advantage of indifference and confusion to launch attacks. In previous sections of this chapter, we talked about how to get victims to unknowingly execute malware; predesignated patch days is the perfect time to launch our attacks. We may be able to blend our attacks into the noise of seemingly chaotic activity, and if our malware requires a reboot of the system or additional annoyances, the victim will take it in stride.

It should be noted that the operating system is not the only types of patch processes that we can exploit – we may want to target different applications other than those provided by the operating system's company, such as Adobe, Firefox, and Quicktime. The concepts are the same, but implementation may be different.

Third-Party Support

In some organizations that do not maintain their own IT or security staff, they turn to third-party companies to provide support for systems. We will examine impersonation later in Chapter 6, but one technique that is useful with patch management is playing the part of tech support, also known as "quid pro quo." Although there are many scenarios that could be devised, the simplest would be to contact our target victim and instruct them on how to install an emergency patch. An e-mail shortly before the call indicating that tech support would be contacting them shortly would add legitimacy to the attack.

This type of attack is successful because the victim has an established trust relationship with the third-party organization that does indeed supply support for IT matters. It is also successful because a "quid pro quo" attack promises unsolicited help by IT to the victim, which is a welcomed anomaly.

Summary

Exploitation of current events takes advantage of people's curiosity and fears, in order to exploit their systems. Although we briefly touched on some technical skills that can be employed during these types of attacks, overall human nature allows us to exploit their systems without necessarily requiring complex tools and advanced skills.

The challenge unique to ninja hacking when it comes to exploiting human nature is that we must do so with extreme care to avoid detection or the raising of suspicions. Typical penetration tests often lack time to conduct the attack due to pressures of cost; ninja hacking attacks have a different goal, which is successful completion of the campaign without discovery, and regardless of the constraints in place. To achieve these goals, we may target fewer victims, pinpoint our attacks against specific IP ranges, and tailor our exploits more carefully. The flip side is that we must be even more thorough in our intelligence gathering, so that we can assume the guise of a trusted entity. We must do whatever it takes to manipulate the target victim's actions and make them act against their better judgment and training.

Endnotes

1. Millington T. Email attack spoofs New York Times. http://www.searchsecurityasia.com/content/email-attack-spoofs-new-york-times; 2010 [accessed 1.07.10].
2. Claburn T. Law firm suing China hit by cyber attack. http://www.informationweek.com/news/security/attacks/showArticle.jhtml?articleID=222301001; 2010 [accessed 1.07.10].
3. Higgins KJ. Spear-phishing attacks out of China targeted source code, intellectual property. http://www.informationweek.com/news/security/attacks/showArticle.jhtml?articleID=222301157; 2010 [accessed 1.07.10].
4. Mann J. Google purges thousands of malware sites from search. http://www.techspot.com/news/28050-google-purges-thousands-of-malware-sites-from-search.html; 2007.
5. Landesman M. Weekend run of malvertisements. http://blog.scansafe.com/journal/2009/9/24/weekend-run-of-malvertisements.html; 2009 [accessed 1.07.10].
6. Brumley D, Poosankam P, Song D, Zheng J. Automatic patch-based exploit generation is possible: techniques and implications. http://www.cs.cmu.edu/~dbrumley/pubs/apeg.pdf; [accessed 1.07.10].
7. National Institute of Standards and Technology (NIST). Creating a patch vulnerability program. http://csrc.nist.gov/publications/nistpubs/800-40-Ver2/SP800-40v2.pdf; 2005 [accessed 1.07.10].

Disguise

5

People tend to trust authority, especially in a workspace. People also tend to trust anyone who appears to be an official representative of an external organization. Trust, combined with the talents for disguise among the ancient ninja, is powerful and effective force during a penetration test effort.

Authority appears in different ways, the most effective being visually. Movies have been made that show criminals wearing the uniforms of police agents, security guards, janitors, and technicians, with the goal of convincing others to do the will of the criminals. In this chapter, we will discuss how we can acquire the same level of trust by using uniforms and badges to gain elevated access.

Trust does not only come with visual cues, such as uniforms; trust can also be inherited through established job roles, such as IT support or facility maintenance. While a uniform may or may not be part of these types of jobs, assuming the guise of tech support will afford greater penetration into a corporate facility than other authority professions. We will take a look at how best to assume these roles to gain access to sensitive material.

Fooling people is all well and good and easier than others would imagine, but what about fooling machines? Computer systems do not provide access because of what someone looks like – they require preestablished proof of identity. In this chapter, we will discuss some of the tools and techniques available to us that can convince computer systems that we are communicating with them through legitimate systems.

We will begin by examining how the traditional ninja used these techniques successfully and to what extremes they assumed their disguises. During a modern penetration test, if we are caught, we get to walk away and try something different; in ancient Japan, if the disguise of a ninja was pierced and exposed, it typically resulted in death. Far different results for certain, but by learning the extent the ninja went to in order to successfully disguise their true nature and intent, we can improve our own techniques and conduct better penetration tests.

Ninja Hacking. DOI: 10.1016/B978-1-59749-588-2.00005-6

HENSŌJUTSU (DISGUISE)

In feudal Japan, it was uncommon for people to leave their villages or provinces to journey across the country. Anyone traveling who did not fall into a handful of professions (such as entertainers or merchants) was automatically viewed with suspicion; it was culturally abnormal to travel the countryside without a specific purpose or job. However, some professions had to travel in order to make a living. These *shichi ho de* ("seven ways of going") included[1] the following:

- *Akindo* (merchant or tradesman)
- *Hokashi* (musician)
- *Komuso* (itinerant priest)
- *Sarugaku* (entertainer, showman)
- *Shukke* (Buddhist monk)
- *Tsunegata* or *rōnin* (wandering samurai for hire)
- *Yamabushi* (mountain warrior ascetic)

These were not the only guises ninja would assume, but they did permit them to travel to different provinces in order to conduct their espionage or infiltration assignments. The problem was that the soldiers of each province were tasked with identifying and capturing anyone who might pose a danger to their lands, especially during times of war. If a ninja wasn't really good at disguising himself, he could end up captured, tortured, and executed. Because of this risk, ninja had to be skilled at "thoroughly impersonating the character adopted. Personality traits, areas of knowledge, and body dynamics of the identity assumed were ingrained in the ninja's way of thinking and reacting. He or she literally became the new personality."[2]

Impersonating People

The concept of *shichi ho de* permitted ninja to intermingle in foreign provinces, even if their accent betrayed their origin to be different. As mentioned, the ninja had to literally become the identity they portrayed in order to reduce suspicion about their true mission. This included not only dress but mannerisms and knowledge specific to the assumed profession – a ninja pretending to be a musician had to be talented in a musical instrument; if pretending to be a rōnin, or a masterless samurai (Figure 5.1), they had to act and dress appropriately and have the appropriate martial skills. Simply assuming the clothing would not be sufficient.

Extreme attention to detail was critical beyond just the mannerisms, knowledge, and dress of the ninja. Details such as age, skin texture, dialect, and jargon were also taken into consideration as to which disguise the ninja would assume.[1] It would be ineffective if the ninja did not have rough hands if he was trying to portray himself as a farmer on the way to market, or if he had a full head of hair and was trying to portray a Shukke. Kunoichi could not take on the guise of most of the *shichi ho de*, but could assume other personas as needed, including farmer wives, geisha, entertainers, fortune-tellers, servants, and shrine attendants.

FIGURE 5.1 "Rōnin, or Masterless Samurai, Grimacing Fiercely."[3]

Miscellaneous Items in High Demand, Prints & Photographs Division, Library of Congress, LC-USZC4-8657

(color film copy transparency)

To successfully imitate the mannerisms, knowledge, and appearance of these different characters from ancient Japan, *hengen kasha no jutsu* (immersion in the illusion) was employed, which consisted of the following states of awareness[4]:

- Appearance
- Knowledge

- Language
- Geography
- Psychology

SHINOBI-IRI (Stealth and Entering Methods)

Society portrayed ninja as something otherworldly and referred to them as winged demons – as Zukin – we do not have the same aura; however, we should be cognizant that many people still don't understand how computers work, and take advantage of our victims' ignorance of how we can exploit their systems.

We will examine each of these in greater detail later in this chapter, but there are a couple that are worth discussing now.

Appearance

In the next section, we will apply these states of awareness to today's corporate environment, but attention to detail was critical. When considering appearance, the following traits were examined before considering disguise[4]:

- Sex
- Race
- Height, weight, and build
- Age
- Speech quality and accent
- Facial features
- Hair color, style, and length
- Scars
- Deformities or injuries
- Walking stride and pace
- Clothing details and badges

Certain characteristics may predispose the selection of a disguise; the chance of entertainers having battle scars would naturally be low, while Buddhist priests would not be quick in their pace because of their philosophies. By understanding one's own habits and personality traits, the ninja could better select the disguise most appropriate for themselves and the particular mission that they are undertaking.

Psychology

Adoption of a disguise in ancient Japan required a different level of mental readiness than would be required in today's world of penetration testing. In order to survive, the ninja had to understand not only others and how they may react, but also their own psychological makeup and how to control their reactions in a stressful or confrontational situation. Ninja had to "maintain alertness while appearing outwardly calm [and] avoid the danger of being too stereotypically posed when affecting a temporary illusion."[4]

THE MODERN "SEVEN WAYS OF GOING"

A lot has changed since the ancient *shichi ho de* characters were utilized. A modern interpretation of these characters has been suggested by Stephen K. Hayes[4]:

- Scholastic
- Business
- Rural
- Religious
- Public figures
- Labor
- Uniformed

Depending on the penetration test, some of these modern disguises could be used with different levels of effectiveness. It would certainly be possible that a pentest project required the attackers to conceal themselves in the guise of teachers, priests, or manual laborers; however, the more common method of disguising one's true intent is to appear as an employee, vendor, or someone involved in commerce (such as delivery personnel, solicitors, or businessmen).

Employees

Posing as an employee allows an infiltrator the opportunity to access the deeper recesses of corporate facilities. Numerous exploits using disguises have been printed in both media and books, and of course, Hollywood has provided their fair share of stories; while there may be some hype surrounding the particulars of the actual infiltration using disguises, the reality is that it is quite possible to enter a facility through disguise.

TIP

It is advisable to fine-tune a disguise through practice before attempting to use the disguise in a real-world penetration test. Just as ancient ninja did, we should be constantly striving to perfect our art, including disguise.

Books and media cannot describe the feelings encountered when conducting your first infiltration – adrenaline pumps, the heart pounds, and the mind races with scenarios in which your deceit is discovered. Strangely enough, most of the time the ruse is successful – except in high-security areas – assuming that the disguise is believable. Let's take Vincent Sneed from Nashville, Tennessee, as an example. Sneed was arrested for several counts of theft, in which he reportedly stole unattended laptops during business hours, posing as an employee or as someone who belonged on the premises.[5]

More impressive was the escapades of Preston Vanderbergh in Roseville, California. Vanderbergh was accused of stealing data from SureWest Communications, a telecommunications company. Similar to Sneed, Vanderbergh was able to steal multiple laptops from the victim company. However, Vanderbergh was able to also obtain a SureWest ID card, keys, a uniform, and – more amazingly – a company vehicle; according to police, he was able to be successful in his deceit because "he was just confident and played the part, and looked the part."[6] Vanderbergh fell under suspicion when he began showing up after hours, but employees have no idea how long he had been "working" at the building, attempting to access customer and corporate data.[6]

A similarity between Sneed's and Vanderbergh's success was the size of the facility. Both criminals targeted larger companies with expansive facilities. Additionally, both assumed the guise of an employee to succeed for as long as they did. Although it was not detailed as to Sneed's activities during the heists, Vanderbergh was able to imitate the knowledge, appearance, and attitude necessary to assume the disguise of the average employee.

IT Support

Successfully assuming the guise of IT support allows for additional privileges beyond those of the average employee. Network systems, production systems, and work stations are all available as targets. In the previous example, Vanderbergh had access to employee laptops, but nothing greater; although he attempted to steal customer data, he was reportedly unsuccessful.[6] Had he had access to production systems posed as an administrator, he may have been able to get what he was truly after.

There are some examples in the news regarding how criminals were able to access systems posed as IT, but a more personal example will probably suffice. Many years ago, at a nearby university, criminals posing as IT and tech support stole multiple projectors in various lecture halls. More interestingly, they also pulled off their heists while some classes were in session. Even more interestingly, one of the heists successfully occurred while the department head of computer security was lecturing. The moral of the story is that anyone can be deceived; it simply requires the right attitude, confidence, disguise … and in this case, a ladder.

Security Employees

Information security personnel have a large responsibility within an organization; through the course of their daily activities, they have access to the "keys of the kingdom." Network security engineers have access to systems that collect network traffic, system security engineers can manipulate access to data on systems, and penetration test engineers know the vulnerabilities and weaknesses to critical corporate systems. There has to be a strong trust relationship between a company and its security engineers; that trust relationship extends throughout the organization as well.

A personal example of how the trust relationship between a company and its security engineers occurred during a walkthrough of a large facility with a pentest team member is shown. During that walkthrough, we decided to try and access a part of the facility that contained a large number of production systems, which accounted for a lion's share of the company's total business. Since we didn't know anyone who might have legitimately had access to the system, we decided to simply pose as security personnel. We walked into the production center and requested access; after a brief discussion with the sole staff member on duty responsible for controlling access to the production center, we were permitted to enter without escort by implying we were with the company's security team and needed to look around.

The attack was successful because we appeared and acted as expected. Untold damage could have resulted from a similar attack by those with malicious intent. The attack did not require much in the way of knowledge, but our background in security and system administration would probably have been sufficient had we been challenged with more tenacity.

Badges and Uniforms

The ability to pose as a person of authority requires more than simple persuasion – it requires symbols that are commonly accepted as one of authority; badges and uniforms provide those symbols to those authorized to carry them, as well as those who want to use them nefariously. To obtain symbols of authority without actually having the authority is risky – they have to be either fabricated or stolen.

Stolen Badges and Uniforms

We already examined the story of Vanderbergh who stole both a SureWest ID card and a company uniform; had he desired, he could have posed as a SureWest employee and accessed the inner workings of local companies. While that is of significant concern, worse offenses have occurred.

On March 5, 2010, the following was stolen from the home of a Dallas Texas police officer[5]:

- 2 loaded 9mm magazines
- 2 handcuffs with cases
- 1 radio with holder
- 1 Badge #9319
- 1 OC (oleoresin capsicum "pepper") spray with case
- 1 Sam Browne belt
- 1 short sleeve Class B uniform
- 1 inner belt
- 1 wallet badge
- 1 streamlight flashlight
- 1 stingray flashlight
- 1 warrant of appointment
- 1 Texas Commission on Law Enforcement Officers Standards license

Considering that most of our society has been taught at an early age to identify anyone in a police uniform as someone of authority, using such a disguise could be a disaster for any intended target. The items stolen in Dallas would certainly allow the thief to lower victim's suspicions if used during the initial stages of a crime, or information-gathering phase leading up to something malicious. However, what if the target is the police itself?

In 2007, a man disguised himself as a constable and assumed the responsibilities of one at a police station in the town of Ocean View, South Africa. Ricardo Voight was able to pose as a constable for 7 months, using a stolen police uniform,[7] despite working among and with other police officers. Voight was able to successfully disguise himself under an incredible and challenging situation. Although there are no specifics about how he was able to convince the other officers that he was a transfer from Cape Town, the incident did provide some clues as to why he was not caught earlier. It was reported that organizational procedures were not followed when Voight presented himself to the Ocean View station, which required transfer documents.[7] Voight was able to use his position at the police station to assist in illegal activity; as part of a gang of thieves, Voight allegedly passed information onto his criminal colleagues.[7]

Voight's example shows the extent in which a disguise can be successfully employed, even in modern times. Despite heightened security around the world due to recent terrorist activities, it is still possible to successfully assume the guise of our society's most empowered authority figures. However, theft isn't the only way to obtain the symbols of authority – they can be simply purchased.

Fabricated Badges and Uniforms

Not all police badges are stolen – some are counterfeit. Although federal law prohibits the sale or the purchase of fake police badges, they are created nonetheless and used by both criminals and officers of the law. According to the *New York Times*, counterfeit badges can be purchased for anywhere between $25 and $75 through the Internet and police equipment stores.[8]

In the story of the *New York Times*, the purchasers of the counterfeit badges were New York police officers, who used them instead of their issued badges, primarily to keep the originals safe. However, not all counterfeit items are used so innocently. In February 2010, Iraqi officials began to work with tailors in the country to reduce or eliminate the creation of counterfeit police and military uniforms, including those imitating uniforms worn by U.S. military forces. The crackdown was in response to multiple suicide bombings in Baghdad where the attackers used uniforms to disguise their true identity and intent.[9]

Whether uniforms and badges are fabricated or stolen, there is plenty of stories that show they can be convincing and useful in gaining access to information or garnering trust from unsuspecting victims. Some of them are less than threatening, such as fake badges used to enter conventions as those regularly seen at DEF CON; however, successfully counterfeited, they are extremely beneficial and advantageous to any physical penetration test – or nefarious attack.

Vendors

Vendors have a unique relationship in corporate society – companies use vendors to provide additional services and allow the vendors to access corporate systems and their facilities including those that handle critical production. However, vendors also perform the same services for competitors, and as such, are also a danger to the companies they serve.

As a vendor, the level and means of access to a company's systems varies; sometimes, the vendors are required to work on-site, and other times, it is through remote connectivity. From an attack perspective, on-site vendors are fair game for the use of disguise to infiltrate a company; we can use uniforms and badges, exploit our knowledge of systems and networks, imitate mannerisms, use specialized vernacular, and exploit the psychological expectations of our target victims.

Disguising ourselves as vendors remotely pose a different challenge; we are prevented from using uniforms and badges to lend authenticity to our disguise. Although it may seem more along the lines of impersonation, which we will cover in Chapter 6, "Impersonation," we can still assume the disguise of a vendor that doesn't actually come into physical contact with their clients, albeit without the same level of ease.

On-site Vendors

Customers rely on vendors to identify, prevent, and remediate problems. However, if corporate processes are not in place and used to prevent unauthorized personnel from accessing sensitive systems, anyone posing as a vendor could compromise the target company. An excellent example of exploiting such an attack was viewed by audiences of Court TV during the pilot episode titled "Tiger Team." During the filming of the television show, Luke McOmie was able to access a car dealership's computer system posing as a vendor which provided network tech support. McOmie was able to retrieve and delete sensitive information during the penetration test, as well as obtain passcodes to the company's alarm system.[10] He was able to do so because the victim accepted his identity at face value, rather than vet his claim to be working for the car company's vendor.

Remote Vendors

There are two ways to attack someone as a remote vendor – either posing as a legitimate vendor currently employed or working with the target company or creating a company that sounds like a legitimate vendor working with the target. We can disguise our identity would be to create legitimate-sounding companies (in reality or in name only) in such a way as to reduce suspicion in the target victim's mind. One method used extensively is to create companies or Web sites that have names very similar to legitimate companies; the traditional method is to use legitimate names, just slightly misspelled. An example would be googl.com, facebooks.com, or whatever is appropriate for the penetration test project.

A real-world example of how this type of attack truly works is the case of Angella Muthoni Chegge-Kraszeski who assumed the name "Christina Ann Clay," while bilking the state of West Virginia for over $3 million. To succeed in her scam, she created companies named Deloite Consulting, Unisyss Corp., Acenture Corp., and Electronic Data System Corp. – these names are based on legitimate companies that worked for the state of West Virginia, but created by Chegge-Kraszeski with slight misspellings.[11] Using the bogus, but recognizable, company names, Chegge-Kraszeski was able to bill state organizations for services never performed.

Chegge-Kraszeski's success was based on her ability to select legitimate companies that supported clientele that would not be able to recognize the dupe; clientele that were large, bureaucratic, and disparate. Had Chegge-Kraszeski selected victims that were smaller in size, her chances and rewards would have slimmer.

VIRTUAL DISGUISES

Computers that process sensitive and critical information for an organization (hopefully) have safeguards in place to prevent mistakes from occurring, especially when attacked by unauthorized systems across network domains. During a typical penetration test, the attack team will look for weaknesses or an absence of such safeguards. To probe against computer systems that employ strong security is a nightmare, since it may take an unacceptable time to compromise the target; after all, in a traditional penetration test, time is money, and a client is hesitant to spend additional funds for an expansive and comprehensive test, especially when the extra time holds little promise of additional discoveries.

If we employ the lessons of the ninja and recognize that time is often an ally, we will want to spend the time necessary in order to succeed in our mission to compromise the target systems and networks without being caught. For us, that time might be best spent setting up virtual disguises, targeting systems that require validation of a sender's identity. For those systems that don't really care about the identity of the sender, we can hide ourselves by disguising ourselves through the anonymity of the Internet. Either way, we will be virtually disguising ourselves as someone other than our true selves.

Anonymous Relays

The Holy Grail for malicious attackers is the ability to conduct an untraceable attack anonymously. Numerous ideas have been bantered in Internet forums, but there are weaknesses and flaws in all of them. Some implementations are better than others, but none have been truly successful in being both untraceable and anonymous. Regardless, there are some ways to disguise ourselves on the Internet – one being anonymous relays.

One of the better-known anonymous relays available is the Tor project, which uses proxies scattered across the Internet. Available at www.torproject.org, the application allows users to enter a virtual, encrypted network with random pathways that connect the user to their target server.[12] There are some issues with using Tor; however, if we understand the limitations, we can provide a better way to disguise our attack as ninja hackers.

The Tor Network

The first problem we encounter with Tor is that the endpoints of the Tor network have the ability to sniff our traffic, assuming the traffic is not encrypted. In 2007, Dan Egerstad, a security researcher, announced that he had intercepted usernames and passwords using systems set up as Tor exit nodes.[13] If we were conducting a malicious attack against a target victim using Tor, we may not care if the victim's sensitive information is disclosed. However, as Zukin, we must try and eliminate all traces of our attack – spilling out data does not seem like a logical way of hiding our tracks.

WARNING

One of the disadvantages with using Tor is that numerous exit systems have been identified, recorded, and placed on blacklists. The result is that attempts to connect to a system may be impossible if that system blocks Tor exit nodes. To overcome this, you can add those nodes that present problems in the Tor "torrc" configuration file. If you use Tor regularly, you will end up adding a lot of exit nodes to this list.

Another problem with Tor is that if both the entrance and exit endpoints of the Tor network we use are monitored, our identity could be revealed simply by matching traffic at each point. If this were to happen (which is possible under the U.S. wiretapping law titled "Communications Assistance for Law Enforcement Act" [CALEA]), our use of Tor is negated and our identity compromised, since traffic we send to Tor could be traced backwards from the Tor entry point.

We could provide some additional security by encrypting all our data going through the Tor networking tunnel; however, that is not always practical, especially if the service we are targeting remotely does not use an encrypted protocol. Nor would encrypting the data protect our identity. In short, the use of Tor – intended to provide anonymity and untraceability – does not guarantee either.

A proposal on improving Tor was published in August 2009 by Joel Reardon of Google and Ian Goldberg of the University of Waterloo. The proposal suggests that the data sent across the Tor network, using TCP, would be better protected by encapsulating the entire TCP data segment be encapsulated within the Datagram Transport Layer Security (DTLS) protocol; this would "protect the TCP headers – which would otherwise give stream identification information to an attacker."[14]

Peer-to-Peer Networks

Although Reardon and Goldberg's proposal sounds practical and would improve our ability to remain anonymous, the Tor network has not adopted such a modification to their network. Another option is to use a peer-to-peer network, which provides a decentralized network that can push data anonymously between nodes. An example of a very secure peer-to-peer network is Freenet, which allows users to obtain data from other users without fear of being traced. The problem with most peer-to-peer networks is that it requires each endpoint to be part of the network and only allows access to files, not services. Peer-to-peer networks are not really intended to tunnel traffic to Internet-facing systems as proxies.

What we need is something that provides true anonymity and untraceability that exists now. The proposal by Reardon and Goldberg does point a way to achieving such functionality – blended protocols. If we use the Tor network as a way to secure part of our network, instead using it as our only network, we can increase our ability to remain anonymous and untraceable. This is known as "daisy-chaining" anonymizers.

Blended Anonymized Networks

Tor itself is considered a "daisy-chaining" anonymizer, but it is self-contained. Our goal, as Zukin, is to use multiple anonymizer systems to provide additional security during our attack. One type of peer-to-peer network we need to discuss before progressing in our examination of anonymity is called a wireless mesh network. Similar to a wireless network, systems connect wirelessly to an access point. The difference is that the access point in a wireless mesh network is simply a radio node – it could be a wireless router, or it could be another computer with a wireless receiver.

NOTE

The use of any anonymous network, especially wireless mesh networks, is overkill in traditional penetration tests – the network can be slow, applications must be able to use proxies, and the exit points may be blocked by systems on the Internet. However, if we are extremely concerned with staying anonymous to the point of near-paranoia, anonymous networks are invaluable. In a ninja hacking situation, this level of paranoia is rational. For examples of wireless mesh networks, check out www.cuwireless.net and http://pdos.csail .mit.edu/roofnet.

In a wireless mesh network, our attack system may hop through multiple radio nodes before connecting to one that has Internet access through an Internet service provider. The advantage to this type of network is that the peer-to-peer relationship is established ad hoc; with a large wireless mesh network, such as one that extends across a city, the access point into the network, as well as the router accessing the Internet, might be different each and every time we connect. Our activity can only be traced back to hardware information (the MAC address), which we can also change every time we access the wireless mesh network. This increases our anonymity dramatically and allows us to conduct our attack with greater stealth and disguise.

Summary

In this chapter, we examined ways that both the ninja and modern criminals have used people's predisposition to trust authority to their advantage. By following their examples, and most importantly creating our own ways of disguising ourselves, we can acquire the same level of trust, whether it is by using uniforms and badges to gain elevated access, posing as vendors, or presenting ourselves as someone the victim might do business with. The key in any such endeavor is to maintain the composure necessary to complete the task and maintain the knowledge, appearance, and skills necessary to deceive during the task. Remember, trust does not only come with visual cues, such as uniforms. It is our job as Zukin to exploit people's psyche so that we can gain access to sensitive material.

Although we discussed only a couple examples of the "modern seven ways" of disguising ourselves, our creativity should not stop here. Each and every disguise we create, either virtually or physically, loses its ability to convince the more often we assume the guise. Criminals have been caught because they use the same identity repeatedly; if we are to use the knowledge and wisdom of the ninja in our attacks, we cannot afford to risk the effectiveness of our disguise simply for convenience sake. We must constantly strive to change our *modus operandi* each and every time so that we do not fall into a pattern. It is important to remember that during any attack, especially during a small penetration test project, we may only have one shot at successfully disguising ourselves; we cannot waste it and must endeavor to exceed our current skill set and improve on our ability to disguise ourselves, both physically and virtually.

Endnotes

1. Hayes SK. The ninja and their secret fighting art. Rutland (VT): Charles E. Tuttle Company; 1981.
2. Hatsumi M. Ninjutsu: history and tradition. Burbank (CA): Unique Publications; 1981.
3. Miscellaneous Items in High Demand, Prints & Photographs division, Library of Congress, LC-USZC4-8657 (color film copy transparency). http://memory.loc.gov/master/pnp/cph/3 g00000/3g08000/3g08600/3g08657u.tif [accessed 1.07.10].
4. Hayes SK. Ninja vol. III: Warrior path of Togakure. Burbank (CA): Phara Publications; 1983.
5. Dallas Police Department. Dallas police department reports. [Online] http://policereports. dallaspolice.net/publicreports/ReportOutput/584355099.pdf; 2010 [accessed 1.07.10].
6. Gianulias K. Man poses as SureWest employee to steal info. [Online] http://cbs13.com/ local/Man.Poses.As.2.886456.html; 2008 [accessed 1.07.10].
7. Joseph N. Independent online. [Online] www.iol.co.za/index.php?art_id= vn20070731121146263C824187; 2007 [accessed 1.07.10].
8. Rivera R. New York Times. [Online] www.nytimes.com/2009/12/01/nyregion/01badge .html; 2009 [accessed 1.07.10].
9. Al Jazeera. [Online] http://english.aljazeera.net/news/middleeast/2010/02/ 201021616599284385.html; 2010 [accessed 1.07.10].
10. TruTV.com. [Online] www.trutv.com/video/tiger-team/tiger-team-101-2-of-4.html; 2007 [accessed 1.07.10].
11. Messina L. Daily Herald. [Online] www.heraldextra.com/news/state-and-regional/ article_81a942bd-f215-53eb-8a5d-c5f6cd7eac8e.html; 2009 [accessed 1.07.10].
12. Tor Project. [Online] www.torproject.org/overview.html.en; 2010 [accessed 1.07.10].
13. Zetter K. Wired.com. [Online] www.wired.com/politics/security/news/2007/09/embassy_ hacks?currentPage=1; 2007 [accessed 1.07.10].
14. Reardon J. USENIX Security Symposium. [Online] www.usenix.org/event/sec09/tech/ full_papers/reardon.pdf; 2009 [accessed 1.07.10].

Impersonation

In Chapter 5, "Disguise," we examined the use of disguise to overcome people's suspicions in order to access target facilities; in this chapter, we are going to take it a bit further and discuss the use of impersonation to conduct our attacks. Impersonation is a bit more involved because it requires an additional element – pretending to be someone that is known to the victim in one degree or another. In Chapter 5, "Disguise," we saw examples of how to pretend to be someone of authority; but in this chapter, we will go a step further and show examples of how pretending to be someone specific can be useful during an attack.

Ninja were quite skilled at impersonation. *Gisojutsu*, or impersonation, according to Steven K. Hayes, is used by the ninja as a "way of assuming another personality or identity in such a way as to operate in full sight or even with the cooperation of the enemy."[1] Based on Hayes' definition, we can assume correctly that impersonation comes with additional danger of discovery since we now have to interact with and influence our victims in order to obtain our objective.

All the same concepts used in *Hensōjutsu* (disguise) are still valid during the act of impersonation – perhaps even more. If we plan on using impersonation of a known figure, we must replicate their actions, personality, and behavior more closely than we would simply using disguises. As an example, if we were pretending to be a CEO of a Fortune 500 company, it would not make sense to be wearing cheap suits or worn shoes. Luckily, most of our attacks using impersonation will be either over the phone, via e-mail, or some other interaction that does not require face-to-face meetings.

One example of interacting with victims over the phone or e-mail would be the use of pretexting, in which we assume the guise of a manager, customer, reporter, or even a co-worker's family member. Using a fake identity, we will create a believable scenario that elicits the victim to give us confidential or useful information. The disadvantage to pretexting is that we have to know a lot of information beforehand, such as names, job positions, geographical locations, and perhaps even personal information about the victim and/or the persona we are assuming.

A simpler way of social engineering a victim using the technique of impersonation is through conducting a phishing attack. In most cases, phishing involves a broad attack against numerous, potential victims; however, as Zukin, we can conduct spear phishing attacks instead, and target specific individuals or companies to obtain unauthorized access or confidential information from our victims.

Not all impersonations require us to assume the guise of a person – sometimes we need to impersonate a server and its applications. In Chapter 5, "Disguise," we looked at some examples of creating Web sites and companies with names that sound similar to real companies; but what if we want to take it a step further and impersonate the company itself? We can use fraudulent certificates to convince our victims that they should trust us with their information because of who we *say* we are – not who we truly are.

As Zukin, the use of impersonation should be selected as a last resort, and only used if we cannot gather the necessary information in another fashion. By using impersonation, we dramatically increase the chances of getting caught, which was a death sentence to the ninja in feudal Japan. Although we live in less-dangerous times, we still need to be aware of the risks involved in impersonation; we should have the same mental and physical preparedness as the ninja of old – intent on succeeding in their mission and willing to pay whatever cost was necessary. To do otherwise is to follow in the footsteps of the average hacker, adopting traditional methodologies and allowing others to surpass our skills in identifying and protecting corporate assets; if our capabilities are surpassed by malicious attackers, we are doing a disservice to the company paying for our skills as penetration testers.

To achieve success in pretexting and phishing, we have to understand people's weaknesses. In Chapter 10, "Psychological Weaknesses," we will discuss in detail the concept of "the five weaknesses," which are laziness, anger, fear, sympathy, and vanity. These are balanced by "the five needs," – security, sex, wealth, pride, and pleasure.[2] In this chapter, we will only briefly touch on both sets of "the five," in order to understand how to exploit the victim, leaving more detailed discussion for Chapter 10, "Psychological Weaknesses;" but by playing to weaknesses and wants, we will make our victims provide information to us against their better judgment.

PRETEXTING

As mentioned earlier, pretexting involves the creation of a believable scenario, while we pretend to be a manager, customer, reporter, or even a family member. While we can use pretexting in face-to-face encounters or over some communication medium, each of them has their own challenges. Direct, face-to-face encounters require a heightened level of attention to detail about our body language, while indirect encounters, such as over the phone or through e-mail, require us to focus more on verbal mannerisms. However, both types of encounters require strong communication and psychological skills, specialized knowledge, nerves of steel, and a quick mind to be successful.

Walking up to a security guard without any detailed knowledge of the target organization and convincing the guard that they need to allow us access to their facility is quite a challenge, and one that probably would not succeed, unless the guard is incompetent. During a penetration test, this may be an option to try, but a more subtle approach is often better, especially if we want to consider ourselves as Zukin. Pretexting gives us an edge when trying to social engineer a victim; if we can drop names, provide details of the facility, and give the victim sufficient cause to believe we deserve access to the facility, our chances of success increase substantially.

Both direct and indirect encounters require skills in the "modern seven ways" and understanding the "fives" (mentioned previously). As a refresher from Chapter 5, "Disguise," the "modern seven ways" are as follows:

- Scholastic
- Business
- Rural
- Religious
- Public figures
- Labor
- Uniformed

We will look at how each of these "ways" has been used effectively to infiltrate an organization or gather confidential data. As with all examples discussed in this book, the impersonation examples we will be examining should provide inspiration for the Zukin – but should not be exactly replicated. Any time we replicate an attack – even someone else's – we run the risk of getting caught since our victim may have heard about the attack beforehand and would therefore be more diligent in recognizing repetitive attacks.

Scholastic

Although traditional penetration test methodologies focus on exploiting systems, networks, or facilities, accessing college campuses and personal student information could provide a wealth of opportunity, especially for those intent in committing fraud or crimes. One of the more unfortunate cases of impersonation within the field of scholastics was performed by Rickey A. Robbins. Robbins had a history of posing as a professor, in order to access college campus buildings; unfortunately, the purpose behind Robbins' infiltration onto college campuses was to commit crimes, including violent crimes. Robbins was able to extend his crime spree over the years by maintaining different scholastic appearances throughout his criminal history and had been spotted on college campuses throughout the western United States.[3]

Robbins' impersonation did not require much skill – he could simply say he was an educator, in order to obtain access to campus facilities. His ability to be successful with the simplest of impersonation skills demonstrates how easy it can be to make others believe in a false identity. In most cases, however, "proof" of an academic experience is necessary to commit fraud as an academician. In 2008, the Iranian interior minister, Ali Kordan, was terminated for faking a degree from Oxford University.[4] Unfortunately for Kordan, his skill at creating a degree was poor; the "honorary doctorate of law" degree he presented as his own had bad grammar and included forged signatures of professors who did not work in the Oxford University law department.[4]

If we want to learn from these examples, we can walk away with two different points. The first point is that presentation of oneself as an educator does not always require a specific appearance – presentation may be sufficient. The second point is that if we do present documents, we should make sure the documents are similar to real documents and use correct spelling and grammar (it seems ridiculous to mention the last point, but since that is how Kordan was exposed it seems necessary to mention).

NOTE

Impersonating a scholar during a professional penetration test would probably be a rarity. However, as a Zukin, it may be a perfect disguise since it is totally unexpected. Attacks that target research and development shops would certainly be a situation where a scholastic persona could increase the chance of success. Part of the fun of being a Zukin is that we can be extremely creative in what identity we assume.

Posing as scholars is not the only way to commit fraud or a crime – sometimes the target is students themselves. The theft of student personal information is a productive crime since students typically have cleaner credit histories. One method used to obtain student information is the promise of college scholarships in which scammers pose as organizations with grant money and offer students a way to pay for school. In some cases, the scammers had done significant homework before attempting their attack – they have been able to gather birth dates and the last four digits of the target's social security number.[5]

Impersonating scholastic personas take advantage of the authority educators have in higher education. By posing as a professor, we can gain access to facilities often without hindrance. If we chose to pose as a representative of a company that supports scholastic endeavors, we may need to delve deeper into understanding our target during our information gathering phase. Although we may not need to obtain information such as social security numbers, extensive research can pay off dramatically.

Business

Examples of impersonating someone in business are numerous; we have discussed some different scenarios already in this book, including the escapades of Vanderbergh and Voight from Chapter 5, "Disguise." However, Vanderbergh and Voight had to remain somewhat inconspicuous and blend in with the surroundings. In ninja hacking, remaining inconspicuous has its advantages; but sometimes it pays to aim higher up the corporate ladder.

Jide J. Zeitlin, founder of the Independent Mobile Infrastructure, admitted to assuming the identity of his company's rival chief executive officer in an e-mail.

The rival company was American Tower, and the e-mail was sent to two of American Tower's largest investors and contained information considered defaming, according to a law suit against Zeitlin.[6] The law suit was later dropped by American Tower – Zeitlin also had the distinction of being selected for nomination to the United Nations as a representative of the United States by President Obama, a distinction Zeitlin turned down for personal reasons.[7]

Zeitlin's ability to impersonate his competitor's CEO demonstrated how to pinpoint his attack, by choosing a small number of investors. Unfortunately, his ruse failed when the investors contacted the CEO of American Tower.[6] This failure indicates that Zeitlin failed to understand how others would react to his impersonation attempt. In our next example, we will see another failure when other people's reactions are discounted during an impersonation attempt.

Rural

Examining failed attempts provides insight into how to improve one's own skill in impersonation and disguise. The following example involves a high-ranking insurgent in Iraq who attempted to impersonate a rural farmer. The insurgent's disguise failed when Captain Pedro Rasario, of the United States Air Force, noticed some oddities in the impersonation attempt. According to a news report, Rosario stated "his hands are immaculate; his clothes are white as snow … Villagers are coming out: Gawking, bowing, shaking his hand […] I know what a farmer looks like and what a teacher looks like in their culture."[8]

The insurgent failed at both attempting to disguise himself and impersonate a farmer; his disguise failed because of his pristine clothes, and his impersonation failed because of how others interacted with him through demonstrations of obeisance. This example provides some additional insight into additional elements we need to pay attention to when conducting a ninja hacking attack – the reactions of those who surround us play a significant part in our ability to impersonate someone.

Religious

Priests carry a lot of authority for many individuals; under the right circumstances, impersonating a priest can take advantage of that authority. George Persyn would wear a priest's garb to persuade victims to trust him during a sales transaction; Persyn allegedly tried to purchase vehicles "in the name of the Church" from car dealerships from Texas to Arizona.[9] Persyn would also use his fake persona to acquire other items as well, including furniture. In a shop in San Antonio, Persyn was able to convince a furniture dealer to sell him a cherry wood desk, for which he would pay within 30 days time.[10]

A more daring attempt in impersonating a priest occurred at the Vatican; in 2008, a man attempted to enter the Vatican as a priest in an attempt to hear confessions in St. Peter's Basilica. The impersonator had a forged pass and documents on his person that appeared to be valid; the forged pass allowed him to enter the cathedral, and the other forged documents identified him as a priest. Both appeared valid enough that he was able to access the site.[11] However, documents are not enough to pull off a successful impersonation attempt. According to the judge who tried the impersonator, there were inconsistencies in the man's mannerisms during his attempt to act as a priest.[11] The failed attempt to access St. Basilica demonstrates the need to assume the entire persona of the person we are attempting to impersonate – documents are helpful, but should be considered only a part of the overall success of our attacks.

Public Figures

There is a high probability of failure when trying to impersonate a public figure in face-to-face encounters. Unless we can imitate facial features, we cannot expect success in assuming the guise of someone that is in the public eye. Luckily, today's social networking allows us to assume the identity of others without having to replicate their facial features, height, weight, or body gestures.

An example of the use of social networks to impersonate public figures was the fake Twitter account that purported itself to be that of Mayor Nutter of Philadelphia. The purpose behind the creation of the account is unknown since it was not used for gain, and all the messages appeared as legitimate – referencing city programs.[12] Today's Web 3.0 applications, such as Facebook and Twitter, allow us to impersonate anyone, depending on how we present ourselves.

Labor

In businesses, the most obvious persona to impersonate that will have access to all corners of a building is a janitor. They often operate after business hours and do their job without supervision. Our next example illustrates how the position of a janitor can be used to access personal information.

SHINOBI-IRI (Stealth and Entering Methods)

Impersonation can be particularly effective when we use the guise of unskilled or "lower class" labor. Many people tend to ignore janitors, food service workers, landscapers, and the like entirely. Additionally, we can use the excuse of being slow or not speaking the native language if confronted directly in order to escape from sticky situations.

In March 2010, a janitor and her two sisters were charged with identity theft of over 200 individuals; the crimes were committed while Shikila Blount was performing janitorial duties for doctors' offices, which consisted of Blount stealing patient information, such as social security numbers and other personally identifiable information in order to obtain credit cards.[13] It is interesting how organizations may attempt to protect corporate data through tactics such as background checks, security systems, and security guards; however, they allow contractors, such as janitorial personnel, to have unrestricted and unmonitored access to the entire facility.

Uniformed

The story of Frank Abagnale became popular knowledge with the release of the movie *Catch Me if You Can*, in which Abagnale impersonated everything from an airline pilot to a medical doctor. His exploits were exceptional in their ability to garner the trust of people in many industries. The exploits of Voight from Chapter 5, "Disguise," illustrated how someone could impersonate an officer of the law; the motivation behind both Abagnale's and Voight's impersonation attempts were for personal gain, and both were successful because they were able to convince others with their presentation. However, neither of them actually had experience in the field they were infiltrating.

Andrew Madrid from San Jose, California, posed as both an IT employee or a security guard to rob companies, including his previous employer.[14] Madrid's impersonation was different from Abagnale and Voight in that Madrid was a professional network administrator and used his experience to pull off his exploits. Allegedly, Madrid infiltrated his previous employer to destroy company data so that they would "ask him to come back and fix the very problem he created."[14] Madrid conducted other crimes in which he stole laptops or anything else of value; if confronted, he would use his knowledge as a network administrator to convince others that he belonged.[14] Additional ways of gaining and maintaining access to corporations was through impersonation of a security guard, by stealing uniforms or security badges.[14]

Since pretexting involves the creation of a believable scenario (to our victim), it is important to build a believable disguise, depth of relevant knowledge, use of appropriate vernacular (language), understanding the layout – or geography – of the victim's facility, and understanding of psychology to manipulate victims. In this section, we primarily examined failures in pretexting and infiltration; however, these failures can provide some insight into how to achieve success as a Zukin during professional penetration testing targeting a company's facility. The selection of a disguise is not the only component to a successful attack – we must adopt *hengen kashu no jutsu* (immersion in the illusion) to be invisible and successful.

PHISHING

Phishing is a different form of impersonation, in that it is employed entirely through the use of e-mail. Most phishing attacks are broadly cast and involve convincing the potential victim to click a link in the e-mail, in order to send the victim to a fake site designed to collect personal information or to have the victim install malicious software. The fake sites are typically copies of well-known Web sites, such as Amazon, Facebook, and eBay. In some cases, the victim is directed to a fake login page that imitates popular banking sites, to acquire bank account login information and the funds within them.

> **TIP**
>
> For an additional method that can be used in phishing, certificate, and other similar attacks, see the discussion on the internationalized domain name (IDN) homographic attack in Chapter 9, "Discovering Weak Points in Area Defenses."

The problem with most phishing attacks is that unless the target victim actually has an account on the site being faked, the attack will fail; someone who does not have a Chase Bank account will not be convinced by a phishing attack that redirects to a fake Chase Bank Web site. Even if the target victim does have an account, people are beginning to be cautious of unsolicited e-mails from their banks or other Web sites. From a ninja hacking perspective, phishing attacks are messy and have a high chance of discovery; if we plan on conducting e-mail phishing attacks, we need to refine our methods.

Spear phishing is a targeted attack against a specific company, organization, or person. A spear phishing attack requires advanced information gathering so that the e-mail attack will be seen as legitimate, and directs the potential victim to a fake site that the victim would expect, and see as valid. In addition, our e-mail must be seen to come from a valid sender – someone the victim would trust, such as someone from human resources, a manager, the corporate IT support team, a peer, or friend. In a sense, a phishing attack simply requires us to use a disguise; a spear phishing attack requires us to impersonate someone the victim trusts.

The Sender

Similar to pretexting, we need to impersonate someone that the victim will believe; however, with spear phishing, we need to impersonate someone within the victim's company or someone they know personally, in order to get them to read our e-mail and follow our instructions within. The target we intend to impersonate can be a friend, a colleague, a human resources representative, a boss, or a person of higher authority. The trick is to be able to do so with enough credibility.

Although it would be nice to say that we should try to impersonate the person with the greatest authority over our target victim, our efforts to gather information may be insufficient to be successful. Sometimes we will have to simply accept a lesser figure in order to completely convince the target as to our fake identity. Since we are focusing on e-mail attacks, we must make sure that all identifying information in any sent e-mail is accurate and believable; it may be possible that the intended victim is cynical and untrusting by default and will examine any communication with suspicion. Because of losing the initiative if we are caught sending fake e-mails, we cannot afford to make a mistake. This means we have to obtain an e-mail from the person we intend to impersonate, so we know how they address and sign their e-mails, as well as understand how they write – everything must be exact to assure the highest chance of success.

The closer the target victim is to the person we intend to impersonate, the more work is required to successfully perform our impersonation. There are two considerations that we need to be aware of – the first being how well the two individuals know each other's writing mannerisms. The second consideration is what type of knowledge the person we intend to impersonate has.

When trying to imitate someone's writing mannerisms, we need to be aware of what types of words they use and how they address the target victim (first name, last name, and/or nickname). We also need to be familiar with how they indent paragraphs, their use of emoticons, and when they typically send e-mails (mornings or afternoons). All these things add up to build a person's identity, and when closely imitated, it will reduce the potential for suspicion.

The second consideration of what type of knowledge the person we intend to impersonate possesses is intended to prevent us from overreaching in our attempt to pull our victim into the trap. If the person who we are trying to impersonate is not very familiar with technical details about a system that we want to access, we should not be using vernacular used by system administrators. We should also be careful about asking for information that the person we intend to impersonate should not have access to – it would seem odd for HR to want information regarding system configuration, for example.

It is possible to successfully use spear phishing without going to the extent of deception outlined in this section, but the better we craft our understanding of our intended targets and the interrelationship between them, the greater chance of success we enjoy.

The E-mail

A successful spear phishing attack targets a small number of people who believe the authenticity of the e-mail and believe in the authenticity of the sender. By keeping the number of recipients as small as possible, there is less chance of the phishing attack being exposed by the media or within an organization. An example of a spear phishing attack was made public by McAfee's computer security research lab in which an e-mail was purportedly sent by the "United State [sic] Tax Court," which claimed that the "Commissioner of Internal Revenue" had brought a law suit against the potential victims.[15] Rather than sending the e-mail to a large mass of people, the e-mail targeted corporate executives – people who would not be too surprised to receive legal notifications. The objective behind the attack was to get the target victim to click on a link which supposedly downloaded a copy of the legal document filed by the Internal Revenue Service; however, the link would download malware onto the victim's computer instead.

WARNING

In recent years, phishing attacks have become so commonplace as to render the average user much more suspicious of e-mail messages. Although this attack can still be very successful, we must take care to construct phishing e-mails carefully. Small things such as grammatical errors, misspellings, missing logos, etc ... can tip off a target to the e-mail not being legitimate.

Part of the reason this particular phishing attack failed was that it included McAfee in its target list. In addition, there were spelling issues, including in the sender's e-mail name. If we are to conduct an attack as Zukin, with the goal of not raising suspicions to prevent detection, our phishing attacks have to be well written, spelled correctly, and minimal in the number of copies that are released – maybe even as few as one copy.

The Web Site

In a spear phishing attack, we are not concerned with getting personal information to access social networking, auction, or banking sites; we are attempting to collect personal information used within the victim's company. We are after corporate login information, company data, and anything else that will allow us to infiltrate the corporation undetected. We can do this by including a link in our e-mail that downloads malicious software onto the victim's system. If we decide to use malware, we do not really have to worry about the location or domain name of the server since the software is pulled to the victim's computer – the victim does not have to visit the server. If we intend to obtain login information, we need to create a Web site on a server that is convincing to the target victim.

The system we use needs to have a domain that seems valid to the victim. The best choice would be to compromise a system within the target corporation, install a Web server (if not already available) and create a bogus page designed to collect personal information. However, if we already have access to a corporate server, we may not need to conduct phishing attack – we could use the compromised server as a launching point for additional attacks within the network. Therefore, we have to assume we will need to set up a server outside the corporate domain that appears to be valid.

"Typo-squatting" – or using a domain name that is similar to a legitimate company's Web site name – just misspelled has already been discussed in Chapter 5, "Disguise." In that chapter, we examined the case in which Chegge-Kraszeski used misspelled domain names to defraud West Virginia. We can do the same to conduct our spear phishing attack; however, another option is to create a domain name that is an extension of a legitimate domain, such as "microsoftupdater.com," which to the nonskeptical mind may appear to be legitimate. Regardless of which type of domain we use, it has to be convincing to the potential victim. However, a fake domain name that appears legitimate may not be sufficient for our purpose – we may have to convince our victim to trust our site through the use of fraudulent Web site certificates.

Fraudulent Certificates

One other topic that we need to briefly discuss in this chapter is the use of fraudulent certificates. When using fake public key infrastructure (PKI) certificates, we have two options: disguise ourselves as someone trustworthy or impersonate someone that already has an established trust relationship with our victim. Since this chapter is about disguising ourselves, we will limit the conversation to just that.

For those who are not familiar with PKI, it is the framework in which a trust relationship is created through the creation and distribution of digital certificates. We, as consumers, use PKI every time we purchase something from Amazon or eBay. It allows us to create secure communication channels with remote systems and provides some level of assurance as to the identity of the remote system to which we are connecting.

In Chapter 5, "Disguise," we examined the possibility of creating fraudulent Web sites that had names similar to real ones. The creation of SSL certificates is a simple matter – we would just register for a certificate using our domain name. However, if our victim can discern that our domain name is potentially bogus, the certificate is useless in convincing the victim otherwise. If we want to create a Web site with a certificate that appears valid and says we are someone legitimate, we need to hack the public key infrastructure itself.

X.509 is the standard for PKI and is composed of specifications for creation and revocation of public key certificates. In 2009, numerous vulnerabilities within the X.509 standard were identified and exploited – one of them is known as a null prefix attack. The vulnerability was presented at black hat that year and takes advantage of the ability to include null characters in the X.509 request.[16] An example of the exploit would be to request a certificate with the following to the Certificate Authority:

- www.paypal.com\0.heorot.net

The Certificate Authority is only concerned with the identity of heorot.net since it only looks at the root server – not any subdirectories. If we own heorot.net, then we can receive a valid certificate with "www.paypal.com\0.heorot.net" as the verified domain. Once we receive a certificate with "www.paypal.com\0.heorot.net" as the valid site name, anytime someone visits us, we will be able to create secure connections as the legitimate certificate holder. However, the interesting part of the attack is not that heorot.net will appear as the valid Web site, but we can also validate ourselves as paypal.com as well.

When someone visits our heorot.net site where we are using "www.paypal .com\0.heorot.net" as the domain for the certificate, a flaw in many Internet browsers will authenticate us as both heorot.net and paypal.com. If we are trying to get our victim to provide us with their PayPal login information, the certificate will make us appear as a valid PayPal server. We can take it one step further – instead of using paypal.com in our certificate, we could have simply submitted "*\0.heorot.net" as our domain. In this situation, we could pose as any Web site – not just heorot.net or paypal.com. For additional information about the null prefix attack, check out www. thoughtcrime.org/papers/null-prefix-attacks.pdf.

Although the null prefix attack may be fixed by the time this book is published, it does provide proof that there are exploitable vulnerabilities within the X.509 architecture and the public key infrastructure.

Summary

The use of impersonation in a professional penetration test may appear to be a simple thing – assume a disguise and play a role. For most pentest projects, this may be true; if the impersonation fails, we simply note it in our final report for the client we attempted to infiltrate. However, if we need to avoid detection at all costs, impersonation becomes a much more complicated endeavor.

The ninja used *hengen kasha no jutsu* (immersion in the illusion) to actually become the person they impersonated. We can do the same by using the "modern seven ways of going" and adopting the mentality and dedication of the ninja. As we noted in Chapter 5, "Disguise," the ninja had to be "thoroughly impersonating the character adopted. Personality traits, areas of knowledge, and body dynamics of the identity assumed were ingrained in the ninja's way of thinking and reacting. He or she literally became the new personality."[17]

If we decide to conduct an attack using pretexting, we need to make sure that our disguise is perfect and that our knowledge, language, understanding of geography, and understanding of human psychology is exceptional for the task at hand. Although we have a lot of different choices when choosing a disguise and persona to impersonate, we need to be cognizant of the efficacy of the impersonation in our attack; we also need to be aware of how others we know would interact with us while we are in our disguise. Although in this chapter we looked at failures of impersonation, we can learn from the mistake of others and improve our own skill in impersonation and disguise.

If we do not want to go through the effort to create a physical disguise, we can choose to perform e-mail attacks using our spear phishing skills to gain information necessary to access the corporate systems of the target organization. Unlike pretexting, we need to refine the target of our impersonation to be someone familiar with the victim, which requires additional information gathering on our time. Before we can conduct a spear phishing attack, we need to know what type of authority figure – or personal friend – the victim will better respond to and what motivates the victim to react.

The problem with the use of a phishing attack is that we cannot always be assured that we will have access to a server within the target corporation's network in which to conduct our attack. In cases where we have to use remote systems to conduct our spear phishing attack, we may need to generate fraudulent certificates for our servers so that they appear to be legitimate.

Endnotes

1. Hayes SK. Ninja vol. III: warrior path of Togakure. Burbank (CA): Phara Publications, Inc; 1983 [accessed 01.07.10].
2. Hayes S. The ninja and their secret fighting art. Rutland: Tuttle Publishing; 1990. 978-0804816564.

3. Blasko E. Fugitive sex offender possibly spotted at IUSB. WSBT TV. www.wsbt.com/news/local/37674979.html; 2009 [accessed 01.07.10].

4. Parker Q. Iranian minister sacked over fake degree. Guardian News and Media Limited. www.guardian.co.uk/education/2008/nov/04/oxforduniversity-highereducation-iran; 2008 [accessed 01.07.10].

5. Internet Broadcasting Systems, Inc. High school students targeted in scholarship scam. www.thepittsburghchannel.com/education/4136440/detail.html; 2010 [accessed 01.07.10].

6. Reuters. Wireless tower operator sues chief of rival. New York Times. www.nytimes.com/2007/12/29/technology/29lawsuit.html; 2007 [accessed 01.07.10].

7. Rogin J. Execlusive: Controversial Obama U.N. nominee withdraws for "personal reasons," officials say. Foreign Policy. http://thecable.foreignpolicy.com/posts/2009/12/29/exclusive_controversial_obama_un_nominee_withdraws_for_personal_reasons_official_sa; 2009 [accessed 01.07.10].

8. Kelleher C. FSC grad awarded Bronze Star. MediaNews Group, Inc. http://cache.zoominfo.com/CachedPage/?archive_id=0&page_id=1267986199&page_url=%2f%2fwww.sentinelandenterprise.com%2flocal%2fci_3103409&page_last_updated=10%2f11%2f2005+11%3a03%3a34+AM&firstName=Pedro&lastName=Rosario; 2005 [accessed 01.07.10].

9. San Antonio Police Department. Bat-Net arrests. www.sanantonio.gov/sapd/BATNETARRESTS.HTM#priest2; 2003 [accessed 01.07.10].

10. LiveLeak.com. Man accused of posing as a priest (again). Obtained online at www.liveleak.com/view?i=16e_1190691310&p=1; 2007 [accessed 01.07.10].

11. BBC News. 'Fake' priest exposed at Vatican. http://news.bbc.co.uk/2/hi/7491851.stm; 2008 [accessed 01.07.10].

12. Lucey C. Fake Nutter Twitter account disabled. Philadelphia Daily News. www.philly.com/philly/blogs/cityhall/Fake_Nutter_Twitter_Account_Disabled.html; 2009 [accessed 01.07.10].

13. Cox T. ID-theft ring targets patients at medical office. Daily Herald. www.dailyherald.com/story/?id=368621&src=143; 2010 [accessed 01.07.10].

14. McMillan R. IT admin used inside knowledge to hack, steal. IDG News Service. www.csoonline.com/article/462130/IT_Admin_Used_Inside_Knowledge_to_Hack_Steal; 2009 [accessed 01.07.10].

15. McGee K. Beware of spear phishing by 'U.S. Tax Court.' McAfee Labs Blog. www.avertlabs.com/research/blog/index.php/2008/05/22/us-tax-court-spear-phishing; 2008 [accessed 01.07.10].

16. Marlinspike M. Null prefix attacks against SSL/TLS certificates. www.thoughtcrime.org/papers/null-prefix-attacks.pdf; 2009 [accessed 01.07.10].

17. Hatsumi M. In: Furuya D., editor. Ninjutsu: history and tradition. Burbank (CA): Unique Publications, Ltd; 1981.

Infiltration

In Chapter 6, "Impersonation," we discussed using impersonation and pretexting in order to conduct our attacks. This gives us a better chance of moving about undetected, or at least unnoticed, but we may need to access more strongly secured areas in the facility. Even with the Zukin disguised as a network technician, we may still need to bypass a lock, clone a proximity card, or move through an area equipped with alarm sensors, all of which will need to be dealt with in turn.

We may alternately be entering an installation in a virtual sense, instead of a physical sense. When conducting network and system attacks, we want to look for a route that is less monitored and less secure, rather than being swept up with the rest of the unwashed mass of hackers that are attacking the heavily fortified border devices of the company. Regardless of whether we attack virtually or physically, we want to use stealth, concealment, and leave no traces behind to indicate that we were even there.

LOCK PICKING AND SAFE CRACKING

The ability to open locks is a key skill for the Zukin. Being able to enter a place or open a container, collect information, then disappear with no one the wiser was and is a key ability in the ninja arsenal. We will talk about a variety of systems from mechanical locks, to safes, to systems protected with biometric authentication.

Avoiding the Lock

Following the path of the Zukin, the most desirable action when presented with a lock, whether mechanical or electronic in nature, is not to attack it head on, but to avoid it entirely. If another means can be found to reach the objective that does not involve manipulating the locking mechanism, stealing or impressioning keys, or any other method that might leave direct evidence, this is the route that should be taken.

Ninja Hacking. DOI: 10.1016/B978-1-59749-588-2.00007-X

Tailgating

Tailgating refers to entering a secure area directly behind a person or persons who have authenticated into the area, without the tailgater actually authenticating themselves. This can be an extremely effective means of entry to a facility that has a large staff moving in and out of the building, particularly if this happens at regular intervals, that is, shift changes. Tailgating is discussed in more detail in Chapter 8, "Use of Timing to Enter an Area."

Physical Security Design Flaws

When attempting to avoid taking on a lock directly, one of the better routes is often to look for flaws in the design of physical security. These may be doors that blow open or do not close entirely due to oddities in the building architecture, areas that cameras cannot see or are blocked by landscaping, or even entrances with less or no security due to multitenancy in the building. Physical security design flaws will be covered in greater depth in Chapter 9, "Discovering Weak Points in Area Defenses."

Subverting Locks without Leaving Evidence

One of the main issues for the Zukin in lock picking is that of leaving evidence behind. Many of the standard lock picking or subverting techniques will either damage the locking mechanism to a certain extent, as we see in the scratches left by the use of lock picks, or will leave material in the keyway, as we might see in the use of certain materials used to reproduce keys through impressioning. We can use a variety of means to accomplish this goal, most of which relate to either not damaging the lock or doing so in areas that are very difficult to detect.

Bump Keys

Although the existence and usefulness of the bump key has been known since the late 1920s at the latest,[1] the technique was not widely known until the efforts of The Open Organisation of Lockpickers (TOOOL) in publishing a whitepaper on the topic[2] and giving demonstrations at several major security conferences.

The bump key, as shown in Figure 7.1, is, in principle, very simple and uses the same general method of operation as a pick gun. The bump key itself is a key that is cut to the maximum depth in all locations. The key is inserted into the lock, struck sharply on the back with a lightly weighted object, then turned a fraction of a second afterwards.

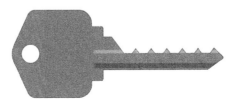

FIGURE 7.1 A Typical Bump Key.

Courtesy of Deviant Ollam

NOTE

The bump key is generally only successful with pin tumbler locks, as shown in Figure 7.2. Additionally, some locks are designed with security features to prevent the use of a bump key. Although this method will be successful on the vast majority of residential and commercial locks, it is best to investigate the target locks in advance, if at all possible.

FIGURE 7.2 A Pin Tumbler Lock.

Courtesy of Deviant Ollam

The way that this enables the cylinder to move is a neat trick of physics. In the same way that the cue ball in pool will impart most of its energy to the other ball and then stop moving itself, the bump key causes all of the key pins to jump, in turn causing all of the driver pins to jump above the shear line. This is the same basic principle of pin movement that we see when using a pick, just done all at once.

For those who are not clear on how exactly the internals of lock mechanisms work, we suggest the book *Practical Lockpicking: A Physical Penetration Tester's Training Guide* (ISBN: 978-1-59749-611-7), by Deviant Ollam, now available from Syngress. He is a true font of lock-picking knowledge, is involved with TOOOL in the United States, and can regularly be seen discussing lock picking and physical security at various security conventions.

Counter to what we might believe, higher quality locks tend to be more susceptible to bump keys than lower quality locks. Due to the tighter machining tolerances in the more expensive locks and the higher quality of material from

> **WARNING**
>
> It is very easy to visibly damage a lock using a bump key. We can not only damage the mechanism of the lock itself but also leave a very noticeable dent on the front face of the cylinder. Worse yet, overzealous bumping can cause the bump key to become stuck in the lock. None of these are positive things from a stealth standpoint. Aside from being gentle with the bump key, a thin piece of hard rubber can be place between the shoulder of the key and the cylinder to mitigate damage to the cylinder. Practicing this technique before hand to gain skill in damage avoidance is always a good suggestion.

which they are constructed, there is less "slop" inside the lock when a bump key is used, meaning that the lock mechanism does not move unnecessarily, allowing for the pins to move more smoothly and more energy to be imparted to them from the bump.

Padlock Shims

Padlock shims are a thin, stiff piece of sheet metal, often made from a beer or soda can, which have been formed into a shape as shown in Figure 7.3. Technically, shims are a bypass tool, not a pick, which is slipped down next to the latching bar of the lock, allowing the shackle of the lock to pull out without actually rotating the cylinder. The padlock shim, if successful, is an excellent tool for surreptitious access as it allows the lock to be opened in seconds, then relocked with no easily visible evidence that the lock was every tampered with.

Padlock shims generally work best on older locks or on less expensive new locks. They also work especially well on many combination locks that fit into the same category. Newer locks tend to have mechanisms to prevent the use of a shim and may actually damage the shim sufficiently as to leave evidence in the lock; the preventative mechanisms may also make the shim very difficult to remove.

Reproducing Keys

Making a reproduction of a key can be an excellent way to bypass a lock, presuming that we can obtain a copy of the legitimate key and have enough time to make some sort of a duplicate of it. The easiest method to duplicate the key would, of course,

FIGURE 7.3 A Typical Padlock Shim.

Courtesy of Deviant Ollam

be to use a key duplication machine. However, such machines are, in general, not terribly portable, somewhat noisy, and take a few minutes to make a duplicate of the key. Despite the drawbacks, the use of a duplication machine is the preferred method of replication if we have an extended period of time in which to keep the key because the precise tolerance of the duplication machine will generally produce very clean and usable copies.

If we only have a shorter period of time to possess a key, we can try to create an impression of it from which we can later make a duplicate by casting. We have often seen this done very quickly in the movies, but the process must be done very carefully in order to make sure that the mold that we will make is not distorted. This is generally done using clay or silicon as a mold material and can be somewhat difficult if the person making the attempt is not familiar with molding and casting small objects. We may also leave evidence on the key itself from the molding process, which might undermine our ability to conduct our attack undetected.

A bit safer means that is related to physical impressioning and avoids many of the issues discussed above is to work from a photograph of a key. This has the benefit of greatly reducing the amount of time that we need to have the key, but may mean that our key is not as accurate as making a direct copy and may need a bit of adjustment in the field. This type of duplication was made rather public in 2007 when Diebold posted a photograph of a key on their Web site for an electronic voting machine. Using the photograph of the key and a few key blanks bought from a local hardware store, Ross Kinard of SploitCast, was able to make two copies of the key that, when later tested in an actual Diebold voting machine, were able to open the lock.[3]

Opening Safes

Safes are used to protect everything from secret military plans to mom's cookie recipe. An enormous variety of mechanisms exist on the market, ranging from simple mechanical safes all the way to complex electronically guarded units with multiple layers of tamper protection mechanisms.

Opening a Combination Safe

The easiest way to open a combination safe is, of course, by having the combination. There are a variety of methods that we can use in an attempt to obtain the combination, some of which will be discussed in Chapter 13, "Covert Listening Devices." Given time, we can search the area for a written copy of the combination in the usual places: a note on the wall, a sticky note on a monitor, or under a keyboard.

Another quick trick to try is to see if the safe is still set to the default combination. When safes leave the manufacturer, they are set to a default combination, with the intent that the owner of the safe will change it. Default combinations are relatively standard and well known to those in the lock and safe industries.

Having failed to obtain the combination through obvious means, we may need to resort to manipulation of the lock. This features heavily in many movies and involves listening to the mechanism inside the door of the safe as the dial is moved.

In less-sophisticated combination locks, when one of the wheels is rotated into the proper position (or close to it), it will make a small click as the mechanism shifts. Given enough time the Zukin can determine roughly which numbers are present in the combination for the safe. Then it is just a matter of trying all of the different arrangements of those numbers. Both software and electronic devices exist that can aid in and theoretically speed up this process for those that are trained in their use.

Opening an Electronic Lock Safe

Electronic safes, meaning those that have a keypad in place of a dial and somewhat different internal mechanisms, present a somewhat more difficult target than combination safes, as they have a considerably smaller attack surface than the combination safe, presuming that we will stay with methods that do not involve physically disassembling or modifying the safe.

The safest route that we can take to reduce the combination space with which we are concerned is to examine the surfaces of the safe buttons themselves. Using a fingerprint dusting kit, it is generally possible to discern the more frequently used keys, thus allowing us a greater chance at entering the proper combination.

Another possible method could be to coat an intervening surface, such as the handle on a door loading to the room where the safe resides with ultraviolet ink or other substance that can easily be transferred between a person's hand and the safe keys without detection. When the safe is accessed by a person with ultraviolet ink-stained hands, residue will be left behind on the keypad and can later be revealed with the use of a small blacklight.

SHINOBI-IRI (Stealth and Entering Methods)

Higher end safes may have security features that will not only make these methods dramatically more difficult, but may also make it possible to detect even a failed attempt at opening the safe, such as the following:

- Mechanisms to prevent the dial from being turned at high speeds
- Disproportionate distances between numbers on the dial
- Very large combination spaces (1,000,000+ possible combinations)
- Time limits for entering the combination
- Limits on the length of continuous dialing
- Lockouts for successive incorrect combinations
- Audit trails

Less Elegant Methods

Although the methods below are more than likely out of scope for the majority of penetration tests, they are valid methods for the ninja, cyber warfare, and criminal enterprises in general. We may not want to use them ourselves, but understanding them is important.

There are a variety of methods that can be used to physically open a safe including the use of explosives, drilling through parts of the housing to gain access to the mechanism, various cutting tools, and multitude of other improbable methods that have graced the silver screen. These methods, some few of which are actually effective, are out of the scope of activities for the Zukin, due to the gross physical evidence left behind. However, if no other option is available and it is essential to enter the device, the Zukin should create a scenario that makes the destruction of the safe appear as an accidental consequence of some larger attack or accident. As an example, if a safe is next to a wall that has a gas main running through it, the Zukin could modify the scene to make it appear that the gas main exploded, which resulted in the accidental destruction of the safe. Regardless of the real circumstances, any attack performed by the Zukin should appear as a natural disaster or simply bad luck.

Compromising Proximity Card Systems

Stealing or cloning a badge and its accompanying proximity card may not seem like the most clandestine way to get around a proximity card lock, but it is highly effective. Many large companies, particularly those in the high-tech industry tend to attract a smattering of small restaurants, dry cleaners, and a variety of other service establishments in their immediate vicinity, if not on the site itself. These locations provide ample opportunity to come in close contact with employee badges working for the target company; these locations provide access to badges often for extended periods of time, in a setting where such activity is very unlikely to be noticed.

Card Cloning

Proximity cards are, almost without exception, implemented with simple RFID tags. The card reader transmits a carrier signal that powers the RFID tag in the proximity card. The proximity card then transmits a simple stored code. If this code is captured by another reader, it can be used to create a duplicate card with the same code or can be played back electronically with a RFID card simulation device. Ultimately, in order to clone a proximity card, we do not even need to touch it. Given a sufficiently powerful and sensitive cloning device, we can do everything that we need to do from several feet away. Restaurants surrounding our target location are a great setting to gain such access without attracting notice.

Although this may sound like technology out of the reach of mere mortals, plans can be found on the Internet to build a wide variety of such devices.[4] These will work for most proximity cards on the market today, although they will not work for more complex systems containing RFID tags, which function on a challenge-response principle. Although these types of tags are not commonplace at present, they are sure to become more so as the number of systems using RFID for various purposes become more numerous.

Stealing Cards

Stealing a proximity card is simplicity itself. Such cards are often displayed externally on some type of lanyard or retractable device, so as to be easily displayed to the physical security personnel at the person's place of employment. Stealing a proximity card is as simple as cutting the retaining device, brushing by the target in a crowded restaurant and unclipping the badge or any of a number of similar activities.

Although this is not as clean of a method to use as cloning a card, it is very efficient, very fast, and does not require a great commitment of resources or technical knowledge. Victims of this technique, due to the general low quality of badge holders, are likely to think that the badge has fallen off on its own and will report it as lost when they next enter the facility. It is, therefore, important to keep in mind that the window of opportunity to use a stolen badge, in general, will be short; likely very short if a high-security facility is concerned.

Defeating Biometric Systems

Biometric identification or authentications systems, that is, systems that work from fingerprints, iris or retina scans, height or weight, voice analysis, or any number of other factors, can be very difficult to defeat. Some of these methods can be extremely difficult to defeat, but one stands out that has been overcome in various demonstrations – the fingerprint.

Fingerprints

One of the better points of using fingerprints as a means to defeat a biometric system is the ease of access to the biometric identifier. We can pick up a fingerprint from a work area with relative ease; items containing easily accessible fingerprints include soda cans, drinking glasses, or any number of everyday items. The methods for lifting fingerprints have been well known for many years and a number of tutorials can be found in various texts or Web pages. Suffice it to say that the materials needed to lift a fingerprint from a small item are easily placed in a pocket.

Once the needed fingerprint has been obtained, we need to go through the process of casting it in order to create our duplicate. After the fingerprint has been lifted, we will need to create a copy of it to be enlarged. The easiest way to do this is to scan it into a graphics file on a computer. Lifted fingerprints are often not as perfect an image as is the enrolled fingerprint in a biometric system. The enrolled fingerprint is often taken under controlled conditions using a specific set of instructions in order to get the cleanest possible print. Our fingerprint will often be obtained under much less precise conditions. Once we have the image of the fingerprint scanned into the computer, we can often clean it up by filling in broken or weak lines, giving us a much better chance of succeeding with our duplicate.

When the image has been cleaned up, we need to make a mold of it using the same process used to etch circuit boards. Hack a Day has an excellent review of this process, including a tutorial video.[5] When we have our finished etching of the fingerprint, we can then cast it in a variety of materials. When copies are cast in a thin enough material, such as latex, they can then be glued over the Zukin's own fingerprint and are not easily noticeable without close inspection. With a little practice, this process works very well and can succeed even on fingerprint readers that test for "liveness," which uses temperature, capacitance, or pulse sensors.[6]

Other Biometric Identifiers

Various attempts have been made at defeating iris or retina scans, most of which have been deemed impractical due to difficulties in obtaining a proper image to use when attempting to bypass the system. Additionally, this is a field that continues to advance in the areas of accuracy and liveness testing.

At Black Hat DC in 2009, a presentation was given by researchers from the Ha Noi University of Technology in Vietnam on defeating facial recognition. Although the research was limited to the systems built into laptops produced by Lenovo, Asus, and Toshiba, the researchers were successful in bypassing all three systems by using photos of the enrolled user.[7] Although this research may not directly relate to bypassing higher-end commercial systems, it does show some promise.

ALARM SYSTEM EVASION

There is a veritable plethora of alarm systems and sensors on the market from any number of glass break sensors, to pressure mats, to magnetic contacts. To cover them all here not only would turn this into a treatise on alarm systems but also would likely lead us into the territory of hardware modifications that would leave evidence behind, which is in stark contrast to the activities and philosophy for the Zukin. We will discuss the systems that we are likely to encounter and can bypass or disable without leaving traces behind.

Creating False Positives

Many alarm systems and sensors are set to be very sensitive to the condition that they detect and are on the proverbial "hair trigger," much to the dismay of security personnel. In some systems due to environmental conditions, doors that never quite latch, and a variety of other factors, we may find alarm sensors that activate erroneously, sometimes on a regular basis. Even when this is not already the case, we can create this situation.

Given an easily accessible alarmed door, motion sensor, or other device, and a way to activate the sensor without being seen, we can trigger the sensor to send an alarm. This can be as simple as throwing small rocks at a window. While the rocks may not be large enough or thrown hard enough to actually cause any damage, they may, depending on the sensor, be enough to set off the alarm. When the guard has come to investigate the alarm for the sixth time that night, they will be considerably less likely to consider themselves under attack than to simply silence the alarm and file a request for maintenance in the morning.

Temporarily Blinding Cameras

The ninja used small containers filled with sand, pepper, metal shavings, or other irritants, called *Metsubishi* (sight removers) to blind opponents.[8] In a similar fashion, we can use technology to blind surveillance cameras. Although various means have been used in movies, such as painting over cameras and interfering with video feeds, we will stick to methods that are not permanent and should leave little or no evidence behind.

Cameras that use infrared illumination, whether on the camera itself or individual illuminators, are prone to being blinded in small areas by overly bright infrared sources. This method is very effective, but only produces spot blindness on the camera image and only in the immediate vicinity of the infrared source. This has been demonstrated to be very effective in disguising the face of an individual wearing a single infrared LED in a headband and reduces the visible image of the person's face on the camera to a bright circle of light.[9]

Cameras that do not use infrared illuminators – that is, many indoor cameras – can still be blinded using lasers. Even a small, low-powered laser pointer on a fixed mounting device can be used to blind a camera at short distances (<20 feet) and will render the majority of the image seen by the sensor a red blur.[10] To achieve the same effect over a longer distance, a more powerful laser coupled with some type of aiming device, such as a scope, is needed; but the same effect can be achieved, presuming a good angle to the camera lens is accessible. These types of devices should not permanently harm a camera, but caution should be used, as with all laser devices.

Alarm Sensors

Alarm sensors are, as a general rule, extremely difficult to defeat without tampering with the alarm system or the sensors themselves. Such systems are best avoided when armed, as the possibility of accidentally setting them off is very high. We will discuss a few methods that might fool some of the different sensors, but there are a wide variety of devices on the market and many of them are implemented with more than one type of sensor in high-security installations.

Thermal Motion Sensors

Thermal motion sensors function by reading, usually through an infrared sensor, the level of heat in the room. When an object of a sufficiently different temperature from the background passes through the area of the sensor, an alert is send to the alarm. A number of different methods have been shown in the movies as being able to fool such sensors, including people covering themselves with mud, using special suits, and a variety of other unlikely methods. These methods generally fail because of the human body warming up the temperature blocking material over time. One successful method that has been demonstrated is to place the blocking material, such as a pane of glass in front of the sensor itself, thus causing the sensor to only read the surface temperature of the material, not the actual area that is supposed to have been monitored.[6] Although this may be a functional method of defeating the sensor itself, it would require access to the sensor without activating it, perhaps through a ceiling tile, and it would need to be done with any sensors in the area where we would be operating. Additionally, we would need to remove all such devices on the way out of the facility.

Ultrasonic Motion Sensors

An ultrasonic motion sensor sends out a high-frequency sound wave that bounces off of the walls and other objects in the area. The receiver in the sensor picks up the reflected sound and registers the amount of time that it took to return. When something changes the timing of the returned sound wave, the sensor sends an alert to the alarm system. Two main methods that show some measure of success have been demonstrated with this type of sensor, the first being to use a sound absorbing material held between the Zukin and the sensor. The material required will likely vary according to the particular model of sensor. The second is to move very, very slowly. The sensor has a threshold of allowed movement so that small movements in the room from events such as the ventilation system do not constantly set the alarm system off. Moving through the room at a speed below this threshold should not trigger an alarm on the sensor.[6]

TRUSTED NETWORKS

When attempting to gain entry to a house with very solid doors and many locks, the best route is often through the window with its single pane of glass. By the same token, when trying to access a network with very strong protections, it is often best to look for an easier and less protected route in.

In many industries, it is necessary to extend the internal network of the organization out to include employees, vendors, partners, and other parties with which we need to interact closely to conduct business. These trusted connections can often provide a point of entry for the Zukin.

Employee or Contractor Home Networks

In this day of ubiquitous computing, many office workers are actually sitting in home basements or coffee shops, connected to the office using VPN software. Although the connections themselves are generally very secure, there are a few factors that may still leave us an opening, such as poor software configurations or missing protective software.

Split Tunneling on VPN Connections

Almost anyone in the security industry will make an ugly face when the topic of split tunneling on a VPN arises. Normally, on a securely configured VPN connection, when the connection is made to the remote network, access to the local network is prevented. In the case of an employee working from home, this means that local devices, such as network printers, will not be accessible from the machine without first disconnecting the VPN. When faced with frustrations such as these, we can often find the enterprising user poking about in the settings for the VPN software.

> **SHINOBI-IRI (Stealth and Entering Methods)**
>
> Operating over a hijacked VPN connection provides an excellent tool of concealment for the Zukin, as it may appear that the traffic is coming directly from a legitimate source. This guise can be made even more effective by adopting the MAC address of a machine already operating on the network in question. These activities make tracing traffic to its true origin very difficult, even if network activity is being logged and should sow the seeds of confusion and misdirection at the very least. Note that operating a duplicate MAC address on a network for an extended period of time may raise flags with network or support teams, so this should be used with care.

In most VPN clients, the feature that prevents split tunneling can be disabled, allowing our user to connect to the VPN and access their printer. This also allows other devices on the local network to potentially access the other end of the VPN connection through the machine running the VPN client. By extension, this could also allow anyone connecting to a wireless access point on the local network to access the VPN connection. In many cases, this would turn the relatively strong security of the VPN connection into a connection available to anyone with the skill to manage a single click allowing access the wireless network.

Poor or Missing Protective Software

The security policies of many organizations stipulate a minimum set of requirements for a machine to be allowed to connect to the corporate network, whether locally or from remote. Many disallow the use of noncompany-owned assets from being connected to the network at all, a policy often scorned by users. Most require the use of antimalware tool and software firewalls. All of the above are put in place in an effort to keep compromised and malware-ridden devices from accessing the network and infecting other devices.

Although controls can be put in place to rigidly enforce the use of these protective measures, they are very uncommon outside of a few, very security sensitive industries such as banking or defense industries. For the majority of targets, the Zukin will find a much easier route into the corporate network by compromising a laptop or home system of an employee and waiting for them to use it access the network of the company.

Vendor or Partner Networks

In the same way that employee-connected networks can enable the existence of areas of weaker security, so can networks that allow connections from vendors or partners. Although many of the same issues exist on vendor network as do in employee networks, they are often exacerbated due to scale. When such relationships are set up to provide services or support, connectivity is often required to various internal systems or networks.

Lower Levels of Security on External Networks

Many organizations are relatively unique in the way that their security policies are written and implemented, largely due to differing focus of the organizations in question. It stands to reason that a company in a partnership with a vendor will differ in the ways that information is handled, systems are secured, networks are restricted, domain structures, and a multitude of other factors. Although there may be policy in place that stipulates that a vendor or partner must comply with the security policies of the other party, this is often paid lip service at best. Where differing levels of security exist, we will find documents not properly protected, improper information exposed on the Internet, unauthorized files shared on peer-to-peer networks, and a multitude of other sins. These all enable the Zukin to locate and exploit such security holes for attach or information gathering purposes.

Site-to-Site VPNs

External network connections can be particularly useful when implemented in the form of semipermanent or permanent site-to-site VPN connections, particularly if there are not a great deal of limitations placed on access. Although the VPN connection itself may be very secure, chances are that some flaw may be found in the network that the VPN is connected to or in the systems on that network.

In many cases, when a weakness is found on the vendor end that would allow access to an attacker in the first place, such a connection could be extended outside of the physical facility on the vendor end through the use of a wireless access point. This would obviate the need for the Zukin to be physically present in order to utilize the VPN access.

Nonstandard Internal Networks

In many organizations, for a variety of reasons, there exist networks that do not comply with the standards set forth by the designers of the network. Although there may be legitimate causes for these types of networks to exist and they may be officially blessed, they may still provide a weaker target for the Zukin to attack than other areas of the overall network infrastructure.

Research and Development Networks

In many organizations, research and development groups are the favored children. They are often working on a variety of project that have needs, sometimes legitimately and sometimes not, that fall outside of the standard services provided to the rank and file of the company. In some cases, they require network connections to the outside world that offer greater bandwidth, less or different firewall protections, or other specialized changes. Although these requirements, in and of themselves, do not pose a threat, it is also the case that these groups often maintain and monitor such connections themselves. Although it is entirely possible that such maintenance will be absolutely top notch, we have often noticed that this job is given to a single engineer and is one among many projects for which this person is responsible, thus allowing a greater chance for mistakes and misconfigurations to be made, than if the connection were being maintained by a full-time network staff. In general, one-off efforts like these tend to have a lower standard of security than deliberately designed and planned efforts.

Unfiltered Security Networks

An issue that we have seen arises during a variety of security surveys, penetration tests, and other security-oriented activity is the convoluted and labyrinthine state of the network interfering with testing. Even when conducting scans against targets internal to an organization, the very construction of the network may prevent security personnel from seeing an accurate picture of what a network or host really looks like. In some cases, the information returned is indicative of the properties of some intervening device, not the target in question at all. Often, this issue is solved by providing the security team with a network connection that has less or no interference from other devices by trying to minimize or remove the number of devices that may get in the way of said scans. Although we would hope that our theoretical security organization would be extremely cognizant of the fact that this may provide a security hole through which an attacker might enter, it still might be worth adding to the list of weaker targets for which our Zukin should to keep an eye open for.

Legacy Networks

Many larger businesses and organizations exist in an organic conglomeration of communications networks. As time goes by and different portions of the company come and go with organization restructuring, projects rise up then die; any number of internal events happen that can make these networks become a bit of a tangle. These networks, designed for special projects, may fall by the wayside to become forgotten or unused, and, in many cases, unmonitored.

Analog Phone lines

The modern corporation, even in this age of largely digital voice communications, is still rife with analog phone lines, many of them providing an easy target for the alert Zukin. Analog lines are used for fax machines, multifunction printer-copier-fax-blender devices, and last, but not least, as out-of-band access to service a variety of equipment.

Although the possibility does exist that a standard fax machine could be compromised over its analog line, the equipment in the machine itself is generally fairly low level and rather limiting. This would still allow it to be used for a variety of distractions and/or denial-of-service attacks, but the real gold is in the multifunction device.

Multifunction devices today are no longer the mechanical monstrosity of old; many are complex devices running actual operating systems (even Windows XP!) that are attached to specialized hardware for printing, faxing, etc. When we consider the possibility of a device running an antiquated operating system that has likely seen few, if any, patches, that is attached to both an analog phone line and a network connection, a better target for exploitation would be difficult to find.

> **TIP**
>
> For those interested in pursuing multifunction device hacking, a couple good places to start are on the Phenoelit[11] and Irongeek[12] Web sites. A few tools can be found there to begin experimenting with multifunction devices and printers, ranging from useful security tools to tools to confuse or distract users. Other information on these sorts of hardware-oriented hacks has been presented at various security conferences, such as Black Hat, in 2006[13] and CanSecWest, in 2003,[14] over the years and more can be found with a bit of searching on Google.

Analog lines are also used to provide out-of-band access to a wide variety of other equipment that is not directly involved in communicating with the outside world, including phone switches, network infrastructure devices, and heating and air conditioning systems. These lines are generally used to allow maintenance or support personnel access to devices that are remote, difficult to physically access, or have lost normal network connectivity. Although some of the connections, on more modern devices, are well protected and require strong authentication and/or the activation of a dial-in feature on the device itself, some of them have no security whatsoever and will simply present the caller with a friendly menu when contacted. Being able to control the environmental settings in a building might prove to be an excellent distraction for the other activities of our Zukin.

Legacy Networks from Acquisitions

In certain industries, particularly in those involving technology, there is a constant Brownian motion between companies. Large companies snap up small ones, then turn right around and close down portions of the new acquisition or sell them to other companies. In some cases, one company might be in the process of buying another, and then itself be bought by yet a third. Clearly, this can cause considerable confusion and can result in communications lines, systems, and even people who have been missed or forgotten. In a situation where entire portions of the network are mislaid, it seems likely that the security for that network will be lax at best. In the case where the target of the Zukin is in an industry in a state of constant flux, it would pay to carefully investigate not only the target organization itself, but also any portion of the organization that have recently arrived or departed.

Summary

The ninja of old had somewhat of an advantage by living in an age bereft of advanced forensics techniques. When infiltrating a facility using the techniques of the Zukin, one of our primary concerns is to not leave evidence that might prepare our target for the possibility of a future attack, thus rendering our painfully gathered intelligence much less useful.

When picking locks we need to be careful not to use some of the more common methods, such as lock picks, that may leave unusual scratches on the pins of the lock. This also makes entering safes much more difficult, as more expedient methods such as drilling through the safe door to access the mechanism will be very obvious to the user of the safe. In our favor, many modern facilities control access through the use of proximity cards, these being easy to copy without even necessarily having to touch them. Facilities and equipment protected by some of the more common biometric systems such as fingerprints or voice recognition systems may be able to be bypassed in some cases, but more advanced systems, or systems using some of the more unusual biometric identifiers may prove more difficult.

When viewing a facility from a network perspective, the common avenues of attack may prove to be very well protected and monitored. The Zukin may find a much easier route in by utilizing peripheral networks that are trusted but are functioning at a lower level of security. Such networks may be connected through vendors or partners, internal groups with special networking needs, or legacy networks that still exist from acquisitions or holdovers from older network infrastructure.

The best path in is often not through the front door.

Endnotes

1. Pulford G. High-security mechanical locks: an encyclopedic reference. New York: Butterworth-Heinemann; 2007. 978-0750684378.
2. Gonggrijp R, Wels B. Toool. [Online]. http://toool.nl/images/7/75/Bumping.pdf; 2005 [accessed 13.04.10].
3. Halderman JA. Freedom to tinker. [Online]. http://freedom-to-tinker.com/blog/jhalderm/diebold-shows-how-make-your-own-voting-machine-key; 2007 [accessed 14.04.10].
4. Westhues J. Proximity cards. [Online]. www.cq.cx/prox.pl; 2003 [accessed 13.04.10].
5. Rollette J. How-to: etch a single sided PCB. Hack a day. [Online]. http://hackaday.com/2008/07/28/how-to-etch-a-single-sided-pcb/; 2008 [accessed 14.04.10].
6. Mythbusters: crimes and myth-demeanors 2. Discovery Channel, LLC; 2006.
7. Minh Nguyen Minh Duc, Bui Quang. Your face is not your password: face authentication bypassing Lenovo - Asus - Toshiba. Blackhat. [Online]. www.blackhat.com/presentations/bh-dc-09/Nguyen/BlackHat-DC-09-Nguyen-Face-not-your-password.pdf; 2009 [accessed 14.04.10].
8. Levy J. Ninja the shadow warrior. New York: Metro books; 2007. 978-0-7607-8998-8.
9. Filoart. Filo art "IRASC" – infra red anti-surveillance-camera. [Online]. www.oberwelt.de/projects/2008/Filo%20art.htm; 2008 [accessed 14.04.10].
10. Naimark M. How to zap a camera. Michael Naimark. [Online]. www.naimark.net/projects/zap/howto.html; 2002 [accessed 14.04.10].
11. Phenoelit. Phenoelit. [Online]. www.phenoelit-us.org/; [accessed 12.04.10].
12. Crenshaw A. Irongeek.com. [Online]. www.irongeek.com/; [accessed 12.04.10].
13. O'Connor B. Vulnerabilities in not-so embedded systems. Black Hat USA; 2006.
14. Felix "FX" Lindner. Attacking networked embedded systems. CanSecWest; 2003.

Use of Timing to Enter an Area

The use of timing, Nyukyo no jutsu, when planning an attack is critical. If we take the time to gather information regarding the regular movement of people in and out of a facility, the timing of the rounds made by guards and where they will be located at a particular time, when patches will be applied to systems, when log books or files are likely to be reviewed, then we can take steps to hide our attacks better, or keep them from being noticed at all. Often gaps in timing can be exploited to considerably reduce, if not avoid entirely, the security measures that we will need to find a method of dealing with.

Even when we have perfect timing, an excellent disguise, and a busy location to provide cover for us, intrusion detection systems may still trip us up. It is important to have a good foundation of knowledge about the various systems that might be in place, whether entering a location on foot or over the network, and what we might do about such systems when we find them. Following the path of the Zukin, we need to understand how to attack or avoid such systems while leaving minimal or no evidence that any activity has taken place.

TAILGATING

Commonly, the term tailgating is used to refer to following someone through a physical access control, such as locked door, without authenticating through the access control ourselves. We define tailgating as the act of closely following an event, in either a physical or logical sense, in order to illegitimately take part in it. In this sense, it can also be used to refer to session hijacking, malware infection, and a wide variety of other activities. In essence, it is a type of attack based on timing, whether of a physical or logical variety.

Physical Tailgating

Physical tailgating also known as "piggybacking" is what most people think of when they hear the term used. Quite simply, this is the act of following someone through an access control point, such as secure door, without having the proper credentials, badge, or key, normally needed to enter the door.

Ninja Hacking. DOI: 10.1016/B978-1-59749-588-2.00008-1

Tailgating is a problem endemic to locations that use technical access controls. In almost any location, unless strong steps have been taken to prevent it, we can see people tailgating. This is partly an issue of laziness, and partly an issue of the desire to avoid confrontation. Particularly in locations where the majority of foot traffic is composed of younger people, we will see tailgating policies flouted, i.e., closed school campuses, apartment buildings, and so on ... often willfully so. Such locations make for particularly easy tailgating targets.

A few tricks of equipment, such as knowing which props to use, and the use of psychology to allow us to play on the sympathies of others, will aid us in our tailgating efforts.

Psychology of Tailgating

The Zukin who is a student of psychology and social engineering (see Chapter 10, "Psychological Weaknesses") will find tailgating a much easier task. One major factor that will aid in our efforts is the desire of people to help those who appear to be in need. When a person is walking toward a door with an armful of boxes, papers, paper cups of coffee, and so on, the impulse of most is to hold the door open. The more precarious our grip appears to be on our props and the more flustered that we seem to be, the better this will work.

An even better tactic is to fake an injury. Wheelchairs are very effective at getting people to open the door (as well as being good for concealing equipment), but crutches tend to work even better to tie up the Zukin's hands, thus making it more difficult to open the door. In general, people do not want to challenge the injured, particularly when it could aggravate the condition of the injured to do so.

Physical Traffic Patterns

Traffic patterns are an excellent tool for the Zukin to use when needing to physically either enter or exit a facility. In larger facilities, there are generally times of the day that see a considerably higher amount of foot traffic, specifically shift changes and meal breaks. In many companies, shift changes happen, at a minimum, at the beginning and end of the day.

At facilities that operate around the clock, such as factories or technical support centers, shift change may happen at various other times of the day as well. Meal breaks often occur in the middle of the day and at the end of the day. Again, this may vary slightly in locations that operate extended hours.

NOTE

Depending on the working environment, country, and culture, we will often see other movement in and out of the building at intervals as employees take breaks. A good example of this can be found in people who smoke. We can often find such individuals clustered outside, smoking and socializing, regularly throughout the day. Similar cycles may be seen involving food, beverages, and so on. We can generally pick such activities up easily by monitoring the site for a short period of time.

At these times of day, we can generally see a large rush of people in a short period of time, as workers are trying to get to or away from their work area, often both at the same time, many carrying backpacks, food and beverages, and sundry other items. This rush of activity makes an excellent cover for the Zukin. Traffic patterns are discussed further in Chapter 9, "Discovering Weak Points in Area Defenses."

Exploiting Weak Entrances

As many buildings are not architected with security in mind, most tend to have one or more entrances that are weak from a security perspective. This may be due to a variety of factors ranging from poor camera coverage to oddities of the security staff.

In certain areas lack of monitoring may provide the Zukin with a good opening. This may be a gap in camera coverage, where a location is out of the camera's range or angle of vision, thus allowing us to proceed unnoticed and unrecorded. It might also be an entrance where no guard is posted, or visits infrequently, due to staffing reasons. This can also be an issue in multitenant buildings where overall security is handled by the building management company, instead of the individual occupants.

Environmental conditions can often cause particular entrances to be weaker. In more tropical locations, it is not unusual to find doors or windows propped open in order to promote ventilation. In windy areas, the pull of the wind blowing by the face of a building is often enough to keep exterior doors from latching entirely, but may let them close enough not to register an alarm for being stuck open. In particularly cold or snowy areas, a variety of equipment may malfunction; causing camera or security system issues, doors to become stuck open or closed, or tree limbs to fall and break windows.

Oddities of security personnel can cause gaps in entrance coverage as well. These may be gaps in remote monitoring, or they may be gaps in actual physical presence. Surveying the area beforehand will often produce evidence of such weaknesses. We may find an excellent opportunity during shift changes, even if the relief shift is on time, due to distraction caused by filing of paperwork and idle conversation, remote video monitors may not be watched or posts may not be manned.

SHINOBI-IRI (Stealth and Entering Methods)

In some high-security facilities, the Zukin may encounter physical access controls that are designed to prevent tailgating. These are often in the form of a turnstile, revolving door, or mantrap that will only physically accommodate a single person at a time. More complex electronic systems exist that can detect more than one person entering for a single set of credentials being used to open a door. It is generally a good idea to observe a planned entrance in advance to watch for strict observance of a no tailgating policy. If everyone whom we see is being particularly scrupulous about not tailgating, there is usually a reason.

If a guard is not relieved on time, his or her emotional state may preclude careful monitoring or execution of duties, particularly if this is a regular occurrence. Last but not least, we may find security personnel who are just not performing their duties at all and are either napping or watching a football game. This is one of the best opportunities for the Zukin because the guard was not only *not* paying attention, but he or she may be forced to ignore signs of our activity in order to avoid being punished for his or her lapse.

Disguises

As discussed in Chapter 5, "Disguise," when transiting into or out of the facility, the use of disguises, or Hengen-kashi no jutsu, can aid the Zukin. Disguises intended for a particular location can often be perfected by the observance of foot traffic at the facility for a short period of time; it would not do to attempt to enter a location in a suit when everyone present was clad in jeans and t-shirts. Similarly, attempting to pass ourselves off as a network technician in a uniform would likely be unsuccessful if the technicians in question did not wear uniforms.

Often, one of the most critical items for disguise is something approximating the correct set of credentials for the location. Even if the Zukin has not been able to obtain the proper proximity card or other physical credentials for the area, being able to flash a badge at a security guard from a distance will diffuse many situations. Although this does not always work, and will likely fail horribly in a high-security location, a little preparation will usually go a long way.

Physically Tailgating on Authentication Credentials

When we successfully enter a facility in disguise and are able to move about unmolested, we are presented with an opportunity to tailgate in a manner that blends the physical and logical. In a given office environment, with the possible exception of a high-security area, dozens or hundreds of unoccupied and unlocked computers can be found.

Although a stranger typing away at a cubicle neighbor's keyboard might draw a great deal of attention, a visit from the "IT department" may not. In a very short period of time, a person claiming to be checking a network drop can install any number of surveillance devices, software, or perhaps even a small wireless access point. Although this type of activity might draw attention at a very small company, at a large one it will likely not even register. In this way, we can tailgate on the logical credentials of the user or system, by penetrating the physical security.

Network and System Tailgating

In the same way that we can tailgate on someone who has authenticated against a logical access control, we can tailgate on virtual systems as well. We can apply ourselves to surveillance of network or system traffic patterns, look for authenticated sessions, and watch for regular patching cycles in order to time our attack against systems and networks.

Network and System Traffic Patterns

As discussed previously, the movement of personnel in and out of a building can disguise the activity of the Zukin. We can put this principle to use in disguising our logical movements as well as by monitoring the actual traffic on the network for a period of time. Although gaining the vantage point to watch for traffic patterns on the target network may be more difficult than watching foot traffic, it is no less important.

In locations that prove more difficult to access for network-monitoring purposes, we can also make inferences regarding the traffic, a task that is often more easily completed than actual monitoring of the traffic, and may provide information that approaches the same level of usefulness. If we research and monitor a target and find that operations between the hours of 6 P.M. and 6 A.M. drop down to a very small staff, then we can infer a reduced level of network activities at these times. Similarly, if we see a large number of people all entering a building at 8 A.M., then we can infer a spike in traffic a few minutes later as people reach their work areas, check e-mail, surf the Web, and so on.

When planning activity, synchronization with these busy periods will help to disguise us in the rush of traffic. Where a large amount of traffic on the network in the middle of the night might trigger an alert on a network intrusion detection system, the same traffic, carried out shortly after the influx of workers first thing in the morning, might not.

Credential Hijacking

Credential hijacking is a perfect example of a logical timing attack. It is usable in a variety of circumstances but basically boils down to waiting for an authorized user to gain access to a system or application, then impersonating the user and using their credentials to take over the session. This can be done by actual session hijacking, either by using cookies from a user machine, or by hijacking the users TCP session, or can be a matter of sniffing credentials directly from the network.

A good illustration of this type of activity can be found in the "Wall of Sheep,"[1] a regular appearance at the well-known DefCon security conference. The Wall of Sheep, using a variety of tools to sniff traffic on the wireless network used at the conference, pulls out the credentials being used to log into various social networking sites, e-mail, and a variety of other services. The gleaned information – including usernames, passwords (partial), and domains connected to – is then put into an application and displayed for all the attendees to see. Although this is done at DefCon to provide a learning experience, there are plenty of users sitting at coffee shops ready to provide the Zukin with the opportunity to gather potentially useful information.

Hardware Upgrades

Computer hardware upgrades provide an excellent opportunity for the Zukin to insert additional items of hardware or software, while systems are in flux and users are distracted by the activity, particularly when upgrades are taking place on a large scale. Many large companies enjoy special processing of computer systems, either directly by the manufacturer or by a third party, in order to load customized operating systems, company specific software, and so on. This adds another attack vector where hardware or software loads may be altered.

> **TIP**
>
> In addition to inserting such items into the hardware upgrade process, another tactic is to simply send hardware to the target. This can be done in the guise of a contest, review hardware from a hardware manufacturer, or any of a number of ruses. Particularly, when the target is the typical geek or computer enthusiast, our trojaned hardware, such as a cutting edge video card, is very unlikely to languish for a long period of time before being installed into a computer.

Some items of hardware that carry onboard flash storage, primarily video cards and motherboards, provide an excellent vehicle for delivering malware. Although this capability has been rumored for some time, successful demonstrations of the technique have occurred in the past several years. A demonstration given at CanSecWest in 2009 displayed malware that resided in the flash storage area of a video card.[2] It consisted of a modified flash file that was capable of infecting freshly loaded operating systems from the storage area on the card, and was capable of surviving a reflash of the card.

Operating System Upgrades

Similarly to timing on hardware upgrades, operating system upgrades provide us with an excellent opportunity to penetrate a system or set of systems. Not only do they often change user interface elements, software shipped with the operating system, tools used by the administrator, and a myriad of other items, but also they reset the expectation of the user for how things are supposed to look. When a new operating system is released, users are likely to chalk up differences and misbehaviors to things that have been changed deliberately or things that are not working correctly because of the operating system being new. This is a good opportunity for the Zukin to slip in malware or altered binaries.

We can also exploit operating systems upgrades for devices other than the standard PC. Numerous other devices have operating systems that are complex enough to be used as tools, including the following:

- Network infrastructure devices
- Portable media players
- Phones
- Cameras
- Printers and multifunction devices

Any number of such devices could be installed with a modified operating system and be carried into a target environment. If performed carefully enough, a device with a minimal user interface, such as a media player, might even be carried in unwittingly by a legitimate user.

Patch Cycles

Regular patch cycles for applications are the perfect opportunity for the Zukin to insert a variety of malware or altered software. Knowing that, within a certain period of time, a large set of the users in a facility will all be installing patches from a certain manufacturer provides us with not only an excellent opportunity but also a sure target. Helpfully, for the attacker, such patch cycles have become commonplace, most notably from major vendors such as Microsoft, and more recently Adobe.

If we can insert an altered file into the process, even just to the point of changing configuration settings, we have an excellent opportunity to provide ourselves with an opening for further activities. In Chapter 7, "Infiltration," we discussed how employee VPN connections could be exploited if software were configured to allow split tunneling. A patch to, or upgrade of, VPN software provides an ideal opportunity to change the setting in the default software install to allow the split tunneling option. We have then provided ourselves with an opportunity to attack the VPN through every instance of the client software that has been installed, or will be going forward. Even when subtle activities like this are found, they are more likely to be attributed to a misconfiguration than to any sort of malicious activity.

INTRUSION DETECTION SYSTEM AVOIDANCE

Avoiding intrusion detection systems is a vital skill for the Zukin, and one that requires practice to develop. Intrusion detection systems can be of physical, logical, or administrative varieties, and many detection mechanisms exist for each.

One of the most important considerations when attempting to avoid the intrusion detection system, whatever variety it may be, is to stay below the clipping level for the system. The clipping level is the threshold at which the system will send an alert, which may trigger some sort of response. A classic example of the clipping level is seen with failed logins. When a user types in a password incorrectly a certain number of times, often three, the account that the user is attempting to login to will be locked out. This type of activity can actually be of service to the Zukin.

As with the password example above, the clipping level can easily be determined on many systems by deliberately supplying bad input. We can enter a password that we know to be bad until the error message changes to let us know that the account has been locked out (the notification may not happen on high-security systems). At this point, we have done two things: we have determined the clipping level, and we have locked the account out. Either or both may be desirable, depending on the circumstances.

If we are actually trying to access an account, we know to allow a longer interval between attempts. If we are trying to prevent access to the system by users, we know just how many bad password attempts that we need to enter to do it. Locking the account out can be a simple denial-of-service attack, it can be part of a social engineering attack, because the user will likely be calling the helpdesk to unlock the account, or it can be a psychological attack on the user in order to cause them to become used to the supposed instability of the system.

Physical Intrusion Detection Systems

Physical intrusion detection systems are generally categorized as alarm systems, but, in fact, they include considerably more complex systems than the standard alarm sensor. We may see more common items such as the following:

- Motion detectors
- Cameras
- Alarm sounders
- Alarm sensors

We may also see computer-based systems such as those that can interpret video to determine whether a person entering a door has tailgated, or whether two people are occupying a physical access control point meant for only one person.[3] A number of such systems exist that can provide more complex physical intrusion detection functions by using video- or audio-monitoring systems.

Complex Physical Intrusion Detection Systems

One type of physical intrusion detection that is particularly difficult both to detect and to evade is the acoustic-based system. These systems use distributed networks of microphones to detect intrusions, and they can very precisely determine the source of the sound that triggered the alarm event. These systems can differentiate between sounds occurring inside of a facility that might indicate an actual intrusion, and sounds that originate outside, such as a small rock being thrown against a window in order to trigger a false positive in the system.[4]

Another problem area in physical intrusion detection systems are multisensor implementations. In Chapter 7, "Infiltration," we discussed a few ways that individual sensors might be defeated, but these methods begin to break down when we are confronted with more than one sensor in an area. Although we might stand a reasonable chance of defeating a thermal motion sensor by screening the sensor itself off from viewing the area, the simple addition of a camera or an acoustic sensor would likely nullify our attack. When faced with such systems, the Zukin can resort to social engineering or perhaps denial-of-service attacks against the system in general, instead of attacking an individual area or sensor.

Denial-of-Service Attacks on Physical Intrusion Detection Systems

Denial-of-service attacks against physical intrusion detection systems follow the standard denial-of-service attack pattern and involve overloading the system. This can be particularly easy with physical intrusion detection systems, as the response to the IDS alert is often physical in nature – i.e., sending guards to the location. This can be of great advantage to the Zukin, as triggering an alarm system can easily call attention away from another location, or another alarm sensor alert. At many facilities, triggering multiple sensors in the middle of the night can often sow a great deal of confusion. This type of activity can be particularly effective if done with some regularity – perhaps over the course of a week – as it can cast doubt on the reliability of the alarm system.

Many techniques exist that can aid in subverting the physical intrusion detection system that are covered in other chapters in this book. See Chapter 7, "Infiltration," for a discussion on alarm system evasion, Chapter 10, "Psychological Weaknesses," for social engineering, and Chapter 11, "Distraction," for the use of large events as a distracter.

Logical Intrusion Detection Systems

A logical intrusion detection system is similar in concept to antivirus software. A logical intrusion detection system uses a variety of methods to detect unauthorized use of, or attacks on, a system or network and can issue alerts to intrusion prevention systems, which may take automatic actions based on the attacks that are believed to be occurring.

Intrusion detection systems are often run on the same devices that run other boundary services such as firewalls and proxies but can also be run as stand-alone devices. Intrusion detection systems are generally thought of in two different ways: by the level that they run at, i.e., host, network, or application, and by the method that they use to detect attacks, i.e., signature or anomaly based. An intrusion detection system can run at three different levels, at the application level, at the host level, and at the network level. Controls used in logical intrusion detection systems may consist of components such as the following:

- Audit trails
- Intrusion detection expert systems
- Vulnerability scans
- Checksums

Application-Based IDS

Application-based intrusion detection systems concentrate on events that occur within a particular application and accompanying protocols. These have the advantage of having a comparatively small number of events to examine, and they can examine them at greater level of detail than some of the other IDSs are capable of. They can often identify the particular user or process that is associated with an event and generally have access to data in plaintext, which may be encrypted outside of the application.

Application-based IDSs can often create a fingerprint or baseline of a particular application in order to detect changes that might be made. This can be seen in newer implementations of Microsoft's operating systems whenever software versions are updated. Such systems may be able to be attacked by altering or removing the stored baseline of the application, so that the IDSs do not have an accurate basic of comparison for modifications that might be made.

Network-Based IDS

Network-based intrusion detection systems, often known as NIDS, are easy to secure and can be more difficult for an attacker to detect. Given the large amount of data that network intrusion detection systems have to analyze, they do have a somewhat lower level of specificity. This means that they may miss attacks in progress, often cannot analyze encrypted traffic on the network, and may require more manual involvement from administrators.

NIDS may also be somewhat subject to an overabundance of focus. When a NIDS is closely following an even on a network in an attempt to discern whether or not it is an attack, other events may be granted a lesser level of attention. These factors give the Zukin a few toeholds when attempting to evade a network IDS.

Host-Based IDS

Host-based intrusion detection systems, commonly called HIDS, are used to analyze the activities on a particular machine. They have many of the same advantages as application level intrusion detection systems do, but on a somewhat reduced scale. A problem with host-based intrusion detection systems is that any information that they might gather needs to be communicated outside of the machine, if a central monitoring system is to be used. If the machine is being actively attacked, particularly in the case of a denial-of-service attack, this may not be possible.

A common implementation of a host-based IDS can be found in many of the antimalware products in use today. Many host-based IDSs depend on signature or string matching to detect threats, and they can be defeated by simply changing a tool enough that the signature no longer matches.

Signature- and Anomaly-Based IDS

Another way of looking at intrusion detection systems is by the method used to detect attacks. The two main categories of detection are signature based, similar to most antivirus solutions, or anomaly based.

Signature-based systems compare ongoing activity to a database that contains signatures for known attacks. This method generally works very well, with the exception of attacks that are very new and do not have a signature in the database. The main drawback to this method is its reliance on continuous updates to its signature database. With many attack tools, malware in particular, updating the tool just enough to change the signature is a relatively trivial task. Especially with malware, we can often access the same antimalware tools that are being used by the target and can test against them in order to ensure that any software that we put into the environment is not detected. This is an ongoing task for the attacker, as signatures for such IDSs are updated very regularly, often on a daily basis.

Anomaly-based systems look for behavior that differs from the normal behavior of the users and can theoretically detect previously unknown attacks. This method requires creating a baseline of normal activity on the network, which can lead to difficulties such as false positives. As Zukin, we can take advantage of the sensitivity of such systems in order to deliberately produce false positives. As with many other similar efforts that we might undertake, false positives can be used to undermine confidence in the system and to dull the reactions of those responsible for taking action on such alerts.

Denial-of-Service Attacks against Logical IDS

Denial-of-service attacks against logical IDS are more in line with the classical DoS attack. In this case, we need to provide a sufficient number of events for the IDS to track, so that it can no longer account for all of the events that are taking place. In environments where wireless network access exists, or where they can be injected, this can be a very easy attack to mount, as it can potentially be performed from remote, and can be used to cover up attacks that are taking place in the actual facility.

Administrative IDS

Administrative intrusion detection systems are concerned with detecting unusual occurrences, usually through the use of processes. Administrative intrusion detection systems are intended to catch activity that physical or logical systems are not able to find. A few examples of the controls used in such systems are as follows:

- Security reviews
- Penetration tests
- Audits
- Inspections
- Rotation of duties
- Required vacations
- Manual log reviews

Although the reviews and penetration tests are not unusual, some of the processes that are designed to disrupt usual activity, such as rotation of duties and forced vacations may be a bit more difficult to deal with.

Denial-of-Service Attacks against Administrative IDS

Denial-of-service attacks against administrative intrusion detection systems largely revolve around attempting to make sure that the processes that are designed to catch issues through processes either do not happen or do not see the correct information. As in other forms of denial-of-service attack, this type of attack revolves in overloading the system. In the case of administrative controls, this can be somewhat easier to do because such reviews are normally done by individuals instead of automation.

A successful attack of this type will likely revolve around the disruption or distraction of a particular person or persons. If we can cause distractions in the life of the administrative reviewer, such as reoccurring car troubles, financial issues, marital issues, or any of a number of stressful events, being very precise with administrative reviews and processes will be considerably more difficult for them. If possible, arranging the transfer or firing of the individual concerned may provide an excellent cover for the activities of the Zukin. Some such activities may be out of scope for a standard penetration test, but we may see them used in actual attacks. This is discussed in depth in Chapter 11, "Distraction."

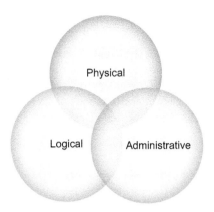

FIGURE 8.1 Out-of-Band Attacks.

Out-of-Band Attacks

Out-of-band attacks are attacks that are not easily detectable within particular category of detective control. For example, if the Zukin has properly cloned a proximity card from a legitimate user, as discussed in Chapter 7, "Infiltration," unless other controls are in place besides the logical measure of the proximity card system, this lapse in security will not be caught. In order to catch our cloned card, a detective measure from the physical control domain, such as a guard, or a requirement for inspection or independent validation of the credentials, from the administrative domain would be needed.

In most cases, when looking at physical, logical, and administrative controls, attacks that come from opposing areas will be the most effective. As shown in Figure 8.1, the overlapping areas between each control present our best opportunity for attack. This is because of the inability of detective controls to handle concepts or actions outside of their particular domain.

Out-of-Band Attacks against Physical Controls

Physical controls are particularly vulnerable to attack, given the propensity of people to trust electronic systems. In the excellent novel *Daemon*, by Daniel Suarez,[5] an inmate is entirely released from prison by manipulation of the records stored in the computer system concerning his status. Although this is a fictionalized account, it is by no means a stretch of the truth regarding trust of technology.

In the physical security world, if a legitimate set of credentials exists, conferring a certain identity on our Zukin and allowing them a set of privileges, a logical control, such as an audit trail in the credential-granting system, or an administrative control, such as an audit-of-said system, would be required to uncover the deception. Even in secure facilities, such an event is very unlikely to randomly occur without an event to trigger a higher than normal state of security.

Out-of-Band Attacks against Logical Controls

A variety of out-of-band attacks can be perpetrated against logical controls. The principal remains the same in that we need to remove ourselves from the normal channels that network and host intrusion detection systems (IDS) monitor.

Network intrusion detection systems are highly focused tools. They are concerned with traffic going over wired and wireless networks through Ethernet and a stack of common protocols. When we can either move to a communications medium that they cannot monitor, or a protocol that they cannot understand, we have largely removed ourselves from their view. If we can route traffic over modem or voice lines, these are generally not monitored. Additionally, for the time being, many networks are ignorant of IPv6 traffic, to the point of such traffic being invisible to many infrastructure devices. In such cases, we have either physically changed the route of communications, or have logically changed to what amounts to a separate communications line.

From the viewpoint of the host intrusion detection system, we must either remove our activities outside of the view of the IDS, or we must disguise them as something else entirely. An excellent tool for blinding a host-based IDS is the rootkit. If we can manage to get it onto the machine under the radar of any monitoring tools, perhaps using trojaned hardware as we discussed earlier, then we can control what the operating system and the IDS are seeing. In this case, we have combined a physical and administrative control attack, by subverting the hardware upgrade process in order to get malware into a machine past the logical controls that are normally in place.

Out-of-Band Attacks against Administrative Controls

Following the out-of-band triangle, effective attacks against administrative controls would largely be physical or logical in nature. In the case of a security review, such as an audit or penetration test, we can take steps to ensure that such reviews do not find any evidence of our trespass, or any reason to launch a more detailed analysis of security measures that we have compromised.

When the Zukin has logically compromised a system, one of the recommended steps is to clean up after the attack, this not only involves cleaning up log files, tools used in the attack, and other evidence, but also it may actually involve further securing the system. This is necessary not only to keep others from following the same path that was used to enter the system in the first place, but also to prevent attention from being called to the system from the security staff that should have been protecting it. If the holes in a system can be safe patched, there is a much smaller chance that the system will be called out for further attention during a security review. In this way, the relationship with the Zukin becomes almost symbiotic in nature. Many of these same concepts apply to attacks on physical security.

In a sense, attacks against administrative controls must be more subtle than attacks against physical or logical controls. Where we can attack a physical or logical control directly, we must concentrate more on escaping the notice of the administrative control, or must work much more diligently to subvert it. A good example of administrative controls that require a much larger degree of effort to attack, on the part of the Zukin, are some of the administrative controls used in the banking industry.

In industries that handle high-value assets, such as the banking industry, rotation of duties and forced vacation are administrative controls that are often used to detect improper behavior on the part of the employee. Tasks change hands on a regular basis and many employees are forced to take a certain block of vacation at regular intervals. This is done so that a new person periodically takes over a task and any nefarious activity such as unusual transfer of assets, theft, or manipulation of automated systems become obvious to the newly assigned person. Although this may seem like an insurmountable obstacle, it simply becomes a problem of a larger scale, to be approached logically (pun intended) and with careful planning.

Honeypots

The idea of the honeypot is a common one, in a logical sense, that is, pertaining to computer systems. The Zukin also needs to be concerned with honeypots that are physical or administrative in nature, as all of our careful planning could come to an abrupt halt if the facility being penetrated or the process being subverted is actually an elaborate trap.

Logical honeypots are systems or software that exist solely to fool attackers into thinking that they are real and contain real data where, in fact, they are nothing of the sort. Simply speaking, logical honeypots are systems, which produce false application and operating system signatures in an effort to lure attackers in. Once the attackers have entered the honeypot, their activities can be examined, methods of attack and tools used can be inspected, and the attackers can potentially be traced back to their source. Many projects such as the Honeynet Project[6] exist to provide software and support for security personnel using honeypots as a tool to examine attackers. Some tools do exist that can detect certain characteristics of honeypots that vary from the actual software, but many of these are ineffective.

> **WARNING**
>
> A broad variety of security designs can include the use of honeypots. Security professionals traditionally think of the honeypot as a logical device, and this is a dangerous limitation for us to allow ourselves. When investigating the security of a network, physical location, or even a process, look with suspicious eyes on a security stance that seems to be woefully low. In many cases, we will actually be looking at a truly pitiful level of security, but in a few, we may actually be looking at a honeypot.

Physical honeypots, following the same general design, are facilities or intentional weaknesses in facilities that exist solely to draw in the attacker. These may be apparently weak entrances, places where cameras are not in place or are blocked, or any number of areas that might look tempting to the Zukin. In short, these are the areas that we would normally choose to make an entrance. Unfortunately, other than observing the area for some period of time and perhaps noticing an unusual traffic pattern, or lack thereof, a physical honeypot may be very difficult to detect.

In all cases, it is a good idea to have a backup exit plan should such a physical entry go awry.

Administrative honeypots, again, follow the same general pattern of flawed processes that might be tempting to an attacker. In this case, the possible tip off to the Zukin would be based on the subtlety of the honeypot in question. Where a process looks too easy to subvert, or a target looks overly ripe for social engineering, it may very well be.

Summary

When entering a location, whether from a physical or logical standpoint, timing is a key component to the attack. Timing can allow us to pass completely unnoticed, walking into a building with a crowd, or sending a cache of covertly collected data out over the network.

Tailgating can allow us to enter a facility or network behind a legitimate user, avoiding the notice of security systems and physical access controls. It can enable us to take of the session of a user logged into an application, or sit down at a machine that a user has left logged on and walked away from. Although there are systems that can detect such activities, the careful Zukin can avoid or disable them.

When intrusion detection systems are present in the environment, we may need to take careful steps to avoid triggering them, or trigger them in a manner that covers other activities. Intrusion detection systems can be physical, logical, or administrative in nature, and each covers up the weaknesses of the others. When attacking or avoiding intrusion detection systems, it is best to approach them from an angle that the system itself is not capable of detecting; out-of-band attacks can allow the Zukin to work around the intrusion detection system by using the areas that are in shadow to it. For physical systems, attacks come from the logical or administrative; for logical systems, attacks come from the physical or administrative; and for administrative, attack come from the physical or logical.

When researching and planning attacks against a target, we need to be careful that we have not happened upon a target that is too easy to attack and is actually a honeypot. Although traditionally logical in nature, honeypots can also be physical or administrative traps. Careful surveillance of the environment can sometimes detect such deceptions.

Endnotes

1. Wall of Sheep. Wall of sheep. [Online]. www.wallofsheep.com/; 2010 [accessed 19.04.10].
2. Fisher D. Threat Post. [Online]. http://threatpost.com/en_us/blogs/researchers-unveil-persistent-bios-attack-methods-031909; 2009 [accessed 19.04.10].
3. FIRS Technology CO., LTD. TailCatch intelligent tailgating detection system. [Online]. www.firscom.net/en/system.asp?name=Tailcatch%E2%84%A2%20Tailgating%20System&scn=PRODUCTS&id=230932&pid=194&smallproid=36; 2010 [accessed 20.04.10].

4. Zieger C, Svaizer P. Acoustic based surveillance system for intrusion detection. Sixth IEEE international conference on advanced video and signal based surveillance. Washington, DC: IEEE Computer Society; 2009. 978-1-4244-4755-8.

5. Suarez D. Daemon. New York, NY: Signet; 2009. 978-0451228734.

6. The Honeynet Project. The Honeynet Project. [Online]. www.honeynet.org/; 2010. [accessed 19.04.10].

Discovering Weak Points in Area Defenses

Discovering the weak points in an area defense is a great skill for the Zukin to develop. When we can find such weaknesses, whether from a physical security stand-point, or from a logical security standpoint, they give us a very good starting point to plan future attacks. It is always wise to thoroughly surveil a target in order to find any weaknesses, watch for traffic patterns (as discussed in Chapter 8, "Use of Timing to Enter an Area"), and become familiar enough with the location to be able to notice oddities in the normal flow of things. It's not always possible to do this thoroughly, but it is definitely useful when we have the luxury of doing so.

We will be discussing traffic patterns, guns, gates and guards, and information diving, each from the physical and logical angles. Given this information, we will be better able to gather information, avoid attack, and attack in turn, all the while work-ing stealthily and not leaving evidence behind of our presence.

Ninjutsu espouses the use of *Sutemi*, or "self-sacrifice," in cases when the ninja's enemies are too numerous to simply evade. Sutemi stipulates that in order to evade, sometimes a direct thrust is needed which is aimed at the weakest among the enemy.[1] Although this seems logical, it means that as Zukin, we need to identify those groups of people who are weakest in their employment of corporate security measures and policies. As we will see in this chapter, the weakest link in any organization's secu-rity plan is people.

TRAFFIC PATTERNS

Knowledge of traffic patterns, in both the physical and the logical sense, can be invaluable to the Zukin. They can assist us in entering or exiting a facility undetected or unnoticed; they can aid us in social engineering attempts; and they can help us conduct activities on networks or systems without being detected in the normal noise of business being carried out. A variety of tools exist that can aid us in locating such patterns.

Ninja Hacking. DOI: 10.1016/B978-1-59749-588-2.00009-3

Physical Traffic

The monitoring of foot traffic in and out of a facility or location is an excellent tool for determining both the number of people at the location and what percentage of them is coming or going at any given time. As we discussed in Chapter 8, "Use of Timing to Enter an Area," people largely tend to enter or leave a facility at relatively predictable intervals, such as shift changes, or meal breaks, and these events can be used to make efforts such as tailgating through a physical access control easier.

Satellite Maps

Satellite maps can be useful for examining traffic patterns at a facility over time. Even when not entirely up-to-date, such maps can indicate areas where employees park, buildings that are and are not frequently used, and a number of other such items. Many such maps are openly provided by Google, Microsoft, and a plethora of others, with a reasonable level of detail and occasional updates.

A variety of commercial satellite imagery offerings also exist, for the well-funded Zukin. These images are often of considerably higher resolution, for example, the offering from GeoEye is capable of a ground resolution of approximately 16 in., with a second satellite launching in 2011 to provide 9.5-in. resolution.[2] With the available resolution and the ability to get up-to-date imagery, offerings such as these can provide a considerably more useful and specific tool for tracking traffic and movement patterns.

Disrupting Physical Traffic Patterns

The disruption of normal physical traffic patterns can be an excellent aid in covering the activities of the Zukin. In outdoor locations, a broken down car that is inconveniently placed at the entry to a parking lot or on a frontage road loading to a facility can cause great disruption. Such blockages can be used to prevent or delay people from either entering or exiting a facility, can be used to distract physical security away from another location, prevent people from being on time to a location, or as cover for any number of activities. Although such activities would rarely be used in the pentesting world, we may see attackers use them.

Such a disruption can be carried out by the Zukin or support staff, giving us the ability for the vehicle trouble to magically evaporate when it becomes convenient for us to restore the normal pattern of movement. Difficulties such as these can also be imposed on others, perhaps a legitimate employee of the target company, with the simple scattering of broken glass or a few nails across the road leading into a parking lot.

Logical Traffic

Understanding the logical traffic patterns of the target can be of great use when planning attacks. As discussed in Chapter 8, "Use of Timing to Enter an Area," timing attacks or transfer of data during peak periods of network traffic can be used to disguise the activity of the Zukin. Tools such as wireless security surveys and network sniffing can be used to determine what patterns of traffic may exist on a network.

Wireless Security Surveys

Wireless security surveys, often known as war driving (walking, kayaking, hovercrafting, biking, and so on), can be a very useful part of collecting network information on a target and can, sometimes, present a gilded path directly into a network. Such surveys, with a small bit of planning, can generally be done inconspicuously at all but the most secure of facilities. Eavesdropping on, or entering through, a wireless network can provide us an excellent window through which we can view the traffic going over the network.

Depending on how the network is structured and how the wireless portion of the network has been segmented from the wired portion, we may not be able to easily see beyond the wireless traffic. Even of this is the case, being able to observe the wireless traffic can be useful.

The equipment needed for a wireless security survey is very minimal and, in some cases can even be pocket sized. The basic equipments needed are as follows:

- Wireless survey software
- A computer, PDA, or phone
- A wireless network card

There are a wide variety of software solutions available on the market today, ranging from free and open source software, to expensive commercial packages that require proprietary hardware devices to run properly. Two of the more popular, and free, software packages are Kismet[A] and NetStumbler.[B]

Kismet is a wireless security survey package primarily intended for use on Linux- or Unix-based operating systems, although less fully featured version does exist for Windows. Kismet's functionality provides for network detection, packet sniffing, and intrusion detection for 802.11 wireless networks. Kismet is generally considered to be a more robust and feature-rich tool than NetStumbler (see below), although it does require a bit more technical know-how to use.

Netstumbler is a tool in a similar vein as Kismet and provides many of the same features. NetStumbler runs on Windows and Windows CE operating systems, with the reported exception of Windows Vista and Windows 7. NetStumbler does lack some of the features of Kismet, such as the ability to use multiple wireless cards simultaneously and intrusion detection.

Both Kismet and NetStumbler are capable of being integrated with, or exporting data to, other software. This capability allows for the overlay of collected data on satellite maps, the construction of signal strength maps, and a variety of other useful tools. GISKismet, located at www.giskismet.org, is one such tool that allows integration of wireless location data with Google Maps.

The hardware needed to run such tools can vary greatly and does not need to be overly complex. Most modern laptops that are equipped with internal wireless network cards will suffice when equipped with an appropriate operating system. PDAs

---

[A]www.kismetwireless.net/.

[B]www.netstumbler.com/.

and phones can be equipped similarly, in many cases, providing a clandestine wireless survey tool that can easily be concealed in a pocket.

Wireless network cards used for this purpose can vary widely. Interfaces for such cards are generally PCI PCI-Express, Mini PCI, PCMCIA, or USB, depending on the equipment that the card will be connected to. Most laptops with internal cards use a Mini PCI interface. When choosing a card, the particular revision of 802.11 that will be targeted is important, as we need to match the card hardware with the revision.

Although they can be more difficult to get working with both operating systems and software, cards that can cover multiple revisions in one piece of hardware can be useful. Such cards commonly cover 802.11a, b, and g or 802.11a, b, g, and n. Careful research before purchase is required for these cards, as some are not suitable for this purpose, due to the chipset, lack of drivers, lack of external antenna connectors, or any number of other reasons.

TIP

External antennas can be of great use to the Zukin in conducting a wireless security survey. Although most people realize that the signal from a wireless device can be picked up from quite a distance away, many do not realize quite how far away that it can be received. Even a fairly minimal external antenna can allow a signal to be picked up several miles away. Under ideal conditions and with the proper receiving equipment, an 802.11 signal at normal broadcast strength can be picked up hundreds of miles away.

When using an external, we will need a wireless network card with an accessible external antenna connector, a feature that some manufacturers provide only on certain models of card. External antennas can not only enable extended range, as mentioned above, but also can be used to add directional specificity in order to allow the origin of signals to be more easily pinpointed, or to prevent interference from other devices.

Network Sniffing

Network sniffing, whether attached to a wireless or wired network, is the primary tool of discovering logical traffic patterns. Sniffing is covered in more detail in Chapter 16, "Sabotage," but for traffic pattern determination purposes, we are primarily concerned with a high level view of the traffic, rather than the contents of individual packets. Many excellent tools exist for network sniffing, but one of the more common tools used is Wireshark.[c] Specifically, the protocol hierarchy statistics dialog, as shown in Figure 9.1 will provide us with an excellent overview of the traffic going over the network, presuming the sniffer is positioned properly.

Of main interest to the Zukin are the protocols in use and the amount of traffic that these represent. In many organizations, Web, e-mail, and instant messenger traffic will constitute the bulk of the traffic produced by users.

---

[c]www.wireshark.org/.

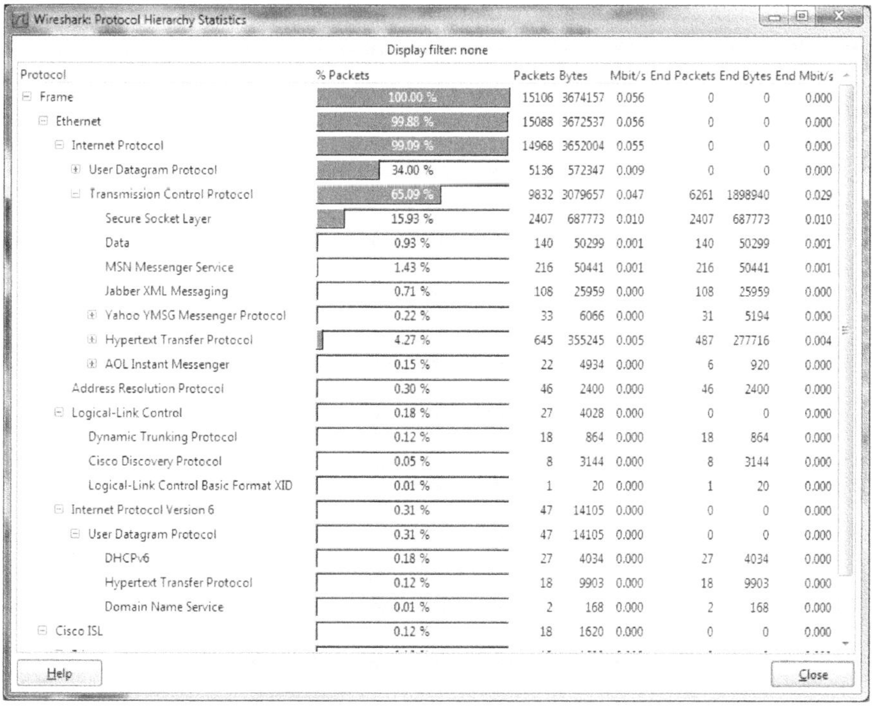
Wireshark: Protocol Hierarchy Statistics

Display filter: none

Protocol	% Packets	Packets	Bytes	Mbit/s	End Packets	End Bytes	End Mbit/s
Frame	100.00 %	15106	3674157	0.056	0	0	0.000
Ethernet	99.88 %	15088	3672537	0.056	0	0	0.000
Internet Protocol	99.09 %	14968	3652004	0.055	0	0	0.000
User Datagram Protocol	34.00 %	5136	572347	0.009	0	0	0.000
Transmission Control Protocol	65.09 %	9832	3079657	0.047	6261	1898940	0.029
Secure Socket Layer	15.93 %	2407	687773	0.010	2407	687773	0.010
Data	0.93 %	140	50299	0.001	140	50299	0.001
MSN Messenger Service	1.43 %	216	50441	0.001	216	50441	0.001
Jabber XML Messaging	0.71 %	108	25959	0.000	108	25959	0.000
Yahoo YMSG Messenger Protocol	0.22 %	33	6066	0.000	31	5194	0.000
Hypertext Transfer Protocol	4.27 %	645	355245	0.005	487	277716	0.004
AOL Instant Messenger	0.15 %	22	4934	0.000	6	920	0.000
Address Resolution Protocol	0.30 %	46	2400	0.000	46	2400	0.000
Logical-Link Control	0.18 %	27	4028	0.000	0	0	0.000
Dynamic Trunking Protocol	0.12 %	18	864	0.000	18	864	0.000
Cisco Discovery Protocol	0.05 %	8	3144	0.000	8	3144	0.000
Logical-Link Control Basic Format XID	0.01 %	1	20	0.000	1	20	0.000
Internet Protocol Version 6	0.31 %	47	14105	0.000	0	0	0.000
User Datagram Protocol	0.31 %	47	14105	0.000	0	0	0.000
DHCPv6	0.18 %	27	4034	0.000	27	4034	0.000
Hypertext Transfer Protocol	0.12 %	18	9903	0.000	18	9903	0.000
Domain Name Service	0.01 %	2	168	0.000	2	168	0.000
Cisco ISL	0.12 %	18	1620	0.000	0	0	0.000

Help Close

FIGURE 9.1 Wireshark Protocol Hierarchy Statistics View.

> **NOTE**
>
> For those of you who are unfamiliar with Wireshark, it is really a great tool for the Zukin. You can find free introductory Wireshark classes online, given by Laura Chappell, at chapellseminars.com. Of course, Laura would also love it if you stuck around for some of the paid classes as well.

Such traffic will usually peak, simultaneously, with the physical headcount of people at the location. When we are able to see what such traffic patterns exist for a given location, we can begin to plan how to hide attacks or movement of data, in order to best disguise them.

Disrupting Logical Traffic Patterns

Logical traffic patterns, as with physical ones can be disrupted in a variety of ways to a variety of effects. We can use something as simple as a denial-of-service attack against a server to temporarily halt conducting business over e-mail or VoIP phones at a location. Such attacks are an excellent tool for the Zukin because of the ease of use and the near impossibility of tracing the attack back to the actual initiator.

We can also be considerably more subtle in our logical traffic disruption and attack the protocols or remote administration interfaces that are used by network infrastructure, such as routers and switches. Such attacks, when carried out with a certain amount of subtlety, are likely to be attributed to a hiccup on the device, or to an error in configuration.

Additionally, we can place devices on or near the network of the facility that will disrupt traffic, but may not look like an attack. Misconfigurations on compromised machines will serve nicely for this purpose, and they can be used to flood the network with a variety of havoc-causing packets. Wireless networks are particularly vulnerable to this type of attack as they are broadcasting for the world to hear.

The Zukin can frustrate the network staff to their very limit by bringing a portable jamming device onto a site and jamming the frequencies used by the wireless networks that are present. If such a device is used sporadically and moved from one location to another at random intervals, it will be virtually impossible to operate a wireless network until the device is shut down. Such jamming can be done either with more complex radio equipment or with field expedient tools such as other wireless devices or cordless phones.

GATES, GUNS, AND GUARDS

This section discusses gates, guns, and guards, in both a physical and a logical sense. For example, when looking at gates, we may be discussing actual physical gates, or we may be talking about logical access controls. It is very important for the Zukin to be able to see everything from both perspectives, as many of the items with which we are concerned may have aspects in both areas. Access through a physical gate may be controlled, ultimately, by a logical system, and it may be much simpler to subvert the logical system than it would be to attack the physical gates. As technology marches on, it becomes far easier, in many cases, to defeat such a mechanism by taking the unexpected approach when attacking it.

Gates

In the classic sense, gates are an object of physical security. However, in the world of the Zukin, we must consider both gates as physical access controls, and as logical access controls. We must understand both what they are and how to defeat or avoid them. Such controls generally present a hardened surface to the expected direction of attack, but may be much softer from other angles.

Physical Gates

Physical access controls, whether they be gates, locked doors, mantraps, turnstiles, or any of a number of other mechanisms, can potentially cause a great deal of trouble for the Zukin. When such systems are properly maintained and the set of policies accompanying them that govern their use is followed, they can be very difficult to defeat.

In many cases, a physical access control is merely a front end for a logical system. If the logical system can be breached, this may be a far more effective way of attacking the physical control. As was discussed in Chapter 8, "Use of Timing to Enter an Area," the most effective attacks are often out-of-band attacks against a particular type of control. In this case, if we can obtain a legitimate, or at least functional, credential for the physical access control in question, then it will likely cease to be an issue.

In the case of very secure systems, it is often best to find another route around or through the control, rather than attempting to attack it directly. If we can find another route in which is less secure, or find another means of obtaining the information that is our target, then this is often the better path to take.

As discussed in Chapter 8, "Use of Timing to Enter an Area," timing can be a major factor in successfully passing through a physical access control. If we can enter by using the credentials of someone who is legitimately allowed entry, then a large part of the task of penetrating a facility may be solved.

Logical Gates

In much the same way that the ninja faced the task of entering fortified physical structures, the Zukin often faces the task of entering fortified logical structures. When looking for gates into such logical structures, we often find a variety of devices, collectively referred to as bastion devices, which may be Web servers, mail servers, proxy servers, VPN gateways, or even honeypots.

Bastion devices, whatever their main function may be, have been specifically constructed to withstand attack from the outside, as they are generally directly exposed to the Internet, or in a DMZ (or demilitarized zone, which refers to an organization's systems accessible to the Internet). Such devices are stripped of every application and service that they do not directly require, and generally do not have any extraneous ports open to traffic. Because of their position directly on the Internet, bastion devices are often very carefully maintained and patched, lest an attacker slip in.

Attacking such devices is often best done through the indirect methods of the Zukin. As with any heavily fortified structure, a frontal attack on the directly exposed interface is often not the best route. Many such devices serve a single application; for instance, a mail server will allow what appears to be legitimate traffic for the application. In this case, an attack using a malformed PDF document may slip through where a direct attack may simply be ignored.

Our PDF file, although malicious in nature, is a common enough file in the business world, and blocking all such files is a difficult proposition. Although scanning for attacks such as these in files is certainly possible, we are still more likely to succeed with such an attack. Although our attack may not always be successful, with the use of recent exploit code, it will likely succeed more often than not because of our difference in goals from the standard attacker.

Much of the malware that exists on the Internet is working toward the aim of only a few goals; recently one of the main goals is recruiting machines into botnets. Such malware attacks are anything but subtle and need only to have a very small success rate due to their mass distribution. Our goal is to be quiet and unnoticed. Sending out one or two very carefully crafted items of malware stands a much greater chance of slipping through the protective mechanisms such as a bastion device.

Guns

Guns are an item that does not typically come to mind when we think of the ninja. Guns are loud, and leave a variety of evidence behind, including their targets. To take the Zukin approach to guns, we need to remove some of the less desirable features of the gun, while keeping some of the more useful aspects.

Such direct physical attacks were used historically by the ninja, in some cases, and would likely be used in the case of a true cyber conflict. Even with such considerations, weapons are a tool that we would clearly not use in a penetration testing environment.

Physical Guns

On the receiving end of the firearms issue, the Zukin should do their absolute best to avoid confrontations with armed security personnel. In a situation where such security is present and it is not possible to avoid contact with them, it is often better to retreat and make plans for a future attack using a different method. Although most security personnel will typically not initiate violence, a bullet-riddled Zukin will not only leave an undesirable amount of evidence behind, but will generally ruin the entire operation from a stealth perspective.

Although the use of a gun is likely to be outside of the scope of activities for the Zukin, we should be aware of the types of devices that we could conceivably want to use, or may face the business end of. In many locations, the use of nonlethal devices, such as bean bag guns, rubber bullets, tasers, and so on has become more popular. The weapon portion of many projectile devices is generally a shotgun or rifle with a special adapter, so these are not a terribly concealable or stealthy device. Tasers, however, can be very portable.

WARNING

It is *entirely* possible to kill someone with a nonlethal weapon. In the case of a bean bag or rubber bullet, hitting someone in the chest with such a round may provide a sufficient impact to stop their heart. Strikes to the head or face will likely break bones, crush eyes, or worse. Strikes at close range will often still penetrate unprotected skin. Tasers have been implicated in multiple deaths. These are not toys and should not be used by those who lack sufficient training in their use.

Such devices can be used to temporarily disable physical security personnel while leaving a minimal amount of physical evidence behind. Bean bag rounds and rubber bullets generally expend most of their energy on the target and can usually be found close by, for purposes of evidence recovery.

On unprotected or lightly covered skin, the impact of the projectile will, at the very least, leave a very nasty bruise. Taser rounds are usually at the end of a long wire and can be collected easily. These leave far less evidence on the target, although they may leave small burns or puncture marks. In the event that we need to use such tools, all possible physical evidence of their use should be removed afterwards.

SHINOBI-IRI (Stealth and Entering Methods)

We should be aware of the potential consequences of using less-than-lethal devices. If we render a person, particularly a person responsible for physical security at a location, unable to report in at a designated interval, we may alert the entire staff to our presence. Second, depending on the tool used and the individual in question, a less-than-lethal device, such as a taser, may not keep them down for any significant period of time.

Logical Guns?

From a logical perspective, we could call various forms of malware a gun, but this might be a bit of a stretch. If we were to continue with this idea, the most seemingly fitting concept would seem to be the denial-of-service attack. As common as the botnet is today, we do have a logical device that we can aim at a particular target and pull to trigger, through our command and control channel, to launch an attack. This analogy falls down somewhat as the result is likely not a single impact from a single source, but a sustained impact from multiple sources. In any case, the concept is there, if we care to shoehorn it into the idea of a gun.

Such offensive devices are not often used by organizations outside of those that would be considered military in nature. In the last few years, a number of governments, including China and, more recently, the United States, have been working on developing a more offensive capability in this area. It is very unlikely that the Zukin, in the course of our activities, would find a commercial or government target that is willing to use such offensive capability. We should, however, keep in mind that this is likely to change as we move into the future and cyber warfare becomes more common, as it seem inevitable that it will.

Guards

Guards are the bane of the Zukin. Where many other systems can be easily manipulated and will tend to stay that way, the guard, whether physical or logical, is in place to provide a protective mechanism with some measure of judgment. Although this is obviously more the case with human or animal guards, the concept still persists in logical systems.

Physical Guards

Human guards can be both dangerous from the standpoint of having independent judgment, and convenient due most being inherently flawed in some fashion. Where an alarm sensor might be fooled by manipulation of its environment or special equipment, such tools would be very obviously out of place to even the slowest and most inept of guards. However, guards are vulnerable to psychological manipulation and social engineering attacks, where a machine would completely ignore both. We will talk more about social engineering in Chapter 10, "Psychological Weaknesses."

Facilities that utilize guard dogs can be a very tricky prospect for the Zukin. Although human guards have a variety of flaws that can be exploited, and can be lazy or easily distracted, such problems are rarely present in dogs. Dogs have a much keener sense of smell and hearing, and stand a much greater chance of detecting a clandestine attack than a human guard.

On the Mythbusters episode, "Dog Myths"[3] attempts were made to confuse scent-tracking dogs and to sneak past guard dogs. Both sets of attempts failed miserably. Although it may be possible to wound or kill a dog in order to bypass the area that it guarded, this would be a most un-Zukin-like activity. Not only would evidence be left behind, but it would be a questionable plan in the first place, as guard dogs are often accompanied by a human counterpart. The best solution to dealing with a guard dog is to entirely avoid it.

Logical Guards

The logical equivalent of a guard would most likely be one or more of the various intrusion detection systems crafted for systems and networks. Such systems can watch for unusual activity on networks, on systems, and within specific applications or protocols used by such systems. Although logical guards can certainly be called more vigilant and focused than human guards, such systems can be easily fooled when approached from an unusual angle, or when they are presented with credentials that are legitimate as far as the system is concerned. Where a human guard might pick up on subtle cues to give them the sense that something was "just not right" when confronting someone, logical guards do not have this type of flexibility.

When attempting to avoid logical intrusion detection systems, the important points to remember are to stay below the clipping level for the IDS, and to try to attack from an angle from which the IDS is not prepared to detect attacks.

See Chapter 8, "Use of Timing to Enter an Area," for a more in-depth discussion on avoiding and subverting intrusion detection systems.

INFORMATION DIVING

Information diving is the practice of gleaning information from either physical materials that have been discarded or disposed of, from logical sources that have been left available by our target, such as job descriptions, or from information-based attacks, such as phishing.

Physical Information Diving

Physical information diving can be a somewhat risky and potentially messy effort, but it can provide great rewards to the Zukin. Many companies are careless with how things are disposed of, both in the sense of actual trash and in the sense of surplus or obsolete hardware. We can use such discards to our advantage in many cases, by going through them in order to sieve out any remaining information. Such activities can result in slim threads, such as a name or telephone number, or can produce a recoverable hard disk containing an entire human resources database.

Dumpster Diving

We can discover a great deal of information by going through the trash of our target. We may find banner pages from printers that can give us user or machine names, memos indicating names, e-mail addresses, or other personal information, equipment manuals, or any number of other information-rich resources.

Although restrictions on disposal of data containing personal information have tightened in recent years due to HIPAA, FERPA, and other such data protection acts, people still have a tendency to be lazy and careless. Even though the disposal of such data may not be of immediate use as an aid in penetrating our target, it can serve the Zukin well as a distractor. If we were to find a printout of customer data and expose such information to a news agency, this might focus the attention of our target away from our activities, as well as being psychologically injurious to those concerned with maintaining the data.

Dumpster diving has become more difficult in recent years, as the awareness of uncontrolled access of trash bins to the public has become more commonly recognized as a threat. Although this does tend to make access to such materials more difficult for the Zukin, it can actually aid us in our activities.

Because many organizations recognize the need to securely dispose of certain materials, such as printed paper that needs to be shredded, such items are often placed in special shred bins for later pickup. Given a reasonable amount of access to a facility, we can simply empty the contents of the bin. Such bins are generally enclosed and locked, so the disappearance of the contents of the bin would only be visible to someone else opening it. Once our conveniently segregated sensitive materials have been removed, we can then refill the bin with scrap paper in order to avoid arousing suspicion on the part of the service normally responsible for emptying it.

Depending on the geographical location, dumpster diving either may or may not be a legal activity. In some countries, trash is considered to be in the public domain, and we can freely remove it with no need for secrecy. In other countries, such activities may result in fees or imprisonment. In either case, it pays to be careful and research such issues before proceeding, as digging through trash in some locations may be a sensitive issue, even when clad in a situationally appropriate disguise, such as that of the homeless or vagrant. In countries where the legality of dumpster diving is an issue, we should be careful to obtain permission first when using this as a penetration testing tool.

For further reading on dumpster diving, see the Syngress book *No Tech Hacking: A Guide to Social Engineering, Dumpster Diving, and Shoulder Surfing* by Johnny Long (ISBN: 978-1-59749-215-7).

Surplus Hardware

Surplus hardware is a virtual goldmine for the Zukin. Although many organizations are now sensitive enough to information security requirements to make some attempt to scrub outgoing hardware of data, the efforts are often incomplete or ineffective.

Many companies that are not security conscious dispose of surplus hardware in a very insecure manner, leaving it in piles or containers outdoors to be picked up and disposed of by contract agencies. Even equipment that does not contain data that is inherently critical may still have records of login names and passwords that are recoverable.

Even in situations where storage devices in equipment have been cleaned, they may not be beyond hope of recovery. Although formatting storage media, such as a hard disk or backup tape may be enough to render stored data immediately unreadable, such data can generally be recovered with a certain amount of effort. Technologies exist today, such as spin stand imaging that make data extremely difficult to erase beyond recovery; however, these are generally not necessary unless unusually thorough means have been used to erase a disk.

We can also consider the storage of data by devices that are not normally considered to be computers, such as printers and copiers. Many such devices of recent manufacture actually do contain a mass storage device, such as a hard drive, and use this storage space to retain copies of printer or scanned images. When these devices are disposed of, or the Zukin engineers the need for one to be replaced or repaired, the storage device can be collected and the documents recovered. On some devices, the hard drive is externally accessible, and can be removed quickly with the aid of a screwdriver. In such a case, the drive could be quickly removed and copied during off hours, then reinserted in the machine with none the wiser.

Logical Information Diving

Information diving, in a logical sense, differs slightly from the physical effort. While we might have a clear sense of what is and is not refuse in the physical world, and may work to dispose of it properly, this is not always true for the logical world. For information that has, at any point, been exposed to the public, particularly on the Internet, there is no real sense of being able to resecure it or throw it away. This can work to the advantage of the Zukin, as we work to discover information on our targets, and, perhaps, encourage them to volunteer information to us.

Phishing

Phishing attacks are well known, at this point, to most of the computer literate world. One of the standard phishing attacks arrives in the form of an e-mail purporting to be from a bank at which the target is a customer. The e-mail might say that the target needs to log into their account immediately, because suspicious account activity has been noticed, and verify that no spurious charged have been made. The e-mail will generally include a link to the login page for the bank, which will actually direct the target to another Web site. Once at the false Web site, the target will enter his or her credentials, which will then be recorded by the attacker. The target may or may not be redirected to the real Web site at this point.

This attack is well known enough now to cause suspicion in many of the recipients of such a communication. These can usually be sussed out due to the poor construction of the e-mail and the false Web site, many of which are full of spelling and grammatical errors and do not make a real effort to fool the user. For the Zukin, this type of attack does still provide us with a good tool; we only need to execute it more carefully.

A well-constructed phishing attack should come from an e-mail address that is a cleanly spoofed internal address, if not actually sent from a genuine mail server on the target network. The utmost care should be taken in crafting the e-mail, in order for it to look as much like a genuine e-mail as possible, including proper spelling, grammar, and use of logos, as well as replicating, as closely as possible, any anti-phishing countermeasures that are present in legitimate e-mail from the source.

Links embedded in the e-mail should either point to a redirected or compromised internal server, or we can attempt to use an internationalized domain name (IDN) homographic attack.[4] This attack utilizes international alphabets, now allowed in domain name registration, to create domain names that look similar to English characters, but are actually partially composed of characters from another alphabet, such as Unicode or Cyrillic. Using an attack of this sort, we could construct something along the lines of domain.com, where the "o" and the "e" were actually Cyrillic characters, thus providing us with a legitimate and distinct domain name that would appear exactly as the name to most users.

Although some security professionals are aware of this type of attack and tools do exist that will detect it, many are still entirely ignorant of its existence. As such domain names become a more popular tool for the crude phishers that flood such e-mails out by the thousands, we can be sure to see detection mechanisms for these attacks become more prevalent. If possible, it would pay to avoid sending such a well-crafted phishing attack to our target before verifying that these tools are not part of the common software load for users. If this type of attack was detected, our target would be alerted to the presence of skilled attackers and would likely be more alert.

Google Hacking

Search engines can provide a virtually limitless cache of information for the informed researcher. Google, given the proper search terms can be used to find information on target systems, hardware, usernames, and passwords, social security numbers, and a plethora of other information. Detailed results from penetration tests can be found online, as can control interfaces for network cameras. Such methods are of great benefit to the Zukin, as they can be done from remote and with very little risk of detection. Syngress publishes an excellent book on this subject, *Google Hacking for Penetration Testers, Volume 2*, by Johnny Long (ISBN: 978-1-59749-176-1), which we highly recommend.

Metagoofil[D] is a great tool for aiding in searches for externally available documents. It allows a domain to be searched for common document types, such as PDFs or Microsoft Office documents, through the use of a script and Google's search engine. Once the search has been completed, a report is produced which shows the information that has been extracted from the documents, including names, usernames,

---

[D]www.edge-security.com/metagoofil.php.

paths, and Mac addresses. In many cases, large corporations do not have a good grasp of what exactly they have published on the Internet, and are sharing more than they might care to be. Such information can be used to locate targets to attack, or can aid in social engineering efforts.

In addition to utilizing search engines, it can pay to directly examine Web sites that are hosted by, or are providing a service to, our target. Often bits of seemingly innocuous information that are spread over user forums, job-posting sites, and the myriad of other Web-hosted applications and documents that are found in the mass of data produced by a large company, can be assembled to produce interesting results. Although such searches can prove to be taxing, tool exists to pull data from these sources as well.

Another tool in a similar vein to Metagoofil, Maltego,[E] allows information to be gathered from a wide variety of sources, and will attempt to determine links between pieces of information. Maltego can be used to collect information on people, organizations, domain names, affiliations, documents, and more, thus allowing us to look at a much bigger picture from an information standpoint. Although somewhat more complicated to use than Metagoofil, Maltego provides a large superset of features and can be very useful in researching a target.

Summary

In this chapter, we looked at a variety of methods to discover weak points in area defenses. We discussed traffic patterns, both from a physical and a logical standpoint, tools that we might use to find such patterns where they exist, and how we can go about disrupting traffic patterns in order to cover our other activities and stop or delay other events from happening.

We looked at guns, gates, and guards, again from both logical and physical angles. Gates, which may be referring to physical devices or to special hardened servers, can often be subverted by taking on the appearance of legitimate traffic and are often not best attacked head on. Whenever we can, we should attempt to utilize a functional set of credentials to pass these types of controls.

Guns, from a physical sense, are best avoided by the Zukin, on the receiving end, but we may also want to consider the use of nonlethal devices against our targets. From a logical perspective, we could also refer to the use of distributed denial-of-service attacks as a gun-type attack. Although we are unlikely to be on the receiving end of such an attack from a commercial or government institution, these can certainly make an effective tool for us.

Physical and logical guards can be problematic for the Zukin. Human guards, with their capacity to make judgment calls can be problematic, but they are susceptible to a variety of human foibles and can often be worked around with social engineering attacks. Dogs, however, with their heightened senses and extreme vigilance, can be

---

[E]www.paterva.com/web4/index.php/maltego.

very problematic and should best be avoided. On the logical side of the guard discussion, we have intrusion detection systems. Such systems can be very dependable, within their parameters of operation, and we should do our best to attack outside of those parameters. Although such systems are smart, they are by no means infallible.

Finally, we discussed information diving. Again, we can look at this from a physical and a logical standpoint. Physically, we can look at dumpster diving, and we can attempt to gain access to surplus or discarded equipment. Often, even though the issue is well known, organizations are careless with what they dispose of in an informational sense. In the trash, we can look for name, account names, telephone numbers, and a laundry list of other information. Such findings can be used to plan attacks, distract, or discredit a company.

From a logical sense, we looked at phishing attacks and at Google hacking. Phishing can be used to obtain information directly from the source and can be a very successful attack, if carried out diligently. Most phishing attacks today fail because of their crudity, and they would actually succeed otherwise. We discussed some of the tactics that can be used to craft a successful phishing attack.

We also covered Google hacking to gain information on our targets. This can be done by searching Google or other search engines directly, and can be done through the use of search tools such as Metagoofil or Maltego. We can also search a variety of external sources such as job boards or forums, to locate information that pertains to our target. Once such information has been gathered, and we can use it to either carry out social engineering attacks or plan other attacks, based on the knowledge of people, systems, accounts, and so on that we have gathered, using the concept of *Sutemi*. Taken as a whole, all the techniques we described will allow us to target the weakest link in an organization's physical and technical security model, and slip in and out of the target because of mistakes or oversights made by the people within the compromised organization.

Endnotes

1. Hatsumi M. The way of the ninja: secret techniques. New York: Kodansha International; 2004.
2. GeoEye. GeoEye | high resolution imagery, earth imagery & geospatial services. [Online] www.geoeye.com/CorpSite; 2010 [accessed 23.04.2010].
3. Mythbusters. Dog Myths. Discover Channel, LLC; 2007.
4. Gabrilovich E, Gontmakher A. The homographic attack. Communications of the ACM; 2002.

Psychological Weaknesses 10

Baiting and social engineering, both psychology-based attacks, can be some of the best tools in the arsenal of the Zukin. While systems can be patched, better intrusion detection systems can be brought online, and higher grade locks can be installed, there is no fix for human gullibility.

Even when processes and training exist, in an attempt to shore up the human weakness, most people still want to be helpful and still want to avoid confrontation. Given basic knowledge of how to conduct social engineering attacks, we can bypass some of the most sophisticated security on the market, simply by being invited in.

BAITING

According to legend, a (probably fictional) hero in the Ninjutsu history named Sasuke Sarutobi was training with a master swordsman, who offered Sasuke the following advice: "Don't you have your eyes in your back? How handicapped you are! You'll be a failure unless you know how to defend your weak point, even if you know the unguarded point of your opponent. The secret of defense in martial arts is to always be alert. Unless one knows his own weak point, he can never be certain that the weak point of his opponent is not a decoy."[1]

Baiting is the practice of offering a desirable item to the target, either directly or by simply leaving it for them to find, as a delivery mechanism for a generally malicious payload. Such a tool can be seen in the classic story of the Trojan horse used during the siege of Troy:

Wearied of the war,

and by ill-fortune crushed, year after year,

the kings of Greece, by Pallas' skill divine,

build a huge horse, a thing of mountain size,

with timbered ribs of fir. They falsely say

it has been vowed to Heaven for safe return,

and spread this lie abroad. Then they conceal

choice bands of warriors in the deep, dark side,

and fill the caverns of that monstrous womb

with arms and soldiery.[2]

In broad strokes, the Greeks constructed a giant wooden horse, filled it with soldiers, and then appeared to leave. After they were gone, the Trojans, taking the horse as a trophy of their victory, brought it inside the city walls. When night fell, the soldiers left the horse and opened the gates to allow the Greek army, who had returned under cover of darkness, in to destroy the city. The tactic of the Greeks has since been applied to modern times through the vehicle of technology.

The Modern Trojan Horse

The Trojan horse is alive and well today and is used regularly to spread malware and various other maliciously oriented tools. The basic technique is still the same; using an interesting item of hardware or software to lure in the target, then delivering the payload quietly in the background. Trojans do have application in penetration testing, but we need to be sure that we are able to maintain control of their activities.

Trojans in Software

The process of using a Trojan horse in software is simple; create a simple application, perhaps a flash game and release it via the Web or e-mail. While your victims are busy flinging elves about, run a process in the background that scans for credit card numbers on the machine, sends out spam e-mail, downloads other malware, or most anything else that we would care to do.

Trojans can also be attached to more complex applications, even commercial ones such as Microsoft Office. In this case, instead of creating software specifically as a vehicle for our Trojan, we simply integrate it into the install routine of the host software. Many install applications conveniently have the capability to install software dependencies already, so, if present, we can add our package to the list and have it install silently in the background.

If the ability to integrate our Trojan with the installer is not present or overly difficult, we can write a wrapper for the host installer. In this case, we replace the actual executable file for the software install with our own, which will install our Trojan for us silently, then call the actual software installer from ours.

The library of methods for inserting Trojans is vast and has been developing for several decades now. The Zukin has a great deal of information and expertise in developing malware to fall back on, merely by browsing the Internet. Software development tools and libraries have been tuned over the years, and creating malware is now a considerably easier task than it once was. Researchers have also been working for some time on the other side of the malware issue. Both sources of information will prove invaluable to the Zukin planning such a software-based attack.

Trojans in Hardware

Trojans resident in hardware are often just a slight variant of a software implementation, running on or stored on a hardware device. This can be as simple as a USB flash drive or as complex as a completely custom operating system running on a phone or media device. The benefit in running such tools on hardware is in the additional lure for the target to actually use the device.

USB Trojan devices are very simple indeed. We create our Trojan software, with no particular need for even a game or program to disguise it and place it on the USB device.

This can either be the ubiquitous flash drive, as shown in Figure 10.1, or a larger USB hard disk, either will work just fine. We then create an autorun file, which will be processed by the host machine when the device is plugged in, thus running our Trojan software automatically.

The U.S. military had such large issues with exactly this sort of attack that, in 2008, the Department of Defense banned removable media and storage devices from use in government computers.[3] At the time, this was done to prevent the spread of worms that used removable media to transport themselves, but, as of the time of this writing, the ban has been relaxed only slightly and such media is only allowed under very controlled conditions.

FIGURE 10.1 A Trojaned USB Device.

> **TIP**
>
> It should be clear that USB Trojans will generally only work on a Windows-based machine. Even on the proper system, it is possible that the autorun functionality may be turned off for removable drives. While this could conceivably be made to work on an OS X or Linux/ UNIX system, the attempt is very likely to fail. Researching your target first will help determine the viability of this type of attack in a given environment.

Trojans can also be placed on more complex computing devices such as phones or portable media players. Such devices generally present a relatively limited view of the user interface to the user, so hiding a Trojan in the background would not be a difficult task, given sufficient programming skill. Many such devices have comparatively vast amounts of storage that could be utilized for the storage of the actual Trojan code, as well as information that might be cleaned from a host computer. The vast majority of these device also have USB connections to allow them to transfer data between the mobile device and a computer, thus providing us with another mechanism to infect, either from the mobile device to the computer or vice versa.

> **SHINOBI-IRI (Stealth and Entering Methods)**
>
> USB devices are not the only tools that we can use to carry out such attacks. We can utilize most anything with storage space that connects to a computer for similar attacks, including phones, digital picture frames, MP3 players, and other similar hardware. We will discuss this further in Chapter 16, "Sabotage."

When using such devices, we also need to take care that they have not been reversed on us and are not being used to provide us false information. In a security conscious and highly technical target, it is entirely possible that our activities could be noticed and turned against us. As with all software tools used by the Zukin, we need to carefully test and validate the behavior of any tools that we send out into a noncontrolled computing environment. Trojaned USB devices make excellent tools for penetration tests. By using them, we can test security in a variety of areas in one strike, including social engineering, antimalware tools, network security, and others, depending on the way that they are used.

The Con

The con, otherwise known as a confidence trick or a scam, often used by the attacker, called a con man, to separate the victim, called the mark, from money or property. Cons have likely existed for the majority of known history and have been well recorded for hundreds of years. While the goal of the Zukin should not be to gain money for personal reasons, such tactics can be used to strip a target of their resources or provide an opportunity for them to be publically ridiculed or discredited for their gullibility.

The mark, the victim of the con, is often chosen because of their greedy nature, making them a much easier target for such tactics. The infirm or elderly are also common targets, as they tend to have impaired judgment. The goal of the con man is to leave the mark completely unaware that anything is out of the ordinary, until they have been able to make their exit with the target of their labors, generally money.

Con men often use assistants in their efforts, commonly referred to as shills. The shill, while actually working with the con man, pretends to be an interested third party, such as a customer or investor. The shill is used to goad the mark into taking action when they might be hesitant to do so, by pretending to be very interested in, or compete for, whatever the con man is offering.

WARNING

The con should be used with great caution. Not only can a con require a great deal of social engineering skill, but it has the potential to backfire in a way that is disproportionate to its gain. When a con has been discovered, our Zukin may be in physical danger or may be arrested, and information on our operation may be compromised. We should take care to plan cons out thoroughly and make sure that all of the players are familiar with and skilled at their tasks. Such tactics may be appropriate in a penetration testing environment, but we would need to be careful to obtain permission before using them.

There is a virtually limitless variety of cons available for use to the Zukin. Though many cons focus specifically on separating the mark from their valuables, many cons are easily adapted to fit our tactics. In many cases, they can be invaluable for distracting, discrediting, embarrassing, or blackmailing our target.

The Spanish Prisoner

The Spanish Prisoner con, a story of great antiquity, repeated in both the film[A] and the short story,[B] of the same name, has a premise that should be familiar to most anyone that is even slightly Internet savvy. In this con, the con man tells the mark that his compatriot has been imprisoned in Spain, and that he is raising money to get him released. The con man tells the mark that he will allow him to contribute money to the cause, in exchange for which he will be richly rewarded. Once the con man gets the money from the mark, he learns that a problem has come up and more money will be required. This continues until the mark is out of funds or refuses to contribute further, at which point the con man disappears.

This same general formula is used in the present day Nigerian 419 scams, generally revolving around money needing to be moved out of a country. In this case, a large share of it is offered to the mark if they will provide funds to pay for the

---

[A]**Mamet, David**. *The Spanish Prisoner.* Sony Pictures, 1997.

[B]**Train, Arthur**. The Spanish Prisoner. *The Cosmopolitan Magazine.* 1910, March.

transfer fees. Such scams are referred to as Nigerian 419 scams, as a very large percentage of them originate from that country.

The Spanish Prisoner and its variants can be useful to the Zukin when we are looking to separate our target from their resources or to discredit them if we are looking to have them removed from a particular position. Such cons can be very effective at moving large amounts of money or valuables.

The Melon Drop

The Melon Drop is a much smaller scale and simpler scam than the Spanish Prisoner. In this case, the con man, carrying a package containing an already broken item, glass works well, will bump into the mark and fall down, ostensibly breaking the contents of the package. At this point, the con man will berate the mark, often loudly so as to draw a crowd. The con man will demand that the mark replace the contents, often setting a price far above the actual value. Though the story may be apocryphal, this scam is supposedly called the Melon Drop, due to its success using cheap watermelons and targeting Japanese tourists, the price of watermelons in Japan being rather high. While the Melon Drop has very limited potential for financial gain, it is an excellent tactic to use for a delay or diversion. The Zukin can very loudly rant at the target about their broken item for some time and the gathered crowd can cover a variety of activities. Cons such as the Melon Drop can also be of great aid in social engineering scenarios, as they can cause the target to become flustered and distracted, thus more easily taken in.

Scam Baiting

On the flipside of baiting, we have scam baiting, also known as counter scamming. The potential exists here for the Zukin to arrive on either side of a baiting situation, either as the one being bated or the one doing the baiting. Scam baiting refers to the situation where the baiting target realizes what is going on and decides to turn the tables on the attacker. This happens frequently with crudely constructed scams, like the Nigerian scam, discussed later in this chapter.

The goal of scam baiters is generally to inconvenience and humiliate, often publically, the scammer, all the while wasting their time and resources whenever possible. Successful scam baiters have even managed to reverse entire scams and collect large sums of money from scammers (oddly enough, often from the Nigerians).

NOTE

For those of you interested in the world of scam baiting, quite a bit of information can be found on the Internet, including documentation of such tactics being used against scammers. One of the more famous sites on the subject is 419eater.com, equipped with scam baiting tips, videos, and a forum.

For purposes of the Zukin, we need to be aware, of running a scam or con, that the other party may very well discover the true situation. We need to be vigilant in ensuring that we are not being led into a counter scam.

Stings

While scam baiting is generally done at the hands of the amateur or vigilante, law enforcement agencies have been known to use this tactic as well, commonly referred to as a sting operation or just sting. In the case of a sting, such tactics are used to catch people who are in the midst of violating the laws for which the agency has jurisdiction. The legality of this practice varies, but it is permitted in some countries.

Such activities, when successful, often appear in the media. The television show *To Catch a Predator*[C] is a reality show based on the baiting and subsequent arrest of pedophiles attempting to rendezvous with the actors that pose as underage girls. The pedophiles are then shown being questioned and arrested on national television. Similar publicity has been enjoyed by the participants in many similar incidents.

As we have said many times now, it is very important to research a target or a resource very carefully before approaching. Sting operations such as these would, of course, be very bad news for the Zukin that had the misfortune to be caught up in them and would destroy the covert nature of the operation, at the very least. If we stick to safer and simpler cons, such as the Melon Drop, we can greatly limit the consequences of being detected. In this case, if there is an issue, we can simply walk away, as nothing inherently illegal has been done.

SOCIAL ENGINEERING

While we have discussed some of the more simple psychological attacks, such as baiting and the con, these are a somewhat limited implementation of the overall framework of social engineering. Good social engineering requires the study and understanding of the factors that drive people, most of them very emotional in nature.

Similarly to our discussion in Chapter 8, "Use of Timing to Enter an Area," on avoiding detective controls, the ninja believed that social engineering attacks could be best carried out by approaching them from the opposite angle for which the target was prepared. They expressed this through the use of the five elements: earth, air, fire, water, and void, with each element having another in opposition.[4]

The ninja made a detailed study of what we now call social engineering and divided the overall area into three main pieces; the five elements, the five weaknesses, and the five needs. The five weaknesses – laziness, anger, fear, sympathy, and vanity – allow us to play on the areas to which people are the most likely to respond well. The five needs – security, sex, wealth, pride, and pleasure – are the tools with which we can manipulate those needs.[4]

The Five Elements

The ninja categorized psychological and emotional activities into five main groupings, which they classified as the elements earth, air, fire, water, and void. Each element

---

[C]*To Catch a Predator.* Dateline NBC, 2010.

reflected a particular emotional tendency or emotional state. The understanding of the element being exhibited by a person would give us a good indication for how we would need to approach them or how to best attack them. The five elements were considered to be indicative of the levels of consciousness, with earth being the lowest and void being the highest.

The earth element, known as chi, indicates a stable emotional environment. A person exhibiting signs of the earth element will be stable and difficult to upset, but will also be resistant to change.[4]

The water element, known as sui, indicates a shifting emotional environment. A person showing signs of the water element will show fluctuating feelings and will react emotionally to environmental changes.[4]

The element of fire, known as ka, indicates a strong emotional environment. A fire element person may display aggressiveness, feelings of power, and will feel in control of their environment.[4]

The wind element, known as fu, is the manifestation of intellect and love. The wind element will display wisdom and benevolence and will be very conscious of human interaction.[4]

The last element, void or ku, was considered to be the source of creativity. Those exhibiting void can direct their energies to display the properties of any of the other elements.[4]

For each level of consciousness, there is a corresponding weakness, as shown in Table 10.1. When we are attacking a target through social engineering, we may see those that tend toward the properties of one particular element, this exhibiting a particular weakness to accompany it. We may also see those, as described in the void element, the change from one element to another, thus changing weaknesses as well. In any case, the five elements give us a good framework on which to hang our social engineering efforts. It allows us to classify our target by emotional type or emotional state and gives us a starting place when planning a social engineering attack.

The Five Weaknesses

Laziness, which corresponds to the earth element, is one of the weaknesses that is the most useful to the Zukin. Laziness can cause even the most complex of

Table 10.1 The Relationship Between the Elements and the Five Weaknesses	
Earth	Laziness
Water	Anger
Fire	Fear
Wind	Sympathy
Void	Vanity

security systems to fail, if the security personnel who should be paying attention to the alerts from the system are not paying attention.

Laziness can be particularly useful in situations where the Zukin has adopted a disguise as a worker or employee in a facility. While we should always do our absolute best to make our disguises and the accompanying credentials as authentic as possible, often even a passing imitation will do. With the exception of those employed in very high-security facilities, most security guards will wave our Zukin through after they have flashed their counterfeit credentials from a distance.

Laziness can also work to our advantage when the Zukin must infiltrate or exfiltrate physical or logical items from a facility. Even in locations where physical search is standard, such searches often stop at the level of briefly opening bags, or perhaps running items to be searched through an x-ray machine. Seldom would such a search find small and carefully hidden items. Likewise for logical information. Most intrusion detection systems are operating on the standard settings that the intrusion detection system shipped or installed with. If we take the marginal extra trouble to locate these settings and be sure to stay outside of them, our likelihood of being detected is very low.

Anger, associated with the water element, is another excellent tool for the Zukin. Those who are angry tend to act rashly, without taking the time to think things through, and also tend to not be very thorough. If we can make our targets angry, we may be able to get by with activities that would seem out of place, if the target were calm enough to notice them.

Anger is a very easy state to provoke in most targets. We can flatten the tire on their car to make them late, falsify a call from the school that their children attend to tell them that the child has been misbehaving, send false e-mails from or to managers, or any number of such activities. Additionally, once provoked, many people are more easily angered again in the near future.

Angering physical security personnel can provide an excellent distraction when we need to physically infiltrate a facility. With a little advance preparation, we can lure security guards into chasing "teenagers" who have been vandalizing a facility recently. Anger will lead the guard to pursue our supposed miscreants much farther and for a longer period of time that they normally would have. Such activities can give us ample time to carry out our activities unnoticed. Angering a target can be useful as it tends to shortcut rational thought and make them more susceptible to other attacks and social engineering activities.

Fear, an emotion linked to the fire element, causes many people to lose connection with rational thought. When a person is truly afraid, they do not see things as they really are and may react very inappropriately to a situation.

The Zukin can use fear as a very strong lever in social engineering activities. If we can put ourselves into the role of a person who intimidates and has power over the target, we will have a much easier time influencing them to act in the desired manner. An example of such a ploy might be to phone the security staff in the middle of the night posing as an angry supervisor. We might then command the security personnel to stay away from a certain part of the building, reminding them of a memo that they were not actually sent. Such manipulations tend to work best with very new personnel who are not yet sure of the position and how things are normally done.

Fear can also be used as an interrogation tool. A good example of such a tactic is the practice of waterboarding, recently publicized through use by the U.S. military when operating in the Middle East. Waterboarding has been used since the time of the Spanish Inquisition (unexpectedly) and is used to simulate drowning without actually physically harming the target. The target is strapped to an inclined board, head down, and is immobilized. The targets head is generally covered with cloth, and water is poured over the cloth, causing the target to choke and experience a feeling purported to be very similar to drowning.[5] Such an interrogation technique is almost entirely fear based. While we are very unlikely to waterboard someone in the course of a penetration test, such methods have been used historically and are still used today in larger conflicts and by criminals. We will discuss such methods further in Chapter 14, "Intelligence."

Sympathy is connected to the element of wind. Sympathy can be particularly powerful in social engineering activities. As discussed in Chapter 8, "Use of Timing to Enter an Area," when we looked at tailgating, we can often get someone to hold a door open for us by pretending to be distressed in some fashion. Whether this is through carrying a heavy load and not having a hand free to get the door or through presenting the appearance of being injured by using crutches or a wheelchair.

Sympathy can also be used in an attempt to gain access to locations or systems for which we do not have credentials and cannot tailgate. We can play on the sympathy of security personnel or cleaning staff to allow us into an office space, for example, by claiming to have lost our keys or badge and needing to get materials for an important presentation first thing in the morning. These may all seem like very transparent ploys, but, as a general rule, people's desire to help their fellow man will often outweigh common sense.

Sympathy can also be used in reverse circumstances, as a tool to influence people. A good example of this sort of social engineering appears in *The Adventures of Tom Sawyer*.[D] Tom is given the task of whitewashing a fence and is able to convince the other children that the job is actually a privilege. In exchange for a variety of treasures, Tom allows the children to whitewash the fence for him. In the end, he does very little of the work on the fence and has quite a hoard to show for it. The moral of the story being that making something hard to get makes it desirable. We can use similar tactics in social engineering attempts by pretending to have sympathy on other to allow them to do something that we would really like them to do.

Vanity is a weakness associated with the element of void. Vanity can be a very powerful too indeed, as it can completely blind the target to the activity of the Zukin. Using vanity, we can approach the target from a deliberately lower social or economic position, in order to foster their felling of being superior to us. In many cases, the target will have such a low opinion of us that they cannot even conceive of the idea that we might be doing things with ulterior motives or might be deliberately sabotaging them.

[D]**Twain, Mark**. *The Adventures of Tom Sawyer*. s.l.: Oxford University Press, 2007. 978-0192719997.

Vanity can also be useful in placing Zukin in social situations which will allow them access to people or information. We can play on the vain in order to allow them to think nothing of being approached by an attractive member of the opposite sex or being propositioned by this person. Such tactics can be very useful in inserting kunoichi into a social situation, and we will discuss them in more depth later in this chapter.

The Five Needs

The five needs can be used as an aid to manipulation and social engineering of our targets. Each of the five needs can be used negatively or positively in our activities, that is, we can use them as either the carrot or the stick. The five needs, as previously stated, are security, sex, wealth, pride, and pleasure.

The need for security can be a very strong one indeed. This can be security in a financial sense, in an emotional sense, the security of loved ones, or any number of things. In the sense of being able to offer security, the Zukin can offer security in the form of money, physical security, or any number of things. Although such offerings may be easy enough to provide to our targets, we should be cautious when doing so, in order to not provide lasting evidence of such transactions having taken place.

Sex can be a powerful measure to use, but we should be very cautious when attempting to use it for social engineering. There are a variety of different orientations and tastes that we may encounter and we may anger or sorely offend our target if we miscalculate in our efforts. Such an operation should be very carefully researched beforehand to ensure that we are working from correct information. See the section on kunoichi later in this chapter for more coverage on the use of sex as a tool for the Zukin.

Money can be a strong influencer, and can be, in many cases, easy to use. Money can be used for outright bribes paid to our target or can be used for more subtle machinations. Money can be a somewhat dangerous tactic to use, as the movements of large amounts of it are often tracked by governments. Although this can be a bad thing from the standpoint of attempting to actually move funds, it can be a good thing when we need to deliberately trigger such controls to call attention to a target.

Even when dealing with someone who is well supplied in the other categories of need, pride can still be a good tool with which to reach them. We can use pride in a positive way, to offer redemption to our targets, for example, to restore the damage to a reputation or we can use it in a negative way, to destroy the same reputation. Many of the classic examples of blackmail have to do with damage to pride.

Pleasure is a somewhat amorphous concept to use in social engineering. Pleasure can come from physical contact, money, power, influence, food, or any number of things. When attempting to use pleasure, we must know our targets well, in order to use the correct item to satisfy their weakness. This, like sex, is an area where the kunoichi and their ability to integrate closely to the target on a social level can be extremely useful.

Social Engineering and the Kunoichi

The kunoichi of old, as discussed briefly in Chapter 3, "Strategies and Tactics," was the female version of the ninja. Although the ninja was adept at stealth and covert operations, their role was still considered to be rather physical in nature. The kunoichi, while still undergoing rigorous training, specialized more in tactics that were psychological in nature, what we would now call manipulation or social engineering. When the kunoichi did need to take direct action, they were more likely to use more covert techniques such as the use of drugs or small concealable weapons.[6]

Kunoichi were also used to infiltrate an organization using their feminine wiles, often as a courtesan or member of the household staff. Once in place the kunoichi could lure the, presumably male, target into a bedroom or out of the way place, then drug or kill them, or collect evidence for later blackmail attempts.

The Modern Kunoichi

Although many of the situations used by the kunoichi no longer exist in modern society, the general tactics used by them still remain just as effective as they originally were. Particularly, when dealing with targets that work in the technical or science industries, the stereotypical geek or nerd, the kunoichi can be frighteningly effective. While this may seem harsh to some, it is the reality of the situation. The use of blackmail, drugs, secrets gained from pillow talk, and access to high-profile targets make the kunoichi truly formidable weapon.

Kunoichi, posing as escorts, prostitutes, or simply as available women have very easy access to high-profile targets. Very often in the media, we can see senators, mayors, various government officials, and a parade of others consorting with persons of questionable reputations that are not their spouses. While these people often do, at some later date, take advantage of such situations, the kunoichi has the tools and wherewithal to do considerably more with such a generous supply of opportunity.

The kunoichi has great opportunity to gain information from targets with which she has been intimate. Conversation taking place after sex, often known as "pillow talk" can be very fruitful, as our target has other things on their mind and will often attempt to impress her. Cases of public officials later being embarrassed by such conversations are liberally sprinkled throughout history, including a scandal from 2009 involving the prime minister of Italy.[7]

When the kunoichi is faced with a particularly recalcitrant target, she may need to resort to the use of alcohol or drugs in order to persuade them down the desired path. The use of such substances should be carried about carefully, lest the target or later investigators realize that something out of the ordinary has taken place. If the use of such substances is restricted to alcohol or recreational drugs that are generally available to the public, inquiries will likely trend in the direction of the moral failings of the target, not the use of them as a manipulator by another party.

When given access to high-level targets and having been able to entice them into compromising positions, whether through substance abuse, sex, or a combination of factors, the kunoichi is in an excellent position to blackmail the target. Such blackmail might consist of coercion of the target into a particular activity, extortion of money or information, or it might be used to influence actions or decisions. Given the moral flexibility of many of our high-ranking officials, this can provide an excellent opportunity for the kunoichi to access information or materials that might not otherwise be possible.

Using the Kunoichi

Preferred targets for the kunoichi, as mentioned briefly previously, include those with a certain moral flexibility, as often found in various government roles and those with a certain lack of social skills with women. When we are selecting targets for the kunoichi to approach in a social situation, such factors must be considered.

When we approach a target, the most success will likely be found at either extreme of the social spectrum; either the very outgoing and philandering type or the very introverted loner. For each of these types, we need to take a slightly different approach.

In the case of our philanderer, we have an easy task when attempting to insert the kunoichi into the parade of suitors going by. Nothing should seem unusual to anyone accustomed to seeing the person with a constantly changing variety of companions. This is often the easiest type of target with which to integrate the kunoichi, as they are used to being approached by such persons and will likely find nothing odd about it.

In the case of the introverted loner, our typical geek, we need to take a somewhat more careful approach. This type of person is often not used to the kind of attention that our kunoichi will lavish upon them and may not be comfortable when in close proximity to an attractive person of the opposite sex. We need to approach them much more slowly and will likely need to take on somewhat of an introverted role ourselves. In such cases, research into the hobbies and likes of the target may considerably ease the process. We also need to be careful that those who know or work in proximity of the target do not become suspicious of this newfound relationship with our kunoichi, as this may seem to be considerably out of character for the target.

We must be very careful when approaching those who do not rest on either extreme of the social scale. People in the middle of the spectrum are more likely to be well adjusted and already in relationships, thus more capable of resisting the advances of the kunoichi. For particularly perceptive targets, we need to be very careful that we do not tip our hand by being overly forceful or insistent. As in many other types of operation, it pays to do advanced research and reconnaissance on our target so that we can avoid such issues.

When we are planning to put them in place, we need to consider that the kunoichi may be in place for longer periods of time than an operation that might be typical for the Zukin. Although certain situations might call for a brief dalliance, simple reputational blackmail or information gathering, for instance, some might call for a relationship more on the scale of months or years. This should be considered when planning an operation, as the selection of personnel may need to depend on specific factors, such as availability and personal attachments. We must also consider that, if left in place for very long periods of time, the kunoichi may begin to be sympathetic toward the target or may develop feelings for them. This has the potential of turning our source into a double agent who may deliberately provide us with bad information or may betray us to the target. The handler of the kunoichi should watch very carefully for such signs and should exfiltrate them as soon as possible if they suspect anything of the sort.

To address an item that is bound to come up in certain social situations, while the kunoichi is, by definition, female, we may have need to place a man into this role. It is a very likely situation that we will face the need to socially approach or otherwise socially engineer a female target and we should be prepared to do so. In addition, we should be able to accommodate the sexual preferences of either gender.

Since our selection of targets will vary at roughly half between male and female and the inclination of each gender may be heterosexual or homosexual, we need to be equally flexible in providing kunoichi to fit each role. Although this idea may seem distasteful to some, it is a reality of the social engineering methodology, and we need to, in some fashion, be able to address such needs when planning an operation. Whether this means one of our regular personnel playing this role, or that a "specialist" needs to be brought in, we must plan for this eventuality. If we have not done our research properly in advance, we may blunder greatly by approaching our target with a kunoichi of the wrong gender or the wrong sexual preference. Depending on the target, we may lose our only opportunity through such a misstep.

Summary

In this chapter, we discussed the use of psychological weaknesses to manipulate our targets. We discussed baiting, through the use of the Trojan horse concept, implemented in either software or hardware. This allows us to use something desirable to the target, such as a game, application, USB drive, and so on, in order to bait them into willingly accepting the package containing our payload. Such tactics are generally very successful, due to human curiosity and desire.

We also discussed the con, in which we use the greed, dishonesty, or gullibility of our target in order to separate them from their resources, embarrass them, or blackmail them. We also discussed a few of the common types of cons and how they might be adapted to the use of the Zukin. Also covered was the need to carefully evaluate situations in which we might be running a run, in case we are actually the target of a counter con, either by a scam baiter or through a law enforcement sting. In these cases, we are best sticking with more simple cons that do not inherently violate the law.

When discussing social engineering as a science, we referred to the framework used by the ninja; the five elements: earth, air, fire, water, and void; the five weaknesses: laziness, anger, fear, sympathy, and vanity; and the five needs: security, sex, wealth, pride, and pleasure. Knowledge of these three main concepts will greatly aid the Zukin in social engineering attempts.

Lastly, we talked about the use of the kunoichi in social engineering. The kunoichi was the female ninja and specialized more in the softer tactics. This concept translates well into the modern day and can be a very useful tool for the Zukin. We can use the kunoichi to gain information on our targets, blackmail them, discredit them, and a host of other similar tasks. The kunoichi works so well because they are able to integrate with the target on a social level, often forming personal relationships to gain access to them.

Endnotes

1. Hatsumi M. Essence of ninjutsu: the nine traditions. New York: McGraw Hill; 1988.
2. Virgil. Aeneid. [Williams TC, Trans.]. Houghton Mifflin Co.; 1920.
3. Shachtman N. Under worm assault, military bans disks, USB drives. Wired. [Online] www .wired.com/dangerroom/2008/11/army-bans-usb-d; 2008 [accessed 27.04.2010].
4. Hayes S. The ninja and their secret fighting art. Tuttle Publishing; 1990. 978-0804816564.
5. The New York Times. Waterboarding. The New York Times. May 15, 2009.
6. Levy J. Ninja the shadow warrior. Metro Books; 2007. 978-0-7607-8998-8.
7. Hooper J. 'We didn't sleep a wink': escort releases recording of her night with Berlusconi. Guardian.co.uk. [Online] www.guardian.co.uk/world/2009/jul/20/italian-prime-minister-escort-girls; 2009 [accessed 28.04.2010].

Distraction

The use of distraction to carry out an attack can be critical. Often security systems, security personnel, and bystanders will notice something unusual when we carry out an attack, either physical or logical, if we do not give them something else more interesting to look at or some problem to occupy their minds. Among the many types of distraction that we can provide for such occasions, we can use big events to distract them, such as holidays or sporting events, we can sow false information regarding people or company events and we can use distractors or specific attack timing to ensure that they are looking elsewhere.

In ancient Japan, the ninja were considered to be possessed with magical and otherworldly gifts that would allow them to change into the shapes of animals, physically disappear, fly, and cast magic; the ninja were happy to take advantage of people's misconceptions and use their notoriety to cause fear in their enemies.[1] The use of fear and deception became such an integral part of Ninpō that a formal method of studying incantation was developed, called *hachimon tonko jujutsu* (eight methods of incantation), in which the ninja learned how to distract their enemies.[1] Although we will not be discussing how to use magic in this chapter, our attacks and distractions need to be just as effective and viewed with awe and belief, regardless of reality.

USE OF BIG EVENTS

The use of large or popular events to cover an attack can be a very effective tool for the Zukin. If we can catch everyone while they are distracted, get in and go about our business, then leave before they notice, then we may very well have executed a text-book ninja operation. We can use such events as holidays, sporting events, company activities, and environmental conditions as a cover for our activities. Such tactics can be used as distractions when conduction penetration tests, but we must be careful in their use and ensure that we have appropriate permission beforehand.

Holidays

Holidays can provide excellent cover for the activities of the Zukin. If we can pick a major holiday, such as those few that are recognized by the government and are a religious holiday to boot, we will likely not find a more distracted population. Many people will be busy with their various observances, and the majority of companies and organizations will be running on a skeleton staff at most. These are ideal conditions under which we can conduct our operations.

Religious Holidays

Religious holidays, depending on the country and population, will likely find a large portion of the population occupied. In some countries where a theocracy holds control, it may be all or nearly all of the population. While these occasions provide us an excellent distraction, we must be sure to research the local customs so that we can properly coordinate and justify any public appearances that we might need to make. We may be noticeable if our activity does not match the expectations of the local population for the occasion.

Depending on the location and religious orientation of the event, we may find some sort of violent event already happening spontaneously. We can often see such happenings in countries where differences in religion exist between the residents of the country and neighboring countries, or even between residents of the country.

An example of such differences between the Christian and Shi'ite Muslim populations of Iraq occurred in December 2009. Not only did we see small-scale fighting between Christians and Muslims but we saw two car bombs detonated, killing at least seven people, and four other people killed in various violent acts. These events appeared to be largely based around the minority Christian population celebrating the Christmas holiday. Great care should be taken by the Zukin when operating in such religiously charged environments.

Government Holidays

While government holidays are not necessarily a good disguise or distraction, in and of themselves, they are a great tool to empty out a building. On government holidays, many organizations are closed entirely, not even leaving a skeleton staff behind. On such holidays, we may be able to work entirely unmolested, as long as we are careful to watch for the occasional workaholic who may drop by the office or for a routine security patrol. Generally, such days are expected to be quiet, although they tend to not occur with great frequency on the calendar.

Sporting Events

Large-scale sporting events make for a particularly good distraction. In many countries, events such as football or soccer games draw enormous crowds and even have the attention of those not able to attend. We may find staff absent to attend such events and security personnel who could not go distracted by watching or listening in remotely. Such occasions are a good opportunity for the Zukin to strike, either physically or logically.

Country-Specific Sports

In certain countries, there are large sporting events which make for particularly good distractors. In the United States, one such event is the Super Bowl,[A] the annual championship for American professional football. The Super Bowl is traditionally played on a Sunday, not a work day for many large businesses. The Zukin may find that the skeleton staff manning a location on Super Bowl Sunday will be even leaner than usual and may be distracted with the game. Typically, the Super Bowl is viewed from homes or sports bars in groups.

Another such large event is the World Cup,[B] a similar championship for the sport referred to as football in most of Europe, and in some places as soccer. The World Cup is taken very seriously, particularly in European countries, with many travelling to see the event in person. Similarly to the Super Bowl, we can expect to see diminished or distracted staff for the duration of the event.

Event-Based Violence

For some of the more popular sports, we can often see a strong reaction from the spectators physically attending the game, often from those supporting the losing side. In some cases, we can see full-scale riots and destruction of property. In February 2010, at a soccer game in Brazil, 17 people were injured and one killed at just such an occurrence.[2] Such events, when naturally occurring, are often, but not always, short lived and restricted to small groups of people. For those trained in social engineering, such as our Zukin, the possibility exists for such violence to be incited.

WARNING

Inciting a riot is not a tool to take lightly, nor one that we can necessarily keep any measure of control over. Once the Zukin has started such an event, it is likely to get out of hand and we will see destruction, injuries, and perhaps even fatalities, for which we did not plan. At any riot of large scale, we will also see law enforcement appear in large groups, bearing crowd suppression weapons and equipment. We may very well end up being the victims of our own attack if such tactics are not used carefully. These tactics are NOT RECOMMENDED for use in anything but the most dire of emergencies and would never be used in a penetration testing scenario. We may find such tactics used in a larger scale conflict or by criminal organizations.

As a tool of distraction, event-based violence can be a particularly strong one. Sporting events are occurring on a regular basis and are well spread out geographically. As many sports fans are already in a heightened emotional state and full of adrenaline after a game, it should be a simple matter for the Zukin to goad them into a fully fledged riot.

[A]**NFL Enterprises LLC**. National Football League: Super Bowl XLIV. *NFL.com.* [Online] 2010. [Cited: May 6, 2010.] www.nfl.com/superbowl.

[B]**Fédération Internationale de Football Association**. The Official Web site of the FIFA World Cup. [Online] 2010. [Cited: May 6, 2010.] www.fifa.com/worldcup/index.html.

> **SHINOBI-IRI (Stealth and Entering Methods)**
>
> Timing based around events makes a very good tactic for penetration testers. Although some of the items that we discuss in this chapter involve activities that we might not be able to use in a standard penetration test, the use of timing can often be used with few objections. We must, of course, be able to obtain the proper permission before conducting our penetration test, but this is an excellent aid to penetration testing, particularly when using a black box approach.

We can use such tactics as attacking an individual or group of people, while dressed in the regalia of the opposing team, minor vandalism, and so on to get things started, but once started, they will usually gain momentum and take on a life of their own. We can use the distraction and cover of such events to perform a variety of activities which might otherwise be noticed.

Company Events

Company events can provide the Zukin with a good opportunity to infiltrate, in either a physical or a social engineering sense. Such events are often not graced with any additional security, but can occur in settings outside of the normal site security or can include much larger gatherings of people than what we would otherwise see. In addition, for particularly large events, we may see catering staff and other workers who are not a normal fixture of the location.

Outside Events

Outside events are generally a common occurrence at larger companies, particular during warmer seasons. We can generally count on seeing such events once or twice a year, often with food and diversions for the employees. We can take advantage of these occasions, as they will cause a distraction for the entire facility, get many of them out of the building, and allow us to move about with less chance of being detected in the larger than normal gatherings of people moving in and out of the building.

Large Meetings or Conferences

Many large companies have yearly staff meetings or hold conferences for the industry in which they operate. Again, this provides us with an opportunity, as many people will attend such events, even when not mandatory, as they are an opportunity to escape the cubicle world. We will often find these events to be catered, with the attending catering staff, event staff, and attendees adding to the crowd. Even when such events are not hosted in our target facility, they will still benefit us by emptying the facility of many of the people that we would normally find present.

Environmental Events

Environmental events can provide an excellent distraction for the activities of the Zukin. We can use the cover of heavy rains, snow, flooding, power outages, and other such events to carry out our activities while others deal with the situation. In many cases, if the environmental activity is severe or disruptive enough, we may find entire facilities shut down, security personnel, and all. In cases where there is danger to personnel, such as a very bad storm, this will almost surely be the case. Depending on the event, we may also be able to be somewhat less careful about leaving evidence behind as, in the case of severe flooding, any evidence will likely be destroyed in the process.

Storms

Although we cannot predict them very far in advance, storms can provide ideal conditions under which to conduct operations, as long as we take into consideration the peculiarities of the conditions. We must prepare for operating in such conditions and be willing to face the possibility of the additional dangers of doing so. In the case of severe flooding, we will likely need access to watercraft of some sort and perhaps diving gear. For blizzard conditions, we will need appropriate clothing and will have to be careful about leaving tracks in the snow that will stay for any period of time and so on.

Storms may also provide us with additional difficulties, as we may experience power outages, lines of communications that are down, lock mechanisms that are frozen shut, or any number of other factors. We should prepare adequately so that we can cope with such conditions when we find them.

Fires

Fires can make a fine cover for the activities of the Zukin, but we need to be extremely careful in their use. Fire can be a two-edged sword and will definitely bite us, given the opportunity. Fire can be used to clear a facility of all personnel, but will also call in a variety of emergency services, including the fire department, which will be entering the facility at some point.

TIP

Many tactics will trigger fire alarm systems and fire suppression systems that are not actually fires. Some such systems actually measure the quantity of particles in the air, in order to detect smoke, and can be set off by other substances such as dust. On such trick that can be used in data centers with detectors under the raised flooring is to quickly cycle the ventilation system off then on again. This can raise a cloud of dust sufficient to trigger the sensors and trigger the fire suppression system. Of course, we should be aware that damage to property may be caused by using this tactic.

We must be cautious in the use of fire, we will not only be likely to leave evidence of how and where exactly the fire was started, but we may very well damage the target facility in which we are interested. We will be far better off to contain such tactics to those that will be just enough to produce a small amount of smoke and trigger the fire alarm or fire suppression system, than we will be to use any devices that will actually cause harm and leave evidence. Such heavy-handed tactics would be cross purpose and outside the scope of the Zukin. Additionally, fire investigators are generally very sharp and will easily be able to distinguish between fires caused by accident and those set intentionally. In a penetration testing scenario, we would not set an actual fire. We could potentially use something to simulate one, as discussed in the TIP, but we would still need to do so cautiously. If we trigger fire suppression systems in doing so, we may cause extensive damage to property and potentially harm people in the area.

Utility Interruptions

Extended utility interruptions can be a friend of the Zukin as they will likely empty a facility of workers, with the potential exception of a skeleton security staff. Unlike storms, we can initiate a utility failure, so they can be of a bit more use to use in the way of planning and timing.

Depending on the failure, or failures, we may be able to disable security systems and prevent communications from going out, other than through backup systems. This may ease the task of penetrating the physical security of an installation, in addition to rendering it much more sparsely populated. Such factors can be used to our advantage as solely as a distraction or as part of a more complex plan of attack. Depending on the particulars of the situation, we may be able to use such tactics in a penetration test, given proper permission.

SHILL WEB SITES

With the ease of posting information on the Web and the lack of checking and verification for such data, using Web sites to host false or biased information is an extremely easy type of distraction attack to carry out. We can supply false information on companies, either internally or externally, we can manipulate search engine results or create false results entirely, and last, but certainly not least, we can falsify information on social networking sites. Such attacks can be distracting, damaging, and demoralizing. Due to the potential for very strong reactions and out of control results, we would likely not do this during a penetration test.

Spurious Company Data

Supplying false information about a company and its circumstances can be extremely distracting to the people employed there. For those who have worked in such environments, we know that even when false rumors of company troubles can be very difficult to suppress and that the faintest of evidence to support them can result in a wide-scale panic.

When manipulating company data, we can "leak" our planted information on external sites, such as forums or news agency Web sites, or we can plant information on intranets for employees to find. While internally planted information may be more effective, it will be much more easily suppressed when detected by the company. Information released onto the Internet can be nearly impossible to get rid of. If we plant information both internally and externally, the internal information disappearing will only tend to make people believe that something is being covered up by the company in question.

False Layoffs

False rumors of layoffs are a wonderful tactic to cause a panic and get everyone distracted from their duties. When a person is concerned that they may not have a job at all soon, they are less likely to be as conscientious when going about their job and may not notice the activities of the Zukin. If we have carried out our task well enough, we may see people begin to desert the company for other positions, which always causes a bit of chaos.

False layoff rumors can be spread in a variety of ways. A good starting point is with the social networking Web sites, particularly those with a business or professional focus. Here we can create false employees of the company who can claim to be being laid off in the near future, we can create a large number of false employees who are all looking for jobs at the same time, we can drop hints regarding the layoff in forums and a number of other similar activities. Once such rumors get started on social networking sites, they tend to assume a life of their own and will spread far beyond our original efforts.

Company Troubles

Rumors of a company in trouble are another good tool to use when falsifying information for distraction purposes. If we can get such information reported by a news agency, we also have the possibility of causing actual company troubles with our fabricated report. We saw such an incident happen in 2008 with news regarding UAL Corporation, the parent company of United Airlines. Information regarding UAL's 2002 bankruptcy filing was supposedly picked up from a search engine and posted on the South Florida Sun-Sentinel Web site.

From there the story was picked up by Income Securities Advisors and posted on Bloomberg News as a one-line statement.[3] Ultimately, UAL stocks dropped from $12.30 to $3.00 over the course of the day, although they did rebound after it was discovered that the story was false. Not only did UAL stocks go down significantly but the stocks of the other airlines went down to some extent as well. We can easily see where such a tactic, when done deliberately, might be even more effective.

WARNING

Such tactics, similarly to using fire, should be used very carefully. Unintentionally crashing the company that is our target would likely be a very bad thing for the Zukin behind the operation. Although we may deliberately trigger such packages of false information such as these, we should have a backup plan to defuse the situation, in case things begin to get out of control. We will, of course, likely not gain permission to use such tactics in penetration testing.

In the example above, where a news story was, in theory, accidentally picked up again by the media, the damage was short term and relatively limited because the story was easily proven to be incorrectly reported. When planning such a distraction, we will more than likely want to keep things going for a bit longer than just a day. We might manage this by giving accounts that are similar, but differing in some details, to a few different sources. We should also avoid giving details that are easily proven or disproven using sources other than our target. If we can provoke the target into making a public response to our planted stories, we only lend credence to them and cause rumors to circulate even further.

Many tactics similar to these can work at a company level. The main idea here is to promote our falsified or exaggerated information into the public eye, where it can spread even further. We will talk next about using similar methods at a personal level. In such cases, we will be targeting a specific group of people or individuals and will want to approach things from a slightly different angle.

Social Networking

The Zukin could hardly ask for a more perfect tool for slandering an individual than the social networking site. We have many to choose from, such as Facebook, MySpace, LinkedIn, Twitter, and hordes of others, and such sites are very heavily used. Entire search engines exist to comb details from them, and these details are in no way authenticated. We can easily post a new account to one of these sites with the name and information to match our target and it will likely be taken at face value. In fact, if we have sufficient notice that we might need such an identity posted, we can set one up and allow it to become entrenched in various search engines and the Web of people that are actually associated with our real target.

False Personal Information

The use of false personal information can be a very good distractor. We can use social networking sites to plant false information, in a negative sense, regarding the targets sexual preferences, political affiliation, extracurricular activities, substance abuse or misuse, and a number of similar items. Such information can be backed up with altered pictures or even posts from other social networking accounts of a similar nature.

We can use details such as these to discredit people, to prevent them from being hired, or to get them let go from a position due to inappropriate comments or activities. Again, such information is generally taken at face value and the media is full of examples of people suffering from sharing too much information.

We can also use these tactics in a more subtle fashion by planting less obvious information for potential searchers to find. Companies that carry out background checks and investigators have begun to use these sites as an information mining source, and we can plant things such as false job histories or false educational backgrounds for them to find. Since this information is often regarded as the truth, this can put the target into a bit of distress when questioned about the deliberate inconstancies that we have put in place.

Hijacking Accounts

In addition to posting duplicate accounts with false information, we must also look at hijacking the accounts that legitimately belong to our targets. This would not only allow us to assume a portion of the online identity of the target but it will allow us access to any nonpublic information that they have posted to the hosting site. This may very well lead us to embarrassing information, photographs, or videos that can be used in other distraction-based attacks.

When using this tactic, we must be very subtle, in order to let allow our target to know that their account has been compromised. We can see the results of the heavy-handed use of such tactics in the hacking of then-vice-presidential candidate, Sarah Palin's Yahoo Mail account in 2008.[4] The attacker in this case used weak security questions to set the password for the account and was able to gain access to it.

Such an approach will likely alert the owner of the account, and it will be immediately obvious that an attack has taken place. We should instead, attempt to gain access to the account through the use of the legitimate credentials or use another exploit to gain access to the account. The use of a planted keystroke logger, as discussed in Chapter 13 "Covert Listening Devices," can provide a very clean route to discover such credentials, presuming that it is not discovered.

Advertising Negative Information

Another tactic that we can use is to advertise information that is true, but is negative or embarrassing in nature. This type of distractor will be somewhat harder for the target to deal with, as the information itself is not actually false, but is not something that they would generally want revealed to the public. We can use pictures of the target in compromising situations, such as nude or drunk at a party. We can reveal jobs from which they were fired, tests that were cheated on, illicit encounters with someone of the same gender, drug use, or any number of things. Such information can often be found by the enterprising Zukin with a little bit of digging and investigative work.

Using Restraint

While we can cause an enormous amount of chaos and distraction with social networking sites, we should be cautious in their use. Such tactics definitely have the possibility of causing terminations of employment, divorces, physical violence, and other nasty effects. While these can sometimes be exactly the results that we are seeking, we need to be careful not to make a situation more difficult for ourselves by overdoing our distractions.

We must also consider that information release onto the public Internet is nearly impossible to completely remove. When we use such tactics, we will very likely not be able to undo what we have done. We should plan carefully and release the minimal amount of this type of information that we need to accomplish our goals. Not only could it backfire on us later if circumstances change, but it could also tip our hand by creating a body of information that is so over the top as to be obviously false.

Additionally, when we are integrating an account on a social networking site with actual people who know the target, we need to be very cautious. We should be careful to avoid chat rooms or e-mail messages where we might say something that would indicate that we are obviously not the target that we are impersonating. This can be very easy to do if we are contacted by someone who knows the target well and would notice an inconsistency in their likes or dislikes, knowledge of their friends and personal life, or knowledge of events. Generally, there are settings on most social networking sites that will allow us to avoid the opportunity for such close contact.

False Search Engine Results

False search engine results can be a good general tactic for sowing chaos linked to a particular target or term. These types of attacks are often used to spread malware, or to promote particular products, and are easily adapted to our cause. A variety of tactics are available for making particular terms or sites show up high in search engine results, from planting pages with a great number of keywords in the background, to just outright paying for links.

Malware

Malware attached to a particular topic is a common occurrence. We can see a flood of such attacks surrounding the death of Michael Jackson, including links to malware from search engines, spam, social engineering attempts, fake CNN articles, scareware, and fake videos.[5] We can easily use such tactics ourselves to connect the name of a target company, event, or person to results from a search engine.

NOTE

We should be very cautious when using malware in such situations. We need to very carefully limit our activities to our target and thoroughly test such tools before releasing them. Malware has a habit of getting out of the control of its authors and causing considerably more havoc than was originally intended. Such mistakes could not only draw unwanted attention but actually damage the targets or assets that we are attempting to reach in the first place.

We should be aware that, as common as such tactics are, our attack will likely be short lived and less than subtle. While this might be a problem for longer term attacks that are actually concerned with causing actual damage or collecting information, this is just fine for a distractor. Such a tactic might not be very effective by itself, but as part of a well-planned series of distractions, it will work nicely for our purposes.

MULTIPRONGED ATTACKS

Attacks coming from multiple angles can be used to distract, confuse, and frustrate out targets. We can use attacks that are specifically for the purpose of distraction and have no other goal, which will particularly confound security personnel who are attempting to combat or investigate them. If we have no specific target, other than to cause a distraction, this frees us to behave in ways that do not conform to normal attacks.

We can disrupt monitoring mechanisms, then not attack at that location or we can deliberately trigger monitoring mechanisms and then melt away. We can use attacks that occur on multiple fronts, physical coinciding with logical attacks, or inside attacks occurring at the same time as outside attacks. We can also time attacks to coincide with shift changes or other times that personnel will be distracted or absent. Many different possibilities exist for attacks focused on distraction.

Distractors

Distractors are a type of attack with only one focus, to provide a distraction. This may be a ploy to gain the targets attention at a particular location just for the sake of disruption or it may be as a cover for another attack. Distractors are often showy and noisy deliberately so as to gain the attention of the target. This may sound like it runs counter to the philosophy of the Zukin, but, if executed properly, such attacks can be carried off without leaving any significant evidence. Distractors can often be useful in penetration testing, we just need to be sure that we have permission to do so and do not cause property damage or harm anyone in the process.

Flashy Attacks

One main feature of the distractor is that we want it to be noticed. We want it to be loud, bright, to create enormous spikes in network activity, or anything else that will draw attention. We still do not want to be seen or leave physical or logical evidence behind, so distracters must be carefully placed and triggered.

Physical distractors will often involve loud noises, bright lights, or fire. Ideally would should not leave behind devices, such as igniters, or cause physical damage to property, as this would leave evidence that could later be the subject of an investigators attention.

Logical distractors will generally involve generating unusual network traffic. This can be done internally or externally, ideally in such a way as to intentionally alert any intrusion detection systems that might be monitoring the network or hosts involved. From an external perspective, the easiest tool to use for this task would be a botnet. A good sized botnet will be capable of generating a massive amount of traffic and will be effectively untraceable. Internally, we can configure a compromised host on the network to generate our traffic or attacks, but this will need to be done very carefully so as to not leave any significant evidence behind.

Misdirection

One of the primary uses of a good distraction is misdirection. If we can focus the attention of the target on a particular physical location or a particular attack on the network, we have a much greater chance of sneaking in at another place while security personnel are busy with our distraction. If we can make a large enough noise, such as a sustained attack from a botnet, then we can hopefully get in and out with no notice whatsoever.

One of the main points of using misdirection, of course, is to not only not get caught but to present the distractor used in the misdirection attempt as something that does not look like part of an attack. If we take an extreme physical measure that looks like a direct attack, and then our follow-up actual attack is noticeable, then we have produced something that looks a great deal more like a concerted attack. This is not a desirable feature when we are attempting to be stealthy and not leave behind evidence.

The distractor, in this case, should be something that is easily explainable, but unusual. For example, a car on fire can provide a very nice distractor, particularly when the local fire department arrives to put it out, ambulances are called, and all of the other ensuing chaos that accompanies such an event takes place. While we would theoretically achieve much of the same effect by igniting a random can in the parking lot, it would be much more difficult to explain. If we carry out the same distractor, but do so in a vehicle that we bring onsite, properly modified to catch on fire "accidentally," then we have a much more feasible story, and there will be no need for law enforcement to investigate the accident deeply.

Attacking on Multiple Fronts

Although using a distractor can be a good preface for other attacks, the attacks themselves can often cause a fine distraction when carried out properly. If we launch multiple attacks simultaneously or sequentially, we can cause no end of confusion and chaos. We can trigger physical attacks to coincide with logical attacks, inside attacks with outside attacks, or any number of combinations.

Combining Physical and Logical Attacks

A variety of physical and logical attack combinations can be used to add additional confusion and distraction to the mix. If we arrange for a fire alarm to go off when we are starting out logical attack run, even though the intrusion detection system might be sending alerts, there will not be anyone in the facility to see them. If such alerts are being received on mobile devices by personnel who have evacuated the facility, there will likely be a delay before they can access a device to login in remotely and see what is happening. In such cases, it will generally be some time before the fire department has cleared the building and will allow people to enter it again, allowing the Zukin time to conduct our operation.

Conversely, we can attack logical systems to cover for a physical attack. If we can compromise the security system that receives alerts from the physical intrusion detection system, we can cause not only a distraction but a complete lack of confidence in the functionality of the system. If we repeatedly cause alerts to happen in areas where there has clearly been no intrusion and we mask the alert for the area that we have actually penetrated, this will provide us with a good cover, as well as a distraction.

Local and Remote Attacks

A combination of internally sourced and externally sourced attacks can also sow a great deal of confusion. For example, using this tactic during a logical attack will not only cause it to be considerably less clear where exactly the attack is coming from and what systems and networks have actually been penetrated, but it may also allow us to approach from a different direction entirely while the other two attacks are taking place. We can further add to the chaos by attacking internally from very unexpected networks or systems, such as using a compromised network printer or other device that is not commonly recognized as being a computing platform.

We can use such tactics for physical attacks as well, perhaps by setting off alarm sensors for both internal and external intrusions simultaneously. Of course, as previously discussed, combining physical and logical attacks will only make such tactics even more confusing and distracting. With a little planning, we can watch gleefully as our targets try in vain to discover what has gone wrong with their systems, all the while making a clean getaway.

Attack Timing

The timing of attacks, particularly when using distractors, can be critical. We must be able to synchronize our attacks with any distractions that are to be used, with other phases of the attack, and, potentially, with activities going on at our target location, such as shift changes or maintenance. If we can successfully carry off such timing, then we will be faced with a target that is being pulled in many directions at once, instead of one that has the resources to focus on the true attack that will actually accomplish our goal.

Synchronizing Attacks

The synchronization of attacks can be critical, particularly when using distractors. We will likely need to cause a distraction closely times with our actual attack and will need to be able to do so in a timed manner. When we are planning attacks to go off simultaneously, time is the best trigger that we can use, as we are not depending on a previous event to have taken place.

When attempting to synchronize our attacks, it is critical that we be able to execute with very precise timing. If we are planning one or more distractors, a physical attack and a logical attack, this is a very complex arrangement and generally will not happen on a very specific schedule without significant practice. If at all possible, we should run through the attack several times before actually attempting the real thing. We should try to setup practice environments for all components of the operation, physical, logical, or otherwise, as closely approximating real conditions as we are able to do based on available information and resources.

Sequential Attacks

One possible, perhaps even likely, scenario when conducting operations is the need to conduct sequential attacks. We may need to trigger a distraction before attempting a physical attack, compromise a logical system in order to pass through a physical access control, and so on, with one attack preparing the way for the next. This will normally be a very common fixture of a complex attack.

When attempting to carry out attacks in sequence, we will need to develop a trigger to allow the next attack in the sequence to proceed. We can try to use time alone for this trigger, but this leaves us with little or no room for error or delay and will likely result in a failed attack, in the very best case. If at all possible, some sort of direct signaling, such as voice communications or visible or auditory signals, present us with the best possibility of carrying out our attack sequence properly. When using distractions, it may very well be that the distraction itself will be obvious enough to server as such a signal. In any case, direct signaling will allow us to know that the necessary previous steps of the operation have been carried out properly and that we are ok to proceed.

Attacking between Shifts

As we discussed in Chapter 8, "Use of Timing to Enter an Area," the use of timing to enter an area can greatly aid us in attacking. When looking at things from the point of view of distractions, our environment can often produce distractions of its own, without us even needing to take action. Shift changes are a major feature at many facilities where large numbers of personnel are employed and can aid the Zukin. At such times, there will be movements of people in and out of the facility, security may be changing personnel out, and many people will be generally distracted by plans to leave work or to journey home. In this chaos, we can find many distractions.

Attacking during Maintenance

Maintenance of facilities or networks also provides us with distractors. During network maintenance, the operation of the network may be decreased or absent, allowing us to plant equipment, take systems offline, or send unusual network traffic without drawing attention. We may also find that administrators and network security personnel are distracted by the maintenance taking place and may not be paying attention to other things taking place on the network, to the degree that they normally would.

Physical maintenance to the facility also provides us with an excellent opportunity. This can include cleaning, construction or remodeling, pest control, utility or generator maintenance, and a host of other activities. In such cases, we will often see people moving about the facility that are not normally there and who will not be recognizable, one way or the other, to the building and security staff. This can greatly work to our advantage as it eases the task of entering the facility and moving about and provides us with a convenient excuse as to why we are there and why we are carrying odd equipment or tools.

Summary

In this chapter, we discussed the use of big events to distract the targets of our attack. Using such distractions can ensure that we are able to carry out our main attack unmolested while everyone is concerned with the deliberately noticeable attack that we have set to draw their attention.

We talked about using big events, such as holidays, sporting events, company activities, and environmental events, to draw attention away from the Zukin. Most any event that will gather the attention or physical presence of large groups of people will function for such a distraction. If we are fortunate, we may even be able to cause such an event to draw even more attention than it normally would, such as the tactic of inciting a riot at a sporting event.

The use of shill Web sites to cause a distraction has the benefit of not only being extremely distracting but very easy to carry out. We can use internal servers, social networking sites, and search engine results to sow a variety of spurious information, malware, and other similar devices in order to create confusion. We can even, if done properly, affect the financial status of a company or cause the employment of an individual to come to a screeching halt.

Multipronged attacks can allow us to approach a target from multiple angles, as well as using timing to make our attacks more effective by including distractors, or by causing a distraction with the attacks themselves. We can also use the synchronization between attacks or sequential attacks to make our efforts more effective. In addition, we can time attacks so that they fall between shifts or occur during maintenance activities for physical or logical systems.

Endnotes

1. Hatsumi M. Essence of ninjutsu: the nine traditions. New York: McGraw Hill; 1988.
2. Associated Press. Fan does in Brazil soccer violence. CBS News Sports. [Online] www .cbsnews.com/stories/2010/02/22/sports/main6231165.shtml; 2010 [accessed 6.05.2010].
3. Petruno T. Old web news causes crash in UAL Shares. Los Angeles Times. [Online] articles .latimes.com/2008/sep/09/business/fi-moneyblog9; 2008 [accessed 4.05.2010].
4. Stephey MJ. Sarah Palin's E-Mail Hacked. Time. [Online] www.time.com/time/politics/ article/0,8599,1842097,00.html; 2008 [accessed 6.04.2010].
5. Danchev D. Michael Jackson's death themed malware campaigns spreading. Zero Day. [Online] blogs.zdnet.com/security/?p=3682; 2009 [accessed 4.05.2010].

Concealment Devices

Since the primary purpose for historical ninja was espionage, there was a need to transmit messages secretly across the countryside. Clever methods of concealing messages include the following[1]:

- The bottom of the ninja sword's scabbard
- Hollowed-out canes and walking sticks
- Inside specially constructed arrows
- Umbrellas
- Food, such as walnut hulls and eggs with wax plugs

The ninja demonstrated extreme creativity in designing ways to conceal information in everyday items; the impetus for going to extreme lengths was the fact that they faced death if discovered. In traditional professional penetration testing, the risk of life or limb just does not exist – however, in cyber warfare between governments, the risks associated with discovery are just as high as in ancient Japan.

Although the stakes are not as high in traditional penetration testing as they are in the government arena, being able to inject listening or collecting devices into a target corporate environment is a worthwhile endeavor. With today's advancing technologies and as ninja hackers, we should be able to create mobile listening devices that will appear to be legitimate, everyday items that can be used to collect audio, video, or data; we should also be able to conceal these devices so that they blend in with the surroundings.

Once we obtain the data, we may need to remove it out of the corporate environment or at least conceal it so that if searched, the data will not be found. In some facilities, bags are searched when exiting in order to find printed material or data media leaving the premises – in situations such as these, we need to be able to smuggle our collected data out.

In Chapter 13, "Covert Listening Devices," we will examine covert listening devices, such as key loggers and radio wave interceptors – equipment that was built specifically for spying and exploitation. In this chapter, we will focus strictly on items that serve a function unconnected to hacking, which has been repurposed to clandestine activities, which is much more in line with traditional ninja tactics.

Ninja Hacking. DOI: 10.1016/B978-1-59749-588-2.00012-3

183

Although most covert listening devices, such as key loggers, are extremely useful tools, they are easier to detect and prevent than what we will discuss in this chapter – concealment devices.

MOBILE DEVICES

Mobile phones and personal data assistant (PDA) appliances used to be limited in their functionality; however, today there are wireless devices that operate using advanced operating systems and support applications that are incredibly useful for conducting clandestine activities. As an example, Apple's iPod touch runs on the UNIX-Darwin kernel, which is open source,[2] POSIX compliant, and single UNIX specification version 3 (SUSv3) compliant. Because of this, advanced hacker applications can be built and installed onto the device, making the iPod touch a powerful hacking platform.

However, before we begin to imagine ways to modify innocuous devices into nefarious attack platforms, we need to understand the existing countermeasures available to governments and corporations to detect spy devices. Once we understand what we are up against as Zukin, we can design our tactics to overcome these obstacles.

Detection Methods

Because we are going to focus on mobile devices, we need to be aware of the electronic signals that could betray our use of these devices. Just as the ninja understood the full extent of their weapons, we need to be aware of ours; with electronic devices, we have some advantages and disadvantages.

NOTE

In the following examples, we are going to look at the iPod touch pretty extensively. Although there are other mobile devices that could be used instead, the iPod touch has some advantages, including the operating system, the wireless capabilities, the price, and most importantly – the anonymity. Purchasing an iPod touch does not require a contract with a telecommunication provider and is less expensive. There are some disadvantages (video capturing ability, for example), but overall the iPod touch has numerous benefits and few drawbacks. However, it is by no means the only option available for a hacking platform and will probably be replaced by a better choice in the future.

The primary advantages of mobile devices are processing power, size, and remote communication abilities; the primary disadvantages are that such devices give off very distinct signatures that can be detected. We may be able to disguise some of these signatures (such as wireless connectivity) if we intermingle our devices with similar ones, but we need to know what signatures we need to disguise in the first place.

Radio Transmissions

If we want to use our mobile device as a remote attacking platform, we need to have network connectivity. Most mobile devices, including phones, can connect to local wireless networks. Phones can connect over telecommunication towers, but the ability to bridge networks is difficult at best, if not impossible, with mobile phones. Regardless, once a mobile device connects with a wireless station, whether it is a local access point or a cell tower, those transmissions can be captured. With the right hardware, the exact location of the wireless mobile device can be discerned.

Another concern is interception of data while transmitted over the airwaves. Encryption is a logical step toward concealing the true nature of the transmissions. The use of encryption may trigger suspicion as to the nature of the communication, but if we use well-known ports that use encryption (TLS, for example) to tunnel our remote connection, suspicion may be deflected.

There is not much we can do to hide our wireless communication since radio waves emitting from phones or PDAs are omnidirectional. One method of disguise is to employ it in a location where a lot of other radio traffic exists; a signal from a PDA configured as a hacking platform would be obfuscated if it was located in an area with numerous employees, but would stand out in a facility which prohibits wireless devices. If there is an assumption that rogue systems (such as a hacker-configured PDA) will be searched out, then the only real option is to hide it among the noise (other systems).

Heat Detection

Because mobile devices give off heat, they are easy to locate when using heat detection methods. To remove the heat signature, there are a couple different solutions – the most effective is to cover it in dense material. Sheet rock is a poor shield against heat detection, but wood and glass are much more effective and does not limit radio wave transmissions; the problem is that if the mobile device is employed as a listening device, the greater the insulation, the weaker the audio reception.

Although it is possible to disguise some of the heat signature by locating the mobile device close to another heat source, the device will still stand out to the trained eye when using a heat detection device, due to the shape and patterns of the signature.

Frequency Analysis

One way to detect covert devices is to examine the broadcast spectrum. More and more devices are using wireless transmissions to push data to the collection site, and mobile devices, such as cell phones and PDAs, are heavily reliant on radio waves to communicate. Cell phones and network wireless access points operate on very specific wavelengths, and interception of these radio transmissions are trivial. However, the bigger threat when discussing frequency analysis relates to the electronic components within the mobile device, such as semiconductors, diodes, and transistors. It is possible to excite these components with radio waves in such a way that they will emit a detectable signature; the best part of this technique is that it works against devices that are powered off, which will defeat even the most stealthiest attempts at placing a rouge system in a corporate environment.

Mobile Device Trends

Some of the devices we will examine in this section will become obsolete within a few years – newer models will have capabilities that far exceed what is currently available. Regardless, there are some interesting trends that we can examine and use to our advantage.

The first trend is the use of open-source operating systems. As already mentioned, the iPod touch and the iPhone, both products of Apple Inc., uses the Darwin operating system. Additional proprietary applications, including graphic interface software, have been added to these portable devices; however, the core system is undeniably UNIX based.

The second trend is the increase in computing power and memory. Although the iPod touch does not have the processing capabilities of desktops or even laptops, they are quite capable of processing large amounts of data rapidly. As a benchmark test, the iPod touch (first generation) was able to process 577 MD5 hashes per second using the password cracking tool "John the Ripper." In comparison, the MacBook Pro with a 2.8GHz Intel Core Duo processor was able to process 7674 per second. Although about one-twelfth the capability of the MacBook Pro, the iPod touch results are still impressive for what many consider as simply a fancy MP3 player.

The method of obtaining applications needed for penetration testing or covert audio and video communication will vary, depending on the mobile platform. In the case of the Droid and Palm Pre, access to the underlying operating system is available by design. However, in the case of the iPod touch, access to the operating system can only be achieved by "jailbreaking" the phone, which circumvents protection mechanisms installed by Apple.

> **TIP**
>
> Although we will focus on the iPod touch, the iPhone is just as capable as the iPod touch for conducting similar attacks and can be jailbroken just as the iPod touch. Overall, the iPhone is actually a better attack platform than the iPod touch since audio and video can also be recorded with the iPhone.

The actual method of jailbreaking varies, depending on the generation of the iPod touch and the version of the installed software. Once jailbroken, we can place applications on our device through different repositories – the most notable is called "Cydia." More information on Cydia can be found at http://cydia.saurik.com/.

> **WARNING**
>
> It is entirely possible that using modified firmware or making alterations to the operating system of a mobile device could have bad results. If we are lucky, such results may only be the odd application or operating system instability. If we are not lucky, we may have just gained a very expensive paperweight in the form of a completely nonfunctional device, commonly known as "bricking" it.

To understand the true capabilities of such devices, let us look at some of the different stages conducted during a professional penetration test and see how we can use mobile devices in each stage. Although availability of tools will vary with each mobile device, we will examine those tools available to the iPod touch.

Information Gathering

To gather information about a target network, we can use functionality already built into most mobile devices. An Internet Web browser is a natural starting tool to gather information on corporations, employees, and networks. However, a browser can only give us so much information – additional tools we can install include Nmap and Telnet, which allows us to scan a target system or network and connect with discovered systems. Figure 12.1 shows the Nmap application installed on an iPod touch through Cydia.

The advantage of using a repository like Cydia is that the program has already been compiled and can be installed on the iPod touch with no more than a click of a button. In fact, the number of applications available for the iPod touch through the Cydia repository are so numerous that very few hacker applications need to be compiled separately – the work has almost been entirely done for us.

WARNING

By using Cydia, instead of compiling the hacker applications personally, some functionality may be absent in the application. It is still a best practice to compile the application, instead of acquiring someone else's build, so that we can better tailor the application to our platform and needs.

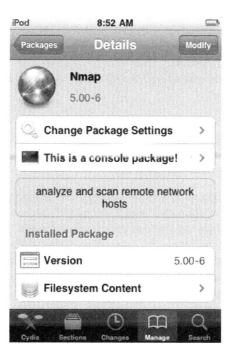

FIGURE 12.1   Installation Screen for Nmap.

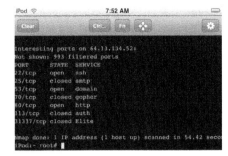

FIGURE 12.2   Nmap Running on the iPod Touch.

FIGURE 12.3   Running Nmap Using On-Screen Keyboard.

In Figure 12.2, we see a screenshot of Nmap running on the iPod touch. The command window in Figure 12.2 is on the actual iPod itself and is not the result of remotely logging into the system (which we will talk about later in this chapter). By employing Nmap directly on the device, we can locate ourselves within a facility in a manner that does not arouse suspicion, unlike plugging into a network drop in an empty cubicle.

There are some drawbacks in using the mobile device as an attack platform, and that is the size of the screen on the devices. In Figure 12.3, we see that the majority of the screen is consumed by the on-screen keyboard; this makes attacking directly from the device almost impractical, unless we set up scripts in advance. A better alternative is to connect to the iPod touch remotely, which we will discuss when we get to section "Maintaining Access."

Nmap will allow us to grab the following information regarding a target system and its applications:

- Operating system and version information
- Open ports
- Applications running on open ports (best guess)
- Application version information

Although Nmap does perform some banner-grabbing functionality, it is important to verify this information with a second tool, such as Telnet or netcat.

Netcat is another tool that can also be easily installed using Cydia. Figure 12.4 is a screenshot of a netcat session connecting to Google.com. There are some advantages to using netcat over Telnet, in that netcat does not inject or extract control characters; this means we can download files using netcat without worrying about data corruption by the application itself.

We can also use secure tunnel to connect to remote systems using OpenSSH, in case we need to mask our activity. An example of the use of OpenSSH is presented later in this chapter when we discuss remote connectivity under section "Maintaining Access."

Vulnerability Identification

There are numerous commercial tools available to a professional penetration tester who conducts vulnerability identification analysis – unfortunately, none have been ported to the iPod touch. The Nmap application has the ability to use scripts that interpret the Nmap findings and attempt to identify vulnerability; however, the development of Nmap as a vulnerability scanning application does not have the support that other programs do, like Nessus or Core IMPACT (to name a couple).

Perhaps a better alternative is to use the iPod touch as a pivot for more robust vulnerability scanners. Figure 12.5 is a screenshot of how we can install an agent onto a remote system, such as the iPod touch; this agent will allow us to use the agent to conduct scans on other systems within the target network.

In Figure 12.6, we see how an agent can be used to compromise systems deeper in the target network. If we look at it closely, we see that the server with the IP

FIGURE 12.4   Netcat Session on iPod Touch.

FIGURE 12.5   Core IMPACT Agent Installed.

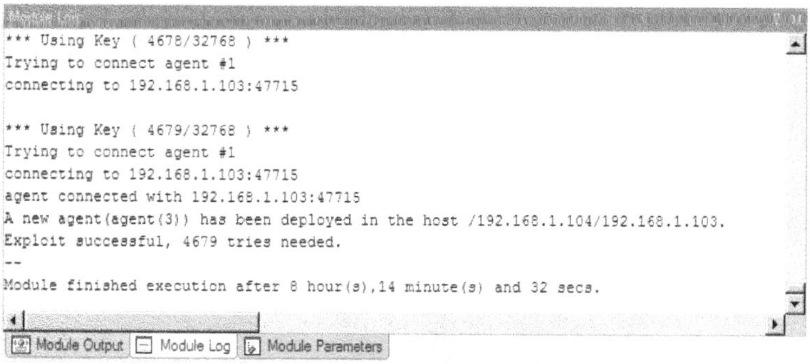

FIGURE 12.6   Example of Using an Agent to Pivot an Attack.

address of 192.168.1.103 was exploited through the agent located on 192.168.1.104. This is an example of using an installed agent to conduct a pivot attack.

The use of the iPod touch as a platform to conduct a pivot attack seems to be the best option for conducting a vulnerability identification scan than trying to use Nmap or do the identification manually.

Vulnerability Exploitation

We can use an agent deployed on the iPod touch to conduct vulnerability exploitation, similar to the way an agent can be used to perform vulnerability identification. Again, Core IMPACT would be a good choice for such an attack. However, there is an application framework that can perform vulnerability exploitation, which can be installed using Cydia – the Metasploit 3.0 Framework. Figure 12.7 is a screenshot of the Cydia package for the Metasploit Framework.

Similar to the traditional application installed on laptops or desktops, the Metasploit application can be run from the command line from the iPhone touch (Figure 12.8). In this configuration, we can launch exploits against servers with greater certainty of stability and accuracy.

For those who prefer the Metasploit Web-based exploit application, we can use that on the iPod touch as well. In Figure 12.9, we see the front Web page of the

FIGURE 12.7   Installation Screen for Metasploit.

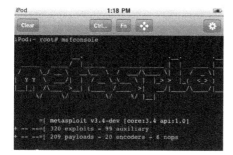

FIGURE 12.8   Metasploit Framework Command Line.

FIGURE 12.9   Metasploit 3.4 Web Console on iPod Touch.

```
iPod:~ root# perl --version
This is perl, v5.10.0 built for arm-iphoneos

Copyright 1987-2007, Larry Wall

Perl may be copied only under the terms of either the Artistic License or the
GNU General Public License, which may be found in the Perl 5 source kit.

Complete documentation for Perl, including FAQ lists, should be found on
this system using "man perl" or "perldoc perl".  If you have access to the
Internet, point your browser at http://www.perl.org/, the Perl Home Page.

iPod:~ root# python --version
Python 2.5.1
iPod:~ root#
iPod:~ root# bash --version
GNU bash, version 4.0.17(1)-release (arm-apple-darwin9)
Copyright (C) 2009 Free Software Foundation, Inc.
License GPLv3+: GNU GPL version 3 or later <http://gnu.org/licenses/gpl.html>

This is free software; you are free to change and redistribute it.
There is NO WARRANTY, to the extent permitted by law.
iPod:~ root#
iPod:~ root# ruby -v
ruby 1.8.6 (2007-09-24 patchlevel 111) [arm-darwin9]
iPod:~ root# _
```

FIGURE 12.10   Program Languages and Version Numbers.

Metasploit Framework Web console (to be able to view the Web console, the command had to rerun to read as follows, which places the process in the background: `iPod:~ root# msfweb &`). Although not as reliable as the command-line method, the Web console makes it easier to visualize attacks and select payloads. The preference of one over the other is up to the user.

Another alternative to vulnerability exploitation is to create our own exploit code or download it from a Web site, such as milw0rm.org. In order to take advantage of the scripts available on the milw0rm.org site, we need to have some program languages installed. Figure 12.10 shows some of the languages that can be installed on the iPod touch with minimal effort.

FIGURE 12.11   GNU C Compiler.

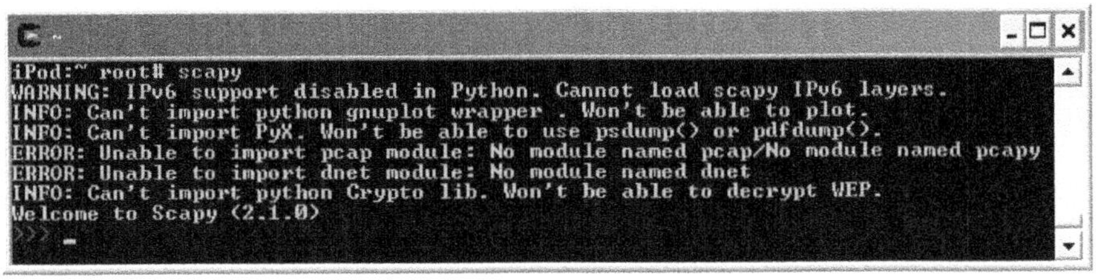

FIGURE 12.12   Scapy Installed on iPod Touch.

As we can see, Perl, Python, bash, and Ruby are available for use. The GNU C Compiler can also be installed (Figure 12.11), which will allow us use those exploits that need to be compiled. With these different programming languages available, we should be able to compile any exploit we find on the Internet.

If we need to do some packet manipulation, we can install the scapy application, available at www.secdev.org/projects/scapy/. Figure 12.12 shows a screenshot of the scapy program installed on the iPod touch; as an application that runs on top of Python, scapy can use Python commands to add additional versatility to packet manipulation projects.

One disadvantage with the iPod touch is that there are no applications that can be installed which will read and display pcap files, which are captured packets. To view the packets, it is necessary to download any pcap files onto a remote system, and read offline. This will be a problem also when we conduct wireless attacks using the iPod touch.

Web Hacking

Although we cannot get more robust applications loaded onto the iPod touch, such as Core IMPACT or HP WebInspect, there are still some good applications available. Figure 12.13 is a screenshot of the Nikto open-source (GPL) Web server scanner version information; Nikto is a Perl application available for download at http://cirt.net/nikto2.

Ranked #12 of the top 100 network security tools by Insecure.org, Nikto will scan a server for configuration files, cgi applications, outdated version information, and a multitude of other bits of data that can be useful in a penetration test. Although most of the work done by Nikto focuses on information gathering, it does a pretty good job of identifying potential vulnerabilities when found, as seen in Figure 12.14.

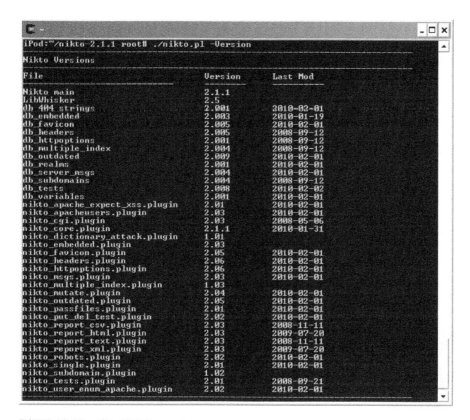

FIGURE 12.13   Nikto Web Server Scanner.

```
iPod:~/nikto-2.1.1 root# ./nikto.pl -host google.com
- ***** SSL support not available (see docs for SSL install instructions) *****
- Nikto v2.1.1

+ Target IP:        74.125.127.147
+ Target Hostname:  google.com
+ Target Port:      80
+ Start Time:       2010-06-04 14:42:34

+ Server: gws
+ All CGI directories 'found', use '-C none' to test none
+ Uncommon header 'x-xss-protection' found, with contents: 1; mode=block
+ /modules.php?op=modload&name=FAQ&file=index&myfaq=yes&id_cat=1&categories=%3Ci
mg%20src=javascript:alert(document.cookie);%3E&parent_id=0: Post Nuke 0.7.2.3-Ph
oenix is vulnerable to Cross Site Scripting (XSS). http://www.cert.org/advisorie
s/CA-2000-02.html.
+ /modules.php?letter=%22%3E%3Cimg%20src=javascript:alert(document.cookie);%3E&o
p=modload&name=Members_List&file=index: Post Nuke 0.7.2.3-Phoenix is vulnerable
to Cross Site Scripting (XSS). http://www.cert.org/advisories/CA-2000-02.html.
```

FIGURE 12.14   Nikto Scan Results.

Based on our results in Figure 12.14, it looks like we might have a starting point in which to look for exploits; the nice thing about Nikto is that it provides URL references regarding the discovered (potential) vulnerabilities, allowing us to find out more if we need.

Wireless Attacks

Unfortunately, the iPod touch's wireless chip cannot be placed into promiscuous or monitor mode, meaning we cannot obtain wireless data necessary to conduct brute force attacks against wireless access points using encryption. There are other mobile devices that can be set for promiscuous or monitor mode, so if a brute force attack is an absolute necessity, there are options available. However, there is an application that can intercept traffic on a wireless network called "Pirni," written by Axel Moller. Figure 12.15 is the configuration screen for the Pirni application, available through Cydia.

The program is configured to intercept all traffic intended for the default router (192.168.1.1 in this particular network) through ARP spoofing. Based on the Berkley Packet Filter (BPF) values, the only traffic that will be collected is TCP segments leaving the network, destined for port 80. The BPF can be modified to capture whatever type of traffic we are after. The Regex Options are used to immediately capture interesting packets, such as usernames and passwords. Figure 12.16 illustrates the three default regular expressions we will be presented on the Live Feed page, when they are collected.

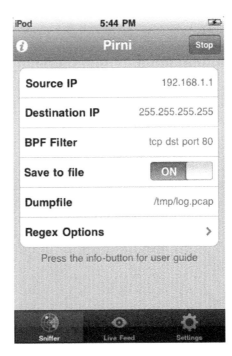

FIGURE 12.15   Sniffer Screen for Pirni Pro.

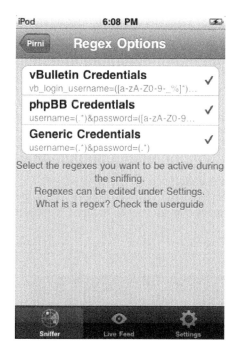

FIGURE 12.16 Pirni Default Regular Expressions.

FIGURE 12.17 Captured Username and Password.

Once we are satisfied with the regular expressions we want to use to present us with live data, we launch Pirni and wait until an unsecure connection is made. In Figure 12.17, we see an example of what a live capture of a username and password looks like. We can also see that we captured over 10,000 packets as well, which we can review later to see if there is any additional information we can use to exploit the target system.

The application presented here is a commercial version of the Pirni application (written by the original Pirni author); however, there is a free command-line version of Pirni, and some scripts that have been written to provide the same functionality as the Pirni Pro application demonstrated above. The Pirni project can be found at http://code.google.com/p/n1mda-dev/wiki/PirniUsageGuide, and the additional scripts can be found at http://code.google.com/p/Pirni-derv/.

Maintaining Access

Later in this chapter, we will be talking about concealing mobile devices; due to their small size, phones and PDAs are perfect candidates for leaving behind within the target corporation's facility similar to key loggers (discussed in Chapter 13, "Covert Listening Devices"). If we decide to leave them behind, it would be beneficial to maintain access to the device – if we compromise systems within the victim's network, we will also want to have applications at the ready to maintain access with them as well. The two applications typically associated with remote logins and backdoors are netcat and SSH.

Earlier we took a look at netcat as an information gathering tool. However, it can also be used as a backdoor as well. Figure 12.18 shows a remote connection established using netcat, in which a shell is spawned when connected.

With the right scripts, we can set up a reverse shell that can connect back to our attack server. A good resource of how to use netcat to its fullest and to set up a reverse shell can be found in *Netcat Power Tools* (ISBN: 978-1-59749-257-7, Syngress).

OpenSSH is one of more handy tools on the iPod touch and is one of the first tools recommended for installation once the iPod touch is jailbroken. Figure 12.19 is a screenshot of the SSH service running on the iPod touch.

Besides providing secure communication, SSH can also be set up as a reverse shell as well and used to create encrypted tunnels that allow us to use the iPod touch

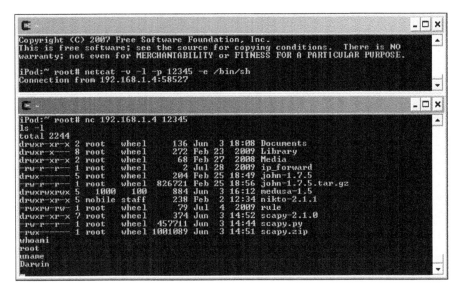

FIGURE 12.18 Netcat Backdoor on iPod Touch.

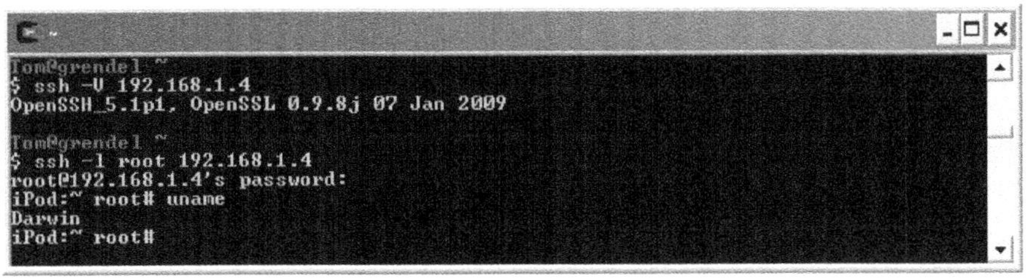

FIGURE 12.19 SSH Server Information on iPod Touch.

as a remote attack platform. Although a valuable technique, we would not be examining how to set up encrypted tunnels or reverse shells using SSH. For more information on this topic, check out Chapter 13, "Maintaining Access" in *Professional Penetration Testing: Creating and Operating a Formal Hacking Lab*, (ISBN: 978-1-59749-425-0, Syngress).

SHINOBI-IRI (Stealth and Entering Methods)

When we connect to networks with our mobile devices, the device's signature will show up differently than typical systems.

There are plenty of other tools that can be installed on the iPod touch and other mobile devices, than those mentioned here. Table 12.1 provides a list of some of the tools that can be installed on an iPod touch, presented at the DEF CON hacker conference in 2009.

The following applications were installed manually: libssh2, john the ripper (brute force password cracker), scapy, and medusa (used for remote brute force attacks). The Apple Store provided a few applications as well, including TouchTerm, Ping, and Speed Test. Altogether, these programs provide an array of tools that make the iPod touch an effective hacking platform, whether handheld or used as a remote attack platform.

Table 12.1 Tools Installed on iPod Touch Through Cydia

adv-cmds	APT	AutomaticSSH	Backgrounder
Base structure	Berkeley DB	Bourne again shell	bzip2
Core utilities	csu	Cydia installer	Darwin CC Tools
Darwin tools	Debian packager	Dev-Team	developer-cmds
Diff utilities	diskdev-cmds	dns2tcp	Docs
Find utilities	Gawk	gettext	GNU C Compiler
GNU cryptography	GNU debugger	GNU privacy guard	GNU PG errors
Grep	gzip	iBrowser	inetutils
iPhone Firmware	less	libffi	libgcc
Libnet	libpcap	libutil	libxml2
Libxslt	Link identity editor	Lynx	Make
mDNSResponder	Metasploit	Mobile substrate	nano

Continued

Table 12.1 Tools Installed on iPod Touch Through Cydia *Continued*

Netatalk	netcat	Network-cmds	New curses
Nmap	OpenSSH	OpenSSL	Perl
Pcre	pirni	Python	readline
Ruby	RubyGems	SBSettings	sed
shell-cmds	SpoofMAC	Stealth MAC	Stumbler plus
Stunnel	Sudo	system-cmds	Tape archive (tar)
Tcpdump	unzip	Vi IMproved (VIM)	wget
Whois	WinterBoard	XML parser toolkit	

Although other mobile devices may not have the same depth of precompiled applications available for download as the iPod touch and iPhone, they are still quite capable devices and can serve the same capacity (maybe even better) than the iPod touch – just as the ancient ninja, it is incumbent on the Zukin to thoroughly understand their weapons' capabilities and use those tools that provide the greatest advantage and concealment during a mission.

DATA SMUGGLING

Collecting data at a remote site requires that we remove it somehow – if we have a continuous connection, such as a reverse shell, then we can collect the data real time. However, if we deposit our mobile device with the intention of concealing it for an extended period of time, then we need to worry about a few issues as follows:

1. Preventing discovery of our collected data while on-site
2. Providing concealment during the duration of the event
3. Extracting the data safely

Extracting the data from the facility will be covered in greater detail when we talk about key loggers in Chapter 13, "Covert Listening Devices"; to emphasize again, in this chapter, we will only be talking about everyday items that can be used for espionage – not hardware or software specifically designed for a single purpose, such as key loggers.

Encryption

If we use mobile devices to collect and transmit data, we should be selective in our choices of devices and ensure that they are capable of encrypting any data at rest or in motion. Earlier models of most mobile devices are incapable of full disk encryption, which puts the device and us at risk if discovered and forensically examined; we, therefore, need to look for devices that will allow us to keep our activities secret or provide a mechanism for covering our tracks if discovered.

Data at Rest

The newer mobile devices claim to provide something similar to full disk encryption. Although the ability of these devices to be able to protect data against forensic analysis is questionable, the devices are getting better at addressing the security of data at rest. As Zukin, we can do a few additional tasks to encrypt data at rest on our mobile devices to increase our comfort level about our hacking data.

Naturally, we cannot encrypt scripts that we need to run during our collection or attack phases; however, once we have collected the data, we can encrypt the data using strong passwords. The program gpg is one method of securing a file through symmetric encryption. Figure 12.20 is an example of how to encrypt a file with the GNU Privacy Guard (GNU PG) application, which can be installed on a jailbroken iPod touch; in this example, we are encrypting the captured packets collected through the use of Pirni Pro.

GNU Privacy Guard provides different options regarding hashing and cryptographic methods, allowing us to be selective on how secure we want our data to be at rest. In our example in Figure 12.20, we used a symmetric key to encrypt our data; however, if we wanted to create a script that automatically encrypted our data on a regular basis, we could use an asymmetric algorithm and provide it with our public key, which would prevent anyone from being able to reverse our encryption without possessing the corresponding private key.

Data in Motion

If we can establish a (reverse) shell to our mobile device, we need to make sure that we communicate securely and in such a way as to ensure our communication stream blends in with the rest of the compromised organization; the use of SSH to create a tunnel is the surest way to do so. The use of SSH will allow us to set up tunnels or use the iPod touch as a proxy. However, we can also set up the iPod touch to be a

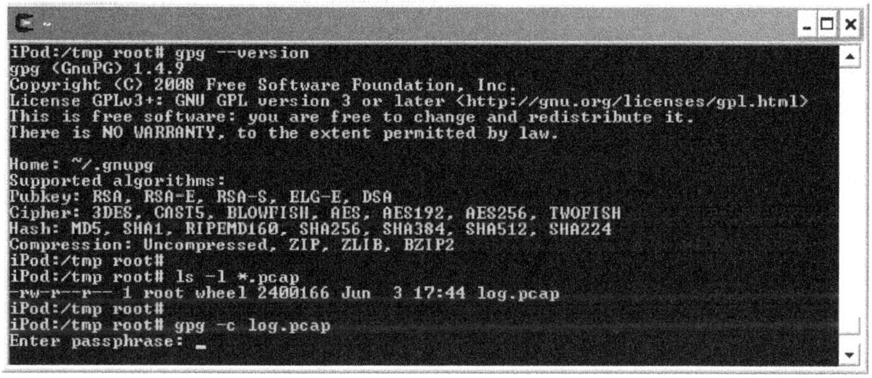

FIGURE 12.20   Encrypting Pcap File.

FIGURE 12.21   OpenVPN Application Information.

VPN server as well. Figure 12.21 provides us with the version information for the OpenVPN application, available through Cydia, which has already been compiled to run on the iPod touch and iPhone. Once configured, we can connect to the iPod touch using VPN software and use the device to conduct our attacks securely.

Both solutions – the VPN and the SSH application – are quite capable of ensuring our communications between the iPod touch and our remote attack platform are encrypted. We also have the flexibility of using our encrypted channels through whichever open port exists within the victim's network; this will permit us to conduct our attacks with much greater stealth since we can avoid detection by intrusion detection systems looking for specific data (such as keywords) traveling across the network.

Concealment

Since all we are discussing in this chapter is the use of common everyday objects such as phones and PDAs, theoretically we should be able to leave such devices out in the open without the fear of attracting attention to our espionage activities. However, since we may need to leave such devices in the victim's facility for extended periods of time (not to mention the cost of the devices), we may want to find ways to hide them in a way that does not arouse suspicion (an iPod duct taped to the underside of a table, for example, would probably make people wonder).

Concealment Limitations

There are a couple concerns that we need to be aware of when concealing mobile devices beyond the obvious, such as heat and moisture. Although technology has advanced quite a bit, we still need to deal with some limitations, including battery life and reception.

The first issue we need to resolve with mobile devices is power. CPU activity and wireless use will quickly draw down battery life within mobile devices. Therefore, we need to be able to connect our devices to power somehow. Most devices use USB connections to power themselves, so we either need to be near a computer with open USB ports or use a power charger that has the appropriate USB end for our device. Most phones come with cables needed to connect either to USB or a power outlet, but most PDAs do not (the iPod touch, for example, requires a separate purchase to connect to a wall socket). Another consideration, however, is that standard power outlet cables are bulky for what we need to do (we will see an example later in this section). Therefore, it may be necessary to purchase a third-party cable regardless of what was included in the device's initial purchase.

The second issue we need to resolve is wireless reception. We must be able to deposit our device in an area where we can be guaranteed a wireless signal. To see available wireless access points and their signal strength, we should be able to use our devices; Figure 12.22 is a screenshot of available access points within reach of our example iPod touch.

The information provided by the wireless access point scanner seen in Figure 12.22 includes additional data, such as the access point's MAC address, the channel it is broadcasting on, the station name, and encryption method used when connected. This particular application also allows us to modify the sensitivity of the signal strength, so we can narrow our search down to just those access points with the strongest signal. By understanding the capabilities of the wireless devices and signal coverage within a facility, we can better identify locations to place our concealment device.

Example Hiding Locations

Once we understand the wireless radio coverage within a facility and understand our device's power needs, we can decide where to locate our covert attack platform. Unless we somehow are able to access the entire facility without any hindrance, we will most likely be restricted to placing our device in a publically accessible location.

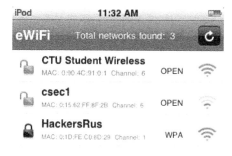

FIGURE 12.22   Wireless Access Point Information.

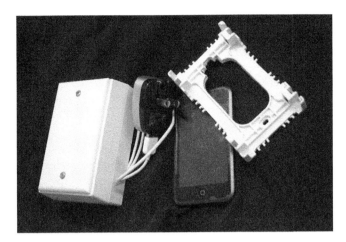

FIGURE 12.23 Concealment Device for iPod Touch.

As a result, our placement options may be limited, especially if we need to use a wall power outlet to keep our mobile device charged.

Some logical places where we might place our device would be behind coffee machines, behind computers (where we can use either an open USB port in the back of the system or an open power socket), near televisions, behind vending machines, or anything else in the facility that will be able to hide the device. The disadvantage with concealing the mobile device in this manner is that we may draw attention messing around behind stuff. What if we brought our own concealment with us, instead of relying on others to provide it for us – that would certainly be more ninja-like?

Figure 12.23 is a photo of tools we can use to conceal our mobile device in plain sight – however, this is only one example. The items within the picture include an iPod touch, a low-profile power cable that attaches to a wall socket and a wall cover box (available at any hardware store).

As we can see, the back piece (located in the upper right corner of the photo) has a hole in the back, which will allow us to place the device over an open wall socket and still have access to power. When completely assembled and placed over a wall outlet, we have something that appears to be an unusable wall outlet, as seen in Figure 12.24. Another advantage to using this particular type of case is that because we are using plastic to conceal the device, we do not interfere with any nearby wireless signals.

In this configuration, a mobile device is much easier to place and extract within a victim's facility and provides us with all the necessary requirements – concealment, power, and reception.

Other Methods of Data Concealment

Another way to extract data from a facility is by smuggling it out on memory cards that have been removed from a mobile device. This accomplishes two things: first, if our mobile device is searched for evidence of espionage, it would not be discovered; secondly, the memory card data can be encrypted in case of discovery. However,

FIGURE 12.24   Concealment Device with Enclosed iPod Touch.

as Zukin, we need to take extra precautions to prevent detection in the first place. Figure 12.25 is an example of how we can hide data within a concealment device that appears as an everyday item.

In Figure 12.25, we see that we can conceal a miniSD card within a hollow nickel. The miniSD used in this photo can retain 2 GB worth of data; this data can be in the form of photos of the victim's facility, photos of documents, or data extracted from the victim's systems and network. Once removed from the mobile device and concealed within the hollow coin, the chances of discovery of our activities within the facility are largely negated.

2D Barcode

Although not practical – but a great example of how to think like a Zukin – is to use 2D barcodes to store data. Applications exist on many of the more powerful mobile devices that allow us to create 2D barcodes, saved as images; these applications allow us to place a very finite amount of data within the barcode. An example of a 2D barcode that contains data can be seen in Figure 12.26.

FIGURE 12.25   MiniSD Chip Concealed in Hollow Coin.

FIGURE 12.26   2D Barcode (QR Code) Containing Text Message.

The amount of text capable of being included in a QR Code barcode is limited – less than 3 K of binary data, but is an example of alternative methods of concealing data through the use of everyday items.

Summary

Although we talked about the use of disguises in Chapter 5, "Disguise," we did not discuss the use of personal items that add to the disguise, yet still allow us to perform our hacking objectives. It would be unusual to see a member of the clergy carrying around a whole bunch of hacker gear, so we must modify everyday items in such a way that will allow us to perform our duties as Zukin without jeopardizing our disguise. The use of concealment devices to collect and extract data from a facility in a manner similar to what has been described in this chapter would certainly afford us the opportunity to surreptitiously attack and exploit target systems while reducing the chances of being detected or discouraged from collecting data from our target.

Mobile devices will certainly be advancing in capability as new technology is developed and component costs are reduced, making PDAs and phones a serious threat to organizations; since it is improbable for most companies to create and enforce a security policy that outright bans cell phones within their facility (government facilities are the most obvious exception), it is a relatively easy task to insert into a facility a mobile device that has been loaded with hacker tools. And once brought into a facility, the mobile device can be placed without arousing suspicion, if done correctly; even if discovered, it is possible that the mobile hacking device will be turned over to the facility's security and deposited in the lost and found box, which would still allow us to retrieve the device and any captured traffic or data.

In situations where extraction of data is more complicated than simply walking out the door with it loaded on a mobile device, there are ways to conceal the information, again using common objects that can be modified to conceal items. Although this chapter has provided a couple ideas on how to conceal devices and items, it is incumbent on the Zukin to devise other ways of creating attack platforms in such a way to reduce suspicion through the use of everyday items, similar to the way ancient ninja modified common items into concealment devices or weapons.

Endnotes

1. Hatsumi M. Ninjutsu: history and tradition. Burbank: Unique Publications; 1981. 0865680272.
2. Kernel Architecture Overview. Retrieved from Mac OS X Reference Library: http://developer.apple.com/mac/library/documentation/Darwin/Conceptual/KernelProgramming/Architecture/Architecture.html#//apple_ref/doc/uid/TP30000905-CH1g-TPXREF101; 2006 [accessed 01.07.10].

Covert Listening Devices

Having the ability to eavesdrop on what are assumed to be private conversations and communications is very useful to the Zukin. Since radio is used as a communications media in so many ways, this leaves us with a very target-rich environment to carry out such attacks. We can listen in on Bluetooth, cell phone conversations, wireless data networks, and a variety of other communications, often entirely undetected.

RADIO FREQUENCY SCANNERS

An enormous number of devices today use radio as a transmission media. We can see it used in cell phones, wireless computer networks, various portable devices, broadband Internet access, and a number of other places. The use of radio is so ubiquitous that many users do not even recognize that it is being used, and they just use these devices as the appliances that the manufacturers intend them to be.

WARNING

Eavesdropping on communications, including wireless and cell traffic, is generally considered to be wiretapping and usually falls under these same laws in the area where it is performed. In other words, this is commonly considered to be illegal and may land anyone caught doing so in serious hot water, including heavy fines and jail time.

For purposes of the Zukin, this is a very good thing. Radio, as a transmission media, is inherently insecure. It is a broadcast, in many cases, far outside of the area in which it is immediately used, and this range can greatly be increased with the appropriate receiving equipment. This can allow us to sit at great distances, potentially miles away, under the right conditions, and eavesdrop on this signal.

While many of these devices have some sort of security in place, it is often a best effort attempt or is seriously flawed. A great many people are interested in attacking the security of such devices, many of them doing so as a hobby. This gives us a large body of work to fall back on and a fairly well-polished set of tools to use.

Ninja Hacking. DOI: 10.1016/B978-1-59749-588-2.00013-5

Bluetooth

Bluetooth headsets are, conveniently for the Zukin, often fairly trivial to eavesdrop on. Such devices often have few or no security features and provide us a good way to bug portable devices without actually having to alter them in any fashion. In many cases, our targets will prefer to carry out conversations on cell phones, believing them to be more secure than using an office or home phone. In the case of headset users, this is often the reverse of the truth.

Bluetooth headsets use a four digit code for security purposes, specifically to prevent the type of eavesdropping or hijacking that we are discussing. Interestingly, on most devices, the pin cannot be changed by the user and is set to 0000. This is the standard among multiple manufacturers of Bluetooth headsets. Since the manufacturer has done us the favor of nullifying their own security, we can, with the proper equipment and software, connect to the headset from a laptop or other Bluetooth-equipped device.

Once connected to the device, we will be able to access it and use the functionality of it in the same ways that a mobile device is allowed it.[1] Of primary interest, we can eavesdrop on the headset, allowing us to hear any conversations taking place. Additionally, we can send audio to it, allowing us to disrupt conversations taking place or distract the user.

While standard Bluetooth equipment is short range, with the appropriate antenna, we can increase the range. For a good discussion on using Yagi rifles, as shown in Figure 13.1, for this purpose, see *Dissecting the Hack: The F0rb1dd3n*

FIGURE 13.1 A Yagi Rifle.

Network, Revised Edition(ISBN: 978-1-59749-568-4), available from Syngress. In deal conditions, we can connect to devices that are over a mile away. This could potentially allow us to eavesdrop on multiple targets in an office, restaurant, or other crowded location.

Cellular

One particularly useful capability for the Zukin is to be able to eavesdrop directly on cell phone conversations. While we discussed how to do this above by accessing devices such as Bluetooth headsets, we cannot always depend on such a device being present, and it may not be used for every conversation. Fortunately, there are a few flaws in the security mechanisms that are in place for common cell phones.

The Global System for Mobile Communications (GSM) is the most commonly used cell phone system today. According to the GSM Alliance, there were nearly 3.5 billion GSM phones in use across the globe in the second quarter of 2009.[2] Fortunately for us, the security measures used in GSM phones are in the area of 20 years old and are very insecure. This leaves us with two main methods that we can use to eavesdrop on such devices.

Intercepting such transmissions can be easily done with the proper equipment. We can effectively set up our own small cellular network and allow phones to connect to it. All that needs to be done is to ensure that our network is used preferentially over any legitimate networks in the area to broadcast a stronger signal.[3] This is a trivially easy attack and is used regularly by a variety of law enforcement agencies for exactly the purpose of this type of eavesdropping. While the equipment for this is a bit expensive, it is available commercially.

As an alternative to intercepting calls, we can attempt to crack the encryption used on GSM networks, known as A5/1. This type of attack is considerably more difficult to carry out than interception, requiring more complex RF equipment and quite a bit of precomputation for cracking. While such attacks are certainly possible, they represent the more difficult route to take.

802.11 Wireless

802.11 wireless networks are those commonly used for consumer and commercial wireless data networks and have been around since the late 1990s, and a large amount of legacy equipment is still in use. While the newer revisions of the 802.11 standard, 802.11g and 802.11n, are capable of utilizing fairly strong security, much of the old equipment still in use is not. The deciding factor in whether an 802.11 network is secure is the type of encryption in use.

For the original revisions of 802.11g devices and the revisions proviso to them, we will likely find WEP or WPA encryption being used. These types of encryption had inherent weaknesses, particularly WEP, and are crackable without a large amount of effort. Most newer 802.11g and 802.11n devices are capable of running WPA2, which, although more difficult to crack, can be broken using cowpatty or aircrack-ng.

> **TIP**
>
> For those of you who are interested in learning more on hacking wireless networks, Syngress has a few books out on the topic, including *Kismet Hacking*[A] and *WarDriving and Wireless Penetration Testing*.[B] These will give you a good start down the path.

With the proper equipment and tools, such as aircrack-ng,[4] we stand a fair chance of being able to penetrate many of the 802.11 wireless networks that are in use.

KEY LOGGING

Key logging, also referred to as keystroke logging, provides the Zukin with a very clean method of collecting information, particularly credentials, presuming that we can get the logger in place without being discovered and that we have a way to collect the information.

Key loggers can collect a variety of information, from just the keystroke being typed on a keyboard, all the way to a full video capture of the screen, all keystrokes, and all clicks of a pointing device. If we are overly concerned with the size of the data being captured, or have a small window of time during which to retrieve the logs, we can stay with a simple log of keystrokes, as this will often provide us with the data that we need.

Software Key Loggers

Software key loggers are a bit of a self-defining tool. They are often installed on the target machine covertly and generally operate in such a way as to not be visible to anyone operating said machine. They usually will not display a window or icon to indicate their presence, and will often take steps to hide the process from which they are running, or disguise it under a name that appears to be a normal component of the operating system.

Software key loggers are generally considered malware, and common or commercial tools may be detected by antimalware tools. We will discuss this issue further on in this chapter in the section on spyware.

Hardware Key Loggers

Hardware key loggers are small devices, generally a bit smaller than a pack of chewing gum, that contain a small bundle of electronics and a storage device. Hardware

---

[A]ISBN: 978-1-59749-117-4, Syngress. Available for purchase at www.syngress.com/hacking-and-penetration-testing/Kismet-Hacking.

[B]ISBN: 978-1-59749-111-2, Syngress. Available for purchase at www.syngress.com/hacking-and-penetration-testing/WarDriving-and-Wireless-Penetration-Testing.

key loggers generally have a PS2 or USB interface that can be used both to collect data from the target machine and to read data from the storage area on the device.

The USB variety can plug into any available USB port on the machine, but must still be between the USB keyboard connector and a USB port, while the PS2 version specifically needs to be plugged in between a PS2 keyboard and the PS2 keyboard port on the machine. Additionally some hardware key loggers have wireless capability to allow the data to be read from the storage area remotely.

Such devices are relatively simple in construction, although the price that they command is not reflected in the complexity of components. At the time of this writing, such devices in the United States were generally above $100. For those of us who have a steady hand at the soldering iron, plans are available on the Internet to build a PS2 key logger,[5] the construction of which is not beyond the ken of mortal man.

Placing Key Loggers

Depending on the environment, getting a key logger in place can be challenging. If we are using a software key logger, we will need to worry about having sufficient access to the target machine, either directly at the console or from remote, and we will need to bypass or avoid any monitoring mechanisms that might be in place. For hardware-based devices, we will need to directly access the machine and be able to plug the device in, which could possibly be detected visually or could interrupt the functioning of the machine. In either case, this is a task to be approached with caution.

Placing Hardware Key Loggers

Putting hardware key loggers in place is simplicity itself, but we do stand a fair chance of being detected in the process, due to having to plug and unplug cables from the machine. Preferably, we would do this at a time when the area surrounding the target machine was unoccupied and unmonitored.

For a USB key logger, we only need to plug it into an available USB port, preferably one on the back of the machine where it is not noticeable, and then plug the USB keyboard into the device. Inserting USB devices will often cause the operating system to sound an audible alert that a new device has been picked up, so we should be aware that this might happen.

SHINOBI-IRI (Stealth and Entering Methods)

When using a PS2 hardware key logger, depending on the computer and keyboard in use at the target, we may disrupt the system's connection with the keyboard by unplugging and plugging it back in with the power on. It is entirely possible that, having done so, the keyboard will not work properly until the system has been rebooted. This may be an issue in an environment where rebooting the target system will draw attention. In this case, we should use a USB key logger instead.

When using a PS2 key logger, we will need to unplug they keyboard, plug the keyboard into one end of the key logger, and then plug the key logger into the PS2 port when the keyboard was plugged in. The key logger is quite obvious when looking at the back of the machine, and it is very unlikely that any legitimate device exists in the environment that would be plugged in like this.

Placing Software Key Loggers

Getting software key loggers in place is generally the same as introducing any type of malware in a system. We will generally need to use similar delivery mechanisms, such as an infected e-mail attachment, or trojaned software. The difference being that we are likely to be targeting an individual or a small group and will need to closely police our infection mechanism to restrict it to our desired targets.

As we have discussed previously when covering the use of Trojans in Chapter 10, "Psychological Weaknesses," we need to take great care in testing malware when we intend to use it in our target environment. In this case, we will need to locate the manufacturer and version of any antimalware tools that are in use in the environment and obtain copies of these tools to test against. If we use a custom or heavily modified key logger, we stand a very good chance of being able to slip it past any monitoring tools, particularly if we are able to test against them first.

Retrieving the Data

Depending on the type of key logger that we have used, the ease of retrieving the information can vary greatly. When pulling data from a software key logger, we will need to be concerned with devices in the environment that might detect our transmission of data, and when dealing with hardware key loggers, we will need to be more concerned with being physically caught. Particularly, when retrieving data from a hardware key logger, we should have a cover story already prepared.

Retrieving Data from Software Key Loggers

In order to retrieve the data from a software key logger, either we will need to collect it from the store directly on the machine or we will need to send it over the network. Collecting the data from the machine will require either accessing it at the actual console of the device or connecting to it from remote. Both of these are somewhat risky tasks and come with a strong possibility of being detected in the process and leaving evidence in logs files on the machine. If this is necessary, we will need to plan not only to collect the information but also to clean up any traces that we have left. Manipulating log files is discussed in Chapter 16, "Sabotage."

If we send the data over the network, although we stand much less of a chance of being physically caught or having our activities logged on the host, we will need to contend with intrusion detection systems on the network, proxies, firewalls, and other similar systems. In this case, our best option is to use a common protocol, such as HTTP, to send out data so that it is not only disguised, but part of a large flow of data that happens regularly.

Additionally, if we plan to automatically send data out at daily or other intervals, we need to make sure that our transmissions are sufficiently irregular so as not to be picked up by devices or software that are monitoring for "phone home" traffic that is used by botnets and other malware to connect to their command and control systems. This can be achieved by varying the interval at which we send the data and by varying the place that we send the data to. If we send our payload out every hour, on the hour, to the same location, we are very likely to be detected.

Retrieving Data from Hardware Key Loggers

The task of retrieving collected information from a hardware key logger can be a bit tricky, depending on the equipment used. If we have used a standard PS2 or USB key logger, we will either need to physically remove the device and attach it to another computer to read it or need to read it on the machine to which it is attached, either option having its disadvantages.

If we remove the device and take it elsewhere to read it, then we will need to access the target machine only briefly, but we will need to reinstall it later, thus increasing our chances of being detected. Likewise, if we read the data directly from the target machine, we can leave the key logger in place, but we will need to sit at the console of the machine long enough to collect the data from it.

SHINOBI-IRI (Stealth and Entering Methods)

When attempting to physically recover data from a hardware key logger or recover the key logger itself, we may be able to provide cover for our activities by using social engineering (see Chapter 10, "Psychological Weaknesses") to adopt a role as a member of the local IT staff. Most nontechnically oriented people will quickly become interested in other things or suddenly discover that they have an appointment to run to when presented with a detailed technical discussion on what might be wrong with their computer.

When using a hardware key logger equipped with wireless capability, we need not concern ourselves with physically accessing the key logger itself or the target machine to retrieve the data, but we will then need to worry about the radio frequency (RF) environment in which the device is being used. Most wireless key loggers use a relatively low-powered and low-range radio, of either a proprietary design or Bluetooth.

In either case, we will need to be fairly close to the device in the best of conditions, generally well under 100 yards. Unfortunately, office settings are not often the best environments for propagating RF signals. We will likely be transmitting in the vicinity of large masses of metal, concrete, plumbing, wiring, file cabinets, and many other RF unfriendly objects. This will likely significantly reduce our range. If at all possible, we should test such devices in an area similar to our target environment before using them against the actual target.

We must also consider the connection type of the hardware key logger that we are using. As mentioned above, while removing or inserting a USB device, we should see no issue, but this may not be the case with a PS2 device.

Not Getting Caught

Placing a software key logger is a relatively low-risk activity, at least from the standpoint of being physically caught. We can generally install such software using the same mechanisms that are common to malware and have been honed over time. In this case, being caught generally means having our delivery mechanism detected. Although our install attempt will likely have failed at this point, it will be disguised in the crowd of malware infections that happen with a regular basis at most companies and will generally not be recognized as having been a targeted attack.

We must also be careful that our retrieval mechanism does not make sufficient noise on the network so as to draw attention to itself and that any protocols that we use are capable of disguising our data transfer. This should be a relatively easy task if we are only moving a text log of keystrokes, as the amount of data being transported is very small. In locations where a very high level of security or network monitoring is in place, we can even break up our transmissions into very small chunks and send them through Web forms, ICMP, or other difficult to detect methods.

While being directly identified as an individual when installing or retrieving data from a software keystroke logger is very unlikely, the possibility of being detected while doing so with a hardware keystroke logger is fairly significant. When removing or installing such a device, we will need to spend at least a short period of time bent over the back of the target computer, a pose that immediately signifies to passers by that someone is "messing with" the target machine.

Additionally, anyone looking at the back of the machine or the contents of our hands will notice the odd little device that does not look like it should be there. Anyone even remotely familiar with information security will immediately be able to identify the device as a keystroke logger, at which point, we have a problem. We can mitigate this issue by using devices that are not immediately identifiable as being a key logger.

For key logging devices that are USB based, we can build them into, or disguise them as, a wide variety of devices, keyboards, mice, USB hubs, and so on. Such devices will attract considerably less notice if we are detected and will provide us with a prop, if needed, for a bit of social engineering to get us out of a sticky situation.

We can also, without the use of specially disguised devices, make our key logger installation somewhat less obvious. If we look at the back of a machine and see a foreign device in a USB port or in between our PS2 keyboard and its port, this will likely stick out to us as being out of place. If we place our key logger on the end of a USB or PS2 extension cable and tuck it out of site, then it will be considerable less noticeable to the casual viewer. Many computers have a nest of cables behind them, and few people will bother to chase them all down unless they are troubleshooting an issue.

SPYWARE

Spyware, generally considered a subset of malware, is simply software that collects information or makes changes on a machine without the knowledge or consent of the machine's owner. While we discussed software key loggers earlier in this chapter, which are often considered a form of spyware, there are many other ways that spyware can be used, most of which revolve around the clandestine collection of information.

Stealing Personal Information

When we consider the information that is stored on machines today, we could hardly hand pick a better point from which the Zukin can spy on an individual. We can often see financial records, credit card and bank account information, credentials, chat logs and e-mail, address lists, phone records, and a plethora of other items. We can often easily collect enough information from the average computer to impersonate an individual, in either personal or professional capacity. At the very least, we will provide ourselves with a rich mine of material on which to hang attacks, social engineering based or otherwise.

Stealing Credentials

Out of all of the personal information that we might have access to when using spyware on a machine, credentials for the user or users will be the most commonly found and the most useful. Such credentials can allow us access to other systems, e-mail accounts, financial institutions, credit information, and much more.

When looking for credentials, we can check stored passwords in applications, cookies from browsers, outgoing network traffic that passes credentials in plaintext, and many other places. Particularly, when dealing with high-security environments that have painful rules regarding password complexity and password reuse, we may very well find a stash of passwords on the system recorded in a text file so that the user is able to function in the environment. In this case, draconian password policies can often work to our distinct advantage.

Working to our advantage when playing the role of attacker is the very poor password hygiene practiced by almost everyone who does not work in the information security field or is not otherwise forced to be more security focused than the average user. We will often find that obtaining one set of credentials for an individual will give us access to most or all the other accounts that they hold, business, personal, or otherwise. When we find a user who uses the same accounts for business and personal logins, we may be able to collect information on their personal activities, some of which may be very useful when planning distractions, social engineering attacks, or blackmail.

Modifying Configurations

When we have managed to get our spyware tools installed on a machine, we can also use them to potentially modify the configuration settings of the various applications installed, or even the operating system itself. We can then use these subverted areas of the user's computer to carry out other attacks, collect other information, or feed misinformation to the user.

One of the most useful areas in which we can take finer control of the target machine is the browser. We can redirect some or all Web page requests that the user enters, we can install tools to the browser to collect further information or to install other items of software or malware, or we can simply disrupt the user's browsing capability. Such change can be made within the browser itself or may be made by modifying other files or settings in the operating system, a common target being the name resolution that depends on entries in the hosts file.

Installing Spyware

Just as our discussion on installing software key loggers earlier in this chapter, installing spyware is much the same as installing any type of malware. We must be careful to avoid any detection mechanisms that might be present or any activities that might unexpectedly prompt the user for permission. We must also be aware of the operating system and applications that the user is running, as well as the browser vendor and revision, if we are using browser-oriented spyware.

Operating Systems and Browsers

When looking to install spyware on a machine, one of the most important items that we can discover before carrying out our attack is the operating system being used. Most spyware attacks are very specific to Windows operating systems and will generally fail if the target is actually running something else, such as Linux or OS X. These operating systems, in most cases, use entirely different compiled binaries and have much more granular access control systems, and this will cause us problems when attempting to introduce spyware.

Windows UAC

On more recent versions of Windows operating systems, Vista and newer, we will likely encounter the Windows user account control (UAC) mechanism.[6] UAC will prompt the user, to the irritation of many, whenever an application makes request to do something that would require administrative privileges. Activities that may set off a UAC alter message include the following:

- Installing or removing applications
- Installing device drivers
- Installing updates
- Configuring remote access
- Installing ActiveX controls

Many other similar tasks will set off such an alert as well. Although UAC prompts have been toned down a bit in newer Microsoft operating systems, such as Windows 7, the capability remains in place.

In order to ensure that UAC alerts to the user do not become an issue, we can take three primary approaches: we can stay below the clipping level for UAC, we can disable UAC, or we can disguise our activities as something else. Each method will have its advantages and disadvantages, but we will need to develop workarounds when targeting these operating systems.

In order to stay below the UAC clipping level, we really cannot perform any of the tasks that will set off a UAC alert. This will severely cripple our efforts and will restrict us to the most basic of attacks. On the plus side, if we can manage to carry out an attack in such restricted circumstances, it will be very light weight and will not leave much evidence behind.

NOTE

Although we may find security measures such as the UAC in most any Microsoft operating system newer than Vista, they do not all work in exactly the same way. Some methods will work on Vista, but not on Windows 7, and so forth. This is definitely something that bears testing on the same operating system and version as the target before we try to use it.

Disabling the UAC can be done by a variety of methods, but the most simple is to use the command line, as shown in Figure 13.2. While this does need to be done from a command prompt run as administrator, it is a very quick and simple method.

The main issue that we need to work around using this method is the prompt that we will get when attempting to open a command prompt with administrator permissions, as shown in Figure 13.3. In order to work around this, we can either social engineer the user into clicking **Yes** by disguising the prompt as part of a software update or depend on the reflex of the user to automatically click **Yes** on any prompts that appear, although this may be a somewhat less reliable method.

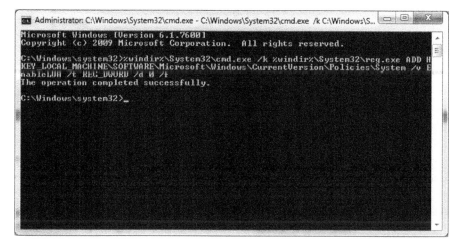

FIGURE 13.2 Disabling UAC via Command Line.

FIGURE 13.3 Dialog Presented When Opening a Command Prompt as Administrator.

Once we have disabled the UAC, we have relatively free reign on the computer without alerting the user. We can change policies, disable the privilege escalation prompt, or any of a number of other changes to help hide our activities and clean up any trails that we have left behind.

Using Spyware Quietly

When using spyware tools or even malware in general, we must take care to do so in a manner that will not alert the users of the system, administrators, network engineers, or anyone else in the environment that something might be out of place. This is a typical failing of malware and is often what leads to it being noticed and quickly eradicated. Typical implementations of spyware are often visible to the user in some fashion, often due to pop-ups, banners in applications, additional toolbars, or unusual activity on the machine. This is all quite contrary to the methods of the Zukin and is generally not useful to us.

When developing such tools for our own use, we should strive to conserve system resources whenever possible and not act in such a fashion as to attract the attention of antimalware tools or intrusion detection systems. It is usually the uncontrolled propagation from one target to another that causes activity or resource drains that are noticeable to the user, and we will generally not have a reason to be doing anything along those lines, unless doing it deliberately for a distraction or as a denial-of-service attack.

Managing System Resources

When we have infected a machine with spyware, we must be careful to conserve system resources. When we look at resource usage, the three most likely areas that will impact performance enough to be noticeable to the user are the CPU usage, memory usage, and network utilization. Since we will most likely be using such tools on a very small scale, we can monitor these areas through the tools present in most operating systems, such as the Resource Monitor in Windows, as shown in Figure 13.4.

If we may have remote access to the machine, we can pull resource reports programmatically and send system summaries along with our data payloads, in order to ensure that we are not taxing the machine to the point that users will begin to notice.

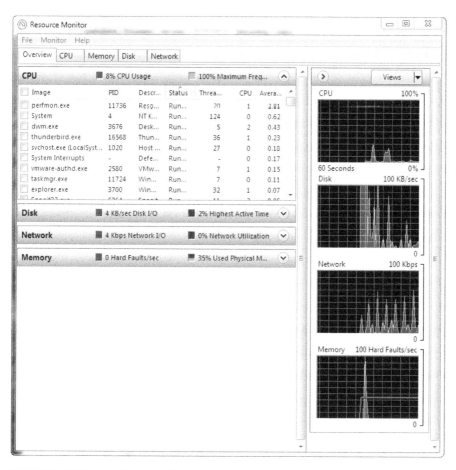

FIGURE 13.4 Windows Resource Monitor.

Antimalware Tools

If we have carried out our spyware development and insertion properly, we should have little to fear from antimalware tools. Such tools are largely signature based, and these signatures are collected from samples of the malware collected in the wild. Since we would be developing a much more specialized version of our spyware tool, likely to be custom in its entirely, we should not be showing up in these sorts of signature databases.

The other way that we might be detected is through carrying out activities that are outside of the baseline for normal system activities. These might include such things as overwriting system files, writing to the master boot record of the hard disks in the system, and so on. Again, these are very typical malware type tasks, and even if we do have a reason to do them, we should really find an alternative as they might cause our spyware to be detected.

Intrusion Detection Systems

One of the other systems that might detect the activity of our spyware is the intrusion detection system. In the case of using spyware tools, we need to be careful of alerting both network-based instruction detection systems and host-based intrusion detection systems. In both cases, the intrusion detection systems will be looking for activity that does not match what is normal on the system or network and possibly for signatures of known malware as well.

In order to successfully avoid host-based intrusion detection systems, we will generally want to leave the system alone as much as is possible once we get the spyware installed. Earlier, we discussed shutting down UAC, potentially changing polices, and other activities that would aid us in getting our spyware onto the machine. In the case of a host-based intrusion detection system, we may need to take additional steps before taking such measures, as the system might catch this type of activity. This depends greatly on exactly what software is being used, and this is something that we would want to research carefully before attempting to compromise the machine. In most any corporate environment, such tools will be part of a standard build for systems, and we may be able to use such standardization to our advantage.

CLANDESTINELY PLACED SENSORS

We can place a variety of sensors in an environment to carry out covert monitoring. We can use audio and video bugs, we can access existing cameras, or we can snoop on the electromagnetic emissions from monitors, keyboards, and a wide variety of other devices. Where possible, it behooves us to use methods that do not involve leaving devices in place at our target location, as these could potentially be discovered and would alert our target to the fact that they were being monitored.

Audio

When eavesdropping on audio only, we can use a relatively simplistic set of equipment to accomplish our goals. While we can use specific audio bugging devices, there are several other methods that we can use that will provide a more stealthy approach. Given the availability of VoIP lines that we can listen in on and microphone-equipped computers scattered everywhere, we should use such devices as a last resort.

Eavesdropping on VoIP

Depending on how exactly VoIP is implemented at a given location, the level of eavesdropping on it can go from trivial to very difficult. In many VoIP implementations, the traffic is routed through a virtual LAN (VLAN) of its own, and this is considered to be a sufficient level of security. In such cases, if we have access to a VoIP phone, we can collect sufficient information from the phone to discover where on the network the VoIP traffic is being routed and connect ourselves to the appropriate VLAN. Having done this, it is relatively trivial to sniff VoIP conversations.[7]

Computer Microphones

Computer microphones can provide another easy audio source that the Zukin can access. Various malware exist that are capable of accessing a microphone, but we have a much easier solution available to use. Many computers today have software installed to utilize the Flash product from Adobe, as it is a large component on many commercial Web sites, and flash is capable of listening to the input from a micro phone. Normally, a user is prompted to authorize such access when it is attempted, but flash can be configured in such as way as to always grant permission when asked.

Audio Bugs

When looking at purpose-built audio bugging devices, a wide variety of them exist for our usage. We can find many such devices for sale on the Internet or in specialty shops, but as we discussed above, we will often be better off subverting devices with audio capabilities that are already in the environment. One of the main issues in using actual audio bugs is the evidence that we will be forced to leave behind. In high-security areas, we may also be faced with security tool that are designed to foil or detect such devices. In the case of audio eavesdropping, we have an excellent alternative that not only removed the requirement for us to place a device but also precludes us having to enter the location on which we would like to eavesdrop.

Laser listening devices work by bouncing a laser beam off of a surface, usually a pane of glass, then reading the reflected beam with a sensor and translating the fluctuations in the beam back into sound. The fluctuations in the beam are caused by vibrations in the surface that the beam strikes, and the vibrations are usually being caused by sounds in the immediate area of the surface. Such devices can easily be used to pick up conversations from a distance. While commercial units are available to perform this task, crude but effective versions of such tools can be made with just a few very low-cost components.[8]

Video

Video devices can be invaluable when surveilling an environment. While audio only device can be useful, they will only give us a partial idea of what is actually taking place. Additionally, video devices often possess an audio component as well, thus giving us a complete monitoring package. When conducting video surveillance, we can use purpose-built video bugs, or we can use video devices that are already in place. The use of existing equipment is preferable, but may not always be available to us.

Video Bugs

A wide variety of equipment exists for the covert monitoring of an area. We can find cameras that are very tiny and that are built into a variety of devices such as smoke detectors, coat buttons, teddy bears, almost anything that we can think of. Such equipment is readily available in various specialty shops and is available from a multitude of sources over the Internet.

While using devices specifically designed for use in concealment is an easy route to take, it does have the strong disadvantage of leaving behind indisputable evidence of covert monitoring. When such a device is discovered, whether by accident or through the use of detection equipment, there is no doubt as to its nature and purpose. Wherever possible, we should attempt to use equipment that is already in place in the environment, as this suits our goal of stealth to a much better degree.

Covertly Using Existing Cameras

In some cases, existing camera systems can be accessed and used to view the areas in which they are installed. Many residences have video baby monitors, webcams, IP cameras, and other such device that are either poorly secured against eavesdropping or not secured at all. These devices work greatly to the advantage of the Zukin, as they require very little effort on our part to access and do not require us to enter the premises to install, potentially leaving noticeable evidence of our presence.

Video baby monitors have become very common in the last few years. Such devices often have a very limited facility for changing the operating frequency, and some have no such option at all. This allows us to monitor only a small range of frequencies and pick up a large number of such devices. If our targets have small children, this is an avenue of video and audio monitoring that we should not ignore.

Webcams are so common now as to have become almost ubiquitous. We can not only see freestanding devices on desks in both homes and businesses but also see them build into many of the laptops that are produced today. Software exists that will allow these devices to be remotely activated, with no permission to do so being required from the user of the device. In 2010, a scandal involving the covert use of webcams built into laptops, in order to monitor the home activities of high school children, took place in Philadelphia.[9] Legal action was still pending at the time of this writing.

Unsecured IP cameras can provide the Zukin with another excellent avenue for easy video monitoring. Such cameras are generally directly connected to a network and run an internal Web server to display the image from the camera, as well as controlling the focus, pan and tilt, and other such features. Families of camera models from the same manufacturer often have the same or similar wording in the titles, or on the pages of their user interfaces, and can be found by inputting those strings into search engines.

WARNING

When accessing an IP camera where we have permission to change the settings, or to alter the pan or title of the camera, we need to be very careful when doing so. If we disrupt the camera image sufficiently and leave it in that state, we may well alert the owner of the device that someone else has been using it. If it is absolutely necessary to change the camera settings, we should return them to the way that we found them on the way out. As with any other operation, the Zukin should strive to leave no evidence of their passing.

FIGURE 13.5 An Unsecured IP Camera.

When we find an open IP camera, we may only be able to view the available images, as was the case with the camera image in Figure 13.5 from one of the author's cameras, or we may have sufficient control to alter the camera settings.

Although we have no guarantee of a camera being present, or being accessible if it is, these do provide us with a great resource when we can get them.

We may also be able to access similar features in commercial surveillance systems. Such systems are often configured to feed to a central server which displays the camera output to a client system. While we can expect such systems to be more secure than off-the-shelf consumer camera systems, if we can gain access to the target network, we may be able to compromise them. This can not only give us the potential to access the entire surveillance system of the target, but the possibility also exists that we can utilize such control over the monitoring system to our advantage in other ways.

Other Electromagnetic Radiation

The electromagnetic spectrum comprises radiation such as radio, microwaves, visible light, and x-rays, just to name a few. In short, most all modern methods of communication fall within this spectrum. Where we become concerned with electromagnetic radiation from a monitoring perspective is in the information that can be picked up from monitoring such emissions. While we have discussed radio frequency scanning earlier in this chapter, and have discussed audio and video surveillance devices, there are other less commonly known areas in which we can listen to similar signals.

Van Eck Phreaking

In 1985, a Dutch computer researcher named Wim van Eck published a paper titled *Electromagnetic Radiation from Video Display Units: An Eavesdropping Risk?*.[10] Van Eck's paper discussed the possibility of monitoring the radio interference produced by monitors and CRT screens at the time, and using this interference to reproduce what was being shown on the target screen. Van Eck was able to prove that this was possible and was able to carry out a successful test of his theories.

Similar work done by Markus Kuhn in 2004[11] was able to show that LCD screens, now much more common than CRTs, are vulnerable to the same sort of eavesdropping. Kuhn was able to construct a low-cost device to read the LCD display from a laptop using a very similar process to that originally described by van Eck.

Monitoring using these methods is a bit more complex than just placing an audio or video bug and may require some electrical engineering or programming skills. While not trivial to carry out, this type of monitoring is not exceedingly difficult for the Zukin with the technical know-how and sufficient resources to gather the needed equipment.

Keyboard Emissions

In 2009 two students, Martin Vuagnoux and Sylvain Pasini, from the Ecole Polytechnique Fédérale de Lausanne in Switzerland presented a paper[12] on eavesdropping on the emissions from both wired and wireless keyboards. Vuagnoux and Pasini composed four different methods, including one based on Kuhn's method for LCD monitors discussed above, for recovering the characters typed on the keyboard and were able to successfully use at least one of the attacks on all the keyboards tested.

Such attacks require a minimal amount of equipment and a software decoding tool and are able to function from some distance away, even through intervening walls and infrastructure. Not only can multiple keyboards be detected, but variations in each cause the emissions to be sufficiently distinct as to be able to tell them apart. While this method may not be quite as visually fulfilling as being able to read the contents of a monitor from remote, it is considerably easier to carry out and can be done with fewer resources.

Blinky Lights

To get even further off into the electromagnetic spectrum, we can also eavesdrop on visible light emissions from some devices equipped with LED indicator lights. While this does not work on all devices, where it has been found to work, the flickering of the LED light as the device operates has been found to carry usable information. This has been shown to work in modems, network infrastructure equipment, PBXs, and other similar equipment. Eavesdropping on such emissions is discussed at length in the paper *Information Leakage from Optical Emanations*.[13]

One of the interesting aspects to this sort of eavesdropping is that it is able to work from a distance and can potentially work from reflected light. In this case, we would potentially sniff traffic from outside of a building by picking up the reflected LED light from an outside window. Other than blocking the light from reaching the outside, or covering the LED, this would be a difficult attack to prevent.

Summary

In this chapter, we discussed a variety of cover listening devices that might be available to the Zukin. Although a range of eavesdropping tools are available, we should gravitate toward passive methods of eavesdropping. Such methods can enable to avoid entering the locations that we wish to monitor and that will not require us to leave devices in place that might later be discovered.

We discussed the use of radio frequency scanners for monitoring several methods of communication. We can use such devices to monitor Bluetooth, cellular and data networks, and other radio sources as well. Although specialized equipment is required for listening to some forms of radio communication, others are accessible with low-cost devices off the shelf or equipment that we can cobble together ourselves.

We discussed the use of key loggers, in both hardware and software forms. Such devices can be used to record everything from keystrokes to complete video of the user's desktop for our later perusal. We also discussed some of the issues in using key loggers, such as placement, retrieving data, and taking steps to not be discovered.

In addition to key loggers, we also discussed the superset of spyware in general. We can use spyware to collect a variety of personal information, credentials, contacts, and a number of other such informational items. Here, we also discussed some of the issues in avoiding intrusion detection systems and antimalware tools when installing and using spyware.

Lastly, we covered clandestinely placed sensors, including video and audio bugs. When using audio and video eavesdropping methods, we are often better in using devices that are already in place in the environment, such as IP cameras or computer microphones, than we are to place a new device. Additionally, we have other methods of listening on communications such as van Eck phreaking, listening to keyboard emissions, and watching fluctuations in LED indicators on devices.

Endnotes

1. Wright J. How to eavesdrop on Bluetooth headsets. Gizmodo. [Online]http://gizmodo .com/328664/how-to-eavesdrop-on-bluetooth-headsets; 2007 [accessed 12.05.2010].
2. GSM Alliance. Market data summary. GSM World. [Online] www.gsmworld.com/ newsroom/market-data/market_data_summary.htm; 2009 [accessed 12.05.2010].
3. Paget C, Nohl K. GSM: SRSLY? 26th Chaos Communications Congress. [Online] http:// events.ccc.de/congress/2009/Fahrplan/events/3654.en.html; 2009 [accessed 12.05.2010].
4. Aircrack-NG. Aircrack-NG. [Online] www.aircrack-ng.org; 2010 [accessed 12.05.2010].
5. KeeLog. Hardware keylogger - keeLog. [Online] www.keelog.com/diy.html; 2010 [accessed 10.05.2010].
6. Microsoft. Understanding and configuring user account control in Windows Vista. Microsoft. com. [Online] http://technet.microsoft.com/en-us/library/cc709628%28WS.10%29.aspx; 2010 [accessed 10.05.2010].
7. Meloche M-A. Eavesdropping on VoIP. *Hakin9*.2010, Vol. 5, 1.

8. Chilton D. DIY laser long-distance listening device. DIY Life. [Online] www.diylife.com/2007/08/22/diy-laser-long-distance-listening-device; 2007 [accessed 12.05.2010].

9. Todt R. School caught in spying scandal admits activating webcams on students laptops. Huffington Post. [Online] www.huffingtonpost.com/2010/02/22/harriton-high-school-admi_n_471321.html; 2010 [accessed 11.05.2010].

10. van Eck, W. Electromagnetic radiation from video display units: an eavesdropping risk? Comput Secur 1985; 4:269–286.

11. Marcus K. Electromagnetic eavesdropping risks of flat-panel displays. 4th Workshop on Privacy Enhancing Technologies; 2004.

12. Martin V., Sylvain P. Compromising electromagmentic emanations of wired and wireless keyboards. 18th USENIX Security Symposium 2009; 2009.

13. Joe L., David U. Information leakage from optical emanations. Vol. 5(3). ACM Transactions on Information and System Security, 2002.

Intelligence

When discussing the methods that we might use to gather information from individuals, there are a few routes that we can take. We can use *human intelligence*, often abbreviated as HUMINT. HUMINT involves the acquisition of information, usually in a non-covert manner, through personal contact with the source of the information. HUMINT includes a variety of interviewing and questioning techniques.

When we acquire human intelligence through clandestine means, commonly known as spying, this is referred to as clandestine HUMINT. Clandestine HUMINT uses techniques such as recruiting those in the employ of a target to provide information, clandestine reporting methods and tools, and a variety of equipment and resources to aid such causes.

While attempting to acquire information in either a covert or a noncovert manner, we may also need to resort to interrogation. Standard interrogation techniques include methods such as suggestion, deception, and repetition. Stronger techniques, although outside of the scope of penetration testing, may include the use of drugs, physical torture, or psychological torture. While these techniques may be of questionable utility, they do enjoy frequent use, even in recent years.

HUMAN INTELLIGENCE

In standard human intelligence gathering operations, as conducted by the U.S. military, there are rules of engagement that are closely regulated and followed. Stepping over such boundaries is generally considered to be breaking the law, although such lines have occasionally been known to blur. In the cases of governments, intelligence agencies, and other such organizations, we may not see such neatly drawn parameters set for intelligence gathering. In some cases, we may cross the line entirely and cross into clandestine HUMINT, colloquially known as spying. Clandestine HUMINT will be discussed later in this chapter.

Standard operating procedure for HUMINT operations involves the selection, screening, and interviewing of sources. How this is carried out will depend on the information that we are seeking, how cooperative our sources are, and various factors that come up during the interview. Different interview techniques may be used, depending on the particular situation and the source in question.

Sources of Human Intelligence

Sources for human intelligence gathering may come from a variety of places. They may be part of our own organization, they may be bystanders to an event, or they may be "the enemy." A wide variety of such groupings exists in any given situation, and they will likely each need to be handled very differently according to what they know and how cooperative they are.

Screening Sources

When we have a group of individuals who are potential sources of information, we will want to prioritize them in the order that will most likely provide us with the most useful information first. In this case, we need to consider two main points: which of them is the most cooperative and which of them is the most likely to actually have useful information. The U.S. army has a set of source screening codes for just such as purpose, as shown in Figure 14.1.

When using such codes, the lowest number and letter correspond to the most useful sources of information, which should be prioritized first. According to the coding system, a 1-A source is the highest priority, and a 3-C source is the lowest. In addition to the coding system, the army also provides a chart, as shown in Figure 14.2, to enable the information to be more easily interpreted.

When categorizing sources in such a way, we also determine the type of interview to which they will be invited. Cooperative sources and uncooperative sources will experience two different types of interview.

Relationship Analysis

When interviewing a source, relationship analysis can lead us to other sources of information. In casual conversation, a person might mention people that they are friends with, places that they shop, and a variety of other trivial information. Depending on the particular reason for the interview, we may be looking for other people who the source knows that have a common linkage. The creation of social network structures may allow us to discover such linkages.

Code	Cooperation level
1	Responds to direct questions.
2	Responds hesitantly to questioning.
3	Does not respond to questioning.
	Knowledgeability level
A	Very likely to possess PIR information.
B	Might have PIR information.
C	Does not appear to have pertinent information.

FIGURE 14.1 Source Screening Codes.[1]

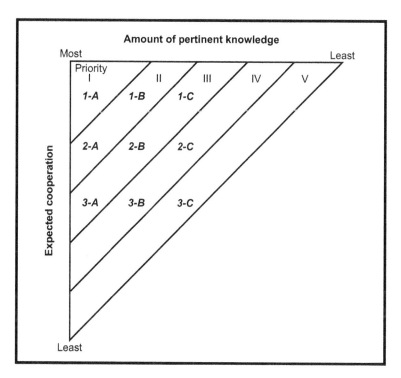

Amount of pertinent knowledge

FIGURE 14.2 Interrogation Priorities by Screening Category.[1]

Social Networks

When discussing human intelligence, we are concerned with social networks, both in the sense of Web-based social networking tools and in the sense of social structures made up of individuals who are connected in some fashion. In actuality, the social networking tools that exist on the Internet are also a type of social network structure, defined by the use of such tools. We may also find social networks that connect at certain points.

For example, if we look at a social network structure composed of those that use social networking tools on the Internet, we may also find parallel networks that are composed of people who attend the same schools, people who work together, people who have or have not met in person, and so on. Once we have mapped out a social network structure, we can quickly add members to it in order to increase our potential pool of sources.

Both types of social networks give us very strong method of discovering new sources for intelligence gathering. The social network structure allows us to use connections between people to verify information that we already have, discover new information, and collect information through inference. It can also allow us to find those who are present in a social network, but have a lack of common connections to others in the network.

For instance, if we look at a social network structure, composed of set of people in a small town, there will likely be a limited set of such structures present. We will likely find the following:

- People that live in the town
- People that went to school there
- People that work there
- People that are related to others in the network

Being a small town, we will also likely see heavy overlap between these network structures. By consulting the sources that we have, whether these are documents, Facebook, interviews, or other sources, we can identify people who do not belong to these networks.

In such cases, these people may be more isolated from others and make more willing sources due to their social isolation. They may also be in the area with ulterior motives and worth our closer attention. Social networks can be a very valuable tool indeed for approaching issues on the basis of relationships.

The use of social networking tools on the Internet can make the task of constructing social network structures considerably easier than it would otherwise be. We would normally suss out such networks through face-to-face interviews with members of the network structure. With the advent of social networking applications on the Internet, we are often free to gather initial information ourselves, to a certain extent, and validate the information during the interview process.

We must also be aware that information gained in both the interview process and in our own research may be spurious, either deliberately or just from honest error. When we encounter such errors during the construction of a social network structure, we should be able to converge on the correct information by collecting the same information from multiple sources. Greatly differing information from multiple sources may be an indication that the data being provided is deliberately false.

Debriefing and Interrogation

Debriefing and interrogation are two sides of the same coin. They represent two different approaches to interviewing a source, generally based on whether said source is or is not cooperative. The line between interrogation and debriefing is not always cleanly drawn, and it is entirely possible that we will see techniques from one being used in the other, depending on the situation.

Debriefing

For those sources that are of a cooperative nature, we will likely use the debriefing process. Debriefing, generally being a nonhostile activity, may involve both foreign sources and sources that are of the organization belonging to the interviewer. For example, in the case of an intelligence gathering operation, the operatives may be debriefed upon their return in order to collect the information from them, as well as a report of their activities.

Debriefing generally allows the interviewer to discuss the situation with the source in comfortable surroundings and enables the interviewer to ask a variety of questions about the information being requested, clarifications to be made to statements, and generally the best information to be obtained.

Interrogation

Interrogation is generally reserved for sources that are not cooperative. While in a debriefing session, we attempt to make the subject as comfortable as possible and avoid being adversarial, as they are cooperating with us. In the case of an interrogation, we will likely not take these steps, although they are not out of the question, depending on the situation.

Interrogations are more likely to use techniques such as deception, suggestion, or in extreme cases, even drugs or torture. While such approaches are generally considered to be distasteful and out of scope for penetration testing, they are still used by militaries and governments around the world. We will discuss interrogation in depth later in this chapter.

Building Rapport

When interviewing or interrogating a source, one of best things that we can do to is to build rapport with the source being questioned. Rapport implies a relationship of trust and cooperation from the source to the interviewer, but not necessarily friendship. Building rapport will enable us to collect information in a swifter, less stressful, and more productive manner.

TIP

Building rapport is an excellent place for us to practice our social engineering skills. Being able to discuss similar likes and dislikes, being from the same state, liking the same sports, and so on can help ingratiate us with our sources. This is not only handy for interrogation but a good skill in life.

In the course of building rapport, particularly during an interrogation, it may be necessary for the interviewer to play the role of someone other than himself or herself, such as taking the guise of clergy, a doctor, or even a fellow source who is waiting to be questioned. Roles that imply a sympathetic relationship with the subject or a common set of circumstances can place the subject in a much more talkative mood. Such roles should be chosen carefully and with a particular subject in mind, as different roles will likely be needed for different subjects.

INTERROGATION TECHNIQUES

Interrogation techniques fall fairly solidly under social engineering, as discussed in Chapter 10, "Psychological Weaknesses"; however, such techniques are of a much more specialized nature. We may use such techniques as deception, suggestion, or lying, in order to get a source to part with the desired information. These are all methods that do not stray from social engineering. In some cases, interrogators do use additional tool sets to aid in questioning a source, potentially involving the use of drugs or torture.

While such methods are quite clearly very far out of scope for penetration testers, they were part of the arsenal of the ninja and are used today around the world. In the case of a large-scale cyber war, it is quite possible that we would also see such methods put to use by the defending or attacking force or perhaps by both. In any case, we will be discussing techniques that may be unpleasant to some, but have been used in real-world scenarios, even by those considered to be "the good guys." This was also covered in Chapter 2, "The Modern Ninja," when we discussed how the appropriateness of some activities can be situational.

Deception

Deception is a commonly used interrogation technique. One of the more common deceptions used in law enforcement interrogations is to separate multiple people who are being questioned so that they cannot hear or see each other, and then tell one of them that the others have indicated that they are the guilty party.

NOTE

For an interesting lecture discussing the use of such tactics and why it may be unwise to talk to law enforcement in an interview situation, Google for "Don't Talk to the Police" by Professor James Duane. At the time of this writing, a copy can be found at http://video. google.com/videoplay?docid=-4097602514885833865#.

Such deceptions can often, out of desperation and the need for revenge, illicit a steady stream of information from the subject. Such tactics are surprising successful, likely because of the heightened emotional state of the source being in an uncomfortable situation.

Good Cop/Bad Cop

The good cop/bad cop strategy uses extremes of behavior on the part of the interrogation team to render the target more compliant. The person playing the bad cop is aggressive toward the subject, yells at them, threatens them, and generally behaves in such as way as to make them nervous and fearful. At the other extreme, the good cop will act to "protect" the subject from the bad cop, often making the bad cop leave the room. The good cop will often offer the subject food, drink, cigarettes, and so on and will attempt to calm the subject, in an attempt to build rapport. The good cop will often encourage the subject to provide the desired data, lest the bad cop return.

Suggestion

Suggestibility is a measure of how willing a subject is to accept a suggestion and act on it. During an interrogation, the interrogator can take various steps to increase the suggestibility of the source, from repetition to deprivation to drugs. Such methods may vary in effectiveness, according to the subject and the situation.

Repetition

Repetition can be very effective in inducing suggestibility in a source. To quote Aldous Huxley "64,200 repetitions make one truth."[2] While this source is, of course, fictional, there is some truth behind it. Psychological research has shown that repetition can not only be used to alter subjects' memory of events, to reflect the information that has been told to them repeatedly, but also be used to create entirely new memories.[3] Suggestion can also take the form of altering subjects memories when they are confronted with repeated questioning, whether the information is true or not.

Deprivation

In combination with heightened emotional states and deprivation of food or sleep, as we might see in an extended interrogation, false memories, as mentioned above, are even more likely to take hold. This will depend on the subject, of course, and what mental state they are in, so results may be inconsistent.

In combination with the use of repetition, deprivation can also be used to put the source in a more compliant physical, mental, and emotional state. Such tactics can take the form of sleep deprivation, lack of food or water, isolation, or any of a number of similar tactics. When taken to extremes, such tactics can cause permanent damage and may be considered torture. We will cover torture in further depth later in this chapter.

Drugs

The use of drugs is an old saw in movie interrogation scenes, but it is based in reality. Drugs to disorient, make subjects more talkative, or induce pain do exist and are used by various intelligence agencies, criminal enterprises, and others. Uses of such techniques were rumored in interrogations at the U.S. detention facility in Guantanamo Bay, Cuba. Detainees reported being given forced injections, and having been given drugs that made them woozy and disoriented, although these allegations were denied.[4]

Drugs and Suggestibility

Through the use of memory-altering drugs, such as propranolol, memories can even be altered or erased in a subject.[5] When used with suggestion and repetition, a person could even conceivably be programmed with entirely new memories regarding a particular situation after being stripped of the previous ones.

> **WARNING**
>
> Although some of the drugs mentioned could potentially be useful for interrogation (although usually not a step in pen testing), they are often intended for use in treating various medical or psychological ailments. The use of such measures without the proper medical training and authorization is likely to end badly.

The use of such techniques can, of course, result in wildly inaccurate or entirely fabricated information being given by the source. As with many techniques involving coercion of information from a source, methods such as these are inferior to other means that might convince them to part with the information willingly.

Truth Drugs

A variety of so-called truth drugs exist and have been used in interrogations with varying results. Some intelligence agencies and governments are rumored to still use these types of drugs. Interrogation under drugs is generally considered to be unreliable for a variety of reasons, differing by the particular drug that is in use.

Sodium thiopental, also known by its more common trademark, sodium pentothal, is one of the more commonly recognized drugs, largely due to its use in books and in movies. Sodium thiopental is a barbiturate and a general anesthetic and is useful in medicine. It is a depressant and is used in interrogations to make subjects more compliant and talkative.[6]

Project MKULTRA was a covert CIA project, run in the 1950s and 1960s to do research in manipulating the human brain. Among other techniques, drugs were used extensively in this program. LSD was given to test subjects in large doses, as was a combination of barbiturates and amphetamines, among other drugs. Subjects were sometimes successfully questioned under these drug regimens, but often just babbled incoherently.[7]

In the 1970s, some knowledge of the MKULTRA experiments became public, resulting in a congressional committee investigation and a presidential executive order banning future such experiments on unwilling or unaware participants. Several subprojects were spawned from MKULTRA and rumors persist of similar projects to this day.

Torture

Torture has been a staple of interrogation back into prehistory. Torture has been used, largely in the sense of physical torture, by governments, churches, law enforcement, criminals, and many others, to extract information from unwilling sources as a matter of course. In more recent years, interrogation techniques of a less immediately injurious nature have become more commonplace during official interrogations, including sleep deprivation and waterboarding.

While such techniques are clearly out of scope for the Zukin and for penetration testing, by any stretch of the imagination, we will be discussing them. In the larger context of actual cyber warfare or criminal activity, such techniques, although pre-cluded by most laws and treaties, have been and will likely continue to be used.

The Legality and Ethics of Torture

It is generally agreed that in most civilized countries, torture is illegal. From a U.S. centric point of view, torture violates the U.N. Convention against Torture, the U.S. Constitution, Section 2340A of the U.S. Federal Criminal Code, and the Geneva Conventions.[8] There are a variety of other laws, statutes, and regulations that are also violated, but those listed are among the largest. In addition to being almost universally considered illegal, torture is also considered to be unethical by most people.

The question of whether or not torture is ethical is a longstanding one. If we torture one person to save another, is that ethical? If we save 10 people, or 100, is it ethical then? Great minds have pondered over this issue, and we will not come to a conclusion on it here. Suffice to say that torture is, at best, on extremely shaky ethical ground. When we decide that torture is acceptable for one reason, it then becomes much easier to accept it for other reasons. To further the discussion on the ethics of torture, we must also examine its effectiveness or lack thereof.

The Utility of Torture

The utility of torturing information out of a source has been questioned for some time, particularly in recent years. The main issue to be considered is whether any information gained in such a fashion can have any great amount of reliability or whether our source is just telling us whatever we want to hear in order to make us stop.

. When we have placed our source into a state of extreme fear or panic, as discussed in Chapter 10, "Psychological Weaknesses," we have approached a state where, in fear for their lives and physical health, our sources will fabricate information out of desperation. Not only will this approach likely be fruitless, but it will more than likely not incline our source to be forthcoming with future information, presuming that they survive such methods of interrogation at all. Many such methods can leave permanent physical and psychological scars, regardless whether "softer" methods are used or not.

Even when using techniques that lead to less physical injury, such as sleep deprivation, waterboarding, or stress positions, we have only changed the overall method of torture, not the end results. When deprived of sleep, for example, for days on end, our sources are no more likely to produce reliable information than if we had tortured them physically and are no less likely to be damaged by the experience. When needing to elicit information from a source, we are far better off using other techniques.

Social engineering, as discussed in Chapter 10, "Psychological Weaknesses," will often yield better, faster, and more accurate information than any torture technique. Particularly when using resources such as the kunoichi to approach the source at a social level or to develop an intimate relationship with them, we can gain access to information that is freely given. Such techniques are an extension of the questioning technique of building rapport, discussed earlier in this chapter when we discussed human intelligence.

Physical Torture

Even when considering physical torture, we should carefully consider the methods that we might use. Disregarding any further discussion on issues of ethics or effectiveness, we come back to the goal of not leaving behind permanent evidence of our operations. While we could revert to medieval techniques involving hot irons or racking our sources, this will not only leave permanent marks but likely have the effect of heavily damaging and disabling those being questioned.

While this may satisfy the personal needs of certain individuals, there really is no gain to be had by using these methods. For illustrative purposes, we will discuss some of the methods used in recent years in places such as the Middle East and Afghanistan, before discussing some of the psychologically based alternatives.

Even when resorting to physical torture, there is still a considerable list of tools to use that do not deal permanent physical injury to sources and that will generally allow for recovery at some point.

We previously discussed waterboarding in Chapter 10, "Psychological Weaknesses," when referring to inducing fear and panic for social engineering purposes. To reiterate briefly, waterboarding is a form of simulated drowning, provoking great fear in the source, but generally not causing them any lasting physical harm. The first appearance of waterboarding in recorded history is purportedly in a French judicial handbook from 1541 and is referred to as Torturae Gallicae Ordinariae or Standard Gallic Torture.[9]

Waterboarding was used by the United States in interrogations that took place in the Middle East following the 9/11 terrorist attacks, reportedly by sanction of the U.S. government.[10] Since then, the practice has been banned[11] but was reported to have produced some useful intelligence.

Another physical method used is the stress position, which is generally not physically harmful in the long term, if properly used. Stress positions involve the use of particular positioning to place stress on individual groups of muscles. For instance, a common stress position is to force the source to remain standing for long periods of time, usually several hours. This can put extreme stress on the muscles of the legs and back and can be very painful.

Submersion, exactly as it sounds, is submerging someone in a body or container of water, in order to simulate drowning. Overall, it is very similar to waterboarding, although in a somewhat less controlled way. It may be very difficult to tell where exactly the line is between almost drowning the subject and actually drowning them.

Psychological Torture

A variety of psychological methods of torture exist as well, and these are theoretically being less harmful than the physical methods. Whether or not this is truly, the case is a frequent matter of discussion in the news media. Some such tactics, such as sleep deprivation, are ancient in origin, while newer tactics, such as Fear Up, used by the U.S. Department of Defense, are more recent.

Fear Up is a tactic discussed in the U.S. army's FM 34-52 manual for human intelligence operations.[1] The tactic is basically for the interrogator to act in an angry and threatening manner, potentially yelling and threatening the source, and perhaps throwing various objects around the room. At this point, the technique is allowed and is considered to be acceptable. Where things begin to move into more questionable territory is when physical or moral coercion are used or when the subject had been humiliated or placed in a degrading environment. In this case, the technique has likely violated the Geneva Conventions, and we have stepped into illegal territory.

Phobias can be used to very great effect, if the subject is forthcoming about what they are or if the information is obtained from another source. Phobias can range from heights to clowns and can vary greatly in degree. There are a few primal phobias that are common to many people, arachnophobia, or the fear of spiders being one of the more common.

Sleep deprivation, also known as sleep adjustment, is the practice of either depriving sources of sleep entirely or reversing the sleep cycle so that night and day are reversed. This can cause a variety of symptoms, including impairment of mental function, memory problems, speech impairment, and other issues. Newer versions of military human intelligence manuals describe this process as being prohibited.[1]

Isolation is a commonly used technique to render a source more cooperative for purposes of interrogation. The source may be isolated with no outside contact and possibly no light for extended periods of time.[1] Effects of such methods are reported to be similar to those experienced with sleep deprivation. In a memo released by the U.S. Pentagon in 2002, it is stated that such tactics should be limited to a maximum of 30 days.[12]

As mentioned previously, when discussing suggestion, various methods of deprivation may be used to render a target more suggestible and potentially more likely to part with information. As we said when we discussed some of the negative effects of drug use in interrogation, deprivation and suggestion may result in incoherent or false information being provided by the source. Such methods are not generally considered to be reliable in interrogation.

CLANDESTINE HUMAN INTELLIGENCE

Clandestine human intelligence is the aspect of human intelligence that most people are referring to when they talk about spying. Such operations can involve the recruitment or turning of those who are in the employ of or are socially close to our targets. It can also involve methods of clandestine reporting and the resources and equipment necessary to carry out such operations.

While some of this will be out of scope for standard penetration testing, portions of it will certainly be usable techniques in many circumstances. For penetration testing of a more extreme nature, such as those that are used by red teams or similar government-sponsored activities, more of these techniques may come into play.

Certainly, such methods were used by the ninja and are used by criminals and governments around the world.

Penetrating Organizations

Throughout the book, we have discussed a variety of methods for penetrating organizations, from impersonation in Chapter 6, "Impersonation," to social engineering in Chapter 10, "Psychological Weaknesses." In the world of clandestine human intelligence, we add the additional tool of recruiting and turning members of the target organization to our own purposes and the use of sleeper agents.

While such tools may not be of great use when conducting a penetration test, due to the long-term nature of such methods, they are undoubtedly of use in actual cyber war situations. We will be discussing this in the context of such uses.

Recruitment

In recruiting those from our target organizations, we can utilize the five needs, as discussed in Chapter 10, "Psychological Weaknesses": security, sex, wealth, pride, and pleasure.[13] When we find weaknesses in people who are present in the target organization, we then have an opportunity to turn such people by using their weakness. Weaknesses can be either naturally existing in the target or artificially created by the attacker.

Security can make an excellent motivator to turn a target to our purposes. This can be physical security, if the target is in a situation where they feel threatened; money, if they are in poor financial straits; social, if the target is in an unstable or poor social situation; or any of a number of other factors.

Sex is clearly a powerful tool and can be used to influence many people. Sex can be used as either the carrot or the stick. We can use sex to enter social proximity of a person, in order to influence them to our purposes, or we can use illicit sex with a person to embarrass them into the same arrangement. A large portion of Chapter 10, "Psychological Weaknesses," covered the use of the kunoichi for this express purpose.

Wealth can provide a powerful and direct motivator for a target to turn against their organization. Money can be used to directly bribe or pay a target so that they comply with our wishes, or it can be used to blackmail a target by deliberately moving money in amounts large enough that it will cause problems for them with anyone monitoring their financial transactions.

Pride is a somewhat more subtle tool to use than the other needs, particularly in the case of attempting to use it to turn a target. It might be used to turn someone when removal of it is threatened, in the case of threats to release information that might cast a shadow on the target themselves or a family member. We could potentially also offer pride as a tool to turn the target, by offering them a better position socially, in their career, or otherwise, in order to gain them for our side.

Pleasure can be a powerful but variable tool to turn a target. As different people gain pleasure from different things, the incentive offered here could be nearly anything. It could encompass one or more of the other needs, it could be fine artwork, or it could be starring in a movie, and so on. Similar to pride, pleasure can also be very subtle and can easily be mistaken for one of the other needs.

Sleepers

Sleeper agents are people who have been placed with a target far in advance of actual need. In such cases, we might place a Zukin in a social situation close to a target, or in the employ of a target, so that we might use them in the future if the need arose. Such agents can be potentially problematic due to the long-term nature of the assignment. Over time, the agent could potentially become sympathetic to the organization or people who they have been placed with and be unwilling to perform their duties when called upon.

Clandestine Reporting

Clandestine methods of reporting back intelligence can be vital when gathering intelligence. In earlier years, many such methods involved physically handing off papers, films, and other such physical documents, and a wide variety of strategies were developed to aid in doing so.

In more recent years, as computers and portable device have become ubiquitous, electronic methods of passing information have become, in many cases, safer, quicker, and easier to carry out. We can use a variety of methods to pass information over computer systems that are not visible to the casual user and may even pass inspection by those looking for such communications methods. Some of the more common means are the use of steganography and covert channels.

Steganography

Steganography is the practice of hiding messages so that the existence of the message is hidden entirely. While this method has been in use for thousands of years, more recently we have been able to use it in a digital sense. We can conceal messages in audio files, in random data, in comments on Web pages, or in any number of other places. This is particularly useful in clandestine reporting, as our opponent will have an incalculably large area to search in an attempt to find such messages, presuming that we have not left accurate evidence behind of our travels on the Internet.

Some of the more common methods of digital steganography involve hiding messages in audio, graphical, or video files. In most of these sorts of files, the least significant bits in the file can be altered without changing the overall image or sound being carried in the file. The image file shown in Figure 14.3 would make a suitable file to contain a hidden steganographic message.

In such a file with a message hidden in it, we might see slightly more noise in the image or hear a fraction more static in the sound, but these will be unnoticeable to most people. The image shown in Figure 14.4 contains a hidden 1500 word message, a transcription of the Declaration of Independence.

FIGURE 14.3 A Carrier File for a Steganographic Message.

FIGURE 14.4 A File Containing a Steganographic Message.

While such alterations can often be detected with software created for the specific purpose, the file would need to be found and checked in order to determine whether a message was present, let alone being able to extract the message.

One of the useful properties of media files that carry steganographic messages is that we have an enormous area in which they can be hidden. In many of the blogs, forums, image posting sites, and other miscellaneous Web pages that exist, an almost innumerable host of media files exists. All that we need to do to get a message out is to encode it in such a file and post the file in a prearranged place somewhere on the Internet and then wait for the other party to pick it up. Our choices are so broad that we need never use the same site twice.

Such techniques are theorized to have been used by the terrorists that planned the 9/11 attacks against the World Trade Center. According to some accounts, images were e-mail and posted to newsgroups that contained images with steganographically hidden messages on planning the attack.[14] While these stories may or may not be apocryphal, using these methods to plan such attacks is certainly within the realm of possibility, and by no means technically difficult.

Covert channels

Covert channels are methods for bypassing access control mechanisms in very high-security systems. Such systems normally prevent data for which a person does not have access from being read or written and prevent information about such data from being communicated outside the system. Although the origin of such terms is in computer science, the concepts hold true even in other environments. According to the Trusted Computer Security Evaluation Criteria (TCSEC), there are two main types of covert channel: storage channels and timing channels.[15]

Storage channels are a type of covert channel that involves one process writing to a storage location and another process monitoring that location. This could be taken advantage of by the monitoring process watching for the presence or absence of a certain file or the storage on the disk being above or below a certain percentage. Such channels can also be used with the storage of physical objects, such as the presence or absence of a coffee cup sitting in a window, or any other similar situation with an object.

Timing channels revolve around using the timing of a process or activity to communicate information. In a computer system, this method might be used by cycling system resources used by a process up or down in order to communicate. Using this approach, we could even communicate complex information via a binary on and off cycle of a particular resource. Outside of a computer system, there are many other similar applications.

SHINOBI-IRI (Stealth and Entering Methods)

An oft-reported timing channel involves pizza deliveries at the Pentagon during high levels of activity. According to the story, during such times, workers stay late at the Pentagon, working on the issue at hand. All the additional personnel are still at work, when they would normally be home eating dinner, hence the larger than usual level of pizza deliveries. Such activity is reported to have signaled the beginning of Operation Desert Storm.[16]

Whether or not the pizza story is true, this type of activity has definitely been marked as a possible covert channel. Regulations have been put in place so that, in the case of large food orders needing to be placed at night in support of an upcoming operation, such orders will be spaced out over time and will be placed to a wide selection of different establishments.[17]

Resources

A variety of resources can be needed to support clandestine human intelligence. We will need to provide equipment with which our Zukin can communicate covertly, safe meeting places when face-to-face meetings are needed, money to fund operations, and any other equipment needed to carry out our tasks.

In an operation of a truly secretive nature, resources should be purchased or procured in such as way as to be as untraceable as possible. Means of funding to purchase such resources should be disassociated from any channels that might allow such funds to be traced back to their sources.

Tools for Clandestine Communications

Tools that allow for clandestine communications are much more easily obtained and used in the age of modern computing than they were in the past. The use of computers, mobile devices, and portable storage are ubiquitous and draw almost no notice when used publically.

When communicating covertly, it is important to be cautious not to use mechanisms that are easily traceable by other interested parties. One particularly problematic device is the cell phone, which can not only be tracked when in use but also be traceable using its internal GPS, as we will discuss in greater detail in Chapter 15, "Surveillance."

In 2003, several CIA agents were discovered in an unauthorized kidnapping operation that took place in Italy. The Italians were able to track the movements of the CIA agents by their cell phone usage, using, ironically, equipment that had been given to them by the United States.[18]

Meeting Places

Safe meeting places for clandestine meetings or face-to-face communication are becoming harder to come by in modern society. Depending on the country and location in question, we may be under the watchful eye of a veritable army of surveillance device that are publicly placed. In some cities, such as London or Washington D.C., this is an almost certainty. Even outside of such heavily monitored areas, we still have a variety of public cameras on street corners, surveillance cameras in stores and on ATM machines, and others in many less obvious places to contend with.

In general, for purposes of avoiding surveillance, two types of meeting place present themselves: open park-like areas and crowded indoor areas.

In large outdoor areas, such as a park or an open field, physical surveillance becomes more noticeable, and monitoring via audio or video is more challenging. Although still possible with the use of longer range monitoring devices, such as powerful parabolic microphones, the equipment and personnel would be more noticeable.

In crowded indoor spaces, although the difficulty of placing monitoring devices is considerably reduced, the noise level may make them less useful. Crowded and enclosed spaces can also make physically tracking a target more difficult, depending on the layout of the area. We must be careful in use of such areas to not become physically trapped or confined.

When choosing meeting places, it is very important to be as unpredictable as possible and to not use the same meeting place repeatedly. Meeting at the coffee shop around the corner every time not only allows surveillance teams to easily be put in place but also allows surveillance devices to be put in the best possible locations for monitoring.

An additional consideration, which falls somewhere between a meeting place and a communications mechanism, is the use of online virtual worlds or massively multiplayer online games (MMOs) to conduct clandestine activities. Software-based worlds such as Second Life or World of Warcraft can provide an excellent meeting place or way to send messages in relative anonymity, all the while hiding such communications in very commonly used protocols.

Money

Financial resources for clandestine operations can be useful in a variety of ways; they can be used for bribes and to buy equipment, travel, and a number of other activates. While such monetary resources have typically been in cash, we must also understand that large cash purchases may now draw the attention of law enforcement under certain circumstances. In the case of purchasing plane tickets, the use of cash has been a reoccurring pattern that is now well known. It would be best to avoid using cash for such purposes and instead use a generic prepaid card or other source.

When larger amounts of money need to change hands, such funds are typically "laundered" so that the source of the funds is not immediately obvious. One common method of laundering is to cycle the funds through some sort of business in the service industry, which does not take, have, or produce any type of tangible goods. When we have a business that handles actual goods of any kind, we could theoretically be expected to produce or show evidence that such goods actually exist, such as the items themselves, bills of lading, shipping manifests, and so on. In a service industry, no such goods exist, and additional hours of service can be fabricated in order to cover additional income. Once the money has been taken in, it can be paid out to employees or investors in the company, who are, in actuality, the clients of the money laundering service.

Other Equipment

Depending on the particular operation in question, the Zukin may need a variety of equipment in order to complete it. This could range from climbing gear, to computers, to a tuxedo. While we can provide discretionary funds for various needs, it would be impractical and dangerous for individuals to obtain all their own equipment and resources.

As part of the planning phase for a given operation, we should compile a list of the needed resources and make them available to the Zukin as needed, where needed. Such acquisition and transport of goods will require considerable planning and strategy to complete and should not be underestimated in the planning effort.

Summary

In this chapter, we covered the various techniques involved in intelligence gathering and interrogation. Such tactics may vary in scope and severity, depending largely on the party doing the interrogation and the setting, in both the political and geographical sense. Some portions of this chapter discussed activities that were out of scope for standard penetration testing, but covered them in the context of both historical use by the ninja and modern use in the real world by various parties.

We discussed human intelligence gathering and the types of sources that we might find, including the use of social network structures to locate additional sources. Sources are generally categorized by what they know and how cooperative they are. Cooperative sources will generally undergo the debriefing process, while noncooperative sources will face interrogation. In either case, it is important to build rapport with the source.

We discussed clandestine human intelligence, commonly known as spying. While much of this type of work has application for the intelligence community, there are some tools from this field that can be used in penetration testing. Covered were penetrating organizations, clandestine reporting, and the various resources that we might need to conduct such operations.

Lastly, we covered interrogation techniques. In the penetration testing world, the use of such tools will revolve largely around light psychological measures, such as good cop/bad cop. Sterner tactics, such as deception or suggestion, are commonly used by law enforcement and similar agencies. Further to the extreme are tools such as the use of drugs and physical or psychological torture. These tools as we mentioned are very much out of scope for the penetration tester, but were used by the ninja, and continue to be used by various governments and their militaries, intelligence organizations, and other similar groups.

Endnotes

1. Department of the Army. FM 2-22.3 (FM 34-52) Human intelligence collector operations. Department of the Army; 2006.
2. Huxley A. Brave new world. Harper & Row, Publishers, Inc.; 1969. B0016RNX8C.
3. Chan J.C., Thomas A.K., Bulevich J.B. Recalling a witnessed event increases eyewitness suggestibility: the reversed testing effect. Psychol Sci. 2009 Jan;20(1):66-73. Epub 2008 Nov 25.
4. Hambling D. Interrogation drugs at Gitmo alleged. Danger Room. [Online] www.wired.com/dangerroom/2008/11/interrogation-d/; 2008 [accessed 20.05.10].

5. Gray R. Scientists find drug to banish bad memories. Telegraph.co.uk. [Online] www .telegraph.co.uk/science/science-news/3298988/Scientists-find-drug-to-banish-bad-memories.html; 2007 [accessed 20.05.10].

6. BBC News Magazine. Can truth serum work?. BBC News Magazine. [Online] http:// news.bbc.co.uk/2/hi/7773261.stm; 2008 [accessed 20.05.10].

7. Otterman M. American torture: from the cold war to Abu Ghraib and beyond. Melbourne University; 2007. 978-0522853339.

8. Lithwick D. Torture bored. Slate. [Online] www.slate.com/id/2243737; 2010 [accessed 18.05.10].

9. McCoy AW. The U.S. has a history of using torture. History News Network. [Online] http://hnn.us/articles/32497.html; 2006 [accessed 14.05.10].

10. Risen J, Johnston D, Lewis N. Harsh C.I.A. methods cited in top Qauda interrogations. The New York Times. [Online] www.nytimes.com/2004/05/13/politics/13DETA.html; 2004 [accessed 14.05.10].

11. Eggen D. Senate passes ban on waterboarding, other techniques. The Washington Post. [Online] www.washingtonpost.com/wp-dyn/content/article/2008/02/13/AR2008021302888.html; 2008 [accessed 14.05.10].

12. Haynes W. Counter-resistance techniques. http://slate.msn.com/features/whatistorture/pdfs/020927.pdf; 2002 [accessed 1.07.10].

13. Hayes S. The ninja and their secret fighting art. Tuttle Publishing; 1990. 978-0804816564.

14. Manjoo F. The case of the missing code. Salon.com. [Online] www.salon.com/technology/feature/2002/07/17/steganography/; 2002 [18.05.10].

15. U.S. Department of Defense. Department of Defense trusted computer system evaluation criteria. http://csrc.nist.gov/publications/history/dod85.pdf. DoD 5200.28-STD; 1985 [accessed 1.07.10].

16. Leipold JD. Army releases new OPSEC regulation. Army.mil. [Online] www.army.mil/news/2007/04/19/2758-army-releases-new-opsec-regulation/; 2007 [accessed 18.05.10].

17. Shachtman N. Army's info-cop speaks. Danger Room. [Online] www.wired.com/dangerroom/2007/05/the_army_has_is/; 2007 [accessed 18.05.10].

18. Stein J. Italian prosecutor is tracking convicted CIA agents. SpyTalk. [Online] http://blog.washingtonpost.com/spy-talk/2010/04/italian_prosecutor_is_tracking.html; 2010 [20.05.10].

Surveillance

When discussing surveillance, we have several different aspects to look at. We can talk about gathering intelligence on organizations or individuals, which we can do through a variety of sources both online and offline. Such sources may be other people, blogs, public records, or government databases.

We can also attempt to physically track the location of our targets, using purpose-built tracking devices, or simply gathering information freely posted by the individual. Many Web sites, applications, and hardware devices are now locationally aware and may be providing this information unbeknownst to the user.

On the other side of the coin, the Zukin must also be aware of surveillance directed at them. Such surveillance could be electronic or physical in nature and could come in a variety of forms or guises. Some such surveillance is easily detectable, given training, but some, including modern tracking devices, can be virtually impossible to detect.

Finally, we should be aware of devices that are able to disrupt surveillance. Using the proper tools, we can disrupt RF signals, locate hidden video devices, and dampen our electromagnetic emissions. Some such tools are trivially simple to construct and operate, but some require a considerable expenditure of resources and extensive training.

"Stealthy reconnaissance is the ninja's chief contribution to victory,"[1] according to Toshitsugu Takamatsu, the thirty-third Grandmaster of the Togakure Ryu. Without a doubt, surveillance is the hallmark of ninja skills, and it was achieved using a large variety of both tactics and tools. The tactics were developed to allow the ninja to gather data without detection, and the tools to get the ninja into areas where they could gather the intelligence.

Kunoichi has been discussed already, but the female ninja had great opportunity to gather information on a day-to-day basis when placed in temples. However, espionage (*cho ho*) was considered part of the ninja "eighteen levels of training."[1] To be successful in espionage, ninja had to undergo very special mental training. The art of Ninjutsu has accumulated wisdom from a variety of different philosophical sources, to understand both man and nature, and how to take advantage of each in order to achieve success in their mission. Combining the understanding of both man and nature, ninja were able to refine their method of concealment (called *ongyoujutsu*),

Ninja Hacking. DOI: 10.1016/B978-1-59749-588-2.00015-9

during their task to gather information. When we see in the movies ninja hiding in water or buried under a thin layer of earth, they are employing *go ton po*. Although we have other, less messy, ways of gathering information, we should develop a similar understanding of both man and the nature of the world we operate in, whether it is in the physical world or networked world.

In Chapter 3, "Strategies and Tactics," we discussed the different types of spies, according to Sun Tzu,[2] which included local spies, inward spies, converted spies, doomed spies, and surviving spies. Although we discuss each of the techniques for gathering information, it would be a great mental exercise to understand which type of spy goes with each technique or situation; this will allow us to understand espionage better and from a historical perspective.

GATHERING INTELLIGENCE

Intelligence gathering on organizations or individuals is more quickly and easily accomplished now than at any time in the past. We have access to a wealth of information in online databases, blogs, and social networking sites, in many cases free for the taking. Many people post detailed personal information and information about their daily activities for the entire world to see.

We also have a variety of devices that provide locational information to several different audiences. In most cell phones, a GPS mechanism exists to provide our location in an emergency, or we may provide it freely, through locationally aware Web sites, or information embedded in media files.

Resumes and Job Postings

Resumes and job listings can provide the Zukin with a wealth of information on both personal and company levels. In resumes, we might find work histories, skill sets, hobbies, and a variety of other personal information. Such information might be used to set up social engineering attacks based on information regarding the target's skills or interests.

In job listings, companies can expose quite a bit of information that might normally be considered to be somewhat sensitive in nature. We may be able to find geographical information, network or security infrastructure details, software being used, and quite a few other items. Such information can be used to plan attacks against, or surveillance on, organizations.

Resumes

Resumes can provide a wealth of personal information on our targets. From a resume, we can discover where a person works, what he or she does there, how long he or she has been employed, and what technologies he or she works with. We may also discover past work histories, professional organizations, hobbies, and a variety of other information.

Resumes can also lead us to false information that can be used to influence, embarrass, or unemploy the target. It is an all too common practice today for people to "enhance" their resumes. Such false information may include fabricated employers, nonexistent degrees or degrees from diploma mills, or any of a number of pieces of false information. Such false information is often solidly constructed enough to pass a cursory background check, and may need detailed research to be discovered.

Resumes can often be found posted on personal Web sites or blogs, or posted on job search Web sites such as Dice.com or Monster.com. Many people keep resumes publically posted at all times, whether actively searching for a job or not. In many cases, if a target has such a document posted, a simple Google search on the target's name will discover it in short order.

Job Postings

Job postings, at a higher level can give us quite a bit of information regarding a company. It can tell us where facilities are located geographically, when such information might not be easily located on a target company. It can also tell us what kind of work is going on in a particular location, and what tools are being used. It can even provide us detailed information on the network and security infrastructure of the company, potentially including the specific manufacturers and models of devices that are in use.

We can often locate job postings directly on a company Web site, usually listed under careers, jobs, or something similar. If not, we can do a targeted search for the company on one of the major job-placement sites, such as those mentioned earlier. If we have the luxury of time, our research will often benefit from being able to look over such data for a period of a few months or longer.

Given such information, we will have ample resources to set up social engineering attack, or find targets for further surveillance.

Blogs and Social Networks

In Chapter 11, "Distraction," we discussed the use of social networking tools, such as infiltrating or falsifying a blog or Facebook account to plant false or misleading information. We can also use such resources passively in order to collect information.

In many cases, a basic account, or no account at all, is required to read information on a social networking or blog Web site. Given this ability, we can follow an individual through his or her blog, Twitter posts, Facebook posts and information, locational information, as discussed in the "Location Tracking" section in this chapter, and numerous other sources.

When our target is someone who actively participates in such tools, it can be trivially easy to virtually follow his or her activities, locate his or her friends and other social contacts, and even keep track of his or her physical location. This information can be used for strictly tracking purposes, or can be used for more direct action, such as blackmail, depending on the activities of the target. In many cases, younger people tend to be a bit more cavalier about documenting questionable activities, and may provide a richer source for this type of information.

Credit Reports

In the United States, credit reports are maintained by three major reporting agencies: Equifax, Experian, and TransUnion. These agencies track information on financial accounts and account status, personal information, employment, addresses of residence, and miscellaneous other information, depending on the agency. Such information is generally considered private and is, in theory, difficult for other individuals besides the person to access.

Credit reports can be accessed by lending agencies, schools, stores, landlords, employers, and a host of others, not only trivially, but regularly. Such information can even be bought over the Internet from a wide variety of background check services.

WARNING

Accessing the credit report of someone else without permission is, in most countries, breaking the law. In the United States, doing so is a violation of the Fair Credit Reporting Act (FCRA), and can be punishable with fines, damages paid to the person in question, costs, and attorney's fees.[3]

In the hands of an attacker, credit information can be used for a variety of purposes. It can be used to gain background information on a target, to conduct fraud or identity theft, for social engineering attacks, or as a step to collect further information. In many cases, obtaining personal information, employment information, educational information, and a list of previous addresses will get an attacker through the more common security questions that are used to grant access to sensitive information or to reset a password for an account.

Public Records

Public records can provide a wealth of information on a target. We can find mortgages, marriages, divorces, legal proceedings, parking tickets, and a variety of other useful data. Through this we can find where a person lives, previous relationships, company information, and a host of other data.

What exactly constitutes a public record can vary by the geographical location of the record itself, and by the agency that hold it. In the United States, the laws in each state are different, and the information that may be legal to access in one state may be illegal in another. We may also find variability in how the data can be accessed and what data may be available. For example, in 2008, the Government Accountability Office produced a report stating that, across the country, 85 percent of large counties and 41 percent of small counties maintain online records that can make social security numbers accessible in bulk.[3]

Sources of Personal Information

Many databases exist for gathering information on individuals, from criminal information to marriage records. As such information is often in local, county, or state record-keeping systems, the means of accessing this data can widely vary. We can find everything from poorly indexed paper records, which are thankfully no longer very common, to easily searched online databases.

Finding the proper location to access individual records can be no small task. The location and methods of access will often depend on what, specifically, the document is, where the activity being documented took place, and when it took place. For very recent events, we can often find information online, but for older events, we may be forced to physically travel to the location and obtain a paper copy.

Some information, such as that regarding deaths or births, may be in federal records and thus slightly more easily accessed. Information revolving around social security numbers and benefits are the most likely to fall into this category.

Much of our research regarding an individual will tend to parallel the activities that accompany genealogical research. A way to start looking for potential sources of information in a particular location is to search for genealogical resources in that area. Many Web sites exist that are dedicated to finding local storehouses of public records, church records, and other similar information.

Social Engineering

In addition to the other sources of personal information that we have already discussed, we can use social engineering to gain information. If we can develop a social relationship with the target, or those close to the target, this can provide a most excellent source of information. In this way, we may be able to gain access to knowledge that if not available through online sources and databases, and may be of a much more personal nature. For a more in-depth discussion on social engineering, see Chapter 10, "Psychological Weaknesses."

Federal Court Filings

The Public Access to Court Electronic Documents (PACER) database, available at www.pacer.gov/, "allows users to obtain case and docket information from federal appellate, district and bankruptcy courts."[4] Information found on PACER, as shown in Figure 15.1, can include the following for federal cases:

- A listing of all parties and participants including judges, attorneys, and trustees
- A compilation of case-related information such as cause of action, nature of suit, and dollar demand
- A chronology of dates of case events entered in the case record
- A claims registry
- A listing of new cases each day in all courts
- Written judicial opinions
- Judgments or case status

This can be a wealth of information when researching a target or targets that are involved with a federal case or bankruptcy. There is a small fee associated with each page viewed on PACER, and an account is required to access the data. A short waiting period is also required before the account can be activated.

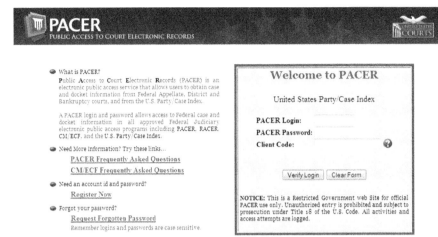

FIGURE 15.1 PACER.[4]

Excluded Parties

The Excluded Parties List System, available at www.epls.gov, provides a list of individual and companies "that are excluded from receiving Federal contracts, certain subcontracts, and certain Federal financial and nonfinancial assistance and benefits."[5] Information can be found on both parties that are actively being excluded, and have been excluded in the past.

We can search this information by company names, names of individuals, social security numbers, or we can simply browse it. In Figure 15.2, we can see that the listed individual has been indefinitely excluded, and if we look further into the CT Code 03-SDGT-01, we will discover that this was done due to ties with terrorism.

In the case of records that are associated with multiple individuals, as would be the case where all members of an organization were excluded, we would see a cross reference to the organizational name at the bottom. We may also see aliases or an individual listed, if the individual were to be known by more than one name.

EDGAR

The Electronic Data Gathering, Analysis, and Retrieval System (EDGAR), available at www.sec.gov/edgar.shtml, is a database run by the U.S. Securities and Exchange Commission. It exists to "increase the efficiency and fairness of the securities market for the benefit of investors, corporations, and the economy by accelerating the receipt, acceptance, dissemination, and analysis of time-sensitive corporate information filed with the agency" and contains data since 1996.[6]

In EDGAR searches, we can find not only information about companies, as we can see in Figure 15.3, but also information about the individuals associated with them. This body of data can allow us to find full names, other business associations,

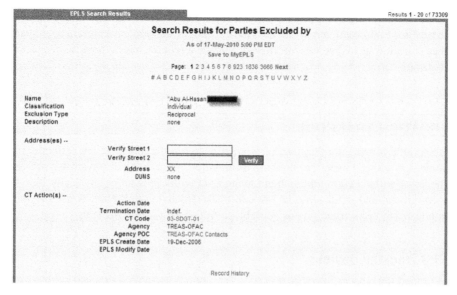

FIGURE 15.2 An EPLS Listing.[5]

FIGURE 15.3 An EDGAR Listing.[6]

addresses, investment information, and a variety of other bits and pieces. Although these bits of information may not always be useful in and of themselves, in aggregate they can allow us to discover information that we might not have otherwise been able to gather.

LOCATION TRACKING

Being able to track the location of a target can considerably ease the difficulty of some operations. Given live tracking information, we can either physically surveil the target without taking the risk of having a surveillance team or physically follow them around and be discovered. We can track targets through phones, use of Web applications, or information posted to blogs and social networking sites.

GPS Tracking Devices

GPS tracking devices have become considerably more sophisticated and compact in recent years. We now have devices that are smaller than a pack of cards and can relay near real-time tracking information over the Internet. Such devices use cellular frequencies to broadcast location information and can be attached to vehicles, people, or nearly any moving object that we would care to track.

Although such devices might be detectable by tracking their broadcasts, many of them go into a sleep mode when not moving and no longer transmit, thus making such detection considerably more difficult. Considering the small size of such units, we could easily conceal one in an area where it would only be found by the most thorough of searches, such as inside a vehicle door or body panel, inside a sealed package, or built into a briefcase.

Vehicle-Based Devices

A variety of GPS devices for tracking the location of vehicles exist. They are primarily divided into two categories: hardwired and nonhardwired types. Hardwired GPS devices are wired into the electrical system of the vehicle and depend on it to provide main power to the device and to recharge its internal backup battery. Such devices are also frequently equipped with external antenna connectors, which can either run to an antenna on the exterior of the vehicle, or can be connected to a nonvisible antenna that runs along the interior or body of the vehicle.

Nonhardwired devices are typically not permanently attached to the vehicle and are not usually connected to the vehicle's electrical system. Such devices are often small and have a magnetic attachment point, allowing them to be quickly attached to a vehicle for covert tracking. Due to their small size, nonhardwired devices often run on a small battery, usually only capable of running for a few days. Their nature makes them very versatile and good for quick and clandestine use, as they are easily placed, but not easily detectable without a thorough search.

Such devices are frequently used by both trucking companies and rental car agencies to ensure that the drivers of such vehicles are obeying local traffic regulations, and policies regarding where such vehicles can and cannot be taken. Such information, although written in the fine print of many rental car agreements, has resulted in surprising fines from the rental car agencies; as such devices were used to track usage out of allowed areas and driving over posted speed limits.[7]

Tracking Systems

Tracking systems for GPS devices, such as those that we have discussed earlier, fall into two main categories, live systems or data loggers.

Live systems offer real-time or semi-real-time tracking of the GPS device. In real-time tracking, the device updates a central tracking system, generally at intervals of less than 1 min. Semi-real-time tracking usually updates the same type of monitoring system, but at considerably less frequent intervals, often upwards of every 15 minutes.

When tracking a target, real-time tracking is, of course, the most desirable option. When tracking updates are less frequent, it is possible to lose the target entirely if they move into an area where the device is unable to access the satellite signals of the GPS constellation in order to obtain tracking information. If the device has moved into such a dead spot, such as an underground or covered parking garage, since the last update, then this can leave us with a rather large radius in which the target could be located nearly anywhere.

Data loggers, while still collecting the location information at some interval, do not report the data out in real time. Instead, the device stores the location information on an internal storage device. When we need to access the location log, the device is either recovered and the storage is accessed, or the storage is accessed wirelessly from somewhere in the immediate area. Data loggers can be considerably less expensive than real-time devices, presuming that we do not need a constantly up-to-date location, but instead just need to see the data over time.

Other Devices that Provide Location Information

A variety of devices, other than those that are strictly GPS devices can provide location information. We can find location information from GPSs embedded in other mobile devices, triangulate from cell phone tower signals, or query location information from wireless access points. We may also find location information embedded in media files, or freely given by people themselves.

Cell Phones

Most cell phones today possess, at the very least, a rudimentary GPS. Even simple devices carry GPS receivers in order to allow location information to be provided in the case of emergency calls, such as those to 911 in the United States. These low-end devices generally do not include fully featured receivers and do not allow the user to access the GPS functionality.

Higher end and more recent cell phones and smart phones usually contain more fully featured GPS functionality and allow users to access this functionality. Such devices often contain features to allow the location information to be used with mapping tools, integrate it with media files, and other similar functions.

For devices that do not possess an internal GPS, a somewhat less granular physical location can usually be arrived at through the use of triangulation and signal strength measurements based on cell tower locations. Additionally, this information can be increased in accuracy through the addition of signals from 802.11 wireless networks.

Cameras and EXIF Data

In devices that include both cameras and GPS receivers, usually mobile devices such as smart phones, but some cameras also have this functionality; we can also look at data contained in the image files themselves. Files produced by such devices contain metadata, called EXIF data, which includes information such as the camera settings, camera hardware, and a variety of other data.

When image files are produced by GPS-containing devices, location information, usually in the form of longitude and latitude, is included in the EXIF data. A very common example of such a device that embeds location information is the iPhone, but many users are not aware of this feature.

TIP

Another useful bit of information, although not necessarily for locational purposes, that may be contained in EXIF data is a thumbnail image of the original picture. We can often find pictures that are cropped, sometimes cutting out useful or interesting bits of information. In 2003, Cat Schwartz, then of TechTV, discovered this the hard way when posting photos of herself to her blog, which contained intact thumbnails of the original images, to her blog. As it turned out, the original pictures were taken with Cat sans a shirt and later cropped down to a more modest form. To make a long story short, the original thumbnails were recovered and posted far and wide on the Internet. Looking through the EXIF data for an image can often produce interesting information.

Google and Others

Google, through the use of the W3C Geolocation API and a browser is able to determine your location, not to the same degree of accuracy as with a GPS receiver, but with a still very useful degree of accuracy. This is accomplished through the use of other 802.11 wireless access points located nearby. Although Google's implementation of these features requires the user to give permission of them to access the location information, we could obviously work around this to include surreptitious location gathering.

Very similarly to Google, Twitter, Lovestruck, Facebook, and a host of other Web sites and applications use geolocation information. These features can be used to find other users, tag posts with location information, play games, or most any application that can be imagined. Although these tools are generally not enabled

---

NOTE

To aid in our information gathering efforts, several search engines exist for the express purpose of aggregating information on people. One such tool is pipl, which can be found at http://pipl.com/. Pipl will pull up an interesting assortment of links and information, including pictures from social networking sites, addresses, dates of birth, e-mail addresses, documents, and a plethora of other information.

---

by default, users often enable them when prompted and leave them enabled. Users often do not look at such tools with security in mind. While we might approach a person on the street and ask him or her where he or she lives, only to be rebuffed, we may find that the person has posted the same information on Facebook for the entire world to see.

Volunteered Location Information

Aside from location information gained by technical means, information volunteered by the target can be surprisingly consistent and reliable from some people. Although we may not see information with the accuracy of GPS coordinates, often even vague information can be useful when we already know the frame of reference for the user. For example, seeing posts, called tweets, on the social networking site Twitter, along the lines of "stepping out for a coffee," we can make an educated guess as to the target's destination if we already know that the target is at work. The Web site PleaseRobMe.com, for a period of time, aggregated messages from Twitter showing such information, primarily as a vehicle to demonstrate how sharing this information is unwise. Although they no longer show the Twitter content, articles discussing the issue are still hosted there.

We can also amass locational information over time using such information. Depending on the tool that has been used to post the location aware information, we may be able to see the historical pattern of the person's movements. From this, we might be able to determine what the person's schedule is, the routes that he or she takes from one location to another, where his or her friends live, and a plethora of similar information. Particularly in the case of EXIF data, as we discussed earlier, we may be able to look at the target's accounts on photo-sharing sites, such as Flikr, to access such historical data.

Such information can be very useful, not only from the standpoint of knowing where the target is, but also where they are not. If we see information saying that the target is going out to dinner and a movie, we can assume that, for a period of at least several hours, they will not be at home or work. These location oriented bit of information can often allow us to know what windows of time that we have, if we need to work uninterrupted in the environment where our target works, lives, and so on. Such information may not always be the most accurate to work with, but is information that even a GPS tracking device could not give us.

DETECTING SURVEILLANCE

Detecting surveillance is, if not more important than, at least as important as, being able to conduct surveillance. We need to be able to find hidden devices, notice monitoring, and detect physical surveillance, so that we can go on about our operations without having untoward eyes on our activities.

Technical Surveillance Countermeasures

The technical term used to connote bug sweeping, counter surveillance, and other similar activities is Technical Surveillance Countermeasures (TSCM). TSCM is terminology used by the U.S. Department of Defense, and is a highly technical field, requiring extensive training and specialized equipment to carry out.

Such searches often involve the use of various equipment to look for emissions of covert devices into the electromagnetic spectrum, very similarly to the eavesdropping on such signals that we discussed in Chapter 13, "Covert Listening Devices." We can look for RF signals that should not be present, odd magnetic fields, electrical noise, or even heat given off by concealed devices.

RF Devices and Wiretapping

The process of detecting various bugs and RF devices is commonly known as bug sweeping. Depending on the device in question, we may or may not be able to pick up its transmissions or interference cause by them, without the use of specialized equipment. Some such devices broadcast over frequencies that are in the standard ranges of other devices, such as FM radios, and may be detectable to such equipment.

In the case of wiretapping on analog phone lines, we may have a somewhat easier task. Many such wiretapping devices are powered using the voltage on the phone like itself, and cause very slight but detectable fluctuations on the line. This may vary somewhat with the quality of the device being used. In more complex wiretapping devices, the tap itself may be placed at long distances from the premises, and may be considerably more difficult to detect.[8] Of additional concern are taps that have been initiated with the cooperation of the phone company themselves. In this case, such a tap may not be detectable at all.

In all likelihood, we will need specialized equipment capable of scanning various RF ranges, such as radio scanners or spectrum analyzers. Such equipment tends to be rather expensive and requires fairly extensive training and experience to use effectively.

In many cases, we may be better off by taking measures to render the device useless, rather than attempting to find it directly. See the "Antisurveillance Devices" section later in this chapter for a more in-depth review of such techniques.

Detecting Laser-Listening Devices

When we are looking for evidence of a laser-listening device, discussed earlier in Chapter 13, "Covert Listening Devices," most methods simply come down to detecting the beam itself, or the visible dot, in the case of a visible light laser. Depending on the equipment being used, we may be able to spot the laser being used on the surface, particularly in the case of a window. Although higher end commercial laser-listening devices often use an infrared laser, which is not visible to the naked eye, lower end devices and handmade devices will likely use a visible laser, as they are a considerably cheaper component, and are easier to obtain. The use of such devices will leave a fairly obvious bright red dot on the surface being eavesdropped upon. If an infrared laser is being used, we may also be able to spot the beam of the device, and be able to trace it back to its source, using an infrared-sensitive tool such as a camera or night vision device.

Detecting Hidden Cameras

We may find video cameras hidden in a variety of devices. Such tools are available commercially and have cameras hidden in smoke detectors, lamps, alarm clocks, teddy bears, and an enormous variety of other equipment. We may also find custom equipment, as miniature wireless cameras are also easily available. Such devices are ideal for surveillance, as they are nearly impossible to detect without a determined search and the proper equipment.

Hidden video cameras can be detected by two main methods. We can try to detect the camera by looking for the lens itself, and we can attempt to detect RF leakage from the device. In most cases, a combination of the two methods will work the best, and devices that will perform both functions in one package are commercially available.

When attempting to locate the camera by finding the lens, we need a very bright source of light and quite a bit of patience. When the lens of a camera that is using focused optics is hit with a bright light, we will see the reflection come back along the same path. To the viewer, this will show as a very bright reflection off of the surface of the camera lens. This same principle is used to detect snipers by using broadly targeted lasers and detecting the reflections from the optics in the scopes of their rifles.[9]

For cameras that are recording using an NTSC video signal, the horizontal synchronization frequency will be at 15.75 kHz, and will likely be detectable over short distances. Such devices often lack good RF shielding, having sacrificed shielding for size, and we will be able to pick the device up in this way.

Although the above method will work for specific devices, video cameras may also be transmitting over 802.11 wireless, Bluetooth, GSM, FM, and any of a number of other frequencies. Commercial devices are available that are able to look for such transmissions.[10]

Although such detective tactics may be useful in many cases, we may still be confounded by equipment that is intentionally shielded, or stores data locally and is not using a wireless transmitter. In these cases, we may need to resort to a physical search of the area for such devices. Such tactics will often be fruitless and are not recommended unless a hidden device is already known to be present.

Physical Surveillance

Detecting physical surveillance revolves around one simple principle; do something out of the ordinary and see if anyone else does the exact same thing. This may be making odd or sudden turns, driving particularly fast or slow, or any of a number of other measures that will cause someone mirroring our movements to stand out.

One such tactic is known as squaring the block[11] and consists of making four turns in the same direction, either left or right, around a block. This will end us up where we started, going in the same direction that we started, and is not a normal set of turns to take while driving. Someone following us through a set of such turns should be viewed with suspicion. On foot, similar measures can be taken by entering and immediately exiting stores by a different route, or similar repetitive or redundant paths.

In such situations, it is best to not behave in ways that will let those following us know that we have detected them, as this may push them into other, less desirable, actions. The best route it to proceed to a place of safety, or a place that the pursuers will be unlikely or unwilling to follow us, such as a police station.

ANTISURVEILLANCE DEVICES

In Chapter 13, "Covert Listening Devices," we discussed a variety of covert listening devices, including cameras, audio bugs and others, and how such devices might be used. We may also find ourselves on the other side of such surveillance, and it is important that we know how to defeat or mitigate the use of such tools.

We can attempt to jam the frequencies that RF devices work on, find cameras, foil laser-listening devices, and limit our emissions into the electromagnetic spectrum, but we must still be vigilant, as these technologies are ever changing.

RF Jammers

Many surveillance devices, audio, video, or otherwise, operate using various radio frequencies. Within a small area, we can generally jam RF frequencies in order to prevent such device from functioning properly. Such devices are illegal for general use in the United States and can result in stiff penalties for the user according to the FCC: "The operation of transmitters designed to jam or block wireless communications is a violation of the Communications Act of 1934.... Fines for a first offense can range as high as $11,000 for each violation or imprisonment for up to one year, and the device used may also be seized and forfeited to the U.S. government."[12]

Despite their illegal status in the United States, commercial jammers do exist and are used by law enforcement for jamming portable communications, among other devices. Such devices are often used to jam cell phone frequencies when law enforcement agencies are conducting large operations and want to avoid cellular communications in the area from warning those concerned or associated with the incident. Such users are given special permission by the FCC to operate these devices.

FIGURE 15.4 Wavebubble – A Self-Tuning, Wide-Bandwidth Portable RF Jammer.[13]

Courtesy of Limor Fried – Adafruit.com

Various home-brewed jamming devices exist as well, such as the Wavebubble, pictured in Figure 15.4. The Wavebubble is particularly useful because of its ability to autotune to multiple frequencies, thus allow it to jam a wide variety of devices. Because of their illegal status, a few plans for such devices exist and are available to the casual user, but kits or assembled units generally do not. Those with skills in electronics or electrical engineering, however, should experience little difficulty in building such devices from the plans available.

Additionally, other devices that operate in or around the same frequency or frequencies can be used as field expedient jamming devices. A classical example of this is commonly seen in 802.11 wireless networks. The 802.11b and 802.11g network devices operate in the 2.4GHz band, a band that receives interference from several household appliances, particularly microwaves and portable phones. Such devices operating in the area of the target frequency many disrupt devices using it entirely, or may, at the very least introduce noise into such signals.

Defeating Laser-Listening Devices

In Chapter 13, "Covert Listening Devices," we discussed the use of laser-listening devices as a good alternative to planting audio bugs. To reiterate briefly, laser-listening devices bounce a laser off of a surface, typically glass, and the vibrations in the surface, often caused by noises in the room, cause the beam to fluctuate. The beam is picked up by a sensor and converted to sound, thus relaying sounds in the vicinity of the target surface.

Laser-listening devices can be easily defeated by introducing spurious vibrations into the surface that is being monitored. One approach that may defeat such a device, as well as drowning out other audio-listening devices in the room would be to place a loud audio source, such as music or a television in the room in order to drown out the conversation. Although this would be an effective approach in most cases, it would make holding a conversation more difficult.

> ### SHINOBI-IRI (Stealth and Entering Methods)
>
> Laser-listening devices are by no means foolproof and undetectable, but they can be very difficult to notice, even when cheaply obtained or constructed. One of the best methods of defense against such tool is to not hold sensitive conversations in areas that present an approach, such as a window, to the laser. Attackers know that windows are the easy targets for this type of eavesdropping, and will be much more likely to eavesdrop in these locations.

Another option and one that specifically targets the laser-listening device would be to vibrate the surface in question directly. This can be done in a field expedient manner by attaching any continuously vibrating source, such as a small battery-powered motor or a massager to the surface of the window. Commercial units that perform this function are available as well.

Blinding Cameras

Surveillance cameras, once detected can be blinded in a variety of ways. In Chapter 7, "Infiltration," we touched briefly on this topic when discussing alarm system evasion. In that particular case, we would be dealing with security cameras, which are generally much more obvious and more easily accessed.

Lasers

In Chapter 7, "Infiltration," we discussed the use of laser to blind surveillance cameras. Security cameras are generally sizeable devices, and we can often count on being able to get a good angle on them to point a laser for blinding purposes. With covert surveillance cameras, we may not have such luxury, as we will likely be looking at a much smaller target that is installed in such a way that it is not noticeable. In such cases, we may need to change equipment slightly, in order to be able to properly blind the device.

We had previously suggested the use of a scoped device in order to reliably be able to hit the camera lens from a distance. In the case of a concealed camera, we are much more likely to be closer to the device. Although still using a laser, we are more likely to find success with the type that produces a split beam over a broader area, or a device that uses multiple beams. This will allow us to blanket the area where the camera lens sits, instead of having to hit a very small spot accurately.

Infrared Lights

Also in Chapter 7, "Infiltration," we talked about using strong infrared light sources to blind cameras that are sensitive to infrared light. In that context, we covered the use of small infrared LEDs to block out the face of individuals passing through areas that are monitored by surveillance cameras. In the case of smaller concealed devices, we will more likely want to blind the entire camera, instead of smaller areas in its viewing area.

To this end, we can use a small, bright, infrared source, preferably one that can be mounted on a wall, or set up on a base, which would allow it to be aimed. We should be aware that, when setting up such a device, we do not pass between the light source and the camera, thus restoring the view of the device. Such tools will more than likely need to be used at a much shorter range than laser camera-blinding devices, as their effective range is much shorter.

Blocking or Dismantling

Finally, we can look at directly blocking the view of the camera itself, or dismantling the device. Although some of the other measures, such as blinding the camera, are temporary in nature and not likely to leave permanent physical evidence behind, tampering with the device itself will almost definitely do so.

We can take two primary approaches using such methods; we can occlude the lens itself or we can simply remove the device. When covering the lens, we can use paint, grease, physical objects, or anything that will sit properly in front of it. Depending on the exact location of the device, we could conceivably take an approach in covering the device that appears to be accidental.

The other alternative is to simply remove or destroy the device. Depending on how the device was placed, it may or may not be immediately accessible, so we may need to take steps in removing other devices which may house it, such as a smoke alarm, and doing so may be a complex task. In some cases, it may be easier to damage or destroy just the lens of the device, rather than removing the whole assembly.

TEMPEST

When discussing TEMPEST, a common argument is on what exactly TEMPEST means. Some say that it is an acronym, the composition of which is unknown, but many guesses exist. Others say that it was the name of a project or series of investigations into emissions in the electromagnetic spectrum.

In Chapter 13, "Covert Listening Devices," we discussed how we can monitor emissions from monitors, keyboards, indicator LEDs, and other equipment. On the other side of the coin is the effort to stop or mitigate such emissions.

Shielded Equipment

Equipment can, through shielding or other methods, be a candidate to be certified by the NSA as a TEMPEST-compliant device. Such devices must comply with, at the time of this writing, *NSTISSAM TEMPEST/1–92, Compromising Emanations Laboratory Test Standard, Electromagnetics*, dated 15 December 1992.[14] This document discusses the construction and testing of such devices, and breaks approved devices into three categories:

- Type 1 – These devices are controlled or classified equipment designed for the protection of classified or sensitive materials.
- Type 2 – These devices are unclassified equipment designed for the protection of unclassified but sensitive materials.
- Type 3 – These devices are unclassified equipment designed for the protection of unclassified sensitive or commercial information.

Shielded Facilities

Entire facilities can be shielded from spurious electromagnetic signals emanating from them. Such undertakings are enormously expensive and difficult to carry out, often being completely unfeasible, on any large scale, outside of new construction. Such rooms or buildings are constructed in such a way that they form a Faraday cage, often accomplished by placing a fine copper mesh in the walls, floor, and ceiling. Such a cage will prevent RF emissions from leaving the area. The other important component is to exclude any unfiltered conductive materials from connecting the shielded are to the outside, as these can act as an antenna to propagate signals outside of the shielding.

Although such areas were more common during the height of the cold war, they are much less so presently. The expense and bother of creating such areas far outweighs that of other security measures that can produce similar results, such as the shielding of equipment discussed earlier.

When eavesdropping on the emissions from CRT or LCD displays, only the high-frequency portions of the video signal are normally available to the eavesdropper, even at very short distances. In order for low-frequency signals to propagate over a distance, a very large antenna is normally needed, which is not a regular feature of a display device.

Jammers

As an alternative to shielding facilities or equipment, it is possible to deliberately broadcast interference on the frequencies that we are concerned with for TEMPEST purposes. Such devices are available commercially and are commonly able to jam signals in the frequencies that leak from monitors, keyboard, and other similar devices, as we discussed in Chapter 13, "Covert Listening Devices."

TEMPEST Fonts

Because the eavesdropper is already missing a portion of the video signal, we can use this to our advantage with specially filtered fonts. If we process a font through a low-band filter and remove a portion of the horizontal information, we can render the text using this font illegible or even invisible to the eavesdropper.[15]

As can be seen in Figure 15.5, the information removed from the font by the filtering process is almost completely unnoticeable to the user. Under strong magnification, however, the change is visible.

Although TEMPEST fonts may render the text on the screen unreadable to us, other methods of eavesdropping will, likely, still be available. In the grand scheme

Normal Font

TEMPEST Font

FIGURE 15.5 Normal and TEMPEST Fonts.

of eavesdropping on emissions, attacks involving the display are actually more challenging than some of the others. We may get better mileage out of eavesdropping on keyboard emissions, and will need to expend fewer resources to carry out the attack.

Summary

In this chapter, we discussed several important surveillance topics, namely gathering intelligence, location tracking, detecting surveillance, and antisurveillance devices.

When discussing intelligence gathering, we talked about some of the places from where we can gather data on companies and individuals. We can search through resumes and job postings, blogs and social networks, and credit reports for personal information. We can also search through multiple government Web sites for information on companies and those associated with them.

We also talked about the tools that we can use for location tracking. We can use purpose-built GPS devices and tracking systems for tracking almost anything that we can place such a device in, or attach a device to. We can also use locational information found in mobile devices, media files, from locationally aware Web sites and applications, or we can simply search for information that has been freely given or posted by our targets.

We covered various methods that might be used to detect surveillance. We could potentially be the target of a variety of surveillance techniques, and should be aware of how to locate or be aware of them. Such methods might include monitoring for RF signals from devices, searching for laser-listening devices, detecting hidden cameras, and how to discover physical surveillance.

Finally, we discussed the use of antisurveillance devices and methods. We talked about how to defeat various listening devices and how to blind or disable cameras. We also talked about TEMPEST and how facilities or equipment might be shielded in order to lessen or mitigate emissions into the electromagnetic spectrum.

Endnotes

1. Hatsumi M. Ninjutsu: history and tradition. Burbank (CA): Unique Publications, Inc.; 1981. 0865680272.
2. Sunzi. The art of war. [Giles L, Trans.]. [Online] www.gutenberg.org/etext/132. [Original work published 1910] [accessed 01.07.10].
3. Schumer C.E. Social security numbers are widely available in bulk and online records, but changes to enhance security are occuring. United States Government Accountability Office; 2008. www.gao.gov/new.items/d081009r.pdf. GAO-08-1009R [accessed 01.07.10].
4. United States Courts. Public Access to Court Electronic Records. [Online] https://pacer .login.uscourts.gov/cgi-bin/login.pl?court_id=00idx.; 2010 [accessed 17.05.10].
5. General Services Administration. Excluded Parties List System. [Online] www.epls.gov/; 2010 [accessed 17.05.10].

6. U.S. Securities and Exchange Commission. Important information about EDGAR. U.S. Securities and Exchange Commission. [Online] www.sec.gov/edgar/aboutedgar.htm; 2010 [accessed 17.05.10].

7. Lemos R. Rental-car firm exceeding the privacy limit. CNET News. [Online] http://news.cnet.com/2100-1040-268747.html; 2001 [accessed 19.05.10].

8. Petersen J.K. Understanding surveillance technologies: spy devices, privacy, history, & applications, revised and expanded. 2nd ed. New York, NY: Auerbach Publications; 2007. 978-0849383199.

9. Shachtman N. Lasers stop snipers before they fire. Danger room. [Online] www.wired.com/dangerroom/2007/04/darpa_countersn/; 2007 [accessed 14.05.10].

10. Defense Devices. Camera detector by radio frequency (RF) or lens capture. DefensiveDevices.com. [Online] www.defensedevices.com/laser-camera-detector.html.; 2010 [accessed 14.05.10].

11. Katz D., Caspi I. Executive's guide to personal security. Hoboken, NJ: Wiley; 2003. 978-0471449874.

12. Federal Communications Commission. FCC: Wireless services: broadband PCS: operations: blocking & jamming. Federal Communications Commission. [Online] http://wireless.fcc.gov/services/index.htm?job=operations_1&id=broadband_pcs; 2010 [accessed 14.05.10].

13. Fried L. Wavebubble. www.ladyada.net/make/wavebubble/index.html [accessed 01.07.10].

14. National Security Telecommunications and Information Systems Security. Compromising emanations laboratory test requirements electromagnetics (U). National Security Agency; 1992. NSTISSAM TEMPEST/1-92.

15. Kuhn M., Anderson R. Soft tempest: hidden data transmission using electromagnetic emanations. Information hiding. www.cl.cam.ac.uk/~mgk25/ih98-tempest.pdf; 1998. [accessed 01.07.10]

Sabotage

During the Sengoku period (1477 to 1600), the demand for ninja by warlords engaged in civil war was high – the ninja families of Iga and Koga were sought after for their abilities to "infiltrate fortified towns considered impenetrable, to commit selected assassinations, and to conduct guerilla warefare."[1] In the histories of ninja comes one story where ninja infiltrated the castle of Ujizane and set fire to structures inside the fortification; that alone qualified as sabotage, but what makes it notable was that the ninja set the fires in a way that the castle inhabitants "believes that traitors coming from their own garrison had attacked them."[1] When we examine the topic of sabotage as Zukin, we need to understand how malicious attackers might conduct their attacks surreptitiously, and in a way to confuse the defenders to misunderstand the origins of the attacks.

Sabotage is the act of disrupting another party, process, mechanism, and so on, in order to hinder it. Many explanations exist for the origin of the term, including throwing wooden shoes into mechanisms, bumbling or unskilled workers, and a few others. In any case, the common usage of the term equates to throwing a monkey wrench into the works of someone or something in order to keep it from functioning properly.

Sabotage can be of logical form, including various denial-of-service attacks, malware, Web vandalism, or any of a number of other tactics. It can also be physical in nature, involving severing communications links, infecting communications and networking hardware with malware, or simply putting glue in the keyway of a lock.

We may also see sabotage from a variety of sources, primarily divided into internal or external sources. Internal sources might be disgruntled employees, or even the slip of a finger by someone editing a configuration file. External sources may be hackers who are compromising systems for the fun of doing so, or they may be terrorists bent on mass destruction.

Some forms of sabotage, mostly in the logical area, but a few physical methods as well, may be available as tools for the penetration tester to use, as some such activities may not be permanently damaging in nature. We can certainly see the use of sabotage both in conflicts between nations and in criminal use on a regular basis.

Ninja Hacking. DOI: 10.1016/B978-1-59749-588-2.00016-0

LOGICAL SABOTAGE

Logical sabotage can involve a variety of different actions and methods of attack. We can work from a purely software perspective and use malware or backdoors. We can also use logical sabotage to effect other types of sabotage, through data manipulation or vandalism, or a combination of both physical and logical approaches, such as the introduction of malware-infected devices or appliances. In either case, logical sabotage measures can be very effective if carried out with subtlety.

Malware

The introduction of malware into an environment can make an excellent agent of sabotage. Depending on the malware in question, we could use such tools to simply cause chaos and confusion in an environment, or we could use it to deliver a more sophisticated payload for carrying out data manipulation, operating system alterations, or other more complex tasks.

Untargeted Malware

The release of untargeted malware into an environment can be an unpredictable tool, and likely not one that we would use during standard penetration testing. Such an attack will sew a variety of chaos and might serve as both an act of sabotage and a distraction, as we discussed in Chapter 11, "Distraction." A successful malware attack will draw the attention of security and IT personnel as they are forced to deal with it.

As we covered in Chapter 9, "Discovering Weak Points in Area Defenses," when using malware in an area, such as a corporate location, it is important that we use malware that has been adapted or created for the particular environment. Most large environments have antimalware tools in place, and the use of malware that already exists in the wild will likely be picked up and dealt with in short order. Custom malware can be tested against the same antimalware tools that are in use in the target environment, so that such tools can be bypassed.

WARNING

Using malware as a tool for penetration testing can be very dangerous. Yes, it does make an excellent tool for conducting client side attacks, and as we mentioned, it can be unpredictable and behave in unexpected ways. The greatest care should be taken when using these tools to ensure that they do not get out of our control and behave in unexpected ways.

We must also be concerned with the potential unboundedness of such malware. Even if the malware is custom built for the purpose, it is entirely possible that because of an error in programming or design, the malware will spread in unpredictable ways. If such an event occurs, our malware may spread into areas that we did not plan for and do not desire; it may generate activity on a level to as to call attention to itself in ways that we cannot control. Such tools should be used carefully and with awareness of the potential consequences.

Backdoors

Backdoors provide us with a method of bypassing the normal authentication process for a given system. Backdoors can be included in an application, either by the application developer or later by an attacker, they can be a freestanding application of their own, such as the command and control interfaces used in the nodes of botnets, or they could be implemented in the hardware or firmware of an actual device.

Backdoors, for the purposes of sabotage can allow us access to a system, outside of the restrictions of the normal authentication mechanism, in order to carry out our activities unimpeded. Such tools might be put in place, in advance of leaving, by former employees in order to give them access after their accounts have been terminated, or they may have been installed by an attacker after compromising a system.

While they can be used as a standalone tool, backdoors are often installed as a single component of an attack or a malware package. An attacker might install a backdoor in order to maintain or ease future access to a system, or a backdoor might be installed by another piece of malware in order to further exploit a machine, beyond the initial attack. Although the installation of a backdoor may or may not constitute sabotage directly, it will certainly ease the path for such activities.

Rootkits

For sabotage purposes, rootkits are a very useful type of tool to install on a system. They can allow a wide variety of activities to take place on systems without the knowledge or consent of either users or protective measures in the operating system, if this is what is desired. Rootkits can be used to bypass access controls on systems, provide backdoors to allow nonprivileged users to act as administrators, disable antimalware tools, or any of a number of activities that would normally require administrative access.

When installing or using tools on a system, rootkits can allow such activities to be hidden entirely and removed from the view of the operating system. This can allow the operation of malware that would normally be detected by antimalware tools, run processes that would normally be suspicious, or conduct activities that would call attention to the presence of such tools of the activities could be seen. Such a tool was used as part of a copy protection system on about 50 music CDs produce by Sony in 2005.

NOTE

The copy protection implemented by Sony, in this particular case, backfired in more ways than just being dodgy software protection. Later in 2005, they recalled the CDs carrying the rootkit, pulled all of the affected CDs from the stores and offered to exchange a version of the CDs to customers that did not carry such software. Additionally, Sony suffered legally and, in some cases, financially at the hands of Texas, New York, California, and the U.S. Federal Trade Commission, and the Electronic Frontier Foundation.

FIGURE 16.1 A Stealthy USB Storage Device.

Photograph by Brian Baskin

The Sony rootkit installed silently and automatically when one of the affected CDs was inserted into a computer, and put measures in place to prevent the music from being copied from the CD. As a part of the copy protection package, the software installed a feature that would hide any registry keys, files, or processes that started with sys, and this functionality was not restricted to Sony's own tools.[2]

Infected Hardware

Many hardware devices today are designed in such a way to make the inclusion of malware an easy task. Products such as digital picture frames, USB storage devices, as shown in Figure 16.1, phones, and quite a bit of other hardware can function as storage devices and, thus, repositories for malicious files.

Digital picture frames seem to crop up every few months as a carrier of malware. Such devices are effectively a display attached to a storage device, which is accessible through a USB port. They have been many occurrences of such devices either shipping with malware already in the storage area of the device, or included in the utility and driver software that accompany it.

Phones and USB flash devices can also provide similar storage areas for malware, and are an oft seen carrier as well. At the 2010, AusCERT conference, IBM gave away flash drives containing an autorun worm. It appears that some, or possibly all, of the drives that they handed out were infected, prompting them to send out an apology/warning to the entire conference attendee list.[3]

We would think that the insertion of malware in such devices would be caught somewhere in the process of quality checking the build for these devices before shipping them, but this often seems not to be the case. Depending on the specific tools that are used in conjunction with the infected hardware, such attacks can be very useful in penetration testing and they certainly would be, and are, used in actual attacks by hackers and criminals.

Data Manipulation

Data manipulation attacks are generally an indirect type of sabotage. Although altering data may not directly compromise a project, decisions based on bad data have the potential to cause great damage later. For an example of how a change in data can cause the failure of an entire operation, we can look at the crash of the Mars Orbiter in 1999.

In this particular case, the difference in measurement of navigational data between two teams involved, one using metric measurements and the other using English measurements caused the craft to go 15 miles further into the atmosphere of Mars than was planned. Instead of orbiting Mars, the Orbiter is believed to have pushed straight through the atmosphere and out the other side, travelling off into space.

To clarify, nothing was mechanically or otherwise wrong with the entire project, just a lack of communication on how to interpret the data. When data manipulation is carried out as a deliberate attack, the results can range from common attacks such as identity theft to potential loss of life, depending on the system in question and the data being altered.

Manipulation for Financial Gain

As we discussed in Chapter 11, "Distraction," when covering the generation of spurious company data, it is possible to heavily impact the financial state of a company through data manipulation. In the example we discussed with UAL, such troubles were caused by an incorrectly reported date on an article discussing an old bankruptcy filing.

Because of the often volatile nature of the various financial markets, attacks that involve manipulation of financial data only have to be moderately effective in order for a huge result to be seen. If the reporting stock prices are manipulated, either up or down, even if these changes are quickly discovered, the financial impact will likely have already been felt by the company in question.

We can also look at other methods of financial manipulation, such as the oft discussed use of "salami fraud." Although the term for it may be unfamiliar, we have all heard of the embezzlement attack in which a fraction of each penny in a transaction is siphoned off to another bank account, collecting enormous amounts of money with no one the wiser for it.

In 1998, in Los Angeles, a salami fraud attack was carried out at a 12 gas stations, overcharging customers out of a total estimated to be more than $1 million. In this particular case, a chip was replaced in the 140 pumps across all 12 stations, causing the quantity of gas dispensed to the customer to be misreported by up to 25 percent. Additionally, as a measure to help avoid detection, the chips were programmed to operate properly when the total amount of gasoline dispensed was 5 or 10 gallons, the increment used by those inspecting the pumps. In this particular case, the activity was caught because of the amount of the data manipulation being too high. Some customers were dispensed gas in amounts that were reported by the pump to be in excess of the capacity of their gas tanks, thus prompting an investigation.[4]

In standard penetration testing efforts, we will likely not see data manipulation designed to commit financial fraud. It is possible, however, that such approaches may at least be discussed, if not carried all the way through, by financial institutions looking to prevent exactly this sort of attack.

User Interface Manipulation

User interface manipulation is a particularly difficult form of data manipulation to detect, unless the tools to do so are already present on the client system. This type of attack alters the user's interface to the application, causing them to take certain actions unintentionally. A perfect example of such an attack is clickjacking.

Clickjacking is a browser-based attack in which portions of the Web page are manipulated by using invisible elements. For example, a user may attempt to click a link or a button that has been overlaid with an invisible element that executes another action entirely. Users can be tricked in this manner into making purchases, altering permissions on Web applications, or any of a number of similar activities.

SHINOBI-IRI (Stealth and Entering Methods)

User interface manipulation is a great tool for penetration testing. If done properly, the user will be completely unaware that anything has taken place, and the end result can be carefully controlled by the penetration tester. In order to prove that we can carry out an attack, we do not even need to do anything that might compromise the system or systems in question in a dangerous way, but can do something simple to indicate success instead, such as incrementing a counter.

Similar user interface manipulation is possible for nearly any application. As with Web pages, it helps if the user is not intimately familiar with the application and if we can render our changes invisible. Other than detecting the effects of clandestine application manipulation, either through direct examination of the application itself or through examination of the output of all parts of the application, potentially including the client, with a packet analysis tool, such modifications can be very difficult to detect.

User interface manipulation can be a useful part of penetration testing, where such activities are considered to be in the scope of the testing effort. Such tactics are used on a very regular basis by criminals, and could be of great use in a cyber conflict.

Vandalism

Simple vandalism may be considered an act of sabotage, particularly when the Web site or service being vandalized is central to the operation of a business or organization. We can say simple vandalism, but in the case of a server being vandalized, it has likely been compromised to some extent to make the alterations, which may leave open other attacks having taken place as well. An act of vandalism, such as the defacement of a Web site, may be used as a distractor to draw attention away from other attacks.

Web site vandalism is very common, with defacement of Web sites being discussed in the media on a seemingly daily basis. Such attacks are often done in support of some type of cause, be it environmental, political, or otherwise. We will discuss such motivations later in this chapter when we talk about hacktivists.

PHYSICAL SABOTAGE

Physical sabotage can take a variety of forms, from disrupted communications, to downed utilities, to unusable physical access controls. Physical damage, particularly to communications infrastructure can be incredibly expensive and time consuming to repair. Breaks in critical infrastructure, such as fiber optic cable, can have enormous impact on very large geographic areas. Acts of physical sabotage are very likely to be completely out of scope for penetration testing.

Network and Communications Infrastructure

Depending on the particular line of communication in question, physical sabotage to communications media can be devastating. In many cases, entire countries, or even multiple countries, are connected to the outside world by a few main fiber optic and satellite connections. In general, a few strategically placed attacks to media or infrastructure equipment can disable communications to a large number of organizations and individuals.

In a roughly 1-month period in 2008, five undersea cables were damaged in the Mediterranean and Arabian seas in the Middle East. These cuts caused outages in data and voice traffic for 60 million users in India, 12 million in Pakistan, 6 million in Egypt, and nearly 5 million in Saudi Arabia.[5] Much speculation took place as to the exact cause of this cluster of cable damage, but few actual causes were ever found.

Network and communications infrastructures, while clearly not a target for penetration testing, are one of the first to be attacked in a conflict that includes cyber warfare elements. It may be possible that some communications targets would be considered fair targets in an extreme penetration test, but permission and very carefully laid out ground rules would need to be established in advance.

Fiber Optic Cables

Not only are fiber optic cables a prime target for sabotage, but they are also quite delicate. As a semiregular occurrence, we can see reports in the media of fiber bundles that have been cut accidentally during excavation for construction or utility projects. Such breaks are not quickly repaired and are very costly.

Additionally, access to fiber optic cables is relatively easily obtained in many places, with fiber running through many of the same underground channels that are used for other utilities. In many cases, manholes and other poorly protected entry points allow easy access directly to these communication lines, and once accessed, fiber optic cables are very easy to damage to the point of no longer functioning.

In 2009, in Santa Clara, San Benito, and Santa Cruz counties in California, 10 fiber optic cables were deliberately cut, affecting cell phones, Internet access, and phone lines for more than 50,000 customers, including 911 services in the area.[6] At the time of this writing, the saboteurs had not been caught. Incidents such as these demonstrate well the frailty of the communications infrastructure in many countries.

Analog Phone Lines

Analog phone lines are very easily sabotaged and present a very lightly secured target. In many locations, both residential and business phone lines truncate in a box, referred to as a demarcation point, or demarc, as shown in Figure 16.2, on the outside of the building. The demarc is often poorly secured, if secured at all, and makes an easy target for a saboteur.

FIGURE 16.2 A Demarcation Point.

Additionally, as with fiber optic lines, phone lines are very easily accessible. Many such lines run unprotected on the outside of buildings, and points of aggregation for multiple lines sit in distinctive looking boxes by the side of the road. In order to sabotage the phone lines for an entire neighborhood or for an industrial or business park, an attacker driving a vehicle over one or two such boxes would likely suffice.

Counterfeit Hardware

Counterfeit hardware has great potential for sabotage. Although much of the counterfeit hardware found on the market appears to be there for purely financial reasons, this may not be the entirety of the reason behind it. At the very least, critical hardware, such as that found in major network infrastructure or medical equipment, will perform at a lesser level when constructed from the cheapest possible components. In the worst case, such hardware could be constructed with additional features that can remotely trigger a failure of the device.

Network Hardware

Network hardware, such as that shown in Figure 16.3, is a particularly sensitive area in which to find sabotaged devices. Such sabotage could be purely disruptive in nature, allowing a device to be remotely disabled, or it could be much more subtle, with the inclusion of features to allow network traffic to be sniffed, altered, or even selectively filtered.

One complicating factor in using such devices is that they are nearly indistinguishable from genuine devices. Since 2007, U.S. customs agents have seized more than 5 million such counterfeit devices.[7] In investigations by the FBI, sales of counterfeit Cisco hardware have been discovered going to the Navy, Marines, Air Force, the FAA, and even the FBI.[8] The FBI is particularly concerned that such devices have been deliberately placed in the Department of Defense for reasons of espionage or sabotage.

FIGURE 16.3 Network Hardware.

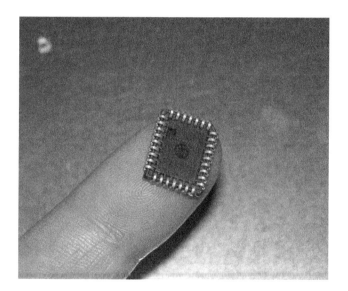

FIGURE 16.4 An Electronics Component.

Components

In addition to entire counterfeit devices, counterfeit components are also very common. U.S. Customs agents regularly seize counterfeit integrated circuits and other small electronic components, such as the one shown in Figure 16.4, which are destined for medical devices, aircraft, weapons systems, and many other sensitive areas. Such components are often low grade and not build to the same specifications as the components that they masquerade as.

Counterfeit hardware items can have a place in penetration testing efforts, but must be used carefully so as not to cause undue or unexpected disruption. Such items definitely have use in cyber-oriented conflicts and may be used to trigger disruptions in services for opponents.

Access Controls

Access control systems can often be sabotaged quite easily, as they are intended to either allow or disallow access to someone or something, and not necessarily robustly resist tampering that is not intended to bypass them. Such systems can often be rendered unusable by damaging or obscuring sensors, in the case of physical access controls, or can be overloaded by denial-of-service attacks, in the case of physical access controls. Additionally, we may find situations where a particular access control spans both areas, and sabotaging one of them will cause the control to no longer function.

Sabotaging access controls can be used as a tactic of delay, distraction, or disruption. If we can prevent an access control system from functioning properly, we can at the very least cause a delay while the issue is sorted out or a manual method is implemented, or we may be able to prevent many activities that require network access or remote access from taking place at all.

Biometric Systems

Biometric systems are generally very easy to sabotage, on either a temporary or a permanent basis. Most biometric systems rely on one or more sensors to measure physical attributes, such as height, weight, fingerprints, characteristics of the eye, and many other such features. Such sensors are generally positioned so that they can conveniently be reached or approached by the person attempting to authenticate, and protective barriers are generally not present between the person and the sensor.

Such sensors can be disabled by disconnecting the sensor, if cabling or connectors are accessible, by obscuring the surface of the sensor with paint, grease, spilled coffee, or other materials, by physically damaging the sensor itself, or any of a number of other methods. The exact methods that we would choose to use would depend on the environment, our desire for stealth, and the reason for the sabotage.

In the case of an all-out attack, as we might find be carried out by a malicious attacker or criminal, in the case of actual cyber warfare, we might be more free to choose methods that are more destructive and more permanent in nature. In such cases, we might choose to physically destroy the sensor itself, thus keeping the system from being used until it could be replaced entirely.

In the case of a penetration test, or other similar operation, we might instead only temporarily disable the device by unplugging a cable, or obscuring the sensor with something viscous and difficult to immediately remove. Such tactics would require troubleshooting the sensor or cleaning the surface before the sensor could be used again, but should not be permanently damaging.

Locks

Physical locks can be easily sabotaged, in ways that are immediately visible or in ways that are much less obvious. In either case, the lock can be disabled in a locked or an unlocked position. Again, as with our discussion on biometric systems above, we can sabotage locks in either permanent or temporary ways.

One of the easiest ways to sabotage a lock is to obstruct the keyway with something, preferably something that is difficult to remove. One of the simplest field expedient measures is to insert a key into the lock as far as it will go and break it off. This can be done with any key that will fit into the keyway of the lock, and can prove difficult to remove, depending on how much of the remaining key protrudes from the lock. As long as a key that is not entirely the wrong size and shape is not forced into the lock, this should not cause any permanent damage, and can be removed by a locksmith.

In the case that the goal is to permanently render the lock unusable, we can use a similar tactic, but from a slightly different angle. In this case, any material that will fit in the keyway will suffice, preferably something metal and slightly larger than the keyway. To permanently disable the lock, we will want to drive the material into it and break it off. If we use another tool, such as a small screwdriver, it will fit into the keyway and then use a blunt instrument to drive the material in further, this will make the obstruction even more difficult to remove.

Last, but certainly not the least, we can use some sort of glue to fill the keyway; superglue will do the job nicely. In this case, we will want to fill as much of the keyway as we can with the glue, so that we can be sure to fix the pins in place and prevent a key from fitting in the keyway. Given considerable time and patience, it may be possible to remove enough residue to use the lock again, but it will likely need to be replaced.

Logical Access Controls

Logical access controls can be one of the easiest access controls to sabotage. Such systems generally have a set limit for the number of incorrect passwords, PINs, and so on that can be entered before the system will lock out the account for some period of time. In this case, we can use something along the lines of a denial-of-service attack to render the system unusable for any accounts that we would care to target in such a manner.

In the case that we have direct access to the logical access control, which could be as simple as the login prompt on a server, we only need to enter the targeted account name and a bad password the required number of times to hit the level of an account lockout. Depending on the system in question, we may or may not see an error message indicating that the account has been locked out.

The duration of such account or system lockouts depends on the configuration of the logical access control in question. Many lockouts will resolve themselves within a specified period of time, often 10 to 20 min. Some systems require the account or system to be manually unlocked by a helpdesk support technician or system administrator. Accounts or systems that require a manual unlock will tend to take longer to regain functionality, even when reported immediately. For systems that unlock accounts automatically, the saboteur will need to either continuously work to keep the account locked, or set up an automated process to do so.

SOURCES OF SABOTAGE

Sabotage can come from two directions: internal or external. Internal sabotage can be deliberate, as we frequently see in cases of internal sabotage, often perpetrated by disgruntled employees. In such cases, particularly, when the saboteur is in a position to have administrative rights on the systems and networks, such sabotage can cripple and entire organization.

We may also see sabotage from external sources. External saboteurs can be from foreign governments, terrorists, joyriding hackers, or any of a number of others. External attacks may be brazen attempts with no degree of subtlety, or they may be stealthy and covert, as the ninja of history would carry out.

Internal

Internal attacks, those that we define as attacks coming from a legitimate member or part of the organization, can be extremely damaging. The potential for using this approach in a penetration-testing scenario is tenuous, at best, but this approach might be used with the aid of a turned member of the target organization, as discussed in Chapter 10, "Psychological Weaknesses." Typically, such attacks come from disgruntled employees, those exploring internal systems or networks, or simple human error.

Disgruntled Employees

Sabotage brought about by disgruntled employees can be one of the single most destructive forms of sabotage that an organization can experience. Such saboteurs usually have intimate knowledge of the applications, systems, and networks that they have worked with, and may have administrative rights or know the details of any backdoors that exist.

Disgruntled employees are often in such a state due to being laid off as a result of outsourcing efforts, reduced pay, demotion, or other similar activities. Unfortunately for the organization in question, such activities often come with ample notice and provide time for the now unhappy employee to plan out their revenge. Such events happen on a quite regular basis and can often be seen being reported in the mainstream media.

In 2008, Terry Childs, a network administrator for the city of San Francisco took control of the network infrastructure running the fiber WAN through which the majority of the network traffic for the city traveled. Although the network was still functioning normally, Childs had locked all of the other administrators out and refused to give up the passwords, even after being arrested.[9]

Childs had reportedly escalated his level of access by sniffing credentials through monitoring devices that he had clandestinely placed on the network for exactly this purpose. He then tampered with the equipment to gain sufficient access to allow him to later lock the other administrators out of the network devices. This tampering was discovered when a new person was brought in to oversee security of the organization and performed an assessment of the devices in question, noting the unusual activity.[10]

A week after the incident, Childs was convinced to surrender the passwords for the devices to the mayor of San Francisco. In 2010, after spending 21 months in jail, Childs was found guilty on one count of felony network tampering and could face a maximum of 5 years in prison. At the time of this writing, he had not been sentenced, and may possibly be released after sentencing because of his time already served.[11]

Such activities, presuming that they do not cause permanent damage, may be entirely within the scope of penetration testing, depending on the situation. In the case of an actual disgruntled employee, malicious hacker, or other attacker with bad intentions, such a situation could be very damaging.

The Curious

One of the most frequently discussed topics in information security is the issue of attacks that originate internally, that is, from someone that legitimately works for the organization in question. Although much discussion has taken place on what percentage of attacks originate internally and externally, we still have to face the fact that such attacks do happen.

Particularly in organizations that are technical in nature, we will find people who are both bored and curious, which can be a dangerous combination for the organization. Such people may explore the network and systems, taking measures to gain elevated levels of access when they find themselves blocked, opening files, accessing storage devices, and just generally poking around at the environment.

When dealing with users who have administrative access to servers containing files or e-mail, we may see snooping for the sake of curiosity. Such access can lead to the discovery of information regarding pay, layoffs, or other privileged information, potentially placing our curious person into the realm of a disgruntled employee, as discussed earlier. Some privileged information may also be of inherent value for intellectual property or strategic reasons.

Additionally, people who have gained privileged access and are exploring systems with which they are unfamiliar may cause inadvertent damage to these systems. In the process of gaining access, manipulating logs to hide their activity, or other similar tasks, the processes and software running on the system may be disrupted or disabled. Although this may blur the line with sabotage due to human error, those investigating such incidents are unlikely to see the situation that way because of the nature of the access to the system or systems in question.

Human Error

Although it might be a bit of a stretch to call such incidents sabotage, human error can produce many or all of the same results as such activities that are deliberately carried out.

Configuration files can be a very rich source of accidental sabotage. Some configuration files are very sensitive to spacing and odd characters, the order of parameters, or settings with dependencies on other settings. When a configuration file has been manipulated in a way that the application or device cannot properly interpret, the results may be unusual or unpredictable. A bad configuration change may cause security settings to be more permissive than they should be, network infrastructure devices to go down or not behave as expected, or various devices to shut down or lose network connectivity entirely. These situations may require someone to be physically present at the device or system in question in order to recover from the issue, and this is not always something that is easily done at remote locations.

Setting up systems or devices while leaving the default configurations and passwords in place is another form of unintentional sabotage. Depending on the device or system in question, an attacker may be able to tell from remote that the default settings are still in place. Even when this is not the case, a standard step when attempting to compromise a system is to try passwords and vulnerabilities that apply to the device as it shipped. Leaving systems in their default state is not only tantamount to inviting the attacker in, but is practically rolling out the red carpet for them.

Upgrades are another area where we can see human error reach into the realm of sabotage. Whether they are software upgrades, firmware upgrades, or hardware upgrades, all such activities have the potential to fail very badly and publicly when carried out in an improper way. We can see cases of mail server upgrades that cause all of the mail in the system to be lost, firmware upgrades both standard and custom, i.e., jailbreaking an iPhone, that "brick" hardware devices, and hardware upgrades that are incompatible with other portions of the system or fail in unpredictable ways.

Although these types of errors may indeed be unintentional, the results are often no less dire than if they had been intentional. When a human error causes the e-mail account of the CEO to be compromised, or a critical server to be down for a week, the problem is still just as painful.

Automated Processes

Automated processes, often in combination with human error, as we just discussed, can make a saboteur out of a simple process or script. Such tools of automation are also ripe with the potential to be exploited by an attacker.

Backup and restore operations are a particularly sensitive place that automation can fail. If the wrong files are backed up or restored, a bad situation can turn into a nightmare in very short order. We may see odd versions of configurations files appear and be written over the proper versions, old data files in the place of current ones, or any of a number of similar catastrophes. Automated routines such as these can also provide us an excellent opportunity to alter the contents of the backup file in aid to an attack, and then trigger the mechanism that causes our altered backup to be restored into place.

Maintenance scripts can cause no end of trouble. In many cases, such tools have been cobbled together by administrators in order to ease their workload, and have not been party to any sort of formal design or testing process, before being rolled out onto production systems. Such scripts, often because of small coding errors may have wildly unpredictable results and wreak havoc on the systems where they run, the network, and possibly other systems on the same network segment.

External

External sabotage is the source from which we can expect to see such attacks arrive in penetration testing, cyber warfare, or just general hacking attacks. Such saboteurs will likely seek to compromise systems in order to take them down entirely or subvert them to their own uses. We may see such attacks from a wide variety of sources, including foreign governments, terrorists, criminal organizations, and a host of others.

Foreign Governments and Terrorists

The activities of foreign governments in hacking and sabotage are generally cloudy, at best. Attacks over the Internet, even when traceable directly back to a machine in a foreign country, are not necessarily attributable to the owner of this machine. Such machines may only be one in a chain of many that lead to the actual source of the attacks.

Attackers in this category will be more likely to conduct outright acts of sabotage or espionage than most. In some cases, such acts may be a small part of an overall larger cyber conflict or even an outright full-blown cyber war.

Hacktivists

Many outright acts of sabotage come from political or environmental activists and some from other random causes as well. Hackers that are attacking for such purposes are commonly known as hacktivists. Hacktivists tend toward public sabotage in very high-profile places, such as highly trafficked Web pages, and either deface the pages in question, or take down the servers entirely with denial-of-service attacks.

We may also see hacktivists conducting acts of espionage, in order to further their particular goals. In 2009, hacktivists compromised the systems of the Climatic Research Unit of the University of East Anglia in the United Kingdom and accessed more than 1000 e-mail and 3000 documents, searching for proof that evidence of global warming had been covered up. The information was then posted on public Web sites.[12]

Hacktivists have great potential for very damaging acts of sabotage, and this is generally their precise goal. Many of the other external sources have other goals in mind and sabotaging systems is largely a matter of collateral damage.

Script Kiddies and Hackers

One frequent external source of sabotage will come from random attacks by various hackers and the unskilled masses of attackers, often known as script kiddies. Such attacks are often not carried out with any overall background goal, other than to penetrate a vulnerable system and find out what is there. Such attacks may involve gratuitous disruption of system processes, destruction of data, or any number of other attacks, based on the whim of the attacker.

Such attacks may target military or government systems for various reasons, including searching for particular information that the attacker believes to be present. A good example of such an attack can be found in the penetrations carried out by Gary McKinnon, a Scottish hacker who compromised nearly 100 systems belonging to the U.S. military and NASA, in a search for, among other things, information involving UFOs. He also left a note in the compromised systems, indicating places where he found holes in security.[13] Efforts to extradite McKinnon to the United States to stand trial have been going on for nearly a decade at the time of this writing.

TIP

Attacks from hackers and script kiddies are often the number one form of attacks that we might see sabotaging our systems. The line between this category of attack and those that fall into the "The Curious" section under internal acts of sabotage earlier in the chapter is often a very fine one. In most cases, it is a matter of whether the attacker is an employee of the company being attacked or not. In some cases, both categories are one and the same.

Attacks from such hackers are generally conducted out of curiosity and in an attempt to prove their hacking skills. Such attackers may or may not care in the slightest of they are affecting the system performance and are there in a largely exploratory capacity.

Criminals

Criminal enterprises often carry out attacks that might be considered sabotage. These can be outright attacks for the purposes of denial of service or extortion, industrial espionage, illegal gambling, recruiting nodes for botnets, or any of a number of other similar activities.

Botnets are one of the primary tools of Internet-oriented criminal operations. Such networks recruit the computing and network resources of thousands or even millions of individual nodes and direct them through command and control mechanisms. Botnets can be used to conduct denial-of-service attacks, crack encryption or password lists, or any of a number of activities that can be approached with distributed computing. Heavy use of botnet nodes can place a serious resource drain on the systems in question, and can cause harm to or disrupt the normal tasks of these systems when they are in use in such a fashion. Additionally, the command and control software can be used to push out new commands, additional malware, or almost anything that those controlling the nodes would care to do to the machine.

Interestingly, there is some discussion of using similar tactics to conduct cyber warfare. Although penetration testers or participants in a cyber conflict might be using a botnet composed of legitimately recruited machines to carry out large-scale tasks, the end results would be very similar.

Pirates

Sometimes software pirates will compromise systems in an effort to gain access to resources with which to aid the spread of their unlicensed software, media files, and other similar items. Such compromised machines can be used as storage space to host download sites for such files, often causing a heavy drain in network and storage resources on the machine in question.

Such compromised servers may be altered to install Web servers, FTP servers, or participate in file-sharing networks such as bittorrent. When popular software, movies, MP3s, and so on are being shared in such a fashion from a compromised machine, this is usually noticeable to the users of the system, due to the drain in resources, such compromised servers do not tend to stay in activity for a long period of time. For the period of time that they are in use in such a fashion, however, this type of compromise may result in a denial-of-service attack to other systems or resources on the network.

Additionally, compromised servers hosting pirated items may present legal liability for the owners of these machines, due to vending such items from their compromised systems and networks. It is entirely possible that organizations like the Motion Picture Association of America (MPAA) or the Business Software Alliance (BSA) would take umbrage to such activity and decide to pursue legal remedies to it.

Summary

In this chapter, we discussed the use of sabotage. Although sabotage is not frequently used in penetration testing, it was used historically by the ninja, and it is regularly put to use in various conflicts and by criminal organizations.

We discussed logical sabotage, which, when used with care, can actually be very useful in a penetration-testing scenario. We talked about various uses for malware, including backdoors, rootkits, and infected hardware such as phones and USB storage devices. We also discussed the use of data manipulation for financial gain, client side attacks, and vandalism.

We covered the use of physical sabotage as well, including communications, hardware, and access controls. The disruption of devices that run critical infrastructure, communications, or control the access of personnel can be very damaging to an organization. Such acts of sabotage may be resulting from substandard parts used to build counterfeit equipment, or they may be because of clandestine disruptive features that were deliberately built in.

Finally, we talked about the various sources for sabotage, the main categories being internal and external. Internal sources can include disgruntled employees, human error, and others. External sources might include foreign governments, hacktivists, and software pirates, just to name a few. Although the motivations driving the efforts of various sources may differ, the end result to the target often looks much the same.

Endnotes

1. Zoughari K. The ninja: ancient shadow warriors of Japan. Rutland (VT): Tuttle Publishing; 2010. 0804839271.
2. Russinovich M. Sony, rootkits and digital rights managment gone too far. Mark's Blog. [Online] http://blogs.technet.com/b/markrussinovich/archive/2005/10/31/sony-rootkits-and-digital-rights-management-gone-too-far.aspx; 2005 [accessed 26.05.10].

3. Cluley G. IBM distributes USB malware at AusCERT Security Conference. Graham Cluley's Blog. [Online] www.sophos.com/blogs/gc/g/2010/05/21/ibm-distributes-usb-malware-cocktail-auscert-security-conference/; 2010 [accessed 26.05.10].

4. Ismael K. Four Accused on high-tech gas pump scam. Los Angeles Times. [Online] http://articles.latimes.com/1998/oct/09/business/fi-30669; 1998 [accessed 27.05.10].

5. Ali Zain A. Cable damage hits one million Internet users in UAE. Khaleej Times Online. [Online] www.khaleejtimes.com/DisplayArticleNew.asp?section=theuae&xfile=data/theuae/2008/february/theuae_february121.xml; 2008 [accessed 28.05.10].

6. Asimov N., Kim R., Fagan K. Sabotage attacks knock out phone service. San Francisco Chronicle. [Online] www.sfgate.com/cgi-bin/article.cgi?f=/c/a/2009/04/09/BAP816VTE6.DTL; 2009 [accessed 28.05.10].

7. U.S. Department of Justice. Departments of Justice and Homeland Security announce 30 convictions, more than $143 million in seizures from initiative targeting traffickers in counterfeit network hardware. Federal Bureau of Investigation. [Online] www.fbi.gov/pressrel/pressrel10/convictions_050610.htm; 2010 [accessed 28.05.10].

8. Lawson S., McMillan R. FBI worried as DoD sold counterfeit Cisco gear. InfoWorld Security Central. [Online] www.infoworld.com/d/security-central/fbi-worried-dod-sold-counterfeit-cisco-gear-266; 2008 [accessed 28.05.10].

9. McGlaun S. Rogue IT admin locks city of San Francisco out of its network. Daily Tech. [Online] www.dailytech.com/article.aspx?newsid=12394; 2010 [accessed 27.05.10].

10. McMillan R. IT admin locks up San Francisco's network. PC World Business Center. [Online] www.pcworld.com/businesscenter/article/148469/it_admin_locks_up_san_franciscos_network.html; 2008 [accessed 27.05.10].

11. Begin B. Network engineer Terry Childs found guilty of network tampering. sfexaminer.com. [Online] www.sfexaminer.com/local/Network-engineer-Terry-Childs-found-guilty-of-network-tampering-92257309.html; 2010 [accessed 27.05.10].

12. Eilperin J. Hackers steal electronic data from top climate research center. The Washington Post. [Online] www.washingtonpost.com/wp-dyn/content/article/2009/11/20/AR2009112004093.html?hpid=sec-nation; 2009 [accessed 28.05.10].

13. Moult J. Gary was just a guy looking for ET. This witch hunt must end (and that's the man from NASA's view). Mail Online. [Online] www.dailymail.co.uk/news/article-1197950/Gary-just-guy-looking-ET-This-witch-hunt-end-thats-man-NASAs-view.html?ITO=1490; 2009 [accessed 27.05.10].

Hiding and Silent Movement

17

Toshitsugu Takamatsu, the thirty-third Grandmaster of Togakure Ryu, provided some guidance on the roles and responsibilities of ninja. According to Takamatsu, "stealthy reconnaissance is the ninja's chief contribution to victory," and that "the ninja accomplishes his mission by concealing his own influence on the situation and preserving the impression that all is going according to fate alone."[1] This puts a lot of pressure on Zukin who want to emulate ancient ninja during efforts to compromise corporate networks. To improve our chances of success, and to avoid detection, we need to perform all of our attacks with the focus of hiding our tracks and moving silently through the victim's network.

Whether we are attacking from outside or inside our victim's network, there are a couple of different tactics that we can use to hide our true attack location. The techniques we will look at have been tried and tested over the years, yet are still effective – these techniques include the use of anonymizers and tunnels. There are some disadvantages in using them, but overall they are effective means of hiding our activities during our attacks. We will also briefly look at the topic of avoiding intrusion detection systems by understanding how they work.

Another method of injecting ourselves into a victim's network without revealing ourselves or objective is the use of hardware that has been preloaded with malware. We can use hardware traditionally used to inject malware into victim systems, such as USB memory sticks; however, there are some new techniques that we should consider that might provide better methods of inserting ourselves into a network.

We also need to be aware of the different logging methods available to system and network security engineers that might detect and report on our activities. We will look at ways to manipulate log files so that our activities are deleted before detection. Using all these different techniques will allow us to mask our activities effectively, in a fashion similar to those of the ancient ninja.

Ninja Hacking. DOI: 10.1016/B978-1-59749-588-2.00017-2

ATTACK LOCATION OBFUSCATION

In Chapter 5, "Disguise," we talked about the use of anonymizers; the examples we used included the Tor network and wireless mesh networks. The use of anonymizers allowed us to present ourselves to the attack system as coming from a location different than our real location. The use of anonymizers is one way to disguise our identity – they can also be used to conceal our movement as well. In this section, we will look at anonymizers a little differently, and that is to use anonymizers to provide a way of hiding our activities, not just our location.

Protocol-Specific Anonymizers

When we use the Tor network, one of the more well-known anonymizers, we use a network of systems (theoretically) dedicated to providing protection of our location. The problem we face with Tor is that we cannot trust the end-systems to not look at our data during ingress or egress. To prevent this type of sniffing or other attacks against our attempt to exploit a target, we can set up protocol-specific anonymizers that allow us to obfuscate our location and protect the data between the attack platform and any system we compromise within the target network. One of the better known ways of hiding our activity is to create a SOCKS proxy and create a tunnel between our two devices. Another advantage in creating a tunnel is that we can use it to avoid firewalls in certain situations.

SOCKS Tunnel

In this example, we will take a look at creating a tunnel using SSH and SOCKS to create a secure connection between systems within an internal network. The objective is to simply demonstrate the ability to both hide our activity and our location of attack; the configuration of the SOCKS proxy can be configured to work with different protocols (such as FTP, SSH, SSL) across any open ports accessible through the victim's firewall; by configuring a SOCKS proxy on the attack platform located within the victim's network, we can push traffic that might normally be sent as cleartext across the victim's network without the victim being able to read our communications. We can also set up the SOCKS proxy to hide our real attack location by using different attack platforms across the globe.

In Figure 17.1, we start off by looking at the IP address of our real attack platform, which is 75.70.246.19. If we were to conduct our attacks from this location, we easily give away our location. In addition, we do not have any secure channel created at this point of our attack, so anything we do will be visible across all the different nodes between the intended victim and our attack platform. In the world of cyber warfare, it would be very evident of who we are, and what side of the "war" we are on.

To set up our proxy, we will use SSH, as seen in Figure 17.2; this will hide any data sent between ourselves and an external system. If we need to export data securely out of our network without being seen by intrusion detection systems or firewalls configured to look for sensitive corporate data, then the SSH tunnel would serve its

FIGURE 17.1 Attack IP Address without SOCKS Configured.

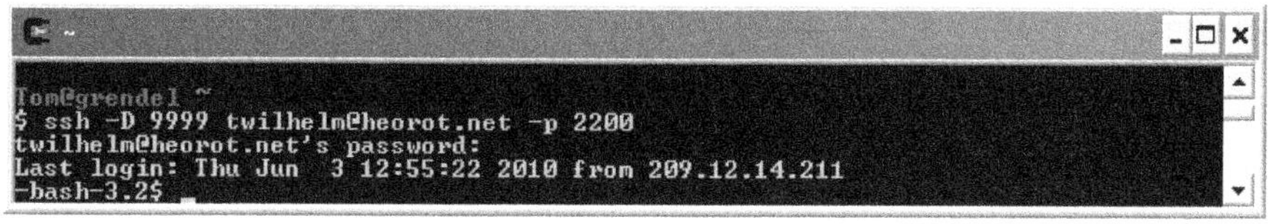

```
C ~                                                    _ □ ×
om@grendel ~
$ ssh -D 9999 twilhelm@heorot.net -p 2200
twilhelm@heorot.net's password:
Last login: Thu Jun  3 12:55:22 2010 from 209.12.14.211
-bash-3.2$
```

FIGURE 17.2 Setting Up SOCKS Proxy on Local Machine.

purpose. However, if we need to conduct additional attacks, for example against an internal corporate Web server, then we can set up a SOCKS proxy that will allow us to continue our attack, as well as hide our activity as it crosses the victim's firewall.

In Figure 17.2, we set up a SOCKS proxy (using the "–D" option) and connect to a remote machine (heorot.net). Once established, we have a secure channel between our local system (sending data out on port 9999) and our remote system (over port 2200). If we needed to, we could configure the SSH server on the remote system to accept traffic on port 80 or port 443, making the traffic appear as if it is communicating with a remote Web server.

To continue our attack and hide our traffic, we need to configure our Web browser to push all traffic through our SSH tunnel, which is set up as a SOCKS proxy. Figure 17.3 illustrates how we can configure the Firefox Web browser to communicate directly with our proxy instead of sending the data directly across the network, pass the default gateway and through the firewall.

Once configured, we can see what our IP address is, assuming we continue our attack using a Web browser. Figure 17.4 indicates that any probes from our local system will appear as coming from 89.185.228.138. All traffic between our attack platform and the remote system is encrypted, and we can communicate over that secure channel using any application that is SOCKS compatible, even if it sends traffic in the clear, such as FTP or netcat.

There are some additional issues that we need to be aware of before we commit to using proxies. One of the minor side effects is that our location may be filtered by our victim. In Figure 17.5, we see that Google has redirected us to their Czech Republic Web page because the remote Web server is actually located in that country.

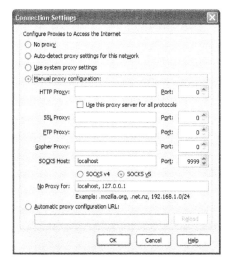

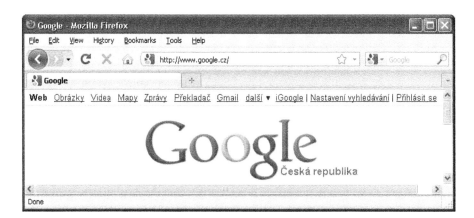

FIGURE 17.3 Configuring Firefox SOCKS Host.

FIGURE 17.4 Attack IP Address without SOCKS Configured.

FIGURE 17.5 Unintentional Results When Using SOCKS.

WARNING

We need to be very selective when choosing the location of a proxy. Each country has different laws regarding hacking, even authorized hacking. Although our actions may be legal in one part of the world, the use of a system located elsewhere may expose us to legal action. Know the laws beforehand to avoid this type of complication.

If our victim is only interested in communicating with potential clients from within the United States and wants to reduce its security exposure, it may filter out any of our connection attempts. In situations like this, we can simply create another proxy to another server in a country that can connect to the victim's Web server.

Another issue we need to understand is that once our traffic leaves the remote system, that traffic will be passed across the network in the clear, assuming we are using a protocol that defaults to cleartext (such as HTTP and FTP). If our remote system was a mobile device configured as an attack platform located within a victim's network, anything we did between the mobile device and another system in the victim's network might be detected by intrusion detection systems (IDS). In cases where IDS platforms are used in the victim's network, we will need to modify the flow of data and the means in which we transmit that data to avoid detection.

Intrusion Detection Avoidance

Although this topic alone could make up an entire book, we will look at some ways to mask our attacks when dealing with intrusion detection systems (IDS). Like any tool, IDS devices have weaknesses that can be exploited. We have already discussed creating secure tunnels, which will hide our traffic, but in many situations, we will not have the luxury of a secure tunnel to conduct our attack.

In cases when we cannot directly avoid detection, we can confuse the IDS in such a way that they do not really know where the attack originates from. We can also slow down our attacks to fall under thresholds that might otherwise alert network security engineers. A third possibility that we will examine later in this chapter, under the section "Local Subnet," is to conduct our attacks within small subnets where IDS might not exist.

IP Address Decoys

There are a couple different tools available to the Zukin that will allow multiple packets to be sent to a target system, which generates fake return IP addresses. The idea is that when we want to send a packet to a target system (such as a scan or exploit code), we send multiple, identical packets – however, each packet contains a different return IP address, and only one of the return addresses is that of our attack system

Figure 17.6 is an example of using decoy IP addresses to confuse the true location of our attack server. Assuming we are using the server assigned with the IP address of 89.185.228.138, we can launch an Nmap decoy scan attack with similar IP addresses. Given enough IP addresses, the IDS system will provide the network security engineer with too much information, and our attack location will blend in with all the false IP addresses.

If we are attacking from within the victim's compromised network, using this technique may be a bad idea unless we think that we might have already been detected by network security engineers; this type of attack increases the number of packets being sent across the network, and might be numerous enough to meet the threshold necessary to trigger an alarm. The use of decoys assumes that our attack will be noticed, and it is best used when trying to mask our identity by hiding in the noise.

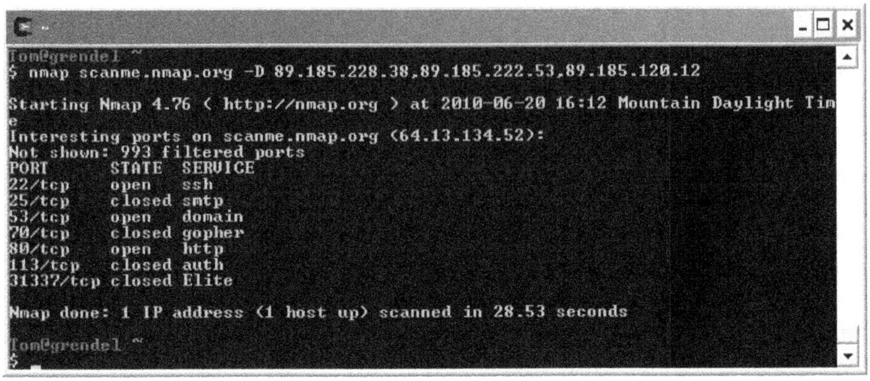

FIGURE 17.6 Nmap Scan Using Decoy IP Addresses.

Staying Under Thresholds

IDS devices often include thresholds in order to reduce the amount of work necessary for the security engineer to perform. These thresholds are based on the number of packets that trigger the rule, and how quickly they come across the network. The following snippet of an IDS rule was written to detect brute force attacks against the POP3 protocol.

```
alert tcp $EXTERNAL_NET any -> $HOME_NET 110 (msg:"POP3 login
brute force attempt"; flow:to_server,established; content:"USER";
fast_pattern:only; detection_filter:track by_dst, count 30, seconds
30; metadata:service pop3; classtype:suspicious-login; sid:2274;
rev:5;)
```

If 30 log-in attempts are tried within a 30-s time span against a system running the POP3 protocol on port 110. To conduct our attack, with the intent of hiding ourselves, we can simply modify the speed of our brute force attack to 29 attempts in 30 s – this will prevent the IDS system from alerting network security.

The tricky part is to know in advance what thresholds exist for our intended attack choice. It would be best if we actually had access to the IDS rules file; that way we would know for certain, exactly, which rules are in effect and how we can tailor our attack to avoid detection. Unfortunately, having access to the rules is rarely possible, so we must make some informed assumptions. It is not unusual for organizations implementing IDS devices to use rules as written. This means we can use published rules to know what thresholds to use; the best place to start is the Sourcefire Vulnerability Research Team (VRT) site found at www.snort.org/vrt. Although free access is limited to rules that are older than 30 days, the Sourcefire VRT provides hundreds of rules in which to begin modification of our attack.

There are other methods to avoid IDS devices on the network. In the next section, we will discuss protocol tunneling, and continue our talk on IDS avoidance with local subnets.

> **TIP**
>
> The use of default IDS rules tend to work better than one would think – many security engineers simply accept the defaults and implement them without any modification whatsoever. If there is some concern about the use of default rules when conducting an attack, simply reduce the number of connections per minute until they are at a comfortable threshold – with ninja hacking, time is our ally.

Filtered Protocol Tunneling

One of the considerations when we decide to create tunnels out is to understand what type of traffic is being monitored within the victim's network. Protocols, such as FTP and telnet are high candidates for detection because of the ease in collecting transmitted data due to the implementation of cleartext communication within those applications. As Zukin, we need to select those protocols that are rarely examined by network security administrators, so that we can silently move data in and out of the victim's network.

We also should be aware of how systems within a network communicate with each other. It is not unusual for critical systems to be located very near to each other, both physically and virtually. It may be possible to use a compromised system to attack other systems within the victim's network without ever passing data across an intrusion detection system, depending on how the systems are used.

Local Subnet

One of the more interesting attacks is when we are launching probes or sending exploit code within a local subnet. In many cases, systems are connected to each other through a switch network, which means that any data traveling from one system to another could be routed only through the connecting switch. When that happens, all communication is constrained and does not continue further down the network, which may contain intrusion detection devices.

Figure 17.7 is a network illustration of attacking systems within a switch subnet. As we can see, we have exploited the Web server, and created a secure channel, whether it is an SSH tunnel or set up a SOCKS proxy as well. Once we have a foothold in the Web server, we can attack other systems connected to the switch without the concern of being detected by the IDS device. The reason this attack works the way it does is because switches will make routing decisions based on the destination's Mac address. If our target and compromised system are both behind a switch, all packets between them will stay constrained to that switch.

The danger in this type of attack is when we, mistakenly, assume that systems are behind a switch, or that they do not have IDS devices sitting in front of each of the servers. Another mistake would be to assume that each system lacks Host IDS (HIDS) software. However, in our effort to compromise the first server (which was the Web server in our example), we may have come across evidence of an IDS. And if we compromise a server, we can examine the running processes to see if any HIDS services are running. Undetected attacks within a local subnet, similar to what we

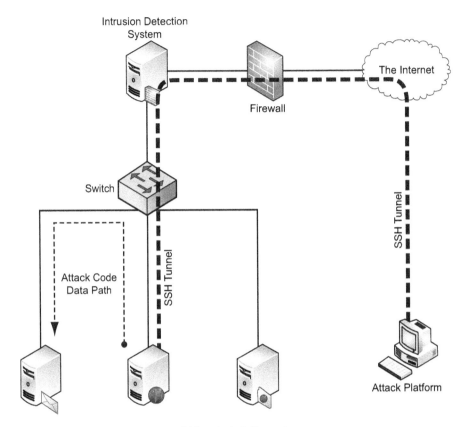

FIGURE 17.7 Data Traffic Pattern within a Switch Network.

see in Figure 17.7, are not an exact science, and there are no guarantees that they will succeed; but with enough system and network enumeration, we can improve our odds.

Protocol Tunneling

As we mentioned earlier, some traffic is closely scrutinized when it leaves an organization's network, such as HTTP or FTP traffic. However, some protocols are not examined; this oversight is not necessarily because of negligence on the part of network security engineers – rather it is because of the voluminous amounts of traffic that is sent across the networks every day. Security engineers simply cannot look at all traffic in and out of the network, and therefore must make some decisions on what protocols to examine, and which ones to ignore. One such protocol is the Internet Control Message Protocol (ICMP), which is used to ping systems across networks and the Internet.

ICMP

The use of ICMP as a method of tunneling information out of a network is fairly straight-forward. All we do is inject additional data into an ICMP ping request/reply message and send it to our remote attack platform. The information being injected into the ping request could be encrypted as well, increasing our stealth; however, the use of ICMP is much slower than sending packets traditionally and might only be worthwhile if we know that ICMP is not blocked at the firewall or if we know that IDS systems are not examining the ICMP protocol.

The ICMP communication structure can be seen in Figure 17.8. What we want to focus on is the data field at the end of the protocol – it is there that we can inject data into the packet.

In Figure 17.9, we see how the ICMP structure can be modified to transmit a TCP packet to a remote system. The ICMP data and the TCP packet are separated by

```
 0                   1                   2                   3
 0 1 2 3 4 5 6 7 8 9 0 1 2 3 4 5 6 7 8 9 0 1 2 3 4 5 6 7 8 9 0 1
+---------------------------------+------------------------------+
|      Type     |      Code       |          Checksum            |
+---------------------------------+------------------------------+
|          Identifier             |       Sequence Number        |
+---------------------------------+------------------------------+
|                          Data ...                              |
+----------------------------------------------------------------+
```

FIGURE 17.8 ICMP Packet Structure.

```
 0                   1                   2                   3
 0 1 2 3 4 5 6 7 8 9 0 1 2 3 4 5 6 7 8 9 0 1 2 3 4 5 6 7 8 9 0 1
+---------------------------------+------------------------------+
|      Type     |      Code       |          Checksum            |
+---------------------------------+------------------------------+
|          Identifier             |       Sequence Number        |
+---------------------------------+------------------------------+
|                        Mgic Number                             |
+----------------------------------------------------------------+
|                             IP                                 |
+----------------------------------------------------------------+
|                            Port                                |
+----------------------------------------------------------------+
|                           State                                |
+----------------------------------------------------------------+
|                   Acknowledgment number                        |
+----------------------------------------------------------------+
|                          Length                                |
+---------------------------------+------------------------------+
|       Sequence Number           |          Reserved            |
+---------------------------------+------------------------------+
|                          Data ...                              |
+----------------------------------------------------------------+
```

FIGURE 17.9 ICMP with Injected TCP Packet.

a "magic number," which will allow the receiving system to accept traditional ping requests, as well as identify those ICMP packets that have injected data.

To inject and extract TCP packets into ICMP messages, both the receiving and sending systems need software designed specifically for ICMP tunneling. It is possible to simply inject data into the ICMP message using a program like Scapy, and then read the message on the other end using packet-capturing software like Wireshark; however, the software available for ICMP tunneling is simple to install and use.

TCP/IP Suite

Another option is to inject data within the TCP/IP suite itself, instead of cramming the entire TCP packet into an ICMP message. The usable areas within the suite include the following:

- The IP packet-identification field
- The TCP initial sequence number field
- The TCP acknowledged sequence number field

The drawback to using these fields are that they are relatively small, and using ASCII values will only hold a single character for each packet sent. The advantage is that these fields are never examined by IDS or network system engineers, so any traffic sent back to our remote system will appear as typical TCP/IP traffic. A good examination of both the ICMP and TCP/IP tunneling method can be read at gray-world.net/papers/ahsan02.pdf.

COMPROMISED HARDWARE

A clever method for injecting malware into a corporate environment uses hardware preloaded with malware; this hardware is passed off as coming from legitimate sources in order to gain acceptance from the victims. By using hardware, we circumvent traditional detection systems, such as firewalls and intrusion detection systems that might catch our attack if it were to be sent over the network against a target system. Another advantage is that while software may be scanned for viruses, some of the more complex hardware items are not examined for malware, simply because the skills needed to do a forensic analysis on hardware is much more advanced than running an antivirus scanner.

Memory Sticks

Memory sticks are an exception to examination by virus scanners; however, they can still be used quite effectively to insert malware into a corporate network without revealing the source of the code. As Zukin, it is best if others do our work for us, so that we can remain undetected. An example of this type of exploit occurred in May of 2010 at the Australian Computer Emergency Response Team (AusCERT) conference. During that time, one of the vendors (IBM) distributed USB memory sticks to conference attendees that contained malware.[2] Although it was not clear in the initial reporting if the malware was inserted onto the USB stick before or during the conference, attendees were undoubtedly under the impression that the memory sticks came from a somewhat trusted source; however, the identity of the actual attacker is not known.

Hard Drives

In 2007, it was reported that 1800 external hard drives, manufactured by Maxtor, had malware installed before they were shipped to retailers.[3] The interesting addendum to this story is that it was suggested that the Chinese government was involved in adding the malware to the drives while in possession of a Chinese subcontractor. The malware on the drives were Trojan horses that would send any data saved to the hard drive to servers in Beijing.[4]

NOTE

Although we may not be able to inject malware on devices built in China, organizations often buy at least some of their equipment locally. It may make more sense to attempt a compromise of hardware obtained locally, because then we can focus specifically on compromising our victim, as opposed to a broad attack against numerous consumers.

Another example of hiding malware in hard drives occurred with the Asus Eee Box desktop computer. In 2008, Asus announced that they had unintentionally sold systems infected with malware to Japanese customers.[5] The installed virus would infect the C: drive when executed, and it would sniff for gaming log-in information.

Cell Phones

In March of 2010, the Android-based Vodafone HTC Magic was discovered to have malware preloaded on some of the devices. The phone would attempt to upload the malware onto any system connected to the phone.[6] The malware was designed to steal passwords, connect to a botnet, and inject the conficker worm onto the connected PC.

In June of 2010, the Samsung S8500 Wave phone was also found to have been shipped to consumers with malware preloaded.[7] In the case of the Samsung phone, the malware was placed on the microSD memory card that was included with the phone. The target of the malware was again any computer that connected to the phone.

Network Devices

There have been some suggestions that malware has come preinstalled in network devices. The proof of this type of attack has not been substantiated; however, it does provide some hint of things to come. It is not unreasonable to assume that legitimate or counterfeit equipment will be inserted into corporate environments containing preinstalled malware; the advantage of having compromised network devices installed within a target network would be incredible, especially if the attacker can access the device directly through a reverse shell or because the network device is part of a botnet.

The ability to compromise hardware before it enters a facility can be achieved in many different ways. However, the most effective way seems to be through social engineering. By using others (such as IBM or Maxtor), we can force the victim to drop their guard and accept the hardware at face-value. Assuming we use social engineering to get others to do our work, if our malware is detected the victims' anger is then directed at the third party, and not us … at least initially.

LOG MANIPULATION

Manipulating log data is a bit tricky – once we achieve a compromise, we rarely have root (or administrative) access. However, to modify log data we need to have elevated privileges. Because of this predicament, once we compromise a system, it becomes imperative to try to achieve administrative access as quickly as possible if we intend to change the logs on the system.

User Log Files

It is important to understand what systems record in their log files before we begin to worry about whether or not we should be modifying the logs. Figure 17.10 examines what happens when someone logs into a system remotely – in this case, we are logging in as the user "root" on a Linux system and attempting to elevate our privileges.

```
bt ~ #
bt ~ # ssh 192.168.1.123
The authenticity of host '192.168.1.123 (192.168.1.123)' can't be established.
RSA key fingerprint is ab:ab:a8:ad:a2:f2:fd:c2:6f:05:99:69:40:54:ec:10.
Are you sure you want to continue connecting (yes/no)? yes
Warning: Permanently added '192.168.1.123' (RSA) to the list of known hosts.
root@192.168.1.123's password:
Linux 2.6.16.
root@slax:~#
root@slax:~# more /var/log/secure
root@slax:~# su -
root@slax:~#
root@slax:~# more /var/log/secure
Apr 29 09:31:23 (none) su[10408]: + pts/0 root-root
root@slax:~#
root@slax:~# ls -l /var/log/secure
-rw-r--r-- 1 root root 52 Apr 29 09:31 /var/log/secure
root@slax:~# █
```

FIGURE 17.10 Log Record of User Activity on Linux System.

We should notice that nothing is added to the log file until we attempt to elevate our privilege using the "su" command; the remote login was not recorded. In Figure 17.11, we see a different situation when we log in locally.

In Figure 17.11, we can see that our local login as root was recorded. If we are doing most of our attacks remotely, then we don't have to worry about our activities being recorded on this particular system; however, if we login as a regular user and need to elevate our privileges, based on what we see in the log files, our login will be recorded, and this may give security engineers advance notice of our intent.

Because we have root privileges, we could simply modify the log file by removing the line indicating our login. However, this produces some additional problems. When entries in the log file are made, the log file gets a new time stamp. If we look inside the log file and compare the time stamp of the last entry to the time stamp of the log file, they need to match – if they don't, there is a probability that someone's been messing with the log data. If there is a time discrepancy, an astute security engineer will act on this information and begin to look for intruders. In Figure 17.12, we see can see a log file that has been manipulated to hide some activity. The last entry in the log file is 9:47, while the timestamp of the file is 10:23.

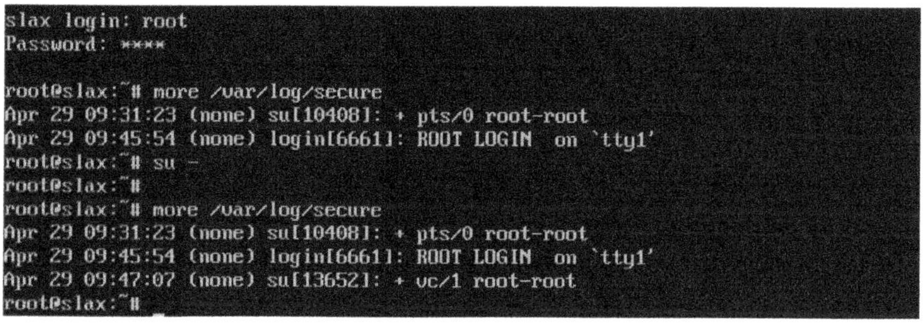

```
slax login: root
Password: ****

root@slax:~# more /var/log/secure
Apr 29 09:31:23 (none) su[10408]: + pts/0 root-root
Apr 29 09:45:54 (none) login[6661]: ROOT LOGIN  on `tty1'
root@slax:~# su -
root@slax:~#
root@slax:~# more /var/log/secure
Apr 29 09:31:23 (none) su[10408]: + pts/0 root-root
Apr 29 09:45:54 (none) login[6661]: ROOT LOGIN  on `tty1'
Apr 29 09:47:07 (none) su[13652]: + vc/1 root-root
root@slax:~#
```

FIGURE 17.11 Log File After Local Login.

```
root@slax:~#
root@slax:~# more /var/log/secure
Apr 29 09:45:54 (none) login[6661]: ROOT LOGIN  on `tty1'
Apr 29 09:47:07 (none) su[13652]: + vc/1 root-root
root@slax:~#
root@slax:~# ls -l /var/log/secure
-rw-r--r-- 1 root root 109 Apr 29 10:23 /var/log/secure
root@slax:~#
root@slax:~# who
root     tty1          Apr 29 09:45
root     pts/0         Apr 29 09:30 (192.168.1.115)
root@slax:~# 
```

FIGURE 17.12 Manipulated Log File.

```
root@slax:~#
root@slax:~# more /var/log/secure
Apr 29 09:45:54 (none) login[6661]: ROOT LOGIN  on `tty1'
Apr 29 09:47:07 (none) su[13652]: + vc/1 root-root
root@slax:~#
root@slax:~# date
Wed Apr 29 11:26:30 GMT 2009
root@slax:~#
root@slax:~# echo 'Apr 29 11:28:08 (none) su[31337]: + vc/1 root-root' >> /var/l
og/secure
root@slax:~# ls -l /var/log/secure
-rw-r--r-- 1 root root 160 Apr 29 11:27 /var/log/secure
root@slax:~#
root@slax:~# date
Wed Apr 29 11:28:08 GMT 2009
root@slax:~# touch /var/log/secure
root@slax:~#
root@slax:~# ls -l /var/log/secure
-rw-r--r-- 1 root root 160 Apr 29 11:28 /var/log/secure
root@slax:~#
root@slax:~# more /var/log/secure
Apr 29 09:45:54 (none) login[6661]: ROOT LOGIN  on `tty1'
Apr 29 09:47:07 (none) su[13652]: + vc/1 root-root
Apr 29 11:28:08 (none) su[31337]: + vc/1 root-root
root@slax:~#
```

FIGURE 17.13 Modification of Log File.

In Figure 17.13, we attempt to match the time stamp of the file with the last log entry. This will alleviate our concern about mismatching time stamps. However, we have an additional problem – knowing what data to insert into the log file. In Figure 17.13, we add a line indicating that another successful "su" attempt occurred. The use of "su" is appropriate under limited circumstances, but too many attempts, or attempts at the wrong time, would put us back into a compromising situation.

Another option besides manipulating a log file is to delete the log file altogether. Although this may not hide the fact we have compromised the system, it does hide our activity, making it much more difficult to understand what we did on the system. Although we may not be "silently moving," we are "hiding" our activities.

Application Log Files

Applications on a system may also log events that we need to be concerned with. In Figure 17.14, we generate some error messages by attempting to log onto a system using SSH. We can see the results of our attempt in Figure 17.15.

As we can see in Figure 17.15, all of our failed attempts were logged. If we are not using valid usernames, a security engineer will quickly come to the realization that something is amiss. By understanding how applications log data, we can adjust our attack to eliminate these types of log messages whether it is to slow down our attack or select a different attack vector that isn't set up to write data to the log file.

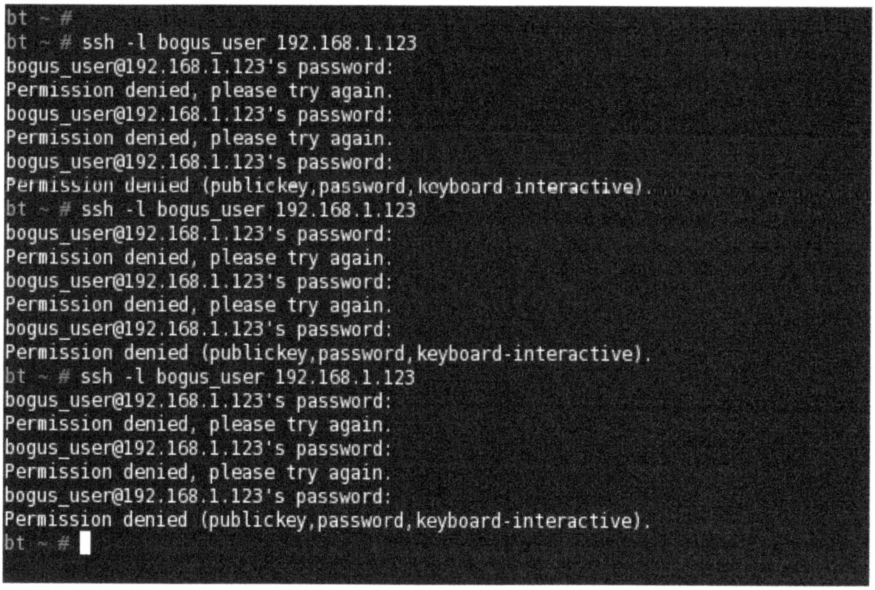

FIGURE 17.14 Logging onto System through SSH.

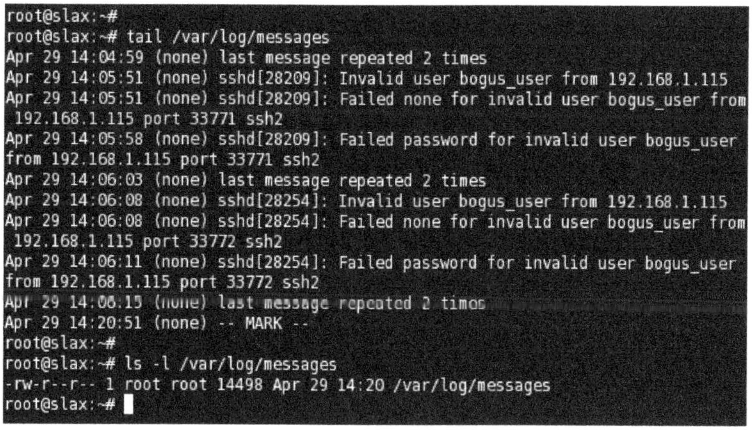

FIGURE 17.15 Results of Failed Logins.

Because the SSH application wrote to the /var/log/messages file, which only the root user can modify, we have to again decide whether or not to attack the system through the SSH application; if we need to modify the log data as part of our effort to hide our activities, then we need to have a plan on how to quickly elevate privileges once we have compromised the system through SSH.

> ### SHINOBI-IRI (Stealth and Entering Methods)
>
> To select attack vectors that do not write data to log files, it is wise to set up a server with the target software, and then conduct attacks locally rather than go directly after the target server. This way we can see which actions and what thresholds exist that would trigger the application to write to a log file. We can also find out what file the application writes to, which can make a difference to our decision: whether to attack the application or not.

The decision to modify the log files is not something that is a *fait accompli*; because system log files are rarely examined until an incident has occurred, modifying log files only hides our activities after the fact. Although it may be possible to set up alarms based on events that happen in log files, security administrators typically use log data as part of a reactive response – not proactively. We also need to be aware that even if we accomplish a compromise on a target system, that system's log files may not reside on the system at all; it is not unusual for system administrators to use remote syslog servers to retain log files. Remote log servers help mitigate other types of attack vectors, including resource consumption (full hard drives) and roll-over attacks (where so much data is written to the log file that the system begins to delete earlier log data). As Zukin, we need to place a high value on attacking a system without being detected. As Grandmaster Takamatsu said, our primary job is stealthy reconnaissance – if we cannot achieve stealth because an application or log-in attack tracks our activities, we may need to abandon the attack vector and select one that is less likely to announce our intent.

Summary

Moving silently and hiding our activity as Zukin should be one of our strongest skills – just like the ninja of ancient Japan, we need to provide a unique service that other hackers and penetration test engineers cannot. By constantly improving our ability to attack a victim's network without being detected, we distinguish ourselves from others. This may mean that some types of attacks, especially brute force attacks, may need to be excluded from our toolset in some cases. Because of our unique role as Zukin, we need to consciously incorporate stealth tactics into all phases of a penetration test, and not just hope that our actions are undetected during the project.

Once we have selected our target and attack vector, we do have options to hide our attacks – the first being anonymization of our true attack location. Through the use of anonymizers and tunnels, we can hide the true actions of our attack and avoid filters, targeting us specifically, that may be in place on firewalls or intrusion detection systems – if security administrators know that we intend to attack their system, they may create firewall rules that will block a range of IP addresses that include our location. But by using proxies located in different regions of the world, security administrators will never really know what traffic is ours and what traffic is from their clients.

We can also avoid firewalls and intrusion detection systems altogether by installing malware on hardware. Designed correctly and distributed through channels the victim believes to be secure we can direct the ire of our victim to another party, should the malware be discovered. The use of compromised hardware may be a better option than attacking the victim's network directly because we can use social engineering to inject the hardware into the victim's facility.

Regardless of which method we use to gain access into a target system, we need to be concerned with how our actions are recorded. Because log files are often used reactively, we may have time to compromise the target system, elevate our privileges, and delete log data before anyone notices. However, we need to know beforehand exactly what types of actions trigger alarms. Again, we should not hope that our actions are undetected – we must selectively choose our attacks to best avoid the detection.

Endnotes

1. Hatsumi M. Ninjutsu: history and tradition. Burbank, CA: Unique Publications; 1981.
2. Naraine R. Threatpost. [Online] http://threatpost.com/en_us/blogs/ibm-distributes-malware-usb-sticks-security-conference-052110; 2010 [accessed 01.07.10].
3. Kingsley-Hughes A. ZDNet. [Online] www.zdnet.com/blog/hardware/malware-found-on-new-hard-drives/928; 2007 [accessed 01.07.10].
4. Yang Kuo-wen LCcaRC. Taipei Times. [Online] www.taipeitimes.com/News/taiwan/archives/2007/11/11/2003387202; 2007 [accessed 01.07.10].
5. Danchev D. ZDnet. [Online] www.zdnet.com/blog/security/asus-ships-eee-box-pcs-with-malware/2016; 2008 [accessed 01.07.10].
6. Mills E. Insecurity complex – CNET. [Online] http://news.cnet.com/8301-27080_3-10466230-245.html; 2010 [accessed 01.07.10].
7. Osborne B. Geek.com. [Online] www.geek.com/articles/mobile/samsung-s8500-wave-phones-shipped-with-malware-2010062/; 2010 [accessed 01.07.10].

Index

Page numbers followed by *f* indicates a figure and *t* indicates a table.

A

Access control systems, 276–277
Administrative honeypots, 133
Administrative intrusion detection systems, 129
Advertisement on search engines, 68–69
Alarm sensors, 112–113
Alarm system evasion, 111–113
    creating false positives, 111–112
Analog phone lines, 116–117, 273–274
Anomaly-based intrusion detection
        systems, 128
Anonymous relays, 84–86
Antimalware tools, 219
Antisurveillance devices, 260–265
Appearance, impersonating people, 78
Application log files, 298–300
Application-based intrusion detection
        systems, 127
Attack IP address, 287*f*, 288*f*
Attack location obfuscation
    filtered protocol tunneling, local
        subnet, 291–292
    IDS avoidance
      IP address decoys, 289
      thresholds, 290
    protocol tunneling, 292–294
      ICMP, 293–294
      TCP/IP suite, 294
    protocol-specific anonymizers, SOCKS
      tunnel, 286–289
Attack timing, 179–180
    attacking between shifts, 180
    attacking during maintenance, 180
Attack vector, 300

B

Backdoors, 269
Badges and uniforms
    fabricated, 82
    stolen, 81–82
Baiting, 151–157
Battlefield, 19–20
Berkley packet filter (BPF), 194
Biometric identifiers, 111
Biometric systems, 110–111, 276

B

Black Hat hackers, 27–28
Blade weapon, 17
Blended anonymized networks, 86
Blinding cameras, 262–263
    ways for blinding
      blocking/dismantling, 263
      infrared light, 262–263
      lasers, 262
Bluetooth, 208–209
Botnets, 282
Brute force attacks, 49–50, 290, 300
Bug sweeping, 258
Building rapport, 231
Bump keys, 104–106
Bushido, 2, 3–8

C

Cameras
    blinding, 262–263
      temporarily, 111–112
    hidden video, detecting, 259
Cell phones, 255–256
Cellular network, 209–210
Chain weapon, 17
Clandestine communications tools, 242
Clandestine human intelligence, 237–244
    clandestine reporting, 239–241
    penetrating organizations, 238–239
    resources, 242–244
Clandestinely placed sensors, 220–224
    audio eavesdropping, 220–221
      audio bugs, 221
      computer microphones, 221
      VoIP, 220
    video eavesdropping, 221–223
      existing camera systems, 222–223
      video bugs, 221–222
Clickjacking, 272
Clothing accessories, 17
Code of Ethics, ISC, 32
Communications Act of 1934, 260
Communications infrastructure, 273–274
Company events, 170
    meetings/conferences, 170
    outside events, 170
    utility interruptions, 172
Complex physical intrusion detection
        systems, 126

Printed and bound by CPI Group (UK) Ltd, Croydon, CR0 4YY

03/10/2024

01040343-0002